THE METALOGICON

THE
METALOGICON
OF
John of Salisbury

*A Twelfth-Century Defense
of the Verbal and Logical Arts
of the Trivium*

Translated with an Introduction and Notes by
DANIEL D. McGARRY

PAUL DRY BOOKS
Philadelphia   2009

First Paul Dry Books edition, 2009

Paul Dry Books, Inc.
Philadelphia, Pennsylvania
www.pauldrybooks.com

Printed in the United States of America

Library of Congress Cataloging-in-Publication Data
John, of Salisbury, Bishop of Chartres, d. 1180.
  [Metalogicus. English]
  The metalogicon : a twelfth-century defense of the verbal and logical arts
of the trivium / John of Salisbury ; translated with an introduction & notes
by Daniel D. McGarry. — 1st Paul Dry Books ed.
      p. cm.
  Originally published: Berkeley : University of California Press, 1955.
  Includes bibliographical references and index.
  ISBN 978-1-58988-058-0 (alk. paper)
  1. Logic—Early works to 1800. 2. Logic, Medieval. I. McGarry, Daniel D.
II. Title.
  B765.J43M43 2009
  160—dc22
                                                          2009033167

To

D A V I D   K N U T H   B J O R K

and

E R N E S T   C A R R O L L   M O O R E

Scholars, Educators, Friends

PREFACE

Horace admonishes us to wait nine years before publishing the product of our pen:

> . . . *If ever you write anything,*
> . . . *Keep it to yourself for nine years,*
> *For what has never been divulged can be destroyed,*
> *But once published, it is beyond recall.*

The somewhat dure prescription of the author of the Ars Poetica *has been more than fulfilled in the present work, begun in 1937, completed in its original form in 1940, and now submitted to publication. During the interim, since 1940, in imitation of many a mediaeval craftsman, the writer has returned to labor on his opus whenever indulgent fate has allowed. Additional sources have been consulted and old references more thoroughly studied, the advice of competent specialists has been solicited, and several revisions have been effected in the interests of accuracy and clarity.*

At length the work is dispatched with fond farewell. Admittedly imperfect, as any translation, especially of this sort, must be, it begs the reader's indulgence. The confession of shortcomings that John of Salisbury quotes from Martial, may well be echoed here, with the same realistic remark that: "Otherwise, oh Avitus, there would be no book."

In accomplishing the present project, the writer has incurred a vast indebtedness. Professor David K. Bjork of the University of California, Los Angeles, his master in mediaevalia *and sage mentor, has consistently encouraged and guided oft faltering footsteps o'er the arduous ways of scholarship. Professor Emeritus Ernest Carroll Moore, former Provost of the same University, who originally suggested this particular endeavor, has ever remained its staunch and efficacious supporter. Without his generous coöperation and that of his wife, Professor Emeritus Kate Gordon Moore, the publication of this work would not have been possible.*

The contributions of the writer's mother, Ana Doyle McGarry, deceased father, Daniel Francis McGarry, and wife, Margaret, defy definition. Edward M., Alice M., and Mae A. Doyle have also aided in many important ways. A fellowship provided by the late Archbishop of Los Angeles, John J. Cantwell, made possible an invaluable year of research in Europe. More recently, aid from the Graduate School of Indiana University permitted active resumption of the project, while a grant from the American Philosophical Society facilitated its successful completion. Nor can enough be said of the patient forbearance and invaluable suggestions of the editorial staff of the University of California Press.

Gratitude is further expressed to the administration of the Corpus Christi College Library at Cambridge, the Bodleian Library at Oxford, and the British Museum for their courtesy in permitting the microfilming of fundamental manuscript codices.

Without the assistance of the dean of Salisbury scholars, Clement C. J. Webb, this undertaking would have been incalculably more difficult. Dr. Webb's critical edition of the Metalogicon *has provided a sound starting point for most of this translation, and the distinguished scholar has been unstinting in his aid to the present writer.*

Among numerous others who deserve thanks for their assistance and encouragement are Frederick W. Householder, Albert L. Kohlmeier, Arthur P. MacKinlay, Bishop Joseph T. McGucken, Charles R. D. Miller, Dayton Philips, Jean R. Redon, Robert Gordon Sproul, Stith Thompson, and Leon Van der Essen.

Even partial realization of the writer's hope that this work will help to further our understanding of the foundations of Western education and learning, and broaden the basis for further research relative to educational theory and practice in the formative Middle Ages will constitute ample repayment for any labors involved in this undertaking.

Saint Louis University   *Daniel D. McGarry*
St. Louis, Missouri

CONTENTS

The Metalogicon

BOOK TWO

[PROLOGUE]

CHAPTER

CONTENTS

CONTENTS

INTRODUCTION

Man's civilization is the sum of his constructive achievement, the substance of his well being, the key of his progress. Yet in the historical development of human culture, one of the most essential and determining factors has ever been education. Paradoxically, education is both a product and producer of civilization. Besides being the regenerative process whereby man transmits his culture, it is also the revitalizing means whereby he reforms it.

In the analysis of this fundamental cultural factor that we term education, as in all research in the social field, the study of genetic development is enlightening. Hence it is that the evolution of educational thought and practice has come to receive increasing attention.

Those who seriously study the history of Western pedagogy come to the inevitable conclusion that the Middle Ages are of fundamental importance. During the mediaeval millennium our education, like so much of the rest of our civilization, was conceived in its essential present-day lineaments. It is true that constituent elements were Greek, Roman, and early Christian in origin, yet it is also true that these received new form and life in the Middle Ages.

If we wish precisely to fix the birth of modern Western pedagogy, it may well be placed in the twelfth century. In that epoch, not only was the curriculum in grammar greatly broadened and deepened, but also logic, the science of rational investigation, was more enthusiastically and intensively cultivated and applied to various categories of human knowledge. As a result, in that and succeeding centuries, fertilization by the rational method continued to beget and improve theology, philosophy, philology, and finally the physical, biological, and social sciences, in a process that knows no end.

For the twelfth-century educational "renaissance," we fortunately possess a most excellent source. The *Metalogicon* of John of Salisbury, completed in 1159, is a defense of logic in its broad sense. This extraordinary treatise summarizes and argues convincingly on behalf of the thorough study of grammar and logic, including rhetoric, as then offered in the higher educational institutions of northern France. During the eight centuries that have since elapsed, this pedagogical classic has never been translated in its entirety. Meanwhile, however, John of Salisbury's parallel treatise on political theory, the *Policraticus*, together with many another mediaeval work of similar significance, has been made available to scholars in careful vernacular rendition. Yet it would be difficult to maintain that any of these treatises contains more important implications for the history of civilization than does the present one.

JOHN OF SALISBURY

The author of the *Metalogicon* was born, of humble origin, at Old Sarum (Salisbury),[1] in southern England, between 1115 and 1120.[2] As a boy, John of Salisbury seems early to have manifested an above-average intellect and been marked as promising ecclesiastical timber. Accordingly, despite his lack of means, we soon find him "learning the Psalter" from a local priest.[3] In quest of further learning, he crossed the Channel to France in 1136.[4] There, in the stimulating cultural atmosphere of Paris and Chartres, he studied for most of twelve years under several of the most brilliant masters of his day. John was a disciple of such great teachers as Peter Abelard,[5] Robert of Melun, later Bishop of Hereford, Thierry of Chartres,[6]

[1] Called at this time Saresberia or Severia, according to John of Salisbury (*Policraticus*, vi, 18; viii, 19); the antecedent of modern Salisbury. See Gleason White, *The Cathedral Church of Salisbury . . . and a Brief History of the See of Sarum.*

[2] The earlier date, 1110, given for his birth by some writers, e.g., H. O. Taylor (*Mediaeval Mind*, II, 201), is not accepted by Poole and Webb. Indeed, it does not accord with John's own statement (*Metalogicon*, ii, 10) that he was but a youth ("adolescens admodum") when he went to Paris to study in 1136.

[3] *Policraticus*, ii, 28.

[4] Most of the information concerning his student life comes from his *Metalogicon* (ii, 10; i, 5). (Hereafter cited as *Met.*)

[5] John refers (*Met.*, ii, 10, 17 ff.) to Abelard as "the Peripatetic from Pallet." The great master was in his fifties when John attended his lectures as an eager student.

[6] Thierry first taught at Chartres, later at Paris, whence he returned to Chartres to become chancellor in 1141.

William of Conches,[7] Richard l'Evêque,[8] Gilbert de la Porrée,[9] and
the English divine, Robert Pullen.[10] With their help, he became
thoroughly grounded in the literary and dialectical Trivium, and
learned something of the mathematical and scientific Quadrivium.
On the completion of his theological studies under Simon of Poissy,[11]
he was ordained to the priesthood, probably at the Abbey Moutier
de la Celle.[12]

After half a dozen or more years of training and service with the
papal court,[13] John was recalled to his native England in 1154 to
assume the important position of secretary to Theobald, Archbishop
of Canterbury. This position had apparently come to him through
the good offices of Bernard of Clairvaux.[14] As secretary to the primate of England, he served on many important diplomatic missions,
and journeyed several times to Italy, as well as to France and about
England.[15] By 1159, when he dispatched the *Metalogicon,* together
with the *Policraticus,* to Henry II's chancellor, Thomas Becket, John
was a kind of plenipotentiary vicar general or "alter ego" for the
aged and ailing Archbishop Theobald.[16] On the latter's death in
1161, John continued as secretary to the new archbishop, Thomas

[7] John studied grammar and philosophy with William for three years. He says that he
learned much from "the most learned and inspiring grammarian since Bernard of Chartres."

[8] Styled "l'Evêque" even before he became Bishop of Avranches in 1171.

[9] John's master in logic and theology, he later became Bishop of Poitiers. See John of
Salisbury, *Historia Pontificalis,* chap. 12.

[10] Eminent theologian, later a cardinal and papal chancellor. See R. L. Poole, "The
Early Lives of Nicholas Breakespeare and Robert Pullen," in *Essays in Mediaeval History
Presented to Thomas Frederick Tout,* pp. 61–64.

[11] Characterized by John (*Met.,* ii, 10) as a "reliable lecturer, but somewhat dull when
it comes to discussion."

[12] See on this, Maurice Demimuid (*Jean de Salisbury,* pp. 37–39), who bases his surmise
on John's *Ep.* 85, and Peter of Celle's *Epp.,* iv, 5, 7, 9; vii, 67; all in J. P. Migne, ed.,
Patrologiae cursus completus. Series latina, CXCIX and CCII. (Hereafter cited as Migne,
P.L.)

[13] See R. L. Poole, "John of Salisbury at the Papal Court," in *English Historical Review,*
XXXVIII (1923), 321–330, whose conclusions are based for the most part on the *Historia Pontificalis.*

[14] John was introduced to Archbishop Theobald by Bernard of Clairvaux at the Council
of Rheims in 1148 (*Hist. Pont.,* chaps. 1–15). The great Bernard also wrote a letter of
recommendation on John's behalf to Theobald (*Ep.* 361, in Migne, *P.L.,* CLXXXII, 562).

[15] John says (*Met.,* iii, Prologue) that he crossed the Alps ten times. See also R. L.
Poole, "Early Correspondence of John of Salisbury," in *Proceedings of the British Academy,*
XI (1924), 51

[16] *Met.,* Prologue; iv, 42.

Becket, whose intimate counsellor he became.[17] It is not unlikely
that much of Becket's dramatic "conversion" and continuation of
the Canterbury tradition of championship of Church liberties and
privileges against royal usurpation are partly traceable to John's
influence. Meanwhile John's activities, including the writing of his
*Policraticus, sive de nugis curialium et vestigiis philosopohorum
libri VIII,* which condoned the assassination of a tyrannical ruler,
as well as his composition of a *Life of St. Anselm,* which lauded
the sanctity of this spirited defender of ecclesiastical prerogatives
against the English monarchy, brought down upon his head re-
current manifestations of the displeasure of King Henry II. Periods
during which the learned cleric was forced to absent himself from
England ensued. Nor was it long before John came to have Archbishop Thomas Becket as his companion in exile. When both returned to Canterbury during an ephemeral reconciliation of king
and primate, John witnessed the murder of Becket by King Henry's
knights in Canterbury Cathedral on December 29, 1170.[18] Six years
later John, befriended by Louis VII, was elevated to the episcopate
of Chartres. There he spent the remaining four years of his life,
dying a revered bishop on October 25, 1180.[19]

Although he was influential in the affairs of his day, John of
Salisbury is especially admired by posterity for his writings. Particu-
larly important are his *Policraticus,* or "Statesman's Book," [20] his
Metalogicon, or "Defense of the Trivium," and his Letters. John's
Policraticus is ranked as a mediaeval classic on political theory. His
Metalogicon occupies a similar position in the history of educational
theory. He is also considered one of the leading letter writers of his
day, and, according to some, of all time. Some three hundred and

[17] Cf. e.g., John's *Epp.,* 113, 138, 142, in Migne, *P.L.,* CXCIX, 98–99, 116–118, 122–
123; as well as Petrus Blesensis, *Ep.* 22, *ibid.,* CCVII, 77–82.
[18] Cf. Willelmus Filius Stephani, *Vita et passio sancti Thomae,* in Migne, *P.L.,* CXC,
183–184; and John's own account in his *Vita sancti Thomae, ibid.,* CXC, 206–208.
[19] His virtues and beneficial administration are warmly praised in "Elogium Johannis
Saresberiensis episcopi Carnotensis," from the *Necrologium Carnotense,* in *Gallia Christiana,*
VIII, 1148–1149.
[20] The Latin text has been critically edited by Clement C. J. Webb in two volumes
(Oxford, 1909). It has been translated, in two parts, by John Dickinson as *The Statesman's Book* (New York, 1927), and by Joseph H. Pike, *Frivolities of Courtiers and
Footprints of Philosophers* (Minneapolis, 1938).

twenty-five of his Epistles are extant in printed form.²¹ His other works include two philosophic poems, each entitled *Entheticus*, the shorter being an introduction to his *Policraticus*, the longer a history of philosophy in 1,852 elegiac verses;²² his *Historia Pontificalis*, an account of the papacy from 1148 to 1152;²³ a *Life of St. Anselm, Archbishop of Canterbury*,²⁴ and a *Life of Thomas, Archbishop of Canterbury*.²⁵

HISTORY OF THE TEXT

Composed to defend the arts of verbal expression and reasoning comprised in the Trivium, the *Metalogicon*, on its completion in the fall of 1159,²⁶ was sent, together with the *Policraticus*, to Chancellor Thomas Becket, to whom both of these works were addressed.²⁷

The principal extant manuscripts of the *Metalogicon* are the *Cantuariensis, De Bello,* and *S. Albani* codices. In each of these the text of the *Metalogicon* is preceded by that of the *Policraticus*, as it was originally presented to Thomas Becket. The *Cantuariensis* (Canterbury or "C") codex, on parchment in folio, is in the Corpus Christi College Library at Cambridge University: MS Cod. 46, fols. 184ʳ–239ʳ. It dates from the twelfth or, at the latest, the thirteenth century. There is little doubt that this was the original copy presented to Becket, for the title page shows the erasure of the follow-

---

²¹ Mostly to be found in Migne, *P.L.*, CXCIX, 1–378.
²² The short *Entheticus* is prefaced to the *Policraticus* in the Webb edition; the long *Entheticus* is in Migne, *P.L.*, CXCIX, 965–1004. The best edition of the long *Entheticus* is that of Christian Petersen (Hamburg, 1843).
²³ The best edition is that of Reginald Lane Poole (Oxford, 1927).
²⁴ *Vita sancti Anselmi archiepiscopi Cantuariensis* in Migne, *P.L.*, CXCIX, 1110–1140.
²⁵ *Vita sancti Thomae Cantuariensis archiepiscopi et martyris, ibid.*, CXC, 195–203.
²⁶ The *Metalogicon* must have been composed after the *Policraticus*, to which it alludes, and which had been completed in August or September, 1159. When John wrote the final chapter, he already knew of the death of Pope Adrian IV, August 31, 1159, and the election of Cardinal Octavian as Antipope Victor IV, in the first week of September, although the news of the lifting of the siege of Toulouse at the close of the same month had not yet reached him. Cf. Webb, *John of Salisbury*, p. 19; and Poole, "Early Correspondence of John of Salisbury," *Proceedings of the British Academy*, XI (1924), 31–32, 36; as well as *Met.*, iv, 42.
²⁷ *Met.*, Prologue, and iv, 42.

ing words: "Sci. Thome archiepiscopi."[28] It is interesting to note that even in this, presumably original copy, the scribe apparently made some mistakes. The *De Bello* (Battle Abbey or "B") codex, also on parchment in folio, is in the Bodleian Library of Oxford University: MS Lat. Misc., c.16, fols. 136^v–170^v. Of the thirteenth, or at the latest, the early fourteenth century, it rarely disagrees with the *Cantuariensis,* except that it breaks off abruptly at Chapter 36 of the concluding book (Bk. IV), which comprises forty-two chapters.[29] A notation on the first page indicates that the codex was given to Battle Abbey by Abbot Richard (+1235). The *S. Albani* (St. Alban's or "A") codex is in the British Museum: MS Reg. 13, D, IV, fols. 161^r–208^r. It is likewise on parchment in folio, and probably dates from the twelfth century. An inscription on the first page states that the manuscript was given to St. Alban's by Abbot Simon, who is known to have died in 1188.

To date, the Latin text of the *Metalogicon* has been published in six printed editions.[30] Three editions appeared in the seventeenth century: Paris, 1610, Leyden, 1639, and Amsterdam, 1664; all of them based on the text of a Cambridge University manuscript.[31] Two editions were published in the nineteenth and one in the twentieth century.[32] The last, the definitive edition, by Clement C. J. Webb, utilizes the principal codices, the "C," "B," and "A," and notes divergent readings in its critical apparatus. This excellent critical edition has been invaluable to the present translator.

Despite its six Latin editions and extensive use by historians, the *Metalogicon* has never before been translated in its entirety. Many

[28] See Montague Rhodes James, *The Ancient Libraries of Canterbury and Dover,* pp. xlii, 85, 158, 510; and *The Sources of Archbishop Parker's Collection of Manuscripts at Corpus Christi College,* pp. 5, 22.
[29] For a description of this manuscript, see Falconer Madan, *Summary Catalogue of Western Manuscripts in the Bodleian Library at Oxford,* VI, no. 32708 (p. 189).
[30] In the early printed editions the title *Metalogicon* was changed to *Metalogicus;* doubtless the modified ending was due to the influence of the *Policraticus.*
[31] Apparently the Cambridge Univ. Lib., MS Codex I, i-ii, 31. See *Catalogue of MSS in the University Library at Cambridge,* III, 400.
[32] In the nineteenth century: that of J. A. Giles: *Ioannis Sarisberiensis . . . , Opera Omnia, nunc primum in unum colligit et cum codicibus manuscriptis contulit,* 5 vols. (Oxford, 1848). The *Metalogicus* is in Vol. V, 1–207. In the same century the Giles edition was reproduced without the critical notes in Migne, *P.L.,* CXCIX. In the twentieth century appeared Clement C. J. Webb's edition: *Ioannis Saresberiensis Episcopi Carnotensis, Metalogicon Libri IIII* (Oxford, 1929).

distinguished scholars have, however, included extensive translated extracts in their own works; for example, Carl Schaarschmidt, Reginald Lane Poole, Jules Alexandre Clerval, Charles Sears Baldwin, Barthélemy Hauréau, Etienne Gilson, Charles Homer Haskins, and Henry Osborn Taylor.[33]

ANALYSIS OF THE METALOGICON

The name "Metalogicon" is of Greek derivation, in accordance with a fad for Greek titles prevalent among twelfth-century writers.[34] It is apparently a synthesis, original with John of Salisbury, of the two Greek words "μετὰ": "about," "for," or "on behalf of," and "λογικῶν": "logic," "logical studies," or "the arts relative to words and reasoning." The author informs us that his title means "a defense of," or "plea for" the studies of the Trivium.[35] He explains that the Greek "λογικῶν" (Lat. *logica*), means both "word" and "reason," and that the term "logic" is here used in its broader sense: embracing not only the science of reasoning but also the arts and sciences of verbal expression.

The *Metalogicon* was composed to refute attacks made on the Trivium by a group whose spokesman John dubs "Cornificius,"[36] after the detractor of Vergil and the liberal arts, who is mentioned by Donatus in his *Life of Vergil*.[37] The work comprises four books, each divided into several chapters. Its contents may be analyzed as follows:

General Prologue: Introduction

Occasion, Purpose, and General Nature of the Work

[33] Schaarschmidt, *Johannes Saresberiensis nach Leben und Studien, Schriften und Philosophie;* Poole, *Illustrations of the History of Mediaeval Thought . . . ;* Clerval, *Les Écoles de Chartres au moyen-âge...* ; Baldwin, *Mediaeval Rhetoric and Poetic;* Hauréau, *Histoire de la philosophie scolastique;* Gilson, *La Philosophie au moyen-âge;* Haskins, *The Renaissance of the Twelfth Century;* Taylor, *Mediaeval Mind.*

[34] Examples are St. Anselm's *Monologium* and *Proslogium;* Hugh of St. Victor's *Didascalion;* William of Champeaux's *Dragmaticon.*

[35] *Met.,* Prologue.

[36] See *Met.,* i, 1–3.

[37] Donatus, *Vita Vergilii interpolata* (ed. Brummer, pp. 30 ff.).

A treatise on education, the *Metalogicon* urges thorough grounding in the arts relative to words (written as well as oral) and reasoning as these were then included in grammar and logic. Warning
against various pedagogical aberrations, it advocates the use of
sound psychological methods. It surveys the proper content of
courses. "Grammar," a much broader subject in that day, embraced
not only grammar as we know it, but also writing, spelling, composition, and "speech," together with general literature, including
poetry and history.[38] Logic, "the science of reasoning," [39] John tells
us, has truth as its object, and is best mastered by study (of the

---

[38] For grammar: *Met.*, i, 13–25
[39] For logic proper: *Met.*, ii, iii, and iv, 1–8, 21–29.

contents, if not always of the text) of Aristotle's *Organon*.[40] This
discussion leads on to a survey of the psychology of cognition.[41]
The successive faculties of sensation and imagination, reason, and
intuitive understanding; together with the ascending cognitive acts
of opinion (from sensation and mental images), scientific knowledge, and wisdom; as well as the relation of faith and reasoning
are all discussed. Truth: cognitive, affective, and practical, is upheld
as the object of human reason and life.[42]

SOURCES

The list of known sources drawn on in composing the *Metalogicon* reads much as might the index for a condensed and combined
edition of Greek and Roman classical authors, together with Pa-
tristic and mediaeval Christian writers (to the middle of the twelfth
century). It is not always certain, of course, whether John had read
the whole or part of the works in question, or merely extracts.
Works of classical antiquity constitute John's principal sources. Although he knew some Greek, he apparently used his Greek sources
in Latin translations. (The bibliography to the present translation
lists works used by John.) Aristotle's *Organon* occupies first place.[43]
Plato's *Timaeus,* together with Chalcidius and Apuleius on Plato's
doctrines, and Porphyry, Cicero, and Lucius Annaeus Seneca, the
Younger, are further philosophical sources. On education in grammar, rhetoric, and the liberal arts, Quintilian, Marcus Annaeus
Seneca, the Elder, Cicero and Martianus Capella are used; and on
scientific subjects, Hippocrates, Pliny, Seneca the Younger, Palladius,
and Vegetius. From the field of general literature John employs
Terence, Catullus, Vergil, Horace, Ovid, Publilius Syrus, Valerius
Maximus, Persius, Martial, Lucan, Statius, Juvenal, Suetonius, Gellius, Macrobius, and Pseudo-Plautus. Extensive use is made of the
works of Church Fathers and subsequent mediaeval writers: Sts.
Hilary of Poitiers, Jerome, Ambrose, Augustine, and Gregory the

[40] See *Met.,* iii, 2–10; iv, 1–8, 21–29.
[41] Discussed in *Met.,* iv, 9–20.
[42] *Met.,* iv, 30–42.
[43] Aristotle's *Organon* is discussed in *Met.,* iii, 2–10; iv, 1–8, 21–29.

Great, together with Dionysius the Pseudo-Areopagite, Nemesius the Bishop, St. Fulgentius, Claudianus Mamertus, Boethius, Cassiodorous, St. Benedict, Alcuin, Angelomus of Luxeuil, Abelard, Gilbert de la Porée, Hugh of St. Victor, Adam du Petit Pont, William of Conches, and Bernard of Chartres. Works on grammar, history, science, and general topics include those of Sts. Augustine, Isidore of Seville, and Venerable Bede, Victorinus, Sidonius Apollinaris, Boethius, Cassiodorus, Remigius of Auxerre, Theodulus, Hugh of St. Victor, Tenred, and Geoffrey of Monmouth. Quotations from both the Old and New Testaments are liberally sprinkled throughout the *Metalogicon*. The *Salernitanum Regimen sanitatis,* the *Digests* from Justinian's *Corpus Juris Civilis,* and the *Mythographi Tres* are also used.

LATIN OF THE METALOGICON

Pronounced to be of the best and purest in the Middle Ages, still John of Salisbury's Latin displays features that mark it as of the twelfth century, when Latin was as yet alive and evolving. Not to mention the special new meanings attached to many words, there are several peculiarities in spelling. The single vowel *e* is always used instead of the diphthongs *æ* and *œ*;[44] *i* and *y* are frequently interchanged,[45] as also are *t* and *c*; and *h* is often omitted or, vice versa, added. John never uses *j* for *i* or *v* for *u,* as do many later Latin writers. Numerous mediaeval Latin words are to be found in the text, such as "diacrisis," "subarrauerunt," "maneries," and "discolor":[46] together with distinctly Christian terms, or words used in a distinctly Christian sense, such as "Christiane," "fidelibus," "ecclesiam," and "episcopus";[47] and Greek words transliterated into the Latin alphabet, such as "logos," "lecton," "lexis," and "idos,"[48] and even provided with Latin endings, as "simplasim," "kirriadoxas," "paradoxas," "Fronesim," and "Alicie."[49] Not only is John's

[44] As in *cecum, estuantis, fedus, cherillus.*
[45] As in *ydolorum* and *hipoteseos.*
[46] Cf. *Met.,* i, 24; ii, Prol., 17; iii, 10.
[47] Cf. *Met.,* iv, 42, 27; ii, 10.
[48] *Met.,* i, 10; ii, 4, 17, 20.
[49] *Met.,* iv, 10, 31; ii, 3.

grammar in general flawless, but his style has been lauded as the most graceful of the twelfth century, and even of the Middle Ages.[50] The text is enlivened by variety, antitheses, apt figures of speech, poetical quotations, classical references, and dashes of humor, which flavor its keen and penetrating thought.[51]

HISTORICAL POSITION

The *Metalogicon* has been termed by Charles Sears Baldwin "the cardinal treatise of mediaeval pedagogy."[52] Whether or not Baldwin's absolute superlative is demonstrable, there can be no doubt that John of Salisbury's spirited "Defense of the Trivium" constitutes a classic in the history of educational theory. Furthermore, as a reasoned presentation of the theoretical bases of an educational prospectus which prevailed, and continued to prevail in Western Europe, it no doubt had some influence on the development of modern education and civilization.

As we have said, on its completion in 1159, the *Metalogicon*, together with the *Policraticus,* was sent to the royal chancellor Thomas Becket, thus assuring its publication and influence. Several manuscript copies of the *Metalogicon* were subsequently made. These continued to circulate, as originally, in company with the *Policraticus.* Although not the kind of work that would attract a large public, the *Metalogicon* was apparently read by intellectual leaders such as Peter of Blois, Peter of Celle, Alexander Neckam, Robert Grosseteste, William of Auvergne, William of Auxerre, Helinand of Froidmont, Vincent of Beauvais, John Waleys, Walter Burley, and Geoffrey Chaucer.[53]

Abiding recognition of the *Metalogicon* is witnessed by the six separate printed editions through the centuries since Gutenberg and Coster. With augmented interest in the genetic development of education, learning, and thought, John's "Defense of the Trivium" has

[50] See Hauréau, *op. cit.,* I, 536; and Clerval, *op. cit.,* p. 230.
[51] For antitheses: *Met.,* iv, 41–42. For figures of speech: *Met.,* i, 18–19. For humor: *Met.,* i, 3; ii, 6, 7.
[52] Baldwin, *op. cit.,* p. 155.
[53] Cf. Webb in the Prolegomena to the *Policraticus,* p. xlviii. For Helinand: H. Hublocher, *Helinand von Froidmont und sein Verhältnis zu Johannes von Salisbury.*

come to be one of our most thumbed sources. Many accounts of the history of Western intellectual culture are liberally sprinkled with footnotes referring to the *Metalogicon;* indeed, some go so far as to quote extensive translated extracts. Representative authorities relying considerably on the *Metalogicon* include: Friedrich Ueberweg, Heinrich Ritter, Barthélemy Hauréau, François Picavet, Martin Grabmann, Etienne Gilson, Maurice de Wulf, and Karl Prantl in the history of philosophy; James Mark Baldwin and George S. Brett in the history of psychology; and Leon Maitre, Augusta Drane, Jules Alexandre Clerval, Hastings Rashdall, G. Robert, Charles S. Baldwin, Bigerius Thorlacius, Reginald Lane Poole, Bishop William Stubbs, J. E. Sandys, G. Paré, A. Brunet, and P. Tremblay, Eduard Norden, F. A. Wright, Charles Homer Haskins, and T. A. Sinclair in the history of education and learning.

The *Metalogicon,* reflecting its versatile author, sparkles with many facets. It is important enough to be something of a landmark in several fields of learning, including philosophy, theology, psychology, and education. In philosophy, it is the first known work to urge and provide the blueprint for a widespread study of the whole of Aristotelian logic.[54] Its convincing arguments for the mastery of the arts relative to deductive and inductive reasoning led naturally, not only into thirteenth-century scholasticism, but also even into modern science. There can be no doubt that modern trends in philosophy and learning are discernible in its frank eclecticism, moderate skepticism, historical approach, and stress on practical applicability.[55] In theology, its concept of the coöperative relation between faith and reason suggests the maxim of mutual corroboration accepted by thirteenth-century thinkers. In psychology, it is classed as both an early instance of empirical psychology, and a crier heralding the possibilities and future evolution of this science.[56] In learning it is a golden example of mediaeval familiarity

---

[54] Thus Karl Prantl in *Geschichte der Logik* . . . , Bd. II (Vol. I), 233–260, where almost thirty pages are given to a discussion of John of Salisbury.

[55] For eclecticism: *Met.*, Prologue; and iii, Prologue. For moderate skepticism: *Met.*, iv, 31, 41. For historical approach: *Met.*, Prologue; i, 1–6, 11–14, 24–25; ii, Prologue, 1–2, 6, 10, 16–20, *passim.*

[56] G. S. Brett, *A History of Psychology*, II, 87, 93, 219–220; and J. M. Baldwin, *History of Psychology*, I, 86 ff., 100.

with classical literary lore, as well as of accomplished Latinity. Finally, it is a treasure-trove of information concerning twelfth-century pedagogy, as well as an enduring classic by its own right in the field of educational theory.

IOANNES
SARESBERIENSIS
METALOGICVS.

*E Codice M S. Academiæ
Cantabrigienſis.*

Nunc primum Editus.

PARISIIS.
Apud HADRIANVM BEYS.
Viâ Iacobæa.

M.ᐧDC. X.

THE METALOGICON

PROLOGUE

I believe that there is hardly anything human, which is so free from defect as to be completely immune from detraction. For what is bad is deservedly denounced; while what is good is maliciously slandered.[1] Reconciled to this, I have steeled myself to bear with patience the darts of detractors. Which resignation is especially necessary, since, in accordance with the divine plan, mother nature has brought us forth in our present day, and in this region of the world, while fate has assigned us the lot of being associated with those who would rather criticize the works of others than look after, order, and reform their own lives. [To the latter applies the saying:]

> Not a one attempts to examine his own conscience,
> Rather, each stares at the bag on the back of the fellow in front.[2]

While it is true that, by keeping silent, I might have avoided being criticized by scholars and those who make a profession of philosophy, I was utterly at a loss to evade the snapping teeth of my fellow members of the court. Being respectful to all and injuring no one used, of yore, to assure one of popularity. Such was the formula given by the comic poet, whereby "One can gain praise unmixed with envy, and win for himself friends."[3] In our day, however, the aforesaid policy rarely even suffices to repress the envy of one's comrades. The habit of obedience is branded as a stigma of servility, and the absence of guilt is deemed an admission of impotence. A

---

[1] Cf. Ovid, *Pont.*, iii, 4, 74. (For full data on references cited, see the bibliography.)
[2] Persius, *Sat.*, iv, 23, 24. This is a reference to the fable that everyone, while conscious of the faults of others, thrusts his own into a bag on his back, where he cannot see them.
[3] Terence, *And.*, i, 1, 35–39 (62–66).

person who is quiet is accused of ignorance, one who is fluent is classed with the garrulous. A man whose manner is serious is suspected of dark designs, one of less gravity is charged with levity and incompetence. Anyone who makes an effort to be modest in word and action is adjudged to be a sycophant, who is courting popularity. Even where actual bickering is absent, ill feeling is hardly ever at rest. Had I wasted my every moment in the company of my fellow members of the court, frittering away all my time in gambling, hunting, and like frivolous pastimes,[4] they could not now be slandering my writings, just as I cannot find any of theirs to challenge.[5] However, I am little concerned if what I write is criticized by persons who magnify the judgment of comedians and actors,[6] and quake as groveling slaves for fear Thais[7] or Thraso,[8] Callirrhoe,[9] or Bathyllus[10] may say or think something deprecatory about them. On the other hand, if professors of philosophy[11] persecute an admirer of those who philosophize, clearly they are doing me an injustice and are poorly repaying my devotion. Even though I cannot be one of them, I am certainly endeavoring to love, honor, and respect them. The support of scholars is due me, inasmuch as I am defending, to the full extent of my capabilities,[12] what they are or what they have been. If I have succeeded, thanks and a reward are due me for the happy event; whereas even if I have failed, I still deserve the same for my good intentions, in accordance with the quotation:

> You declare that I have accomplished naught, and have lost the case;
> But so much the more are you indebted to me, O Sextus, because I have been put to shame.[13]

I do not exclude abler men from pleading the cause of scholarship, when I attest my own devotion. Let the more distinguished author-

---

[4] Cf. *Policraticus*, i, 4 ff.
[5] Evidently a play on the fact that his fellow courtiers, who were criticizing John's writings, had none of their own, since they had wasted all their time on trifles.
[6] Cf. I Corinthians, iv, 3
[7] Thais: a prostitute in Terence's comedy *Eunuchus*.
[8] Thraso: a boastful soldier in the same comedy.
[9] Callirrhoe: probably a female dancer; cf. Persius, *Sat.*, i, 134.
[10] Bathyllus: a comic dancer; cf. Persius, *Sat.*, v, 123.
[11] *philosophie professores*, professors of philosophy: those who teach philosophy or make a profession of philosophizing.
[12] *quali possum aduocatione defendo*, I defend their cause to the utmost of my ability.
[13] Martial, *Epigr.*, viii, 17.

itatively lend their mighty hand to silence all opposition, and to incline the scales in favor of the logicians. Since, however, the labors of the latter [logicians] were being lampooned as a waste of time, and my opponent was goading me on by his almost daily controversies, finally, indignant and objecting, I took up his challenge and determined to strike down his calumnies even as they issued from his mouth. Hence, I have planned my work to answer his objections. I have thus often omitted more important points in order to refute his arguments. It was he, indeed, who determined the course of our discussion. My friends pressed me to compose[14] this work, even if I had practically to throw the words together.[15] For I had neither the leisure nor energy to enter into a subtle analysis of opinions, much less to polish my style. My regular duties have consumed all my time, save that required for eating and sleeping. By the commission of my lord,[16] whom I cannot disappoint, the responsibility[17] for the whole of Britain, as far as ecclesiastical matters[18] are concerned, is on my shoulders. Administrative concerns and the [time-consuming] trifles of court life[19] have precluded study, and the interruptions of friends have used up practically all the time I had left. Consequently, I do not think I should be too harshly judged if any of my statements seem insufficiently considered. On the other hand, the credit for anything that I may say which seems more apt is to be referred to Him without Whom human weakness is powerless.[20] I am by nature too dull to comprehend the subtleties of the ancients; I cannot rely on my memory to retain for long what I have learned; and my style betrays its own lack of polish. This treatise, which I have taken care to divide into four books for the reader's refreshment, is entitled THE METALOGICON.[21] For, in it, I undertake to defend logic. According to the wont of writers, I have included

[14] *dictarem*, to dictate or compose.
[15] *tumultuario sermone;* cf. Quintilian, *Inst. Or.,* x, 7, §§ 12, 13.
[16] Theobald, Archbishop of Canterbury.
[17] *sollicitudo;* cf. *Met.,* iv, 42. A great many of John's letters were written for Archbishop Theobald. Cf. *Epp.,* 1–25.
[18] *causas* (ecclesiastical) business, matters, affairs, or cases.
[19] Occupations connected with his official position in the archbishop's curia.
[20] Cf. John, xv, 5.
[21] *Metalogicon,* probably from μετά and λογικῶν: "about" or "on behalf of logic" or "logical studies" (the Trivium).

various points, which each reader is at liberty to accept or reject as
he sees fit:

> Some things you will read herein are excellent, some mediocre, and
> several defective;
> But this is inevitable—as otherwise, dear Avitus, there would be no
> book.[22]

So says Martial, and I echo him. I prefer thus to speak in lighter
vein, rather than to "start hares" with Ganymede,[23] or to "Reek
of strong wine both night and day." [24] I have not been ashamed
to cite moderns, whose opinions in many instances, I unhesitatingly
prefer over those of the ancients. I trust that posterity will honor our
contemporaries, for I have profound admiration for the extraordinary talents, diligent studies, marvelous memories, fertile minds,
remarkable eloquence, and linguistic proficiency of many of those
of our own day. I have purposely incorporated into this treatise
some observations concerning morals, since I am convinced that
all things read or written are useless except so far as they have
a good influence on one's manner of life. Any pretext of philosophy that does not bear fruit in the cultivation of virtue and the
guidance of one's conduct is futile and false. Being an Academician[25] in matters that are doubtful to a wise man, I cannot swear
to the truth of what I say. Whether such propositions may be true
or false, I am satisfied with probable certitude.[26] It is hoped that, at
your convenience, you[27] will examine all the points that I have made
in detail, since, to rest assured that my labor and expenses will not
be unavailing, I have constituted you the judge of my little works.[28]
But should (as heaven forbid) my Alexis prefer any stageplayer, no
matter whom, to a would-be philosopher, then, "If this Alexis spurns

---

[22] Martial, *Epigr.*, i, 16.

[23] *lepores agitare;* cf. Theodulus, *Eclog.*, v, 78 (ed. Osternacher, p. 35).

[24] Horace, *Ep.*, i, 19, 11. Horace makes reference to an opinion that one must be a
good winebibber in order to be a successful poet.

[25] John here aligns himself with Cicero and the teachers of the Later Academy, who
professed a moderate skepticism.

[26] Cf. *Policraticus*, vii, 2.

[27] "you," namely Thomas Becket, to whom the *Metalogicon* is addressed.

[28] John addressed the *Metalogicon*, the *Policraticus*, the short *Entheticus*, and probably
also the long *Entheticus* to Thomas Becket.

me, I will find another." [29] There are (more fully to explain my purpose) three things that cause me to fear, and that constitute for many writers a danger to their salvation or a loss of merit. These (three) are: ignorance of the truth, misled or wanton statement of falsehood, and the haughty assertion of fact. I concur with the author of the saying that "It is safer to hear the truth than to state it ourselves, for humility is guarded when we listen," [30] while pride often insinuates itself when we speak. I confess that I am at fault in all three respects. Not only am I handicapped by ignorance, but also frequently—indeed, too frequently—I make false statements, or maintain the truth with arrogance and pride, until reproved and corrected by God. Hence it is that I earnestly beseech my reader and listener to remember me in his prayers to the Most High, and to petition God to grant me pardon for my past offenses, security against future falls, knowledge of the truth, love of what is good, and devotion to Himself, as well as that we may accomplish, in thought, word, and action, what is pleasing to His divine will.

END OF PROLOGUE

[30] Augustine, *Tract. in Joann. Evang.*, lvii, § 2 (in Migne, *P.L.*, XXXV, 1790).
[29] Cf. Vergil, *Ecl.*, ii, 7

ʙooᴋ Oɴe

CHAPTER 1.   *The false accusation that has evoked this re-*
joinder to Cornificius.

The malicious wrangler [to whom we have referred] has stirred up against one of the most extraordinary gifts of mother nature and grace, the embers of an outdated charge,[1] long since discredited and dismissed as false and groundless by our ancestors. Barring no means in his effort to console himself for his own want of knowledge, he has contrived to improve his own reputation by making many others ignoramuses like himself. For inflated arrogance is marked by an overweening proclivity both to magnify its own good points, if it has any, and to belittle those of others, so that, measuring itself in comparison, it may count the shortcomings of others as signs of its own proficiency. All who possess real insight agree that nature, the most loving mother and wise[2] arranger of all that exists, has, among the various living creatures which she has brought forth, <u>elevated man by the privilege of reason, and distinguished him by the faculty of speech</u>. She has thus effected, by her affectionate care and well-ordered plan, that, even though he is oppressed and handicapped by the burden of his earthy nature and the sluggishness of his physical body, man may still rise to higher things. Borne aloft, so to speak, on wings of reason and speech, he is thus enabled, by this felicitous shortcut, to outstrip all other beings, and to attain the crown of true happiness. While grace fructifies [human] nature, reason looks after the observation and examination of facts, probes the secret depths of nature, and estimates all utility and worth. In the meantime, the love of good, inborn in all of us, seeks, as our natural appetite asserts

---

[1] See *Met.*, Prologue, above. John's opponent, Cornificius, claimed that logical studies are useless. Cf. also later, in this chapter.
[2] *dispositissima;* cf. Boethius, *Arithm.*, i, 27 (Friedlein, p. 55), and *Consol. Philos.*, iv, pr. i.

9

itself, what alone or particularly seems best adapted to the attainment
of happiness.[3] Since one cannot even imagine how any kind of happiness could exist entirely apart from mutual association and divorced
from human society, whoever assails what contributes to establish
and promote rightful order[4] in the latter [human society] (in a way
the sole and unique fraternity among the children of nature), would
seem to obstruct the way to beatitude for all. Having blocked the
road to peace, he incites the forces of nature to concur for the destruction of the world. This is "To sow discord among brothers,"[5] "to
supply arms"[6] to those at peace, and last, but not least, to establish
a new and "great chasm" between God and man.[7] The creative
Trinity, the one true God, has so arranged the parts of the universe
that each requires the help of the others, and they mutually compensate for their respective deficiencies, all things being, so to speak,
"members one of another."[8] All things lack something when iso-
lated, and are perfected on being united, since they mutually support
one another. What is more reliable, helpful, and efficacious for the
acquisition of happiness than virtue, which is practically the sole
means grace has provided for the attainment of beatitude? Those
who attain blessedness without meriting it by virtue, arrive at this
state by being drawn thither, rather than by going there themselves.
I consequently wonder (though not sufficiently, as it is beyond me)
what is the real aim of one who denies that eloquence should be
studied; who asserts that it comes as a natural gift to one who is not
mute, just as sight does to one who is not blind, and hearing to one
who is not deaf; and who further maintains that although nature's
gift is strengthened by exercise, nothing is to be gained by learning
the art [of eloquence], or at least that the benefit accruing is not
worth the effort that must be expended. Just as eloquence, unen-
lightened by reason, is rash and blind, so wisdom, without the power
of expression, is feeble and maimed. Speechless wisdom may sometimes increase one's personal satisfaction, but it rarely and only

[3] *beatitudo*, beatitude: perfect or complete happiness.
[4] *ius*, right, law, rightful order.
[5] Proverbs, vi, 19.
[6] Vergil, *Aen.*, i, 150.
[7] Luke, xvi, 26.
[8] Romans, xii, 5.

slightly contributes to the welfare of human society. Reason, the mother, nurse, and guardian of knowledge, as well as of virtue, frequently conceives from speech, and by this same means bears more abundant and richer fruit. Reason would remain utterly barren, or at least would fail to yield a plenteous harvest, if the faculty of speech did not bring to light its feeble conceptions, and communicate the perceptions of the prudent exercise of the human mind. Indeed, it is this delightful and fruitful copulation of reason and speech which has given birth to so many outstanding cities, has made friends and allies of so many kingdoms, and has unified and knit together in bonds of love so many peoples. Whoever tries to "thrust asunder what God has joined together" [9] for the common good, should rightly be adjudged a public enemy. One who would eliminate the teaching of eloquence from philosophical studies, begrudges Mercury [Eloquence] [10] his possession of Philology,[11] and wrests from Philology's arms her beloved Mercury.[12] Although he may seem to attack eloquence alone, he undermines and uproots all liberal studies, assails the whole structure of philosophy, tears to shreds humanity's social contract, and destroys the means of brotherly charity and reciprocal interchange of services. Deprived of their gift of speech, men would degenerate to the condition of brute animals, and cities would seem like corrals for livestock, rather than communities composed of human beings united by a common bond for the purpose of living in society, serving one another, and coöperating as friends. If verbal intercommunication were withdrawn, what contract could be duly concluded, what instruction could be given in faith and morals, and what agreement and mutual understanding could subsist among men? It may thus be seen that our "Cornificius," [13] ignorant and malevolent foe of studies pertaining to elo-

[9] Matthew, xix, 6.

[10] Mercury: god of eloquence (among other things); artful eloquence personified.

[11] *Philologia*, philosophy, or literary learning in general, personified.

[12] See Martianus Capella, *De Nuptiis*.

[13] "Cornificius" is the *nom de plume* given by John to the adversary of "logic," the spokesman of those who advocated less attention to "logical" studies (i.e., grammar, rhetoric, and logic). Cornificius was a detractor of Vergil, mentioned in an apparent interpolation in the *Vita Vergilii* by Donatus (in *Vitae Vergilianae*, ed. Jacob Brummer, pp. 10–11, 30–32, note to line 193). The real name of John's "Cornificius" is uncertain.

quence, attacks not merely one, or even a few persons, but all civilization and political organization.

CHAPTER 2.   *A description of Cornificius, without giving his*
name.

I would openly identify Cornificius and call him by his own name,
I would reveal to the public his bloated gluttony, puffed-up pride,[14]
obscene mouth, rapacious greed, irresponsible conduct, loathsome
habits (which nauseate all about him), foul lust, dissipated appearance, evil life, and ill repute, were it not that I am restrained by
reverence for his Christian name. In view of my profession and our
brotherly communion in the Lord, I have thought it better to be
lenient with the person, without ceding any quarter to his error. I
would reverence God, by sparing the nature, which comes from
Him, but attacking the vice, which is opposed to Him, since it cor-
rupts the nature of which He is Author.[15] It is but right, in resisting
an opinion, to avoid defaming the person who has sponsored it.
Nothing is more despicable than to attack the character of the pro-
ponent of a doctrine simply because his views are not to our liking.
It is far better that a false opinion be temporarily spared out of consideration for the person who holds it, provided his error is at all
tolerable, than that the person be calumniated because of his opinion.
All cases should be judged on their own merits, and retribution
should correspond to deserts, but in such a way that gentle mercy
prevails over strict severity. In view of the aforesaid, and lest I seem
to be slandering a personal enemy, rather than seeking the correction
of error, I have omitted mention of the name by which Cornificius is
regularly known. To tell the truth, nothing is farther from fact
[than to presume that I am more interested in discrediting a personal
foe than in establishing the truth]. As far as a Christian may licitly

---

[14] *tumorem uentris et mentis,* the swollen or bloated condition of his belly and mind:
his gluttony and pride.
[15] Cf. Augustine, *De C.D.,* xii, 3.

do so, I would despise both the person and his opinion. But let him
snore away till midday, become drunk in his daily carousals, and
squander his time by wallowing in carnal excesses which would
shame even an Epicurean pig,[16] as much as his heart desires. I will
confine myself to attacking his opinion, which has ruined many, as
not a few believe what he says. Despite the fact that this new Cornificius is less clever than the old one, a host of fools follow him. It
is a motley crowd, made up mostly of the lazy and dull, who are
trying to seem, rather than to become wise.

CHAPTER 3.   *When, how, and by whom Cornificius was edu-
              cated.*

I am not at all surprised that Cornificius, although he has been
hired at a high price, and has been thrashing the air for a long time,
has taught his credulous listeners to know nothing. For this was the
way in which he himself was "untaught" by his own masters. Verbose, rather than eloquent, he is continually tossing to the winds
verbal leaves that lack the fruit of meaning.[17] On the one hand, he
assails with bitter sarcasm the statements of everyone else, without
any concern as to who they may be, in the effort to establish his own
views and overthrow the opinions of others. On the other hand, he
carefully shuns engaging in hand-to-hand combat, and avoids bas-
ing his arguments on reason or consenting to walk together in the
field of the scriptures.[18] Really, I cannot imagine what extraordinary
thing, hidden from all the wise, Cornificius has conceived in the
swollen bellows of his windy lungs, wherefore he disdains to answer
or to listen with patience to anyone else. No matter what proposition

[16] *porcum Epicuri,* a pig or hog of Epicurus, or of the Epicurean herd; Horace, *Ep.,*
i, 4, 16.

[17] Cf. Vergil, *Aen.,* iii, 444 ff.; vi, 74 f. The Sibyl in the cave is said to inscribe notes
and names on leaves, which are subsequently swirled about and mixed by winds howling
through the cave.

[18] John says that Cornificius refuses to come down to earth and argue out questions, either
on the basis of reason or of revelation. Cf. Jerome, *Ep.,* lxxxii, 1 (in Migne, *P.L.,* XXII,
736). The word *scripturarum* might also mean "what has been written" in general,

is advanced, he rejects it as false, or laughs it to scorn. If you expect
him to prove his propositions, he puts you off, and when the day has
ended, you find you have been defrauded of what you were await-
ing. For he does not want to cast his pearls, so he says, before strange
swine.[19] Meanwhile he pastures his [sheepish] listeners on fictions
and foibles. He boasts that he has a shortcut whereby he will make
his disciples eloquent without the benefit of any art, and philosophers
without the need of any work. He himself learned from his own
teachers what he is today passing on to his pupils. He is ladling out
the very same kind of instruction that he himself received. He will
make his disciples his equals in philosophy. What more [could they
wish]? Will they not thus, in accordance with the saying, be perfect?
Do we not read in the Gospel: "Every disciple who becomes like his
master is perfect?"[20] What he now teaches, Cornificius learned at a
time when there was no "letter"[21] in liberal studies, and everyone
sought "the spirit," which, so they tell us, lies hidden in the letter.
He has carefully preserved this, to be heard only by the fortunate
and by "the ears of Jove" (as the saying goes).[22] When Cornificius
went to school, it was a dominant principle that "Hercules begets
Hyllus":[23] namely, that the strength and vigor of the disputant add
up to a valid argument, and that sovereignty resides in the five vowel
sounds.[24] At that time this was considered the proper way to teach
everything. The philosophers of that day argued interminably over
such questions as whether a pig being taken to market is held by
the man or by the rope; and whether one who buys a whole cape
also simultaneously purchases the hood. Speech in which the words
"consistent" and "inconsistent," "argument" and "reason" did not
resound, with negative particles multiplied and transposed through

---

[19] Cf. Matthew, vii, 6.

[20] Luke, vi, 40.

[21] *littera*, the letter as opposed to the spirit, the literal sense, or perhaps learning.

[22] Cf. Horace, *Ep.*, i, 19, 43.

[23] In classical mythology, Hyllus was the son of Hercules and Deianira. Cf. Ovid, *Her.*, ix; and *Metam.*, ix, 279. Evidently the meaning here is that a robust father begets a hearty son.

[24] Literally: "the five vowel sounds are five rights of sovereignty"; cf. Ragewinus, *Gest. Friderici Imp.*, iii, 47: "*Regalia* [rights belonging to the crown] *velut monetam, theloneum, pedaticum, portus, comitatus*," in which the second syllables of the five nouns contain the five vowels: *a, e, i, o, u*.

assertions of existence and non-existence,[25] was entirely unacceptable. So true was this that one had to bring along a counter whenever he went to a disputation, if he was to keep apprized of the force of affirmation or negation. For generally a double negative is equivalent to affirmation, whereas the force of a negation is increased if it is repeated an uneven number of times. At the same time, a negation repeated over and over usually loses its effect, and becomes equivalent to contradiction, as we find stated in the rules. In order, therefore, to discriminate between instances of even and uneven numbers, it was then the custom of those who had prudent foresight to bring a bag of beans and peas[26] to disputations as a reasonable expedient. Even though one might try to get to the root of a question, noisy verbosity would suffice to win the victory, regardless of the kind of arguments advanced.[27] Poets who related history were considered reprobate, and if anyone applied himself to studying the ancients, he became a marked man and the laughingstock of all. For he was deemed both slower than a young Arcadian ass,[28] and duller than lead or stone. Everyone enshrined his own and his master's inventions. Yet even this situation could not abide. Students were soon swept along in the current, and, like their fellows in error, came to spurn what they had learned from their teachers, and to form and found new sects of their own. Of a sudden, they blossomed forth as great philosophers. Those newly arrived in school, unable to read or write, hardly stayed there any longer than it takes a baby bird to sprout its feathers. Then the new masters, fresh from the schools, and fledglings, just leaving their nests, flew off together, after having stayed about the same length of time in school and nest. These "fresh-baked" doctors had spent more hours sleeping than awake in their study of philosophy, and had been educated with less expenditure of effort than those who, according to mythology, after sleeping on [Mount] Parnassus,[29] immediately became prophets. They had been trained more rapidly than those who, after imbibing from the Castalian

[25] *multiplicatis negatiuis particulis et traiectis per esse et non esse.*
[26] Pulse and pease, or beans and peas, with which to keep track of the number of negations.
[27] That is, independently of whether or not the arguments really applied.
[28] Cf. Persius, *Sat.,* iii, 9.
[29] *Ibid.,* prol., 1 ff.

Fountain of the Muses, directly obtained the gift of poetry;[30] or those who, after setting eyes on Apollo, merited not only to be classed as musicians, but even to be accepted into the company of the Muses. What, now, did they teach? How could they allow anything to remain crude and unpolished, old and obsolete? Behold, all things were "renovated."[31] Grammar was [completely] made over; logic was remodeled; rhetoric was despised. Discarding the rules of their predecessors, they brought forth new methods for the whole Quadrivium from the innermost sanctuaries[32] of philosophy. They spoke only of "consistence" or "reason," and the word "argument" was on the lips of all. To mention "an ass," "a man," or any of the works of nature was considered a crime, or improper, crude, and alien to a philosopher. It was deemed impossible to say or do anything "consistently" and "rationally,"[33] without expressly mentioning "consistence" and "reason." Not even an argument was admitted unless it was prefaced by its name. To act with reference to an art and according to the art were (for them) the same. They would probably teach that a poet cannot write poetry unless he at the same time names the verse he is using; and that the carpenter cannot make a bench unless he is simultaneously forming on his lips the word "bench" or "wooden seat."[34] The result is this hodgepodge of verbiage,[35] reveled in by a foolish old man, who rails at those who respect the founders of the arts, since he himself could see nothing useful in these arts when he was pretending to study them.

[30] Cf. Persius, *loc. cit.; Ovid, Am.,* i, 15, 36; Martial, *Epigr.,* iv, 14, 1; xii, 3, 13. The Castalian fountain was on Mount Parnassus, near Delphi, sacred to the Muses and to Apollo.

[31] Cf. Apocalypse, xxi, 5.

[32] *ex aditis:* for *ex adytis,* from the inmost sacred places. Cf. Macrobius, *De. S.S.,* i, 12, 18.

[33] *"conuenienter" et ad "rationis" normam.*

[34] *lignum,* literally, wood.

[35] *sartago loquendi;* cf. Persius, *Sat.,* i, 80.

CHAPTER 4. *The lot of his companions in error.*

After wasting their time, squandering their means, and disappoint-
ing hopes doomed to be frustrated, members of this sect have met
various lots. Some have forsaken the world to become monks or
clerics. Of these, several have subsequently recognized and corrected
their error, realizing and publicly admitting that what they had
learned was "vanity of vanities," and the utmost vanity.[36] I say
"several," because even some of them have persisted in their insanity,
and, puffed up with their old perversity, have preferred remaining
foolish to learning the truth from the humble, to whom God gives
grace.[37] Having prematurely seated themselves in the master's chair,
they blush to descend to the pupil's bench.[38] If you do not believe
me, enter the cloisters and look into the ways of the brothers. You
will discover there the haughtiness of Moab,[39] so extremely intensified that Moab's courage is swallowed up in arrogance. Benedict is
shocked, and laments that, partly through his own fault,[40] [vora-
cious] wolves lurk under the skins of lambs.[41] He remonstrates that
the tonsure and sombre [religious] habit[42] are inconsistent with
pride; or, to put it more precisely, he denounces haughtiness as alien
to the shaven head and the [drab] garb of a monk. Observance of
rules has come to be contemned, while a spirit of false intoxication
has insinuated itself [into the cloisters] under the guise of philosophy. This is a common and well-known fact in all the monastic
orders.[43] Others, becoming cognizant of their inadequate grounding
in philosophy, have departed to Salerno or to Montpellier,[44] where

[36] Ecclesiastes, i, 2; xii, 8.
[37] James, iv, 6; I Peter, v, 5.
[38] *formam discipuli,* the disciple's or pupil's form, class, or bench.
[39] Jeremiah, xlviii, 29.
[40] Because these monks professed to follow the Rule of St. Benedict.
[41] Matthew, vii, 15.
[42] *pullam uestem,* the blackish or dark-colored habit of the monks.
[43] Literally: in every [monastic] habit and [form of] profession.
[44] Salerno was the site of a famous old medical school, while Montpellier had a growing
medical school of more recent origin.

they have become medical students. Then suddenly, in the twinkling
of an eye, they have blossomed forth as the same kind of physicians
that they had previously been philosophers. Stocked with fallacious
empirical rules [for handling various cases] they return after a brief
interval to practice with sedulity what they have learned. Ostenta-
tiously they quote Hippocrates and Galen, pronounce mysterious
words, and have [their] aphorisms ready to apply to all cases. Their
strange terms serve as thunderbolts which stun the minds of their
fellow men. They are revered as omnipotent, because this is what
they boast and promise. However, I have observed that there are
two rules that they are more especially prone to recall and put into
practice. The first is from Hippocrates (whom they here misinterpret): "Where there is indigence, one ought not to labor." [45] Verily
they have judged it unfitting, and foreign to their profession, to
attend the needy and those who are either loath or unable to pay
the full price, if it be only for their words. Their second maxim does
not come, as I recollect, from Hippocrates, but has been added by
enterprising doctors: "Take [your fee] while the patient is in
pain." [46] When a sick person is tortured by suffering, it is a particularly auspicious time for demanding one's price. For then the anguish
of the illness and the avarice of the one affecting to cure it collabo-
rate. If the patient recovers, the credit will go to the doctor, whereas
if he grows worse, the medico's reputation will still be enhanced,
since he has already predicted such an outcome to his intimates. The
wily physician has, indeed, made it impossible for his predictions not
to be realized. To one he has foretold that the patient's health will
be restored; while to another he has declared that it is impossible
for the sick man to recover. If a patient has the good fortune to sur-
vive, he does so easily, except so far as the bungling medico may
delay his recovery. But if he is fated to succumb, then, as Sollius
Sidonius remarks, "he is killed with full rites." [47] How could it be
otherwise? Can the secret and hidden recesses[48] of nature be charted

---

[45] Hippocrates, *Aph.*, ii, 16. What Hippocrates actually says is that a fasting man
should not labor.

[46] *Dum dolet accipe;* cf. *Regimen Sanitatis Salernitanum* (ed. Daremberg), p. 252.

[47] Sollius Sidonius, *Ep.*, ii, 12, § 3.

[48] *cuniculos,* subterranean caves or passages, depths or innermost recesses.

by one who is utterly ignorant of all philosophy? Can they be understood by one who knows neither how to speak correctly, nor to comprehend what is written or spoken? There are practically as many sets of terminology as there are branches of learning, and often authors differ as much in their use of language as they do in physical appearance. One man may resemble another; but not even twins are identical in all respects. Occasionally one voice sounds like another, but not even sisters, nor, if you will, the Muses themselves, have exactly the same tone of speech. Although voices may harmonize, they yet remain distinct, individual entities, and this variety, when properly blended in due proportion, provides a symphony, which is, in a way, more welcome to the ear than would have been the case had similarity meant sameness. Tongues each possess their own idioms, and everyone has his own way of expressing himself. One who fails to take cognizance of this, cannot philosophize any more easily than he could make a magpie that is parroting human words be equivalent to a man.[49] Others have, like myself, fettered themselves to the trifling concerns of court.[50] Borne along by the favor of the great, they can aspire to wealth, which they recognize is not rightfully theirs, and which they know, and admit in their own conscience, they do not deserve, no matter what they may outwardly pretend. I will not here discuss their ways, for my *Policraticus* delves into the latter at length, although it cannot hope to ferret out all their tricks, which would be beyond the powers of any mere human. Still others have, as Cornificius, gravitated to common, worldly occupations. They pay no heed to what philosophy teaches, and what it shows we should seek or shun. They have only one concern: to "Make money, by fair means, if possible, but otherwise in any way at all." [51] They lend out cash at interest,[52] alternately accumulating uneven round-numbered sums and increasing these to even multiple round numbers by their additions.[53] They deem nothing sordid and

[49] Cf. Persius, *Sat.*, prol., 9–10.

[50] *nugis curialibus*, the trifles of the court, or official position; cf. John's *Policraticus*.

[51] Horace, *Ep.*, i, 1, 65, 66.

[52] *fenebrem pecuniam*, money loaned at interest, or usurious money; see Suetonius, *Cal.*, 41.

[53] This is evidently a reference to Horace, where he speaks of "rounding off," in succession, one thousand, two thousand, three thousand, and four thousand talents; cf. Horace, *Ep.*, i, 6, 34.

inane, save the straits of poverty. Wisdom's only fruit, for them, is
wealth. They hold as a maxim those lines of the moral poet:

> Queen Money has within her power the bestowal of both good name
> and beauty,
> While the Goddesses of Persuasion[54] and Charm[55] are consorts of the
> man of means.[56]

At the same time, of course, they do not realize he said it, for they
will have none of him.

All the aforesaid fellows have emerged from this "quasi-Quadriv-
ium," [57] which is indispensable in their eyes, as philosophers baked
over night.[58] Like Cornificius, they had come to despise not only
our Trivium, but also the whole Quadrivium. Subsequently, as we
have said above, they have either merged into the cloisters under the
cloak of religion; or, have sought refuge in medicine, with the pretext of philosophizing and working for the common good; or have
insinuated themselves into illustrious houses, behind a veil of honor,
whereby they would shine and be exalted; or finally, have been
sucked into the abyss of avaricious money-making,[59] pleading need
and duty, but really thirsting for lucre. This is so true that, in comparison with such "proficient philosophers" (or to be more precise,
"deficient philosophers"), any vulgar villain would seem but an
amateur in crime.[60]

[54] Suadela: the goddess of persuasion or eloquence.
[55] Venus: the goddess of love, beauty, or charm.
[56] Horace, *Ep.*, i, 6, 37, 38.
[57] John here evidently refers to the four alternative pursuits mentioned above as open
to students of "the Quadrivium according to Cornificius," namely: service of the Church
as monks or clerics, the medical profession, official position at court, and ordinary
money-making business.
[58] *repentini*, literally, all of a sudden.
[59] See Valerius Maximus, *Fact. et Dict.*, ix, 4. Also cf. Horace, *loc. cit.*
[60] *rudis ad flagitia.*

CHAPTER 5.   *What great men that tribe dares defame, and why they do this.*

Master Gilbert,[61] who was then chancellor at Chartres, and afterwards became the reverend Bishop of Poitiers, was wont to deride
or deplore, I am not sure which, the insanity of his time. When he
would observe the aforesaid individuals scurrying off to the above-
mentioned studies, he used to predict that they would end up as
bakers—the one occupation, which, according to him, usually received all those among his people[62] who were unemployed and
lacked any particular skill. For baking is an easy trade, subsidiary
to the others, and especially suited to those who are more interested
in bread than in skilled workmanship. Others, who were [real]
lovers of learning,[63] set themselves to counteract the error. Among
the latter were Master Thierry,[64] a very assiduous investigator of the
arts; William of Conches,[65] the most accomplished grammarian
since Bernard of Chartres;[66] and the Peripatetic from Pallet,[67] who

[61] In 1137 Gilbert de la Porrée held the office of chancellor at Chartres, in which position he possibly remained until 1139. John, who was in the school at Chartres from
1137 to 1140, came to know him there, and in 1140 again sought him out in Paris,
where he listened to him "on logical and divine subjects." (Cf. *Met.,* ii, 10.) Gilbert
became Bishop of Poitiers in 1142, and lived until 1154. He wrote a *Liber de sex
principiis,* which was appended to earlier editions of Aristotle's *Organon,* and a *Commentarium in Boethii Librum de Trinitate* (in Migne, *P.L.,* LXIV, 1255 ff.).

[62] In Poitou.

[63] *litterarum,* of letters, literature, or learning.

[64] Theodoric or Thierry of Chartres, brother of Bernard of Chartres, was a teacher at
Chartres when Bernard was chancellor there. Thierry may have succeeded Gilbert of
Poitiers as chancellor at Chartres. Cf. Clerval, *Les Écoles de Chartres,* pp. 169 ff., 254 ff.;
and *Met.,* iii, 5; iv, 24.

[65] William of Conches was a disciple of Bernard of Chartres (cf. *Met.,* i, 24). He
wrote a little book called *Philosophia,* as well as the *Dragmaticon,* a work composed
in dramatic style in the form of a dialogue, glosses on Plato's *Timaeus,* and a commentary
on Boethius' *De Consolatione philosophiae.* William taught Henry II of England, as is
evident from what he says in the preface to his *Dragmaticon,* addressed to Henry's father,
Geoffrey (ed. Argentoratum, 1567, pp. 3, 4).

[66] Bernard taught at Chartres in 1115, and was chancellor there in 1124; he died in
1130. Cf. *Met.,* i, 24. See Poole, *Illustrations of the History of Mediaeval Thought,*
App., v, vi, vii.

[67] *Peripateticus Palatinus,* Peter Abelard.

won such distinction in logic over all his contemporaries that it was
thought that he alone really understood Aristotle. But not even all
these [great scholars] were able to cope with the foolish ones. They
themselves became [temporarily] insane while combating insanity,
and for quite a time floundered in error while trying to correct it.
The fog, however, was soon dispelled. Thanks to the work and diligence of these masters, the arts regained their own, and were reinstated in their pristine seat of honor. Their popularity and good fame
were even increased after their exile, as by the right of those who
return home after having been held captive by the enemy.[68] Cornificius begrudged the arts their good fortune. Jealously feeling it
would be a disgrace for one advanced in years to go to school, and
for an old man to be shown up as but a boy in understanding, he
set himself to carping on what he despaired of learning. He criticized everyone else's views, since he saw that all thought differently
from himself. Even so the fox growls at the cherries[69] that he despairs
of reaching, and, in the words of the rustic proverb, he "slurs as
useless what he cannot have." This is the [true] explanation of the
wrath, the tears,[70] and the indignation which the Cornificians have
conceived against the students of the aforesaid wise men. Here is
[the real reason] why they gnash their teeth and "break," as is said,
"their jaw tooth" [71] on the soundness of these masters. They even
presume (though on the sly, because they would not dare do this
openly) to extinguish those most brilliant lights of the Gauls, the
brother theologians Anselm[72] and Rudolph,[73] who have lent luster
to Laon, and whose memory is happy and blessed.[74] They do this
despite the fact that no man has with impunity wounded the aforesaid, who have displeased only heretics[75] and those enmeshed in

---

[68] *iure postliminii,* "the right of postlimium": the right of one returning to the Empire
after having been held captive by the enemy; cf. Justinian, *Instit.,* i, 12, § 5; *Dig.,* xlix,
15, § 5; *Cod.,* viii, 50, § 19.

[69] *cerasa,* cherries; also used in lieu of grapes by Abelard, when he quotes this well-
known fable in his *Invectiva in quendam ignarum dialectices* (*Opp.* ed. Cousin, I, 695).

[70] *hinc lacrime:* Terence, *Andr.,* i, 1, 99.

[71] Persius, *Sat.,* i, 115.

[72] Anselm of Laon, teacher and dean of the school at Laon, died in 1117.

[73] Rudolph of Laon, brother of Anselm, was his successor in the school at Laon.

[74] Ecclesiasticus, xlv, 1.

[75] *hereticis,* may refer to Abelard (cf. *Hist. Cal.,* chaps. 3, 4).

wickedness. They speak plainly and in no proverbs,[76] however, about Alberic of Rheims[77] and Simon of Paris.[78] They not only deny that the followers of the latter are philosophers; they will not even admit they are clerics. They will hardly concede that they are men, but rather ridicule them as "Abraham's oxen" or "Balaamite asses," [79] and call them by the most sarcastic and insulting names they can find. William of Champeaux,[80] according to them, is convicted of error by his own writings.[81] Master Hugh of St. Victor[82] barely escapes, being spared more in consideration of his religious habit, than out of admiration for his learning or doctrines, as they defer not to him, but to God in him. Robert Pullen,[83] whom all good men hold in happy memory, would be called "an ass's foal," [84] were they not held back by their deference for the Apostolic See, which raised this former scholastic doctor[85] to the office of chancellor. Indeed, in order that his sect may have greater license to slander others, the father of the [Cornifician] family externally professes the religious life (though the Lord knows and will judge his [secret] intentions). He

[76] Cf. John, xvi, 29.

[77] John here apparently refers to that Alberic of Rheims mentioned by Abelard in his *Hist. Cal.*, chaps. 4, 9; by St. Bernard in his *Ep.*, 13; and by John himself in his *Hist. Pont.*, chap. 8. Alberic for some time directed the schools of Rheims as archdeacon. He was promoted to the archbishopric of Bourges in 1137; and died in 1141. He was a disciple of William of Champeaux, and an opponent of Abelard.

[78] *Symone Parisiense* may very well be the same as the *Simon Pexiacensis,* who lectured on theology at Paris, according to John, *Met.,* ii, 10.

[79] Cf. Genesis, xxi, 27.

[80] William of Champeaux was a disciple of Anselm of Laon, and an archdeacon of the church of Paris. He went to the old hermitage of St. Victor in the vicinity of Paris in 1108. There, after taking the canonical habit, he founded the famous monastery of that name, where Hugh of St. Victor later became a teacher. The story of the controversy between William and Abelard, at one time William's disciple, is told in Abelard's *Hist. Cal.*, chap. 2. William was consecrated Bishop of Chalons-sur-Marne in 1113, blessed St. Bernard as Abbot of Clairvaux in 1115, and died in 1122.

[81] Cf. Abelard, *Hist. Cal.*, chap. 2.

[82] Hugh of St. Victor, a famous theologian and scholar, was canon in the Abbey of St. Victor at Marseilles, and afterward canon and teacher in the Abbey of St. Victor at Paris. He died in 1141.

[83] Robert Pullen was archdeacon of Rochester from 1138 to 1143. St. Bernard, in his *Ep.,* 205 (in Migne, *P.L.,* CLXXXII, 372), writing to the Bishop of Rochester, says: "I have urged Robert Pullen to spend some time in Paris, because of his recognized sound teaching." Robert was called to Rome in 1144, where he became a cardinal, and held the office of chancellor until 1146. Cf. *Met.,* ii, 10.

[84] *filius subiugalis,* literally a "foal used to the yoke." See Matthew, xxi, 5, where this refers to a young ass (*pullus asine*). This is evidently a play on Robert's cognomen, *Pullus* or Pullen.

[85] Or: Master of the Schools.

has cultivated the friendship of the Cistercians, the Cluniacs, the Premonstratensians, and others of even better reputation, to the end of
acquiring reflected luster. I am resigned to suffering detraction at the
hands of his breed with composure. I admit that I have studied under
some of the aforesaid masters,[86] as well as under their disciples; and
acknowledge that from them I have learned what little I know. For
I have not taught myself as has Cornificius. I have little concern
about what nonsense Cornificius caws[87] into the ears of his followers.
One who will not acknowledge the author of his own progress in ungrateful and perverse. But enough of this. Disregarding the personal
faults of Cornificius, let us refute his erroneous doctrine.

CHAPTER 6.   *The arguments on which Cornificius bases his
contention.*

In the judgment[88] of Cornificius (if a false opinion may be called a
judgment), there is no point in studying the rules of eloquence,
which is a gift that is either conceded or denied to each individual by
nature. Work and diligence are superfluous where nature has spontaneously and gratuitously bestowed eloquence, whereas they are
futile and silly where she has refused to grant it. Generally the
maxim that "A person can do just as much as nature allows," is
accepted as an axiom.[89] Thus prudent and reliable historians are
sure that Daedalus did not really fly, for nature had denied him
wings, but say, rather, that he evaded the wrath of the tyrant by
quickly departing aboard a ship.[90] The device of learning precepts in
order to become eloquent fails to accomplish its object. Even the

[86] Namely, Thierry of Chartres, William of Conches, Abelard, and others.
[87] *cornicetur*, apparently a pun on the name Cornificius.
[88] *sententia*, judgment, doctrine.
[89] *maximarum propositionum*, the highest propositions, first principles; cf. Boethius,
Comm. in Top. Cic., i (in Migne, *P.L.*, LXIV, 1051): "By the highest and greatest propositions we mean those propositions which are universal, and are so well known and
evident that they need no proof, but instead themselves prove things that are in doubt."
[90] Cf. Servius, *Ad. Verg. Aen.*, vi, 14.

most diligent study of rules cannot possibly make one eloquent. The use of language and speech suffices for intercourse among fellow countrymen, whereas he who most assiduously employs his faculty of speech becomes most fluent. This is evident with the Greeks and Latins; the Gauls and Britons will also bear witness to it; nor is it otherwise among the Scythians and Arabs. Everywhere it is true that "Practice makes perfect," [91] and "Persevering application surmounts all obstacles," [92] for assiduous devotion to an art produces the master workman. Even though rules may be of some help in acquiring eloquence, still they involve more trouble than they are worth, and the return never compensates for the investment. The Greeks and Hebrews use their languages to advantage without bothering about rules; and the peoples of Gaul and Britain, as well as others, learn how to talk in their nurses' arms [long] before they receive instruction from doctors who occupy official chairs. The way one talks in manhood often smacks of the manner of speech of one's nurse. Sometimes the [most] strenuous efforts of teachers cannot extricate one from habits imbibed at a tender age. How well and effectively do all the peoples speak in the languages they have been granted by divine providence! Did they first have to await the art of verbal expression[93] or the rules of eloquence? Finally [Cornificius argues], what can eloquence and philosophy possibly have in common? The former relates to language, but the latter seeks after, investigates, and applies itself to learning the ways of wisdom, which it sometimes efficaciously apprehends by its study. Clearly the rules of eloquence confer neither wisdom nor love of wisdom. More often than otherwise, they are not even helpful for the acquisition of wisdom. Philosophy (or wisdom, its object) is concerned not with words, but with facts. From what has been said [if we are to believe Cornificius], it is evident that philosophy eliminates the rules of eloquence from its activities.

[91] *usus magistrum reddit;* cf. Cicero, *De Orat.,* i, 4, § 15.
[92] Vergil, *Georg.,* i, 145.
[93] *artem orationis,* the art of speech, verbal or oral expression, oratory or rhetoric.

CHAPTER 7.   *Praise of Eloquence.*

The foolish flock of Cornificians caws away[94] (in a language all their
own), evidencing that they have contemned every rule of speech.
For, as they themselves inform us, they cannot simultaneously take
care to make sense and also to worry about the troublesome agreement of tenses and cases. We refrain from comment. The sect may
still perceive the truth, even while it is lying, but this condition surely
cannot endure. A man who is a liar in word and spirit will come
to believe the falsehood he peddles. According to the Cornificians,
"Rules of eloquence are superfluous, and the possession or lack of
eloquence is dependent on nature." What could be farther from the
truth? What is eloquence but the faculty of appropriate and effective
verbal expression? [95] As such, it brings to light and in a way pub-
lishes what would otherwise be hidden in the inner recesses of man's
consciousness.[96] Not everyone who speaks, nor even one who says
what he wants to in some fashion, is eloquent. He alone is eloquent
who fittingly and efficaciously[97] expresses himself as he intends. This
appropriate effectiveness[98] postulates a faculty (so called from facility), to follow our wont of imitating the concern of the Stoics about
the etymologies of words as a key to easier understanding of their
meanings. One who can with facility and adequacy verbally express
his mental perceptions is eloquent. The faculty of doing this is
appropriately called "eloquence." For myself, I am at a loss to see
how anything could be more generally useful: more helpful in acquiring wealth, more reliable for winning favor, more suited for
gaining fame, than is eloquence. Nothing, or at least hardly anything, is to be preferred to this [precious] gift of nature and grace.

[94] *Cornicatur,* above, chap. 5.
[95] Literally: "of fittingly saying what our mind wants to express"; cf. Cicero, *De
Orat.,* i, 6, § 21, *passim.*
[96] Literally: "the heart," as the supposed seat of consciousness.
[97] *commode,* fittingly, appropriately, and effectively.
[98] *commoditas,* fitness, appropriate effectiveness, easy adequacy.

Virtue and wisdom, which perhaps, as Victorinus believes,[99] differ in name rather than in substance, rank first among desiderata, but eloquence comes second. Third is health, and after this, in fourth place, the good will of one's associates and an abundance of goods, to provide the material instruments of action. The moralist lists things to be desired in this order, and aptly epitomizes the sequence:

> What more could a fond nurse wish for her sweet charge,
> Than that he be wise and eloquent,
> And that friends, fame, health, good fare,
> And a never failing purse be his without stint? [100]

If man is superior to other living beings in dignity because of his powers of speech and reason, what is more universally efficacious and more likely to win distinction, than to surpass one's fellows, who possess the same human nature, and are members of the same human race, in those sole respects wherein man surpasses other beings? Moreover, while eloquence both illumines and adorns men of whatever age, it especially becomes the young. For youth is in a way to attract favor so that it may make good the potentialities of its natural talent.[101] Who are the most prosperous and wealthy among our fellow citizens? Who the most powerful and successful in all their enterprises? Is it not the eloquent? As Cicero observes "Nothing is so unlikely that words cannot lend an air of probability; nothing is so repulsive and rude that speech cannot polish it and somehow render it attractive, as though it had been remade for the better." [102] He who despises such a great boon [as eloquence] is clearly in error; while he who appreciates, or rather pretends to appreciate it, without actually cultivating it, is grossly negligent and on the brink of insanity.

---

[99] Victorinus, *In Lib. I de Inventione* (in *Opera Ciceronis,* ed. Orellius, V, 3).
[100] Horace, *Ep.,* i, 4, 8–11.
[101] Or: For youth attracts favor and so makes good its claim to intellectual distinction.
[102] Cicero, *Paradox.,* praef., § 3.

CHAPTER 8.   *The necessity of helping nature by use and exercise.*

The Cornificians argue that nature herself gratuitously grants eloquence to anyone who ever comes to possess it, whereas she arbitrarily and irrevocably refuses and denies it to those fated never to become eloquent. They conclude that efforts to acquire eloquence are useless or superfluous. Why, therefore, oh most learned Cornificians, do you not understand [103] all languages? Why do you not at least know Hebrew, which, as we are told, mother nature gave to our first parents and preserved for mankind until human unity was rent by impiety, and the pride which presumed to mount to heaven by physical strength and the construction of a tower, rather than by virtue, was leveled in a babbling chaos of tongues? [104] Why do not the Cornificians speak this language, which is more natural than the others, having been, so to speak, taught by nature herself? Nature is, according to some (although it is not easy to explain this definition) [105] "a certain genitive [106] force, implanted in all things, whereby they can act or be the recipients of action." [107] It is called "genitive," both because everything obtains a nature as a result of being brought into existence, and because this nature is for each being its principle of existence. Everything derives its suitability for this or for that form its composition. This is true whether a thing is composed of what are known as parts; or its composition consists in a union of matter and form, as with simple things that do not admit of an assemblage of parts; or its manner of composition is a consequence solely of the decree of the divine goodness. The latter [the divine decree] is verily "first nature," according to Plato, who, as Victorinus and many

---

[103] *peritiam . . . habetis,* have a practical knowledge or mastery of.
[104] Cf. Augustine, *De C.D.,* xvi, 11.
[105] Cf. Cicero, *De Inv.,* i, 24, § 34; and Victorinus, *loc. cit.*
[106] *genitiua,* genitive, innate or inborn; also dynamic, begetting or originating.
[107] *facere uel pati.*

others attest, asserted that the divine will is the surest nature of all
things, since created nature flows from this fountain, and the activities of all things can ultimately be traced back to God.[108] We exclude, of course, corruption and sin, whereby nature degenerates
from its original state. That force which is originally implanted in
each and every thing and constitutes the source of its activities or
aptitudes is a nature, but a created one. I believe that other definitions [of nature] found among authors generally refer to created
nature. Even that "master artisan, fire," which produces visible effects
in an invisible way,[109] is created; although some, begging leave of
Aristotle[110] and Chalcidius,[111] doubt that it is a nature.[112] I further
believe that the principle of movement as such[113] traces back to God,
and that Aristotle would not deny this. I am sure that Boethius
would agree, since he does not deny that what can act or be acted
upon is created [nature].[114] But the specific differences that provide
forms for every thing either come from Him by Whom all things
have been made, or they are nothing at all. There are also other
descriptions of nature, but anything else that is postulated by a
Platonist must be either nothing at all, or a work of God.[115] For the
present, however, let us use the first definition, which seems best
suited for our purpose. We will grant that the genitive force originally implanted in things is powerful and effective. But, certainly,
just as it can be canceled or hindered by defects, so it can, on the
other hand, be restored or helped by aids. It is not uncommon to
hear children, in their prattle, remark that one lacks the use of a
given natural ability which he otherwise possesses. An animal that
naturally has leg locomotion is sometimes crippled, whereas one who
is by nature two-footed, often lacks either or both of his feet. Care
is accordingly not superfluous. Rather, it assists nature, and makes
easier something that is already possible in one way or another.

[108] Victorinus, *In Lib. I de Inv.* (Cicero, *Opp.,* ed. Orell., V, 70).
[109] Cf. *ibid.*
[110] See Boethius, *Contra Eut. et Nest.,* chap. i (ed. Peiper, p. 190).
[111] Cf. Chalcidius, *Comm. in Tim. Plat.,* §§ 23, 323.
[112] *naturam,* a nature, or simply nature (in general).
[113] *principium motus secundum se;* cf. Boethius, *loc. cit.*
[114] Boethius, *op. cit.* (ed. Peiper, p. 189).
[115] *aut de numero rerum tollendum est aut diuinis operibus ascribendum,* literally: is
either to be separated from the number of things or ascribed to the divine works.

Socrates, we are told,[116] was naturally wanton[117] and overly susceptible to women[118] (to use history's own word).[119] But he subdued
and controlled his passionate nature, which he corrected by philosophy and the exercise of virtue. They say that Scaurus Rufus was far
from naturally bright, but that by assiduously employing his meager
natural talents, he became so accomplished that he even called Cicero
himself "a barbarian." [120] If [more] examples were adduced, it would
everywhere be apparent that, even where nature is sluggish, it is not
unreasonable to apply oneself, and that even though natural endow-
ment might have been more effective in a given case, diligence is
not futile as though it were wasted. Although frequently nature is a
dominant factor, and has greater proclivity in one or in another
person,[121] still, just as natural ability easily deteriorates when neglected, so it is strengthened by cultivation and care.

> The question is raised whether a poem[122] is due to nature or art;
> But I neither see what study can do in the absence of natural talent,
> Nor what natural talent can accomplish without cultivation,
> So much does one demand [123] the assistance of the other, and so closely
>   do they coöperate.[124]

Although the gifts of nature are definitely helpful, they are never or
rarely so effective that they are fully realized without study. Nothing
is so strong and robust that it cannot be enfeebled by neglect,[125]
nothing so well constructed that it cannot be razed. On the other
hand, diligent application can build up and preserve the lowest

---

[116] Cf. Cicero, *De Fato,* 5, § 10.

[117] *petulcus,* inclined to butt with the horns, wanton.

[118] *muliebrosus* (from *mulier*), overly affectionate toward women, or lascivious regarding women.

[119] Namely, to quote the very word used in the story itself.

[120] *Allobroga,* literally: an Allobrogian, a member of a warlike people of Gaul; a barbarian. Cf. Juvenal, *Sat.,* vii, 213, though Juvenal here has "that Rufus, whom they have so often called 'the Allobrogian Cicero.'"

[121] This may mean either: "in one or the other respect," or "in one or the other person."

[122] *carmen,* song, poem.

[123] *poscit* should be substituted here for *possit* in the Webb edition. Cf. MSS C, B, A, as well as the text of Horace.

[124] Horace, *A.P.,* 11, 408–411.

[125] *diligentia* in the Migne and Webb editions is evidently a mistake for *negligentia;* cf. MSS C, B, A.

degree of natural talent. If nature is propitious, it should be industriously cultivated, rather than neglected, so that its fruits may be readily harvested. On the other hand, if nature is unbenign, it should still be nursed even more carefully, so that, with the aid of virtue, it may more happily and gloriously grow strong.

CHAPTER 9.   *That one who attacks logic is trying to rob mankind of eloquence.*[126]

Who has ever, by nature's gift alone, and without study, had the privilege of being most eloquent in all tongues, or even in only one language? If it is good to be eloquent, surely it is better to be very eloquent. The degrees of comparison are not here in inverse ratio to the good proposed, as with "fluent" and "extremely fluent," [127] where the positive term connotes wisdom and eloquence, but wisdom diminishes, and the flow of speech swells to a flood, in proportion as the comparison increases. So [at least] some grammarians have taught. Although some of the arts pertaining to and imparting the power of eloquence are natural, still that art [of eloquence] which is practically as we would want it cannot be known by nature since it is not natural. For it is not the same among all [peoples]. It is imprudent to expect of nature, without human assistance, that which is chiefly the work of man. While this [Cornifician] sect does not condemn eloquence, which is necessary to everyone and approved by all, it holds that the arts which promise eloquence are useless. The Cornificians do not propose to make everyone mute, which would be impossible and inexpedient. Rather, they would do away with logic. The latter, according to them, is the fallacious profession of the verbose, which dissipates the natural talents of many persons, blocks the gateway to philosophical studies, and excludes both sense and success from all undertakings.

[126] *homines enititur elingues facere.*
[127] *disertus . . . aut disertior,* fluent or voluble.

CHAPTER 10.   *What "logic" means, and how we should endeavor to acquire all arts that are not reprobate.*

Behold, the Cornificians disclose their objective, and advance to
attack logic, although, of course, they are equally violent persecutors
of all philosophical pursuits. They have to begin somewhere, and so
they have singled out that branch of philosophy which is the most
widely known and seems the most familiar to their heretical sect.
First, bear with me while we define what "logic" is. "Logic" (in its
broadest sense) is "the science of verbal expression and [argumenta-
tive] reasoning." [128] Sometimes [the term] "logic" is used with more
restricted extension, and limited to rules of [argumentative] reasoning.[129] Whether logic teaches only the ways of reasoning, or embraces
all rules relative to words,[130] surely those who claim that it is useless
are deluded. For either of these services may be proved by incontrovertible arguments, to be very necessary. The twofold meaning of
"logic" stems from its Greek etymology, for in the latter language
"logos" [131] means both "word" and "reason." For the present let us
concede to logic its widest meaning, according to which it includes
all instruction relative to words,[132] in which case it can never be convicted of futility. In this more general sense, there can be no doubt
that all logic is both highly useful and necessary. If, as has been
frequently observed (and as no one denies), the use of speech is so
essential, the more concisely it [the use of speech] is taught, the more
useful and certainly the more reliable will be the teaching. It is
foolish to delay a long time, with much sweat and worry, over

[128] *loquendi uel disserendi ratio,* the rational system or science of speaking or verbal
expression, discussion, argumentation, or reasoning; cf. Boethius, *Comm. in Top. Cic.,* i
(in Migne, *P.L.,* LXVI, 750).
[129] *disserendi,* discussing, arguing, or reasoning: argumentative reasoning.
[130] Literally: "the rule of all words," or "all rules relative to words" [whether spoken
or mental].
[131] *logos,* here John transliterates the Greek word into Latin characters, according to his
practice.
[132] Evidently here John understands mental, as well as written or oral words.

something that could otherwise be easily and quickly expedited. This is a fault common among careless persons who have no sense of the value of time. To safeguard against this mistake, the arts of doing all things that we are to do should be taken up and cultivated. Our devotion to the arts should be augmented by the reflection that the latter stem from nature, the best of all mothers, and attest their noble lineage by the facile and successful accomplishment of their objects. I would say, therefore, that the arts of doing things we are to do[133] should be cultivated, with the exception of those [arts] whose purpose is evil, such as lot-reading and other mathematical methods of divination that are reprobate.[134] Arts such as the latter, which are wrong,[135] should, by the decree of sound philosophers, be banished from human society. This matter, however, is discussed more at length in our *Policraticus*.[136]

CHAPTER 11.   *The nature of art, the various kinds of innate abilities, and the fact that natural talents should be cultivated and developed by the arts.*

Art is a system that reason[137] has devised in order to expedite, by its own short cut, our ability to do things within our natural capabilities. Reason neither provides nor professes to provide the accomplishment of the impossible. Rather, it substitutes for the spendthrift and roundabout ways of nature a concise, direct method of doing things that are possible. It further begets (so to speak) a faculty of accomplishing what is difficult. Wherefore the Greeks also call it[138] *methodon,* that is, so to speak, an efficient plan,[139] which avoids nature's wastefulness, and straightens out her circuitous wanderings,

---

[133] *gerendorum,* "of doing things" or "of things to be done."
[134] *matheseos,* divinatory mathematics; evidently a transliteration of the Greek.
[135] Literally: contrary to our duties.
[136] Cf. *Policraticus.,* ii, 19.
[137] *ratio,* reason, or a rational, scientific system or method.
[138] *eam,* evidently art, or possibly [the system of] reason.
[139] *quasi compendiariam rationem.*

so that we may more correctly and easily accomplish what we are to do. However vigorous it may be, nature cannot attain the facility of an art unless it be trained. At the same time, nature is the mother of all the arts, to which she has given reason as their nurse for their improvement and perfection. Nature first evokes our natural capacity[140] to perceive things, and then, as it were, deposits these perceptions in the secure treasury of our memory.[141] Reason then examines, with its careful study, those things which have been perceived, and which are to be, or have been, commended to memory's custody. After its scrutiny of their nature, reason pronounces true and accurate judgment concerning each of these (unless, perchance, it slips up in some regard). Nature has provided beforehand these three factors [natural capacity, memory, and reason] as both the foundations and the instruments of all the arts. Natural ability (according to Isidore) is "an immanent[142] power infused into one's soul by nature." [143] This description seems to mean that nature has endowed the soul with a certain force, which either constitutes or at least evokes the initial [and fundamental] activity of the soul in its investigations. Natural talent is said to be "immanent" inasmuch as it has need of nothing else as a prerequisite, but precedes and aids all subsequent [abilities]. In our acquisition of [scientific] knowledge, investigation is the first step, and comes before comprehension, analysis, and retention. Innate ability, although it proceeds from nature, is fostered by study and exercise. What is difficult when we first try it, becomes easier after assiduous practice, and once the rules for doing it are mastered, very easy, unless languor creeps in, through lapse of use or carelessness, and impedes our efficiency. This, in short, is how all the arts have originated: Nature, the first fundamental, begets the habit and practice of study, which proceeds to provide an art, and the latter, in turn, finally furnishes the faculty whereof we speak. Natural ability is accordingly effective. So, too, is exercise. And memory likewise, is effective, when employed by

---

[140] *ingenium,* natural or innate capacity, native ability or talent.

[141] Cf. Cicero, *De Orat.,* i, 5, § 18.

[142] *per se valens,* effective of itself, immanent.

[143] John evidently refers here to Hugh of St. Victor (*Erud. Did.,* iii, 8, in Migne, *P.L.,* CLXXVI, 771), rather than to Isidore; cf. Isidore, *Etym.,* x, § 122.

the two aforesaid. With the help of the foregoing, reason waxes strong, and produces the arts, which are proportionate to [man's] natural talents. There are three kinds of these natural capacities [or personalities], as old Bernard of Chartres used to remind his listeners. The first flies, the second creeps, the third takes the intermediate course of walking. The flying one flits about, easily learning, but just as quickly forgetting, for it lacks stability. The creeping one is mired down to earth, and cannot rise, wherefore it can make no progress. But the one that goes to neither extreme [and walks], both because it has its feet on the ground so it can firmly stand, and because it can climb, provides prospect of progress, and is admirably suited for philosophizing. Nature, I believe, has provided in the latter a basis for the arts. For study enhances its effectiveness. "Study" (according to Cicero) "is the diligent and vigorous application of one's mind to the determined accomplishment of something." [144] Memory is, as it were, the mind's treasure chest, a sure and reliable place of safe-deposit for perceptions. Reason, on its part, is that power of the soul which examines and investigates things that make an impression on the senses or intellect. A dependable judge of better things, reason has, after estimating similarities and differences, finally established art, to be, as it were, a circumscribed science of unlimited things. As unlimited names end in "a," the names of the arts terminate in the feminine article, except those which reason has distinguished by some designation of their specific property. Species are unlimited, but reason has circumscribed them, so that every species has a genus. Numbers are unlimited, but reason has classified all of them as either odd or even. Consider an example to illustrate the origin of an art.[145] The first disputation developed by chance, and the practice of disputing grew with repetition. Reason then perceived the form of disputation, the art of this activity. This art, on being cultivated, conferred a corresponding faculty. The mother of the arts is nature, to despise whose progeny amounts to insulting their parent. Natural ability should accordingly be diligently cultivated. At the same time, study should be moderated by recreation, so that while one's natural

[144] Cicero, *De Inv.*, i, 25, § 36.
[145] . . . *et ut duo dicitur, liquido comprobetur exemplo* . . . , *duo* in the Webb edition is a misprint for *quod;* cf. MSS C, B, A.

ability waxes strong with the former, it may be refreshed by the latter. A certain very wise man (whom I thank for his statement) has said: "While innate ability, proceeds from nature, it is fostered by use and sharpened by moderate exercise, but it is dulled by excessive work." If natural ability is properly trained and exercised, it will not only be able to acquire the arts, but will also find direct and expeditious short cuts for the accomplishment of what would otherwise be naturally impossible, and will enable us quickly to learn and teach everything that is necessary or useful.

CHAPTER 12.   *Why some arts are called "liberal."*

While there are many sorts of arts, the first to proffer their services to the natural abilities of those who philosophize are the liberal arts. All of the latter are included in the courses of the Trivium[146] and Quadrivium.[147] The liberal arts are said to have become so efficacious among our ancestors, who studied them diligently, that they enabled them to comprehend everything they read, elevated their understanding to all things, and empowered them to cut through the knots of all problems possible of solution. Those to whom the system of the Trivium has disclosed the significance of all words, or the rules of the Quadrivium have unveiled the secrets of all nature, do not need the help of a teacher in order to understand the meaning of books and to find the solutions of questions. They [the branches of learning included in the Trivium and Quadrivium] are called "arts" [either] because they delimit [*artant*] [148] by rules and precepts; or from virtue, in Greek known as *ares*,[149] which strengthens minds to apprehend the ways of wisdom; or from reason, called

---

[146] Namely, grammar, dialectic, and rhetoric.

[147] Namely, arithmetic, geometry, astronomy, and music.

[148] *artant*, they delimit, circumscribe, compress.

[149] *ares*, evidently for ἀρετή, -ῆς. Cf. Donatus, *Commentum Terenti* (ed. P. Wessner, i, I, 3, and note)

arso[150] by the Greeks, which the arts nourish and cause to grow.[151] They are called "liberal," either because the ancients took care to have their children[152] instructed in them; or because their object is to effect man's liberation,[153] so that, freed from cares, he may devote himself to wisdom. More often than not, they liberate us from cares incompatible with wisdom. They often even free us from worry about [material] necessities, so that the mind may have still greater liberty to apply itself to philosophy.

CHAPTER 13. *Whence grammar gets its name.*

Among all the liberal arts, the first is logic, and specifically that part of logic which gives initial instruction about words. As has already been explained,[154] the word "logic" has a broad meaning, and is not restricted exclusively to the science of argumentative reasoning. [It includes] Grammar [which] is "the science of speaking and writing correctly—the starting point of all liberal studies." [155] Grammar is the cradle of all philosophy, and in a manner of speaking, the first nurse of the whole study of letters.[156] It takes all of us as tender babes, newly born from nature's bosom. It nurses us in our infancy, and guides our every forward step in philosophy. With motherly care, it fosters and protects the philosopher from the start to the finish [of his pursuits]. It is called "grammar" from the basic elements of writing and speaking. *Grama* means a letter or line,[157] and

[150] *arso*, to what Greek word meaning "reason" John here refers, the translator does not know.
[151] See Isidore's *Etym.*, i, 1, § 2, 5, § 2; Cassiodorus, *De Artibus,* praef. (in Migne, *P.L.,* LXX, 1151); Donatus, *In Ter. Andr.*, i, 1, 4; and St. Augustine, *De C.D.*, iv, 21.
[152] *liberos*
[153] *libertatem.*
[154] *Met.*, i, 10.
[155] Isidore, *Etym.*, i, 5, § 1.
[156] Literally: of the whole study of literature, letters, or learning.
[157] For this part of John's discussion, see Isidore, *Etym.*, i, 5, § 1; as well as Macrobius, *In Somn. Scrip.*, i, 5, § 7.

grammar is "literal," since it teaches letters, that is, both the symbols which stand for simple sounds, and the elementary sounds represented by the symbols. It is also [in a way] linear. For in augmenting size, the length of lines is fundamental, and, as it were, the basic dimension of plane surfaces and solids. So also this branch, which teaches language,[158] is the first of the arts to assist those who are aspiring to increase in wisdom. For it introduces wisdom both through ears and eyes by its facilitation of verbal intercourse. Words admitted into our ears knock on and arouse our understanding.[159] The latter (according to Augustine) is a sort of hand of the soul, able to grasp and to perceive.[160] Letters, that is written symbols, in the first place represent sounds. And secondly they stand for things, which they conduct into the mind through the windows of the eyes. Frequently they even communicate, without emitting a sound, the utterances of those who are absent.[161] This art [grammar] accordingly imparts the fundamental elements of language, and also trains our faculties of sight and hearing. One who is ignorant of it [grammar] cannot philosophize any easier than one who lacks sight and hearing from birth can become an eminent philosopher.

CHAPTER 14.   *Although it is not natural, grammar imitates nature.*

Since grammar is arbitrary and subject to man's discretion,[162] it is evidently not a handiwork of nature. Although natural things are everywhere the same, grammar varies from people to people. However, we have already seen that nature is the mother of the arts.[163]

---

[158] Literally: which educates the tongue.

[159] *intellectum.*

[160] Whence John obtains this description, which he attributes to St. Augustine, is undetermined.

[161] Cf. Isidore, *Etym.,* i, 3, § 1.

[162] *ad placitum sit:* is according to our [human] will, pleasure, or discretion; is arbitrary.

[163] *Met.,* i, 11.

While grammar has developed to some extent, and indeed mainly, as
an invention of man, still it imitates nature,[164] from which it partly
derives its origin. Furthermore, it tends, as far as possible, to conform
to nature in all respects. Thus it has, at nature's bidding, limited the
number of elementary vowel-sounds to five[165] among all peoples,
even though with many [peoples] the number of written symbols
may be greater.[166] At the same time, our friend Tenred,[167] a grammarian who has more real scientific knowledge than he has been
given credit for, has demonstrated that the number of elementary
sounds is even greater. According to him, if one carefully notes the
differences of vowel sounds, one will observe that they are seven.
Among the consonants, nature has likewise formed various semivowels and mutes, as well as simple and double consonants; whose
differences cannot remain hidden from one who observes mouths
modulating sounds according to the marvelous laws of nature, and
carefully estimates the vocal quality[168] of these sounds. The very
application of names, and the use of various expressions, although
such depends on the will of man, is in a way subject to nature, which
it probably imitates [at least] to some modest extent.[169] In accordance with the divine plan, and in order to provide verbal intercourse
in human society, man first of all named those things which lay
before him, formed and fashioned by nature's hand out of the four
elements or from matter and form, and so distinguished that they
could be discerned by the senses of rational creatures and have their
diversity designated by names as well as by properties. Hence it is
that (as Boethius observes)[170] one entity is called "man," another
"wood," a third "stone," names being, so to speak, stamped on all
substances. Also, since there are numerous differences among given
substances, some quantitative and some qualitative, some accidental
and some from things more intimately connected with them and

[164] Cf. *Ad Herennium de arte rhetorica*, iii, 22, § 36, erroneously attributed to Cicero.
[165] Namely, *a, e, i, o, u.*
[166] Thus among the Greeks, ε is distinct from η and o from ω.
[167] Tenredus: Webb is of the opinion that this refers to Tenred of Dover, concerning
whom, see the Prolegomena to Webb's edition of the *Met.*, pp. xx–xxi, and note to p. 33.
[168] Literally: force, power.
[169] Cf. Abelard in his *Dialectica* (*Ouvr. Inéd.*, p. 487) and in his *Theol. Christiana*, iii
(*Opp.*, ed. Cousin, II, 481; and in Migne, *P.L.*, CLXXVIII, 1245).
[170] Boethius, *Comm. I in Arist. de Interpr.*, i, 2 (ed. Meiser).

pertaining to their essence,[171] names to express such differences have
been invented so that they can be added to substantive names
[nouns]. These [adjectives] in a way depict the force and nature of
nouns in the same way that the properties of substances indicate
their differences. Just as accidents provide raiment and form for substances, so, with due proportion, adjectives perform a similar function for nouns. And that the devices of reason may cleave even more
closely to nature, since the substance of a thing is not susceptible of
greater or less intensity, a noun does not admit of degrees of comparison. Neither do words referring to substantial differences [admit
of degrees of comparison], despite the fact that they are adjectival,
since they denote substantial qualities. Nor do things added to substances in the category of quantity [admit of degrees of comparison],
inasmuch as a given quantity cannot become greater or less and yet
remain itself.[172] In fine, just as accidents alone, though not all accidents, can be increased or diminished, so only adjectives denoting
accidents, though not all such [adjectives], can be compared. Upon
reflection, one sees that this imitation of nature also maintains in
other parts of speech, as well as in nouns. Since a substance presented
to our senses or intellect cannot exist without some movement,[173]
whereby it undergoes temporal change by acting or being acted
upon, verbs have been invented to denote the changes occurring in
things acting or being acted upon in time. Also, since there is no
movement independent of time, there cannot be a verb without
designation of its tense.[174] Furthermore, as movement is not always
uniform, but has, so to speak, several different shades, and action
or being the recipient of action occurs in diverse places and ways,
as well as at various times, adverbs have evolved for the purpose of
expressing differences in motion, and serve the same function for
verbs as adjectives do for nouns. Moreover, is not the fact that some
verbs do not have certain tenses, as meditative and inchoative verbs
lack a preterite, since the deliberation concerning future action ex-

---

[171] *adesse conducunt,* whose presence is beneficial; or which are conducive to their existence or essence.

[172] Cf. Aristotle, *Cat.,* 6, 6ª, 19–26: "One thing cannot be two cubits long to a greater
degree than another."

[173] *motus,* movement or change.

[174] Boethius, *Comm. I in Arist. de Interpr.,* i, 3 (ed. Meiser).

tends over some time and the things undertaken are not immediately accomplished, is not this a clear footprint of nature impressed on [the devices of] human reason?

CHAPTER 15.   *That adjectives of secondary application should not be copulated with nouns of primary applica-tion,[175] as in the example "a patronymic horse."*

When we proceed to a consideration of the origin of the secondary application, queen nature's authority is likewise apparent, though not so clearly as in the foregoing instances. Man's mind first applied names to things. Then, reflecting on its own processes, it designated the names of things by further names, to facilitate the teaching of language and the communication of thoughts from one mind to another. A word which is declinable, but lacks tenses, is called a "noun" [176] if it signifies a substance or in a substantial way, whereas one which formally, so to speak, refers to what is present in a sub-stance, or something along this line,[177] is called an "adjective." A word which denotes temporal action[178] (provided this is in a tem-poral manner) is called a "verb," and is "active" if it represents the subject as acting, "passive" if it represents the subject as being the recipient of action. Words of secondary application have originated in a way similar to that in which words of primary application were formed. Just as with nouns and adjectives of primary application, some are said to pertain to certain specific things, whereas others are, by their nature, common to several things, so, among words of secondary application, some have a singular and others a general meaning. The words "name" and "enunciation" are properly classi-fied as nouns. When terms such as "appellative" or "categorical" are

[175] *secunde impositionis . . . prime,* second or secondary imposition, origin, or application . . . first or primary imposition, origin, or application. Cf. *Met.,* iii, 1.

[176] Literally: a substantive name.

[177] *aliquid ad imaginem eius,* something like this, apparently with reference to "what is present in a substance," something similar to something present in a substance.

[178] *motus,* in its broad sense, as including all movement, activity, change or action.

predicated of the former, they fulfill the function of adjectives by
determining the quality of nouns. In the works of nature, it requires
much greater subtlety to discern their internal constitution, for example, the simple elements, than to perceive what is presented to the
senses or intellect in a composite state. And if adjectives of secondary
application are not predicated of those things for which they were
by their nature intended, it is close to impossible to know what they
could mean. Substances are by their nature more solid than words,
and the accidents of substances are likewise more substantial than
those of words, since they [the accidents of substances] are more
familiar and more readily perceptible by our senses and intellect.[179]
So true is this that those who refer adjectives of secondary application to nouns of primary institution, either fail to say anything at all,
or talk sheer nonsense. If one speaks of "a patronymic horse" or
"hypothetical shoes," he unites terms that are incompatible. Comprehension is here precluded by the fundamental meaning of the words,
rather than by a mere lack of agreement in accidentals. Although
the adjectives agree sufficiently with their nouns in gender, number,
and case, to join the principals signified is to jabber like an idiot,
as well as to lie. Vergil has been accused of inappropriate wording[180]
for saying *gramineo in campo,*[181] where he should have said *grami-
noso in campo,*[182] but he would certainly have been more at fault,
and far more ridiculous, had he said *in campo cathegorico*[183] or [*in
campo*] *patronomico.*[184] The argument of those who rely on the
mere mutual agreement of accidents is refuted by the fact that not
every consonant followed by a vowel constitutes a syllable. For the
juxtaposition of the consonants "i" [j] and "u" [v] [185] no more suffices to constitute a syllable than the copulation of adjectives of secondary application and nouns of primary origin does to provide

[179] *que sensui aut intellectui familiarius occurunt.*

[180] *acirologie,* see Isidore, *Etym.,* i, 34, § 4; Donatus, *Art. Gram.,* iii, 3 (Keil, *G.L.,* IV,
394). Both Donatus and Isidore define *acrylogia* as *impropria dictio* or *non propria dictio,*
faulty or inappropriate wording.

[181] Vergil, *Aen.,* v, 287; "in a field covered with grass."

[182] In a field full of grass.

[183] In a categorical field.

[184] In a patronymic field.

[185] In Latin, *i* is both the vowel *i* and a consonant equivalent to the later *j*; whereas
u is both the vowel *u* and a consonant equivalent to the later *v*.

correct and balanced [186] speech. Manifestly there are two kinds of faults in speech: lying, and violating the established usages of language. Those who join adjectives of secondary application with nouns of primary application are guilty of at least the second transgression. Furthermore, it is incorrect to add pronouns of the first and second person to verbs, except for purposes of discrimination or emphasis, even though here the accidentals of speech are in sufficient agreement. I would not narrowly restrict futile[187] diction to redundance, as when one perchance adds to a noun an adjective that is already understood in it, for example, by saying, "The rational man walks." Rather, I would extend it to include every form of speech where the copulation of terms is pointless, and in some way falls short of fulfilling its own law. However, a verbal copulation is not futile simply because what it states is false, or because what it clarifies at one time it confuses at another. Grammatical rules do not censure lying, and even things which mean nothing to one who understands the language, may be predicated of each other. From the foregoing it is clear that we should not join adjectives of secondary application with nouns of primary application. But when adjectives are resolved into equivalent words (such as definitions), our mind does not recoil from the apposition of an equivalent term, although it would shudder on hearing the apposition of an adjective of secondary application. The statement: "The proposition is predicative," seems equally to mean that the proposition [in question] states something apodictically, that is, without qualification, and that it has a predicate term. If it be said that "the tunic is categorical," our intellect is perplexed by the incongruity of the adjective, and is probably more likely to charge that the terms have been improperly joined than to accuse one who says this of lying. If one would say, however, that "tunic," of itself, without any condition, "states something," or "has a predicate term," one's listener would straightway argue that this is false, but he would not so quickly complain of a violation of grammatical rules.[188] A "categorical proposition" means "a proposition having a subject and predicate"; whereas a "categori-

---

[186] Literally: equimodal.

[187] *nugatorie,* futile, foolish, trifling, nugatory.

[188] Literally: of an inappropriate copulation of terms.

cal syllogism" refers to a syllogism that consists of categorical propositions. I do not know what "a categorical horse" can possibly signify,
but until convinced otherwise I will maintain that it means nothing.
For I opine that something, which can never be found, is, and will
always be, non-existent. A similar abuse is to say: "*Equus*' [189] ends in
's," and the like. The sentence: "Cato, seated between the Hill of
Janus[190] and the first day of March, is mending the clothes of the
Roman people with the number four or the number six," either is
no speech at all or is more degenerate than the most foolish prattle.
Talk of this sort is styled "stichiology," [191] or "inverted speech," [192]
since the words are combined contrary to the rules of language. For
sticos means a "verse." [193] From it comes the word "distich," signifying a poem of two verses.[194] I have heard many persons arguing
this point, and advocating diverse opinions on the question. Hence
it will not be out of place to recount, nor will it perhaps be unwel-
come to hear, what a Greek interpreter, who also knew the Latin
language very well, told me when I was staying in Apulia. I am
grateful to him, if not for the utility (though there really is some
utility in such), at least for his kindness in endeavoring to enlighten
his hearers. The first point of his judgment or opinion I have already
mentioned: namely, that to join adjectives of secondary application
with nouns of primary application is inconsequential, even according
to grammatical rules. It has an incalculable latent "aphony," [195] that
is, lack of harmony, or (to use Quintilian's expression) *cacozugia*,[196]
namely, lack of suitability. Such apposition, even though we may
be at a loss directly to put our finger on why it is wrong, of itself
[immediately] grates on the ears of those who know grammar.
There are many such things that are directly repugnant, although

---

[189] Horse.
[190] Janiculum: one of the seven hills of Rome.
[191] *stychyologus*, from στίχος (Lat. *uersus*) and λόγος (Lat. *sermo*).
[192] *sermo inuersus*, turned about, inverted, or perverted speech.
[193] *uersus*, a verse, or a turning about.
[194] *uersuum*, verses; probably so called because each new verse involves a "turning about"
and starting a new line.
[195] *aphonie*, that is, ἀσυμφωνίας: *asumphonia*. See Priscian, *Inst.*, viii, 1, § 4 (Keil,
G.L., II, 371).
[196] *cacozugie;* Quintilian discusses not *cacozygia*, but *cacozelia*, that is, bad or perverted
affectation, in his *Inst. Or.*, viii, 6, § 73; cf. viii, 3, §§ 56 ff.

it is not so easy to point out just what is wrong with them. The like occurs with things whose good points or defects are evident. Although grammar overlooks much, it here perceives and argues that the wording is inappropriate.[197] It does not stop with denouncing lack of agreement in accidentals among copulated terms, but also considers absurd the application of words of secondary invention to subjects of primary origin. And absurd it actually is, since the mind becomes, as it were, deaf [198] on being confronted with a copulation of this kind. But what sense of hearing accurately apprehends things to which it is deaf? Are not one's words wasted when uttered to a deaf ear? Therefore, since our intellect[199] is, as it were, the soul's ear, as well as its hand, it derives absolutely no conception from words whose absurdity[200] precludes understanding. However, sometimes a thing may be taken to be absurd, owing to the fact that, at the time, we are not accustomed to hearing the term employed in this unusual manner. "A formless woman" [201] means, not a woman without any figure at all, but a woman with a poor figure. Certain letters are called "mute," not because they completely lack any sound, but because they have very little sound in comparison with other letters. The joining of the terms discussed above is, however, fundamentally absurd, and not just something that sounds false or inconsonant to the listener's ear. Not everything false is absurd, even though one inquiring into the truth will condemn and reject falsehood. Some things are declared absurd by judgment of the appropriate faculties examining the quality of such statements or facts. Grammar considers absurd any incongruous joining of terms, but it does not presume to constitute itself a judge of truth. In his book *On Analogy*,[202] wherein he is a grammarian, Caesar declares that we must avoid whatever may appear absurd to a learned listener. "As sailors steer clear of reefs" he says, "So we should shun unusual and strange

---

[197] *acirologiam;* see above, n. 180.

[198] *absurda . . . obsurdescit,* evidently a play on the words *surdus,* "deaf" and *absurdus,* "absurd."

[199] *intellectus,* intellect, understanding, rational intuition.

[200] Again a play on *surdus,* "deaf."

[201] *mulier informis;* see Priscian, *Inst.,* i, 3, § 10 (Keil, *G.L.,* II, 9).

[202] Gaius Julius Caesar wrote a work on grammar called *De Analogia,* that was much praised by his contemporaries, but it is not now extant.

words." [203] Dialectic it is which accepts only what is or seems true, and brands whatever is remote from the truth as preposterous. But dialectic does not go to the extent of estimating utility or goodness. It remains for political science[204] to measure the latter. For political science treats of degrees of justice, utility, and goodness. Political science accordingly equally abhors whatever falls short of goodness and rightness, whether it be true or false. The like [delimitation of subject matter] is apparent in other branches of knowledge. But let us return to the explanation given by our Greek interpreter. That "Man is rational" is, in view of present reality, in a way necessary. That "Man is able to laugh" [205] is probable. That "Man is white" is possible, but also doubtful, for its chances of being false are about equivalent to its chances of being true. That "Man is able to bray" [206] is impossible, for this positively cannot be true. The grammarian, however, will repudiate none of these statements. For in each of them he finds his own rules observed. Rather than try to correct any of the aforesaid propositions, he alters nothing, and accepts them all without argument. The logician, however, challenges and disproves the last. For it is his function to determine truth and falsity, in view of which he considers it absurd to pay any attention to the last proposition. But now let us suppose that to the foregoing statements we add a fifth to the effect that "Man is categorical." Forthwith the grammarian, who before admitted the doubtful, the false, and even the impossible, jumps up to condemn this as absurd. What does he give as his reason? Simply that his rules are violated: for he has declared it to be ever anathema to combine such adjectives and subjects.

[203] See Gellius, *Noct. Att.*, i, 10, 4.

[204] *ciuilis . . . scientia*, political science, political economy, the science of government and citizenship, here used as Aristotle uses the equivalent Greek word, to include ethics. Cf. Quintilian, *Inst. Or.*, ii, 15.

[205] *risibilis.*

[206] *rudibilis*, able to bray.

CHAPTER 16.   *That adjectives of primary origin are copulated with nouns of primary*[207] *application.*

It is not, however, impossible or inconsequential to reverse matters, and join adjectives of primary application with nouns of secondary origin. Nature is rich and bountiful, and liberally provides human indigence with her untold wealth, with the result that the properties of things overflow into words as our reason endeavors to make words cognate to things discussed.[208] Speech[209] is characterized as "hard" or "soft"; a verb[210] is referred to as "rough" or "smooth";[211] and a name[212] is called "sweet" or "bitter," even though the aforesaid qualities, strictly speaking, pertain to corporeal entities, rather than to words. Many such instances might be alleged, where nothing sounds incongruous to, or is rejected as false by a fair-minded judge or listener. Although faith is a virtue which can be possessed only by a rational creature, yet speech is called "faithful." Again, speech is condemned as "deceitful," although certainly the deceit is in the person speaking, rather than in the words. It is an accepted custom to transfer what I may call "natural" names to supply what "conceptual" [213] names lack; whereas the reverse process is by no means of such frequent occurrence. Transfer is sometimes made from necessity, sometimes for ornamentation, and, as the learned well know, if there be not at least the excuse of ornamentation, it becomes akin to equivocation.[214] When transfer is necessary, words may fittingly

---

[207] MSS C, B, and A of the *Metalogicon* have *prime* (primary) here; this may be a slip for *secunde* (secondary). Cf. the first sentence of the text. But in favor of the present reading, see later in this chapter.

[208] See Abelard, *Theol. Christiana* (*Opp.*, ed. Cousin, II, 481; and in Migne, *P.L.*, CLXXVIII, 1245).

[209] *sermo*, speech, or possibly a word.

[210] *uerbum*, a verb, or possibly a word.

[211] *asperum aut leue*, rough, harsh, strong, or smooth, mild, weak.

[212] *nomen*, a name, or possibly a noun.

[213] *rationalium*, rational, conceptual.

[214] Cicero, *De Orat.*, iii, 38, § 155; Quintilian, *Inst. Or.*, viii, 6, §§ 5, 6.

be applied to many things, and may even frequently change their meaning according to their particular subject, as with words said to be predicated in an accidental manner. No one, however, will charge that this copulation of terms is improper. And even though the less proper or transferred meaning of a word may come to prevail over its original and proper meaning as a result of customary usage, still if we turn about and use the term in its original sense, it is likely that no absurdity will result. At least there will not be as much absurdity in this case as we have said takes place when adjectives that modify words[215] are conscripted to qualify things. By usage, conversion has come to be admissible in the case of terms that delimit one another by mutual predication, as with species, definition, and property. "Finite" and "infinite" are terms that have been applied to names and verbs to designate their qualities; but since these terms were originally derived from things, it is by no means unfitting for them to be brought back home from their wandering, so to speak, so that a thing may also conversely[216] be called "finite" or "infinite." The terms "universal" and "particular," although especially used to refer to words, were originally borrowed from things (for they are not of secondary application). Thus they may, without any absurdity, be referred to names that have been assigned to things. In other words, terms derived from things may revert to things; but terms invented to designate the quality of words cannot be diverted from this special application and employment to refer to the quality of things. The latter terms are something like those called "syncategorematic"[217] in Greek. The meaning of such "consignificative" terms depends on, or is estimated from, their context. When they are associated with terms of like origin, these words each aptly evoke their own proper concept. But if they are transferred to other words, they faint and lose their voice,[218] as though they had

[215] *adiectiua uerborum*, adjectives derived from, or applied to, words rather than things, i.e., adjectives of secondary application.
[216] Literally: "a convertible thing may."
[217] *syncategoremata*, "syncategorematic" [to coin a word in English] or "consignificative." See Priscian, *Inst.*, ii, 4, § 15 (Keil, *G.L.*, II, 54). Priscian tells us that all words are "syncategorematic" or "consignificative," except nouns and verbs, since the latter alone can, without help of other words, make complete sentences when combined.
[218] Literally: they wilt away or lose their voice: they lose their meaning or ability to convey a message.

been drained of their natural vigor. On hearing someone say "a patronymic horse," the grammarian[219] will at once take the person to task, and constrain him to correct his erroneous language. Or perhaps, out of deference to the speaker, he will, with the servant in the comedy, suggest: "Come now, let's have good words."[220] Does not such an exhortation impute a certain defect? One who asks to hear good words, in place of those which have actually been used, evidently does not consider those which have been employed good. Otherwise he would say less rudely: "Come now, let's have better words." If one looks for mood and tense in a name [a noun], or case and comparison in a verb, the grammarian marks him as a silly sort; whence I do not believe he could adjust his powers of endurance to a student who referred to a "horse" as "patronymic." Adjectives of secondary application are so restricted by the limitations of their nature that they not only cannot be applied to the names of things, but also cannot stray far from the words for which they were invented. A proposition may correctly be called "hypothetical," and a name "patronymic"; but if we try to interchange the terms, and refer to a "hypothetical name," or a "patronymic proposition," either we are saying nothing at all, or at least we are speaking incorrectly, according to the grammarian. The supreme arbiter of speech, however, is custom. What usage condemns cannot be reinstated save by usage. Hence the poet:

> Many words that are obsolete, will one day be resurrected, and many now
>   highly esteemed will lapse from use,
> If such be but the will of usage: the judge, the law, and the norm of
>   speech.[221]

Lawyers hold, as an accepted principle, that "Custom is the best interpreter of law."[222] Even so, the practice of those who speak correctly is the most reliable interpreter of grammatical rules. Something that one never finds in writing, or catches on the lips of those who speak correctly, and the like of which one never reads or hears,

---

[219] *gramaticus auditor,* the grammatical listener, a listener who knows grammar, or a grammarian on hearing this.
[220] Words of the servant Davus, in Terence, *Andr.,* i, 2, 33.
[221] Horace, *A.P.,* 70–72.
[222] *Corpus Juris Civilis, Dig.,* i, 3, § 37.

has, I believe, already been long since condemned, or certainly has not yet been approved by grammarians. Still, not all names of primary origin can, in my estimation, be appropriately transferred in all cases, even though their general nature makes them better suited for such transfer.[223] One often finds an instance that does not fit under the rules, and an exception to what we have said above may be uncovered. Still usage generally obtains as we have stated. This reciprocity between things and words, and words and things, whereby they mutually communicate their qualities, as by an exchange of gifts,[224] is more commonly accomplished by words used in a metaphorical sense[225] than by those of secondary origin.[226] Although there may be particular instances which derogate from this general principle, we are speaking of what is usually the case. This force of transferred meaning, whereby properties of things are ascribed to words, and vice versa, gives birth to a certain tolerance, which permits the use of words in varying senses.[227] The latter license serves the learned [228] as a shortcut; yet it confounds and virtually slays the uneducated,[229] preventing them from comprehending the truth. For one who wants to know the truth must weigh, with a judicious mind, even what those who speak in an obscure and faulty way are trying to say as even the latter very often speak the truth.

[223] *transumptionis,* metalepsis: a rhetorical figure whereby a word is transferred from its own proper meaning to another sense. See Quintilian, *Inst. Or.,* viii, 6, § 37.

[224] Or: by mutual investiture.

[225] *translatiuis sermonibus,* words used in transferred or metaphorical senses.

[226] *quam his quos institutio secundaria promulgauit.* It is thought that *institutio secundaria* is here equivalent to *impositio secundaria,* both of which are practically equivalent to "second intention," a term common in later mediaeval logic. John would mean that when words of first and second intention are combined, the adjection is generally of the first intention and metaphorical. See above, for examples.

[227] *indifferentiam loquendi,* impartiality, indifference, tolerance, or latitude in the use of words, whereby, e.g., words may be used with varying meanings.

[228] *compositis ingeniis,* the learned, educated, prudent, broad-minded, judicious.

[229] *indiscreta* [*ingenia*], the uneducated, indiscrete, immature, or simple minded.

CHAPTER 17.   *That grammar also imitates nature in poetry.*

Grammar also imitates nature in further respects. Thus the rules of
poetry clearly reflect the ways of nature, and require anyone who
wishes to become a master in this art to follow nature as his guide.
[So the poet tells us:]

> Nature first adapts our soul to every
> Kind of fate: she delights us, arouses our wrath,
> Or overwhelms and tortures us with woe,
> After which she expresses these emotions employing the tongue as their
>   interpreter.[230]

So true is this [principle] that a poet must never forsake the footsteps of nature. Rather, he should strain to cleave closely to nature
in his bearing and gestures, as well as in his words:[231]

> . . . If you expect me to weep, then first
> You yourself must mourn . . .[232]

Likewise, if you want me to rejoice, you yourself must first be joyful.
Otherwise,

> . . . If you speak your piece poorly,
> I will either drift off to sleep or will laugh at you.[233]

Consequently, we must take into account, not merely poetical feet
and meters, but also age, place, and time, in addition to other circumstances, whose detailed enumeration does not suit our present
purpose. Suffice it to say that all of these are products from nature's
workshop. Indeed, so closely does it cleave to the things of nature
that several have denied that poetry is a subdivision of grammar, and
would have it be a separate art. They maintain that poetry no more
belongs to grammar than it does to rhetoric, although it is related

[230] Horace, *A.P.*, 108–111.
[231] *habitu, gestu, item uerbo.*
[232] Horace, *A.P.*, 102, 103.
[233] *Ibid.*, 104, 105.

to both, inasmuch as it has rules in common with each. Let those who wish, argue this (for I will not extend the controversy). Begging leave of all, however, I venture to opine that poetry belongs to grammar, which is its mother and the nurse of its study. Although neither poetry nor grammar is entirely natural, and each owes most of its content to man, its author and inventor, nevertheless nature successfully asserts some authority in both. Either poetry will remain a part of grammar, or it will be dropped from the roll of liberal studies.

CHAPTER 18.   *What grammar should prescribe, and what it should forbid.*

According to its traditional definition, grammar is "the science of writing and speaking in a correct manner." [234] The qualification "in a correct manner" is added in order to exclude error, so that "orthography" will be observed in writing, and the authority of the [grammatical] art and usage will be respected in speaking. "Orthography," or correct writing, consists in putting every letter in its proper position, and not allowing any alphabetic character to usurp another's place or forsake its own post. [235] Speaking is the articulate and literate verbal expression of our thoughts. The statement ". . . They speak by nods and signs," [236] does not refer to speech proper. One who speaks correctly, shuns the pitfalls of solecisms and barbarisms. A "barbarism" is the corruption of a civilized word, [237] that is, of a Greek or Latin word. [238] Use of a barbarian [239] language in speaking is "barbarolexis" [240] rather than a "barbarism." A solecism, on the

[234] Isidore, *Etym.,* i, 5.
[235] *Ibid.,* i, 27.
[236] Ovid., *Met.,* iv, 63.
[237] *dictionis non barbare,* a non-barbarous or civilized diction or word.
[238] Cf. Isidore, *Etym.,* i, 32; Donatus, *Art. Gram.,* ii, 18 (Keil, *G.L.,* IV, 392).
[239] *barbara,* barbarian; other than Greek or Roman.
[240] *barbarolexis,* barbarian speech or words. See Isidore, *Etym.,* i, 32, § 2; cf. Donatus, *Art. Gram.,* ii, 18 (Keil, *G.L.,* IV, 392).

other hand, is a corruption, not of one word, but of construction, whereby words are joined contrary to the rules of syntax.[241] A solecism may occur either from the parts of speech used, or from accidents in these parts. We have a solecism from parts of speech used when, for instance, a person substitutes one part of speech for another. An example is when one puts a preposition for an adverb, or vice versa. We also have a solecism of this kind when, while using the right part of speech, a person employs one sort of word where he should have used another. An example is when one places a word of secondary origin[242] where one of primary origin is really required. We may also have a solecism that is due to accidents,[243] such as kinds,[244] genders, cases, numbers, and forms[245] [of words]. In addition, there is the metaplasm,[246] which is found in verse. Like the barbarism in prose, the metaplasm occurs in a single word, although it is more permissible than the former, since it is used for the sake of meter. It is called a "metaplasm," or a sort of "transformation" or "deformation," because, as though on its own authority, it modifies or disfigures the form of words.[247] There are also schemata,[248] which we may translate as figures in wording[249] or sense,[250] and which comprise various forms of diction used to embellish speech.[251] Barbarisms and metaplasms occur in single words; solecisms and schemata, not in individual words, but in the joining of a number of words.[252] There are thus three subjects which the grammarian should master; the grammatical art, grammatical errors,

[241] See Isidore, *Etym.*, i, 33, § 1; cf. Donatus, *Art. Gram.*, ii, 19 (Keil, *G.L.*, IV, 393–394).

[242] *inuentionis*, invention, origin, imposition, application.

[243] Isidore, *Etym.*, i, 33, §§ 4–5; Donatus, *Art. Gram.*, ii, 19 (Keil, *G.L.*, IV, 393–394).

[244] *qualitates*, kinds of words, as "proper" or "common" nouns; e.g., putting the proper noun "Dardanus" for the common noun "Dardanius." Cf. Donatus, *loc. cit.*

[245] *figuras*, inflections. John evidently here refers to such forms as the moods, tenses, and persons of verbs. Cf. Donatus, *loc. cit.*

[246] *metaplasmus*, in Greek equivalent to *transformatio* in Latin, means a sort of transformation, deformation, or irregularity.

[247] Concerning metaplasms, see Isidore, *Etym.*, i, 35, § 1; cf. Donatus, *Art. Gram.*, iii, 4 (Keil, *G.L.*, IV, 395). Some examples of metaplasms are the use of *gnato* for *nato*, *sat* for *satis*, and the like.

[248] *scemata;* cf. Isidore, *Etym.*, i, 36; Donatus, *Art. Gram.*, iii, 5 (Keil, *G.L.*, IV, 395–397).

[249] That is, in a number of words together, as is stated in the next sentence.

[250] *sententiis*, evidently meanings. Cf. Donatus, *loc. cit.*

[251] Isidore, *Etym.*, i, 36.

[252] See *ibid.*, i, 35, § 7.

and figures [of speech]. Otherwise he will find it difficult to become
secure in his art, to avoid mistakes, and to imitate the graceful style
of the authors. If someone who is ignorant of the aforesaid [three]
subjects, writes or speaks correctly, he does so more through chance
than as a result of scientific skill. The art [of grammar] is, as it
were, a public highway, on which all have the right to journey,
walk, and act, immune from criticism or molestation. To use faulty
grammar always means that one is forsaking the proper thorough-
fare. He who pursues such devious by-paths is likely either to end
up at a precipice, or to become an easy target for the darts and jousts
of those who may challenge what he says.[253] The figure [of speech],
however, occupies an intermediate position. Since it differs to some
extent from both [regular grammar and grammatical error], it falls
in neither category. All strive to conform to the [grammatical] art,
since it is commanded, and to shun [grammatical] mistakes, since
these are forbidden; but only some use figures, since the latter are
[merely] permissible. Between errors, that is to say, barbarisms and
solecisms, and the art [of grammar], which consists in normal good
speech,[254] stand figures and schemata. With the metaplasm, there
is, for sufficient reason, some modification of a word; with the
schema,[255] for due cause, some deviation from the rules of construction.[256] According to Isidore, a figure is "an excusable departure
from the rule." [257] License to use figures is reserved for authors and
for those like them, namely, the very learned. Such have understood
why [and how] to use certain expressions and not use others. According to Cicero, "by their great and divine good writings they
have merited this privilege," [258] which they still enjoy. The authority
of such persons is by no means slight, and if they have said or done
something, this suffices to win praise for it, or [at least] to absolve
it from stigma. One who has not proved himself deserving of imita-

---

[253] *interpellantium*, of attackers, disturbers, critics.
[254] Literally: which is the virtue and the norm of speech.
[255] *scema*, that is, a figure proper.
[256] Literally: in the context of the words.
[257] *uitium cum ratione*, literally: a fault with reason, an excusable or rational fault.
Figures are discussed by Isidore in his *Etym.*, i, 35, § 7. Texts of the *Etymologies* here
differ.
[258] Cicero, *De Off.*, i, 41, § 148.

tion by such "great and good writings" will, however, vainly try
to expropriate this privilege. The excellence of their other virtues
has rightly made these faults of earlier authors sweet and delectable
to posterity. Whence Augustine says, in the second book of his work
On Order: "Poets have chosen to call the solecisms and barbarisms,
whereby they express themselves, and to which they are addicted,
scemata and *metaplasmos,* preferring to change their names rather
than give up these evident faults. Rob poems of the latter, and we
would keenly miss these delicious condiments. But when we transfer to scenes of informal conversation and forensic discussion,[259] who
will not banish this sort of diction, and bid it be off and hide itself
in the theater? Furthermore, if anyone piles up very many such
expressions together, we become nauseated by the consequent rancid,
ill smelling, and putrid heap.[260] Therefore the moderating principle
of good order will neither allow schemata and metaplasms to be
employed everywhere, nor suffer them to be absolutely banished.
And when these expressions are mixed with ordinary ones, life and
color are breathed into style that would otherwise be dull and commonplace." [261] So says Augustine. Thus we find that one whose
authority we have been admonished to heed,[262] confirms the great
necessity of a knowledge of these forms of speech, which are licitly
used by the more learned, and are found practically throughout the
length and breadth of literature.[263] Consequently one must learn to
discriminate between what is said literally, what is said figuratively,
and what is said incorrectly, if one is ever easily and accurately to
comprehend what he reads.

[259] Literally: free talk and the speech of the forum, market place, or law court.
[260] Augustine, *De Ord.,* ii, 4, § 13.
[261] *Ibid.* The last sentence, though its sense is from Augustine, is evidently not a direct quotation.
[262] *precepta . . . auctoritate,* enjoined, commanded, or prescribed authority.
[263] *scripturarum,* writings, scriptures, literature.

CHAPTER 19.   *That a knowledge of figures [of speech] is most useful.*

Grammar also regulates the use of tropes,[264] special forms of speech[265] whereby, for sufficient cause, speech[266] is used in a transferred sense that differs from its own proper meaning. Examples of tropes are found in metaphors, metonomy, synechdoche, and the like. An enumeration of all the various kinds of tropes would be too lengthy.[267] The employment of tropes, just as the use of schemata, is the exclusive privilege of the very learned. The rules governing tropes are also very strict, so that the latitude in which they may be used is definitely limited. For the rules teach that we may not extend figures. One who is studiously imitating the authors by using metaphors[268] and figures, must take care to avoid crude figures that are hard to interpret. What is primarily desirable in language[269] is lucid clarity and easy comprehensibility. Therefore schemata should be used only out of necessity or for ornamentation. Speech was invented as a means of communicating mental concepts; and figures [of speech] are admitted so far as they compensate by their utility for whatever they lack in conformity to the [rules of the grammatical] art. It is especially necessary to understand those three things which are generally most to blame for blocking comprehension of meaning, namely schemata together with rhetorical tropes; sophisms which envelop the minds of listeners in a fog of fallacies; and the various considerations which prompt the speaker or writer to say what he does, and which, when recognized, make straight the way for understanding. Indeed, as Hilary tells us, "What is said should

[264] *tropos*
[265] *modos locutionum.*
[266] *sermo*, speech, diction.
[267] Cf. Isidore, *Etym.*, i, 37.
[268] *translationibus*, transfers, metaphors.
[269] Quintilian, *Inst. Or.*, i, 6, § 41.

be interpreted in the light of why it is said."[270] Otherwise, even in the canonical scriptures, the Fathers would be at odds, and the Evangelists themselves would be contradicting each other, if we were foolishly to judge only from the surface of their words, without considering their underlying purposes. Such procedure indicates a perverse disposition and disregard of one's own progress. Does not Solomon, in the same book, on the same page, and even in consecutive verses, declare: "Respond not to a fool according to his foolishness, lest you become like him"; and: "Reply to the fool according to his foolishness, lest he be deluded into imagining he is wise."[271] One should learn the rules whereby one can determine what is right and what wrong in speech. One cannot correct mistakes save by rule, and one cannot avoid pitfalls which one fails to recognize owing to one's failure to study. Among the rules of the arts, I do not believe that there are any more useful or more compendious[272] than those which, in addition to taking note of the figures used by authors, clearly point out the merits and defects of their speech.[273] It is a matter of [no small] wonder to me why our contemporaries have so neglected this part [of grammar], for it is very useful, and equally concise, and has been carefully treated by most writers on the art [of grammar]. Donatus,[274] Servius,[275] Priscian,[276] Isidore,[277] Cassiodorus,[278] our Bede,[279] and many others, have all discussed it, so that if one remains ignorant of it, this can only be attributed to negligence. Quintilian[280] also teaches this part of the art. In fact he praises it so highly that he would say that, if one lacks it, it is doubtful whether he has the right to be called a grammarian, and certain that he cannot hope to become a master of the [grammatical] art. The meaning of words should be carefully analyzed, and one should

[270] Hilary, *De Trin.*, iv, 14 (in Migne, *P.L.*, X, 107).
[271] Proverbs, xxvi, 4, 5.
[272] That is, more comprehensively concise.
[273] Quintilian, *Inst. Or.*, i, 5, §§ 1–54.
[274] Donatus, *Art. Gram.*, iii, 5, 6 (Keil, *G.L.*, IV, 397 ff.).
[275] Servius, *Comm. in Donatum*, near the end.
[276] Priscian, *Inst.*, xvii, §§ 166 ff. (Keil, *G.L.*, III, 192 ff.).
[277] Isidore, *Etym.*, ii, 21.
[278] Cassiodorus, *De Artibus liberalibus*, chap. i (in Migne, *P.L.*, LXX, 1153).
[279] Bede, *De Schematibus et tropis sacrae scripturae* (in Migne, *P.L.*, XC, 175 ff.).
[280] Quintilian, *Inst. Or.*, i, 5, § 7.

diligently ascertain the precise force of each and every term, both
in itself and in the given context, so that one may dispel the haze
of sophistries that would otherwise obscure the truth. The considerations prompting the speaker[281] may be surmised from the occasion,
the kind of person he is, and the sort of listeners he has, as well as
from the place, the time, and various other pertinent circumstances
that must be taken into account by one who seriously seeks the
truth. If one applies himself to mastering the above-suggested means
of overcoming the three obstacles to understanding, not only will he
be agreeably surprised by his own increased proficiency in comprehending what he reads and hears, but he will also come to be admired and respected by others.

CHAPTER 20.   *With what the grammarian should concern
himself.*

Grammar also studies other questions.[282] In addition to treating
the nature of letters, syllables, and words,[283] it likewise discusses
metrical feet as well as the accents to be given to syllables. It even
distinguishes and explains the [various] forms of accents, and teaches
whether accents on syllables should be grave, acute, or circumflex.
It further discriminates between punctuations, which are figures
indicating a colon, a comma, or a period, that is to say, where we
should make a slight, a half, or a full stop.[284] Which may be more
easily explained by calling a colon a clause, a comma a phrase, and a
period a sentence[285] comprising the verbal expression of a complete
thought. Some, in order to make matters even clearer, say (whether
or not their opinion is correct) that a colon is put where we commonly pause or inhale, a comma where we divide a verse as it were

[281] *ratio dicendi,* the reason of speaking, the considerations prompting the speaker.
[282] John's chief source in this chapter is Isidore, *Etym.,* i, 19, 20.
[283] *dictionum,* of words or dictions.
[284] *distinctio,* distinction, separation, interpunction, stop.
[285] *periodus circuitus, circuitus* is the Latin equivalent for the Greek περίοδος.

in half, and a period where we conclude a complete verbal statement.[286] There are also notations that indicate the mode of what
is written, and show whether the latter is clear or obscure, certain
or doubtful, and so on. However, this part of the [grammatical] art
has so generally fallen into disuse that those who are most enthusiastic about learned studies justly lament and are brought to the verge
of tears because the art of notations,[287] so highly useful and effective
for both comprehension and retention, has, through the prejudice
or negligence of our predecessors, vanished. That such great import
has existed in such tiny notations should not seem strange, for singers
of music likewise indicate by a few graphic symbols numerous variations in the acuteness and gravity of tones.[288] For which reason such
characters are appropriately known as "the keys of music." [289] If,
however, the little notations we spoke of above gave access to such
great science, I am surprised that our forefathers, who were so
learned, were not aware of this, or that the keys to so much knowledge were lost. Seneca glibly promised to impart the art of memorization,[290] of which I certainly wish I were a master; but as far as
I know, he did not actually teach it. Tullius [Cicero] seems to have
applied himself to this in his *Rhetorical Questions*,[291] but the latter
are not of much help to men like me. There are extant some things,
it is true, which we can scarcely apprehend, but about these we are
very little concerned. On the other hand, rules concerning similar
forms and inflections, etymologies, definitions of terms that need
explanation, and differences,[292] those pointing out the faults of
barbarisms, solecisms, and other grammatical errors to be avoided,
those clarifying the question as to what forms of metaplasms, schemata, and tropes are permissible and ornamental, and those explain-

[286] Cf., in addition to Isidore, *Etym.*, i, 20, also Donatus, *Art. Gram.*, i, 6 (Keil, *G.L.*,
IV, 372).

[287] *ars notaria.*

[288] That is, in pitch.

[289] *musice claues,* the "keys of music" here refers to musical "notes," rather than to
musical "keys" as we understand them today.

[290] Cicero relates this of a certain learned man: *De Orat.*, ii, 74, § 299; cf. *De Fin.*, ii,
32, § 104.

[291] See pseudo-Cicero, *Ad Herennium*, iii, 16 ff.

[292] Literally: analogies, etymologies, glosses, and differences.

ing prose, enunciating the laws of poetry, and stating cases,[293] as well as the method to be followed in historical and fictional narratives,—all must be extremely advantageous. If anyone wants the definitions and forms of the above, he has but to peruse the books of the aforesaid grammarians. If all these volumes are not at hand, one may see what worth knowing he can find in particular books. For, although every one of them does not adequately treat all questions, still each is helpful to some extent. Isidore, especially, is very useful, sufficiently general, and praiseworthy for studied conciseness. If all the books of the grammarians are not available, it is still very helpful, for the interpretation of what we read, to bear in mind [294] even this fragmentary survey.

CHAPTER 21.   *By what great men grammar has been appreciated, and the fact that ignorance of this art is as much a handicap in philosophy as is deafness and dumbness.*

From what has been said, it is clear that [the function of] grammar is not narrowly confined to one subject. Rather, grammar prepares the mind to understand everything that can be taught in words. Consequently, everyone can appreciate how much all other studies depend on grammar. Some of our contemporaries apparently pride themselves on being able to babble along garrulously without benefit of this art. They regard it as useless, openly assail it, and glory in the fact that they have never studied it. But Marcus Tullius [Cicero] did not hate his son, of whom, as is evident in his letters, he insistently required the study of grammar.[295] And Gaius Caesar wrote books *On Analogy,*[296] conscious that, without grammar, one cannot

---

[293] *causas,* John evidently here refers to cases or subjects occasioning discourse. Cf. Quintilian, *Inst. Or.,* ii, 5, § 7.

[294] Literally: to have fixed in our memory.

[295] See Quintilian, *Inst. Or.,* i, 7, § 34.

[296] Or on like word forms in grammar. See above, n. 202. See also Quintilian, *loc. cit.*

master philosophy[297] (with which he was thoroughly familiar) or eloquence (in which he was most proficient).[298] Quintilian also praises this art to the point of declaring that we should continue the use[299] of grammar and the love of reading "not merely during our school days, but to the very end of our life." [300] For grammar equips us both to receive and to impart knowledge. It modulates our accent, and regulates our very voice so that it is suited to all persons and matters. Poetry should be recited in one way; prose in another. The governing principle in pronunciation is at one time harmony, at another rhythm, at still another the sense. The law of harmony reigns in music. Caesar, while still a boy,[301] with fine sarcasm remarked to a certain person: "If you're trying to read, you're singing, and if you're trying to sing, you're doing a miserable job." [302] In similar vein, Martianus, in *The Marriage of Mercury and Philology,* represents grammar as provided with a knife, a rod, and the ointment case carried by physicians.[303] She uses the knife to prune away grammatical errors, and to cleanse the tongues of infants as she instructs them. Nursing and feeding her charges, she conducts them on to the art of philosophy, thoroughly training them beforehand so that they will not babble in barbarisms or solecisms. Grammar employs her rod to punish offenders; while with the ointment of the propriety and utility which derive from her services, she mitigates the sufferings of her patients. Grammar also guides our hand to write correctly, and sharpens our vision so that it is not nonplussed by fine convolutions of letters, or by parchment crowded with intricate and elaborate script. It opens our ears, and accommodates them to all word sounds, including those that are deep or sharp.[304] If, therefore, grammar is so useful, and the key to everything written, as well as the mother and arbiter of all speech, who will [try to]

---

[297] Philosophy or general learning.

[298] Quintilian, *loc. cit.*

[299] *usus,* the use, habit, or practice.

[300] Quintilian, *Inst. Or.,* i, 8, § 12.

[301] *pretextatus,* clad in the toga that was worn by freeborn children until they were seventeen years of age, at which time they assumed the *toga virilis.* Thus: while still a minor; while still under age.

[302] Quintilian, *Inst. Or.,* i, 8, § 2.

[303] Martianus Capella, *De Nupt.,* iii, § 223.

[304] *tam grauibus quam acutis,* grave, deep, or heavy; acute, sharp, or high.

exclude it from the threshold of philosophy, save one who thinks that philosophizing does not require an understanding of what has been said or written? Accordingly those who would banish or condemn grammar are in effect trying to pretend that the blind and deaf are more fit for philosophical studies than those who, by nature's gift, have received and still enjoy the vigor of all their senses.

CHAPTER 22.   *That Cornificius invokes the authority of Seneca to defend his erroneous contentions.*

Cornificius, however, hides behind a great authority, whom he quotes as the source of his erroneous doctrine. This authority [Seneca] indeed deserves the praise he receives from many, and for two reasons. In the first place, he [Seneca] is a strong advocate of virtue and a great teacher of morality. In the second place, his pithy epigrammatic style[305] is admirable for its succinct brevity, while his diction is both beautiful and vivid. Consequently, those who love either virtue or eloquence cannot but be pleased [with Seneca]. With all due respect to Quintilian,[306] there is no, or at least hardly any, other moralist among the pagans, whose words and opinions can be more conveniently alleged in all sorts of discussions. Quintilian, while praising Seneca's intelligence, condemns his judgment, and declares that his writings are full of sugar-coated faults, and that he was popular with immature boys rather than with the learned. Quintilian also complains that Seneca breaks down substantial periods into brief "points," [307] whence one of the emperors characterized his works as sand without lime.[308] Seneca always has some-

---

[305] *comatico genere dicendi;* cf. Jerome, *In Eccles.,* iii, 18 (in Migne, *P.L.,* XXIII, 1095).

[306] Quintilian, *Inst. Or.,* x, 1, §§ 125 ff. Cf. *Policraticus,* viii, 13, for Quintilian's opinion of Seneca.

[307] *summas rerum minutissimis sententiis frangere,* literally: he breaks down composite summaries into very short sentences, that is, substitutes the "sententious" style for the "periodic" one.

[308] Cf. Quintilian, *loc. cit.* The emperor was Caligula, a madman in most things, but showed some keenness in literary judgments.

thing to say. Thus he feels that liberal studies do not make a person good.[309] I agree with him, but I think that the same also holds true of other studies. Knowledge puffeth up; it is charity alone that makes one good.[310] Seneca deflates the arts, but at the same time he does not exclude them from the field of philosophy, since [it may also be said that] those who are merely philosophers are not good men. "The subject of the grammarian," he says, "is language, and if he goes farther, history, and if he proceeds still farther, poetry."[311] Such, however, is no trivial matter, and contributes much to the formation of virtue, which makes a man good. Horace takes pride in the fact that, for virtue's sake, he has reread Homer,[312]

Who tells us what is beautiful and what repulsive, what useful and what disadvantageous,
In [far] more entertaining and effective manner than do Chrysippus and Cantor.[313]

That "Poetry is the cradle of philosophy" is axiomatic. Furthermore, do not our forefathers tell us that the liberal studies are so useful that one who has mastered them can, without a teacher, understand all books and everything written?[314] Indeed, as Quintilian observes, "These studies harm, not those who pass through them, but only those who become bogged down in them."[315]

---

[309] Seneca, *Ep.*, 88, §§ 1–2.

[310] I Corinthians, viii, 1.

[311] Seneca, *Ep.*, 88, § 3.

[312] Seneca (*Ep.*, 88, § 5) denies that Homer was a philosopher.

[313] Horace, *Ep.*, i, 2, 1–4. John has *Cantore*, in place of Horace's *Crantore*.

[314] While preserving the sense, the translator has here changed the direct statement to a question, for stylistic purposes.

[315] Quintilian, *Inst. Or.*, i, 7, § 35. The meaning here is, apparently: "These studies are not in themselves harmful, but only hurt those who after taking them up, become pedantic sticklers."

CHAPTER 23.   *The chief aids to philosophical inquiry and the*
              practice of virtue; as well as how grammar is
              the foundation of both philosophy and virtue.

The chief aids to philosophical inquiry and the practice of virtue
are reading, learning,[316] meditation,[317] and assiduous application.[318]
Reading scrutinizes the written subject matter immediately before
it. Learning likewise generally studies what is written, but also sometimes moves on to what is preserved in the archives of the memory
and is not in the writing, or to those things that become evident
when one understands the given subject. Meditation, however,
reaches out farther to what is unknown, and often even rises to the
incomprehensible by penetrating, not merely the apparent aspects,
but even the hidden recesses of questions. The fourth is assiduous
application. The latter, although it owes its form to previous cognition, and requires scientific knowledge, still smooths the way for
understanding, since, in itself, it constitutes "a good understanding
for all who do it." [319] The heralds of the truth, it is written, "have
proclaimed the works of God, and have understood His doings." [320]
Scientific knowledge, by the nature of things, must precede the
practice and cultivation of virtue, which does not "run without knowing where it is going," and does not merely "beat the air" in its
battle against vice.[321] Rather "it sees its goal, and the target at which
it aims." It does not haphazardly chase ravens with a piece of pottery
and a bit of mud.[322] But scientific knowledge is the product of read-

[316] *doctrina,* study, learning, grasping the doctrinal content; cf. Hugh of St. Victor,
Erud. Didasc., iii, 7, 9, 10, 11; v, 7; together with G. Paré, A. Brunet, and P. Tremblay,
Renaissance du xii° siècle, pp. 113–116.
[317] *meditatio.*
[318] *assiduitas operis,* diligent practical application, action in accordance with knowledge,
virtue. Cf. later in this chapter, and chap. 24.
[319] Psalms, cx, 10. The Psalm refers to practical "fear of the Lord," or observance of
the divine commandments.
[320] Psalms, lxiii, 10.
[321] I Corinthians, ix, 26.
[322] Persius, *Sat.,* iii, 60, 61.

ing, learning, and meditation. It is accordingly evident that grammar, which is the basis and root of scientific knowledge, implants, as it were, the seed [of virtue] in nature's furrow after grace has readied the ground. This seed, provided again that coöperating grace is present, increases in substance and strength until it becomes solid virtue, and it grows in manifold respects until it fructifies in good works, wherefore men are called and actually are "good." At the same time, it is grace alone which makes a man good. For grace brings about both the willing and the doing of good.[323] Furthermore, grace, more than anything else, imparts the faculty of writing and speaking correctly to those to whom it is given, and supplies them with the various arts. Grace should not be scorned when it generously offers itself to the needy, for if despised, it rightly departs, leaving the one who has spurned it no excuse for complaint.

CHAPTER 24.   *Practical observations on reading and lecturing,[324] together with [an account of] the method employed by Bernard of Chartres and his followers.*

One who aspires to become a philosopher should therefore apply himself to reading, learning, and meditation, as well as the performance of good works,[325] lest the Lord become angry and take away what he seems to possess.[326] The word "reading"[327] is equivocal. It may refer either to the activity of teaching and being taught, or to the occupation of studying written things by oneself. Consequently, the former, the intercommunication between teacher and learner, may be termed (to use Quintilian's word) the "lecture";[328]

---

[323] Philippians, ii, 13.
[324] *prelegendi,* reading before, lecturing.
[325] Cf. *Met.,* i, 23.
[326] Matthew, xxv, 29.
[327] *legendi.* The word "reading" is, as John says, ambiguous. One may "read" a book, or may "read" a "lecture" (a "reading" to students or an audience).
[328] *prelectio;* cf. Quintilian, *Inst. Or.,* ii, 5, § 4.

the latter, or the scrutiny by the student, the "reading," [329] simply
so called. On the authority of the same Quintilian,[330] "the teacher
of grammar should, in lecturing,[331] take care of such details as to
have his students analyze verses into their parts of speech, and point
out the nature of the metrical feet which are to be noted in poems.
He should, furthermore, indicate and condemn whatever is barba-
rous, incongruous, or otherwise against the rules of composition." He
should not, however, be overcritical of the poets, in whose case,
because of the requirements of rhythm, so much is overlooked that
their very faults are termed virtues. A departure from the rule that
is excused by necessity, is often praised as a virtue, when observance
of the rule would be detrimental. The grammarian should also point
out metaplasms, schematisms, and oratorical tropes, as well as various
other forms of expression[332] that may be present. He should further
suggest the various possible ways of saying things, and impress them
on the memory of his listeners by repeated reminders. Let him
"shake out" [333] the authors, and, without exciting ridicule, despoil
them of their feathers, which (crow fashion) they have borrowed
from the several branches of learning in order to bedeck their works
and make them more colorful.[334] One will more fully perceive and
more lucidly explain the charming elegance of the authors in proportion to the breadth and thoroughness of his knowledge of various disciplines. The authors by *diacrisis*,[335] which we may translate as "vivid
representation" [336] or "graphic imagery," [337] when they would take
the crude materials of history, arguments,[338] narratives,[339] and other
topics, would so copiously embellish them by the various branches of
knowledge, in such charming style, with such pleasing ornament,

[329] *lectio.*
[330] Quintilian, *Inst. Or.*, i, 8, §§ 13 ff.
[331] *in prelegendo.*
[332] *Met.*, i, 18, 19.
[333] *excutiat*, shake out, search, thoroughly examine or analyze.
[334] Cf. Horace, *Ep.*, i, 3, 18–20.
[335] *diacrisim*, perhaps from διακρῐσις: separation, discernment, solution, interpretation; or perhaps from: διατύπωσις. Cf. Martianus Capella, *De Nupt.*, v, § 524; and Cassiodorus, *In Ps. xxx*, 11; *xc*, 1; *cxxv*, 4 (in Migne, *P.L.*, LXX, 210, 650, 925).
[336] *illustrationem*, illustration, illumination, vivid representation or description; cf. Quintilian, *Inst. Or.*, vi, 2, § 32.
[337] *picturationem.*
[338] Perhaps in the sense of a plot.
[339] *fabule*, a narrative, story, play, fable, talk.

that their finished masterpiece would seem to image all the arts.
Grammar and Poetry are poured without stint over the length and
breadth of their works. Across this field,[340] as it is commonly called,
Logic, which contributes plausibility by its proofs,[341] weaves the
golden lightening of its reasons; while Rhetoric, where persuasion is
in order, supplies the silvery luster of its resplendent eloquence.
Following in the path of the foregoing, Mathematics rides [proudly]
along on the four-wheel chariot of its Quadrivium, intermingling its
fascinating demonstration in manifold variety. Physical philosophy,[342] which explores the secret depths of nature, also brings forth
from her [copious] stores numerous lovely ornaments of diverse
hue. Of all branches of learning, that which confers the greatest
beauty is Ethics, the most excellent part of philosophy, without
which the latter would not even deserve its name. Carefully examine
the works of Vergil or Lucan, and no matter what your philosophy,
you will find therein its seed or seasoning.[343] The fruit of the lecture
on the authors is proportionate both to the capacity of the students
and to the industrious diligence of the teacher. Bernard of Chartres,[344] the greatest font of literary learning[345] in Gaul in recent
times,[346] used to teach grammar in the following way. He would
point out, in reading the authors, what was simple and according
to rule. On the other hand, he would explain grammatical figures,
rhetorical embellishment, and sophistical quibbling, as well as the
relation of given passages to other studies. He would do so, however,
without trying to teach everything at one time. On the contrary, he
would dispense his instruction to his hearers gradually, in a manner
commensurate with their powers of assimilation. And since diction
is lustrous either because the words are well chosen,[347] and the adjec-

---

[340] *campo.*

[341] Literally: its colors of proving (or credible proofs).

[342] *Phisica,* physical or natural philosophy, sometimes called physics.

[343] *eiusdem inuenies condituram,* you will find therein its founding, preparing, or germ;
or you will find it used therein as a seasoning.

[344] See footnotes to *Met.,* i, 5; and cf. Clerval, *Les Écoles de Chartres au moyen-âge,* pp.
158 ff.

[345] *litterarum,* of letters, of literary or grammatical learning.

[346] Literally: in modern times.

[347] *proprietate,* from propriety, fitness, appropriateness.

tives and verbs admirably suited to the nouns with which they are
used, or because of the employment of metaphors,[348] whereby speech
is transferred to some beyond-the-ordinary meaning for sufficient
reason, Bernard used to inculcate this in the minds of his hearers
whenever he had the opportunity. In view of the fact that exercise
both strengthens and sharpens our mind, Bernard would bend every
effort to bring his students to imitate what they were hearing.[349] In
some cases he would rely on exhortation, in others he would resort
to punishments, such as flogging. Each student was daily required
to recite part of what he had heard on the previous day. Some would
recite more, others less. Each succeeding day thus became the
disciple of its predecessor. The evening exercise, known as the
"declination," [350] was so replete with grammatical instruction that if
anyone were to take part in it for an entire year, provided he were
not a dullard, he would become thoroughly familiar with the [cor-
rect] method of speaking and writing, and would not be at a loss
to comprehend expressions in general use. Since, however, it is not
right to allow any school or day to be without religion, subject
matter was presented to foster faith, to build up morals, and to in-
spire those present at this quasicollation[351] to perform good works.
This [evening] "declination," or philosophical collation, closed
with the pious commendation of the souls of the departed to
their Redeemer, by the devout recitation[352] of the Sixth Penetential
Psalm[353] and the Lord's Prayer. He [Bernard] would also explain
the poets and orators who were to serve as models for the boys in
their introductory exercises[354] in imitating prose and poetry. Pointing out how the diction of the authors was so skillfully con-

---

[348] *translatione.*

[349] Literally: what they were hearing, namely, the selections that he read to them [from
the authors].

[350] *declinatio.* This exercise was probably so called from its characteristic part, the declination, or inflections, of nouns and verbs, or possibly from the fact that, at this time, the
light and activity of day were declining (*declinante*) into the darkness and repose of
night.

[351] *collatione,* may mean either a conference or a refreshing repast.

[352] Literally: offering.

[353] Psalms, cxxix ("Out of the Depths" or the *"De profundis"*).

[354] *preexercitamina;* see Priscian, *De Figuris numerorum,* in his preface (Keil, *G.L.,* III,
405, 12).

nected,[355] and what they had to say was so elegantly concluded,[356] he would admonish his students to follow their example. And if, to embellish his work, someone had sewed on a patch of cloth filched from an external source,[357] Bernard, on discovering this, would rebuke him for his plagiary, but would generally refrain from punishing him. After he had reproved the student, if an unsuitable theme had invited this,[358] he would, with modest indulgence, bid the boy to rise to real imitation of the [classical authors], and would bring about that he who had imitated his predecessors would come to be deserving of imitation by his successors.[359] He would also inculcate as fundamental, and impress on the minds of his listeners, what virtue exists in economy;[360] what things are to be commended by facts and what ones by choice of words,[361] where concise and, so to speak, frugal speech is in order, and where fuller, more copious expression is appropriate; as well as where speech is excessive, and wherein consists just measure in all cases.[362] Bernard used also to admonish his students that stories and poems should be read thoroughly, and not as though the reader were being precipitated to flight by spurs. Wherefor he diligently and insistently demanded from each, as a daily debt, something committed to memory.[363] At the same time, he said that we should shun what is superfluous. According to him, the works of distinguished authors

---

[355] *iuncturas dictionum*, literally: connections, or the connecting of things said. Cf. Quintilian, *Inst. Or.*, ix, 4, § 32.

[356] *sermonum clausulas*, the conclusion of speeches. A *clausula*, with Quintilian, means a concise and acute conclusion to a speech.

[357] Horace, *A.P.*, 16; Matthew, ix, 16.

[358] Or: if the inappropriate use had deserved this.

[359] Baldwin (*Med. Rhet. and Poetic*, p. 163), translates this passage as follows: "But if the borrowing was misplaced, with modest kindliness, he bade the boy come down to express his author's likeness; and his own practice was such that in imitating his predecessors, he became a model for his successors." But cf. A. Clerval, *Les Écoles de Chartres*, p. 226, and C. H. Haskins, *Renaissance of the Twelfth Century*, pp. 135–136.

[360] *economia*, that is, *oeconomia*, a fine practical adjustment of means to an end. Cf. Quintilian (*Inst. Or.*, iii, 3, § 9), where he refers to "economy" as including judgment, division, order, and everything relating to expression (according to Hermagoras).

[361] *que in decore rerum, que in uerbis laudanda sint*. John evidently distinguishes here between beauty of content and beauty of expression.

[362] That is, moderation.

[363] Bernard apparently required of each of his students the daily recitation of some passages memorized from their current reading.

suffice. As a matter of fact, to study everything that everyone, no
matter how insignificant, has ever said, is either to be excessively
humble and cautious, or overly vain and ostentatious. It also deters
and stifles minds that would better be freed to go on to other things.
That which preëmpts the place of something that is better is, for this
reason, disadvantageous, and does not deserve to be called "good."
To examine and pore over everything that has been written, regardless of whether it is worth reading, is as pointless as to fritter away
one's time with old wives' tales. As Augustine says in his book *On
Order:* "Who is there who will bear that a man who has never heard
that Daedalus[364] flew should [therefor] be considered unlearned?
And, on the contrary, who will not agree that one who says that
Daedalus did fly should be branded a liar; one who believes it, a
fool; and one who questions [anyone] about it, impudent? I am
wont to have profound pity for those of my associates who are
accused of ignorance because they do not know the name of the
mother of Euryalus,[365] yet who dare not call those who ask such
questions 'conceited and pedantic busy-bodies.' " [366] Augustine summarizes the matter aptly and with truth. The ancients correctly
reckoned that to ignore certain things constituted one of the marks
of a good grammarian. A further feature of Bernard's method was to
have his disciples compose prose and poetry every day, and exercise
their faculties in mutual conferences,[367] for nothing is more useful
in introductory training than actually to accustom one's students to
practice the art they are studying. Nothing serves better to foster
the acquisition of eloquence and the attainment of knowledge than
such conferences, which also have a salutary influence on practical
conduct, provided that charity moderates enthusiasm, and that humility is not lost during progress in learning. A man cannot be the

[364] Daedalus: an Athenian artist, celebrated for his mechanical skill, who was said to
have flown from Crete to Sicily.
[365] *Euriali,* Euryalus: a Trojan, who perished together with his friend Nisus.
[366] See Augustine, *De Ord.,* ii, 12, § 37 (in Migne, *P.L.,* XXXII, 1012, 1013).
[367] *collationibus,* collations, conferences, comparisons. Although "conferences" would
seem to fit here as a translation, Webb holds that "comparisons" is better. Cf. Webb's ed.,
Met., p. 57 (*ad loc.*). Haskins (*Renaissance of the Twelfth Century,* p. 136), also
translates this as "comparisons," though Baldwin (*Med. Rhet. and Poetic,* p. 136), renders
it as "criticisms."

servant of both learning and carnal vice.[368] My own instructors in grammar, William of Conches,[369] and Richard, who is known as "the Bishop,"[370] a good man both in life and conversation,[371] who now holds the office of archdeacon of Coutances, formerly used Bernard's method in training their disciples. But later, when popular opinion veered away from the truth, when men preferred to seem, rather than to be philosophers, and when professors of the arts were promising to impart the whole of philosophy in less than three or even two years, William and Richard were overwhelmed by the onslaught of the ignorant mob, and retired.[372] Since then, less time and attention have been given to the study of grammar. As a result, we find men who profess all the arts, liberal and mechanical, but who are ignorant of this very first one [i.e., grammar], without which it is futile to attempt to go on to the others. But while other studies may also contribute to "letters,"[373] grammar alone has the unique privilege of making one "lettered."[374] Romulus,[375] in fact, refers to grammar as "letters," Varro[376] calls it "making lettered,"[377] and one who teaches or professes grammar is spoken of as "lettered." In times past, the teacher of grammar was styled a "teacher of letters."[378] Thus Catullus says: "Silla, the 'teacher of letters,' gives thee a present."[379] Hence it is probable that anyone who spurns grammar, is not only not a "teacher of letters," but does not even deserve to be called "lettered."

---

[368] See Jerome, *Ep.*, cxxc, § 11 (in Migne, *P.L.*, XXII, 1078): "Love the knowledge of the scriptures, and you will not love the vices of the flesh."

[369] On William of Conches, see *Met.*, i, 5, p. 21, n. 65.

[370] Richard l'Evêque; cf. Clerval, *Les Écoles de Chartres*, pp. 182 f.

[371] *uita et conuersatione uir bonus*, a good man, both in his life or way of life or conduct, and in his conversation or intercourse or deportment. This may also mean a good man, both in his personal life and in his social influence.

[372] *cesserunt*, that is, they stopped school. See Poole, *Medieval Thought*, App., vii, p. 311.

[373] *litteratura*, letters, literature, learning.

[374] *litteratum*, lettered, literate, learned.

[375] *Romulus;* see Martianus Capella, *De Nupt.*, iii, § 229, where *Romulus* is used for Romans.

[376] Cf. Augustine, *De Ord.*, ii, 12, § 35 (in Migne, *P.L.*, XXXII, 1012); and Isidore, *Etym.*, i, 3, § 1.

[377] *litterationem*, instruction in language, making literate, making lettered.

[378] *litterator*.

[379] Catullus, *Carmina*, xiv, 9, evidently cited from Martianus Capella, *De Nupt.*, iii, § 229.

CHAPTER 25.   *A short conclusion concerning the value of
grammar.*

Those who only yesterday were mere boys, being flogged by the rod,
yet who today are [grave] masters, ensconced in the [doctor's] chair
and invested with the [official] stole,[380] claim that those who praise
grammar do so out of ignorance of other studies. Let such patiently
heed the commendation of grammar found in the book, *On the
Education of an Orator.*[381] If the latter is acceptable to them, then let
them [condescend to] spare innocent grammarians. In the aforesaid
work we find this statement: "Let no one despise the principles of
grammar as of small account. Not that it is a great thing to distinguish between consonants and vowels, and subdivide the latter into
semivowels and mutes. But, as one penetrates farther into this (so to
speak) sanctuary, he becomes conscious of the great intricacy of
grammatical questions. The latter are not only well calculated to
sharpen the wits of boys, but also constitute fit subject matter to
exercise the most profound erudition and scientific knowledge."[382]
[Quintilian also says:] "Those who deride this art [of grammar] as
petty and thin, deserve even less toleration. For if grammar does not
lay beforehand a firm foundation for the orator, the [whole] structure will collapse. Grammar is accordingly first among the liberal
arts. Necessary for the young, gratifying to the old, and an agreeable
solace in solitude, it alone, of all branches of learning, has more
utility than show."[383]

END OF BOOK ONE

[380] *stolati,* wearing the stole, the insignia of office.
[381] Quintilian's *De Institutione Oratoris.*
[382] Quintilian, *Inst. Or.,* i, 4, § 6.
[383] *Ibid.,* i, 4, § 5.

ᛒOOK Two

[PROLOGUE]

It has been sufficiently proved in the preceding book, I believe, that grammar is not useless. I feel that we have adequately demonstrated that, in the absence of grammar, not only is perfect eloquence precluded, but also the gateway to other philosophical pursuits[1] is blocked to those who would engage in them. Attention has also been called to the fact that grammar is to be judged leniently, since it is subject both to nature and to the will of man. In like manner, civil laws frequently derive their force from human constitution while what is deemed expedient for the common welfare is considered equivalent to natural justice. But they [the Cornificians] are still not silenced, and refuse to acquit logic. Though maimed, and destined to be yet further mutilated, Cornificius, beating against a solid wall like a blind man, rashly brings to trial, and still more brazenly accuses logic. One who [really] loves the truth hates wrangling, whereas one who is charitable instinctively and spontaneously withdraws from contention. I will pass over the question whether grammar is a part of logic, although logic certainly treats and serves words,[2] despite the fact that it does not, of course, discuss them from every angle.[3] I will leave it to you,[4] who are informed on this matter, to judge the extension of the term [logic], and to decide whether logic includes all speech, or is limited to the critical evaluation of reasoning.[5] I have no misgivings as to your decision. For I have confidence in both the equity of my cause, and the capability[6] and

---

[1] *philosophie professiones,* philosophical or learned professions or pursuits.

[2] *sermonibus,* words, speech, verbal expression.

[3] Cf. Gilbert Crispin, *Disputatio Christiani cum gentili de fide Christi* (Brit. Mus., Add. MS 8166, fols. 29–36); and Hugh of St. Victor, *Erud. Didasc.,* i, 12, and ii, 31.

[4] Namely, Thomas Becket, to whom the *Metalogicon* is addressed.

[5] *ad instantiam rationum,* the criticism or critical evaluation of reasoning or arguments.

[6] *peritia,* learning, capability.

fairness of my judge. Let us pass over the question whether what relates to reasoning[7] is useful, and let us consider the power of logic, notwithstanding the unwillingness of our opponent. My task here will be lightened, since my reader[8] is favorably disposed and does not need persuasion. For all take pride in being logicians: not only those who have become engaged to the science with a few sweet pleasantries, but even those who have not yet made her acquaintance.[9]

CHAPTER 1.   *Because its object is to ascertain the truth, logic is a valuable asset in all fields of philosophy.*[10]

In its narrower sense, logic is the science of argumentative reasoning,[11] which [latter] provides a solid basis for the whole activity of prudence. Of all things the most desirable is wisdom,[12] whose fruit consists in the love of what is good and the practice of virtue. Consequently the human mind must apply itself to the quest of wisdom, and thoroughly study and investigate questions in order to formulate clear and sound judgments concerning each. Logic is exercised in inquiry into the truth. The latter [truth], as Cicero declares in his book *On Offices*,[13] is the subject matter of that primary virtue which is called "prudence"; whereas various utilities and necessities constitute the subject matter of the remaining three [basic virtues]. Prudence consists entirely in insight into the truth, together with a certain skill in investigating the latter; whereas justice embraces the truth and fortitude defends it, while temperance moderates the activities of the aforesaid virtues. Thus it is indubitable that prudence is the root of all the virtues. If this root be severed, then the other virtues

---

[7] *rationalis,* evidently rational science, the science of reasoning.

[8] *auditor,* literally, listener.

[9] *salutauerunt a limine,* greeted her from the threshold, made casual acquaintance with her; cf. Seneca, *Ep.,* 49, § 6.

[10] Literally: for all philosophy, that is, for all learning.

[11] *ratio disserendi,* the science or art of rational discussion or argumentative reasoning. See Cicero, *De Orat.,* ii, 38, § 157.

[12] Cf. 2 *Paralipomenon* i, 11, 12.

[13] Cicero, *De Off.,* i, 5, §§ 15–17.

will wither and die of thirst, even as branches do when they are cut off from their natural source of sustenance. For who can embrace or practice something of which he is ignorant? Truth is the subject matter of prudence, as well as the fountain-head of all the virtues. One who comprehends truth is wise, one who loves it good, "one who orders his life in accordance with it happy." [14] The most learned of our poets, pointing out the secret of happiness, says:[15]

> Happiness comes from understanding the causes of things,
> And nonchalantly treading under foot all fears,
> Including horror of relentless Fate and howling, hungry Hell.[16]

In the words of another poet, more illustrious for his faith[17] and vision of the truth:

> Happy the man who has had the good fortune
> To rest his eyes on the clear fountain of good;
> Happy he who has [at last] succeeded
> In loosing earth's repressive bonds.[18]

While the poets we have quoted express themselves differently, their meaning is the same: "Happy is the man who possesses the gift of understanding." On the one hand, the more intimately what is transitory and momentary comes to be known, the cheaper that which is thus doomed to perish becomes in the estimation of a sensible mind. On the other hand, the truth will set us free, and will lead us from slavery to liberty,[19] relieving us of the oppressive yoke of vice. For it is impossible that one who seeks and embraces the truth with his whole heart should remain a suitor and servant of vanity.[20]

[14] Proverbs, iii, 18.
[15] Vergil, *Georg.*, ii, 490–492.
[16] *Acherontis*: Acheron: river of the infernal regions, hence the infernal regions or Hell.
[17] Namely, Boethius.
[18] Boethius, *Cons. Phil.*, iii, 12 metr. 1–4.
[19] Cf. John, viii, 32.
[20] Augustine opposes vanity to truth in the same way in his *Enarr. in Ps.* cxviii, 37 (in Migne, *P.L.*, XXXVII, 1531).

CHAPTER 2.   *The Peripatetic school, and the origin and founder of logic.*

As a result of the aforesaid considerations, there arose the Peripatetic school, which esteemed knowledge of the truth as the greatest good in human life. These Peripatetics accordingly made careful investigations into the nature of all things, so as to determine which should be avoided as evil, discounted as useless, sought after as good, or preferred as better, and finally which are called "good" or "bad" according to circumstances. There thus developed two branches of philosophy, natural and moral, which are also called ethics and physics. But, through lack of scientific skill in argumentative reasoning, many absurdities were concluded. Thus Epicurus would have the world originate from atoms and a void, and would dispense with God as its author; whereas the Stoics asserted that matter is coeternal with God, and held that all sins are equally grave. It became imperative to devise and make public a science which would distinguish words and meanings, and dissipate foggy fallacies. Such, as Boethius observes in his second commentary on Porphyry,[21] was the origin of the study of logic. There was [evident] need of a science to discriminate between what is true and what is false, and to show which reasoning really adheres to the path of valid argumentative proof, and which [merely] has the [external] appearance of truth, or, in other words, which reasoning warrants assent, and which should be held in suspicion. Otherwise, it would be impossible to ascertain the truth by reasoning. Although Parmenides the Egyptian[22] spent his

[21] John apparently regards the *In Porphyrium Dialogi* . . . of Boethius as Boethius' first commentary on Porphyry, and Boethius' *Commentaria in Porphyrium* as his second commentary on the same writer. Here he obviously refers to Book I of the latter. Both are to be found in Migne, *P.L.,* LXIV.

[22] *Parmenides Egiptius:* John is apparently referring here to the Greek philosopher Parmenides, a native of the town of Elea in lower Italy (*Magna Graecia*), rather than of Egypt, and who lived in the sixth century B.C.

life on a rock[23] in order to invent a scientific system of logic,[24] he has had so many and such illustrious successors in his project that they have appropriated most of the honor for his invention. According to Apuleius,[25] Augustine,[26] and Isidore,[27] the credit for completing philosophy belongs to Plato. For to physics and ethics, which Pythagoras and Socrates respectively had already fully taught, Plato added logic. By the latter, when the causes of things and the bases of the *mores* are being discussed, the real [proving] force of arguments may be determined. Plato, however, did not organize logic into a scientific art. Use came first, for here, as elsewhere, precept followed practice. Subsequently Aristotle perceived and explained the rules of the art [of logic], and he, "the Prince of the Peripatetics," is honored as its principal founder. While Aristotle shares the distinction of being an authority in other branches of learning, he has a monopoly of this one, which is his very own. Although I discuss Aristotle more at length elsewhere,[28] I believe that what Quintilian says about him should not be overlooked here: "I am at a loss to pay tribute to the greatness of Aristotle, for I cannot decide whether he deserves greater praise for his wide knowledge, his numerous writings, his masterful language, his smooth style, the insight of his findings, or the wide diversity of subjects he treats." [29]

[23] *in rupe,* on a rock (or possibly in a cave?).

[24] Cf. Hugh of St. Victor, *Erud. Didasc.,* iii, 2. Hugh has the same story which may have originated from a misinterpretation of Martianus Capella, *De Nupt.,* iv, § 330, where we find: "She [Dialectic] says that she was first reared on a rock in Egypt (or in an Egyptian cave?), whence she made her way into the school of Parmenides and into Attica." Concerning the origins of this story, see R. Klibansky, "The Rock of Parmenides," in *Mediaeval and Renaissance Studies,* I, no. 2, pp. 178–186.

[25] Apuleius, *De Dogm. Plat.,* i, 3, § 187.

[26] Augustine, *De C.D.,* viii, 4.

[27] Isidore, *Etym.,* ii, 24.

[28] See *Met.,* iv.

[29] Quintilian, *Inst. Or.,* x, 1, § 83.

CHAPTER 3.   *That those who would philosophize should be
taught logic.[30] Also the distinction between demonstrative, probable, and sophistical logic.*

The Peripatetics saw that necessity can lead to [the acquisition of]
skill, and the latter result in the development of an art. Accordingly,
they drew up definite rules for what had previously been vague and
arbitrary. They discarded what was erroneous, supplied what was
wanting, eliminated what was superfluous, and prescribed suitable
precepts to cover all cases. In this manner they developed the science
of argumentative reasoning, which discloses manners of disputation
and analyzes the construction of proofs, as well as provides methods
whereby we may distinguish what is true from what is false, and
what is necessary from what is impossible. Although, chronologically,
it came into being subsequent to the other branches of philosophy,
logic still [rightly] precedes all the rest of them [when they are
treated] in order.[31] Logic should be taught to those who are entering
upon philosophical studies, since it serves as an interpreter of both
words and meanings, and since no part of philosophy can be accurately comprehended without it. He who dreams of teaching philosophy without logic, is, in effect, presuming to eliminate the reasons
of things from the quest[32] of wisdom, inasmuch as logic presides over
these reasons. If we may resort to a fable [to illustrate our point],
antiquity considered that Prudence,[33] the sister of Truth,[34] was not
sterile, but bore a wonderful daughter [Philology],[35] whom she
committed to the chaste embrace of Mercury. In other words, Pru-

[30] Literally: logic should be lectured or read [*prelegenda est*] to those who philosophize,
that is, those who study the arts and sciences.
[31] Hugh of St. Victor, *Erud. Didasc.*, vi, 14.
[32] *cultu*, service, cult, quest.
[33] *Fronesis*, prudence.
[34] *Alicie: Alethia*, truth. Cf. Theodulus, *Eclog.*, v, 335. Concerning *Fronesis* [prudence]
as the sister of *Alicia* or *Alethia* [truth], cf. John's *Entheticus*, lines 11–24 (in Migne,
P.L., CXCIX, 965).
[35] See Martianus Capella, *De Nupt.*, ii, § 114.

dence, the sister of Truth, arranged that [her daughter], the Love of [Logical] Reasoning and [Scientific] Knowledge, would acquire fertility and luster from Eloquence. Such is the union of Philology and Mercury [Eloquence]. Logic[36] derives its name from the fact that it is rational. For it both provides and examines reasons. Plato divided logic into dialectic and rhetoric; but those who would further broaden its efficacy attribute even more to it.[37] Indeed, logic includes demonstration, probable proof, and sophistry. Demonstrative logic flourishes in the [basic] principles of [the various] sciences, and progresses further to deducing conclusions from these. It rejoices in necessity. It does not pay much attention to what various people may think about a given proposition. Its sole concern is that a thing must be so. It thus befits the philosophical majesty of those who teach the truth, a majesty which is a result of its own conviction [that it is teaching the truth], and independent of the assent of its listeners. Probable logic [on the other hand] is concerned with propositions which, to all or to many men, or at least to the wise, seem to be valid. It treats either all, or many such propositions, or those that are best known and most probable, or their consequences. Probable logic includes dialectic and rhetoric. For the dialectician and the orator, trying to persuade (respectively) an adversary and a judge, are not too much concerned about the truth or falsity of their arguments, provided only the latter have likelihood. But sophistry, which is "seeming, rather than real" wisdom,[38] merely wears a disguise of probability or necessity. It has no care at all for facts. Its only objective is to lose its adversary in a fog of delusions. Of the aforementioned, dialectic is what all prefer, but few, in my opinion, attain. For dialectic neither aspires to the weighty authority of [apodictical] teaching, nor does it become the plaything of political currents.[39] Neither does it seduce [the unwary] by fallacies. Rather it makes inquiry into the truth, using the ready instrument of moderate probability.

[36] *logica,* from λόγος: speech, reason.
[37] Cf. Boethius, *De Diff. Top.,* iv (in Migne, *P.L.,* LXIV, 1205 ff.).
[38] Aristotle, *Soph. El.,* c. 1 (161a, 21).
[39] Dialectic is unlike rhetoric in this respect.

CHAPTER 4.   *What dialectic is, and whence it gets its name.*

Dialectic, according to Augustine, is the science of effective argumentation.[40] This is to be understood as meaning that the effective
force is to be found in the words themselves.[41] Those who are destitute of the art, and are successful in argumentation simply from luck,
are not to be considered dialecticians. Moreover, one who really fails
to establish with conviction what he is trying to prove is not a
skillful disputant. Our definition is to be understood in such a way
that it excludes both the demonstrator and the sophist, neither of
whom effectively attains the dialectician's objective. For demonstration does not calculate to elicit assent,[42] while sophistry forsakes the
truth. Nevertheless both the demonstrator and the sophist, as far as
their own functions are concerned, argue effectively if they do not
omit anything pertaining to their branch. To argue[43] is to prove or
disprove something that is either doubtful, or denied, or [simply]
proposed in one way or another by alleging reasons.[44] If anyone
accomplishes this with probability[45] by using the art, he achieves the
goal of the dialectician. Aristotle, its founder, gave dialectic this
name.[46] For in and by means of dialectic, disputation concerning
what has been said is effected.[47] Just as grammar, according to
Remigius,[48] is concerned with ways of saying things, dialectic is con-

---

[40] *bene disputandi scientia;* see pseudo-Augustine, *De Dialectica,* c. 1 (in Migne, *P.L.,*
XXXII, 1409).

[41] That is, the speech itself.

[42] *probabilitatem non habet.*

[43] *disputare,* to dispute, to argue.

[44] It is not clear whether this *ratione supposita* goes with "to prove or disprove" or
with "proposed."

[45] *probabiliter.*

[46] Namely, *dialectica* [*ars*], that is, διαλεκτική [τέχνη]: the art of discussion, discursive
reasoning, argumentation.

[47] Cf. the subsequent sentence where John points out that *lecton* means "something said."

[48] Remigius Antissiodorensis (Remigius of Auxerre), in *Art. Don. min.,* c. 5, says
"Grammar is called the literary art because its subject matter is literature"; but I have not
been able to find anything in Remigius corresponding to the present passage. Perhaps
John is referring to the commentary of the same Remigius on Martianus Capella, concerning which see B. Hauréau, in *Notices et extraits,* XX, 2, pp. 1 ff.

cerned with what is said.[49] While grammar chiefly examines the words that express meanings, dialectic investigates the meanings expressed by words. *Lecton* (as Isidore observes) is the Greek word for "something said." [50] It does not matter much whether dialectic derives its name from the Greek *lexis,* which means "speech," as Quintilian opines in his *Preparatory Training,*[51] or from *lecton,* which denotes "something said." To inquire into the effective force of speech and to investigate the truth and meaning of what is said are precisely or practically the same. A word's force consists in its meaning. Without the latter it is empty, useless, and (so to speak) dead. Just as the soul animates the body, so, in a way, meaning breathes life into a word. Those whose words lack sense are "beating the air," [52] rather than [really] speaking.

CHAPTER 5.   *The subdivisions of the dialectical art,*[53] *and the objective of logicians.*

Let us return from the species [dialectic] to the genus [logic]. It is apparent that certain general remarks remain to be made. Authors have divided logic into the science of invention[54] and that of judgment;[55] they have also explained that logic as a whole is concerned with divisions, definitions, and inferences.[56] For logic not only reigns over invention and judgment, but also is skilled in division, definition, and argumentation. In short, it produces a [master] craftsman.

[49] *dictionibus . . . dictis.*

[50] Isidore, *Etym.,* ii, 33, where, however, we find *dictio* (a way of saying something), rather than *dicta* (something said).

[51] Cf. Quintilian, *Inst. Orat.,* ix, 1, § 17; and also i, 5, § 2. *Preexercitamina: Prefatory Exercises* or *Preparatory Exercises:* John seems here to have transferred the title of Priscian's *Preexercitamina* to Quintilian's *Institutio Oratoris,* since the latter consists of *preexercitamina* or preparatory exercises, and *preexercitamina* mean practically the same thing as *institutio.*

[52] Cf. I Corinthians, ix, 26.

[53] *dialectice,* the dialectical art; John discusses here the subdivisions of logic in general.

[54] *inueniendi.*

[55] Cf. Cicero, *Top.,* 2, § 6, and the commentary thereon by Boethius.

[56] *collectionibus,* inferences.

Among the various branches of philosophy, logic has two prerogatives: it has both the honor of coming first[57] and the distinction of
serving as an efficacious instrument throughout the whole body [of
philosophy]. Natural [58] and moral philosophers[59] can construct their
principles only by the forms of proof supplied by logicians. Also, in
order to define and divide correctly, they must borrow and employ
the art of the logicians. And if, perchance, they succeed in this
without logic, their success is due to luck, rather than to science.
Logic is "rational" [60] [philosophy], and we may readily see from the
very name, what progress in philosophy can be expected from one
who [since he lacks logic] lacks reason.[61] Even though one's [natu-
ral] faculty of reason,[62] I refer here to his mental power, may be
very keen, still he will be greatly handicapped in philosophical pursuits if he is without a rational system whereby he may accomplish
his purpose. Such a rational system is a scientific method or compendious [logical] rational plan,[63] to provide and expedite the facile
accomplishment of his object. Those disciplines which we have described as parts of logic supply this very need. Demonstrative, probable, and sophistical logic each include invention and judgment.
Whether they divide, define, or draw inferences, they use in common the same rational systems,[64] even though they differ in subject
matter, purpose, or manner of procedure. Although the word "reason" [or rational method] [65] may have several different meanings,
it is here used in its broadest sense. It is not restricted to actual
rational proof: it also includes what merely seems to be such. Omitting mention of various other meanings of "reason," let me call
attention to the fact that grammarians say that this word is absolute,
since, like the name "God," it needs no added qualification in order
to convey its significance, except for purposes of specification. Thus

---

[57] *principalis* [being] first, initial, or principal.
[58] *physicus,* the physical or natural philosopher.
[59] *ethicus,* the moral or ethical philosopher.
[60] *Rationalis.*
[61] *rationis.*
[62] *rationem.*
[63] *ratio compendiaria,* a succinct, orderly, comprehensive plan.
[64] *domesticis rationibus.*
[65] *ratio,* used above variously to signify reason in general, the faculty of reasoning, rational system, rational methods, and rational proof.

we may speak of "the All-Powerful God," in order to contrast Him
with idols, which have no power at all, or devils, who have very
little power; and in the same way, we may speak of "necessary
reason" or "true reason," to distinguish it from "reason" which
may be vitiated by accident or deceit. The last mentioned "reason"
includes whatever is advanced or may be proposed in order to win
acceptance of an opinion[66] or to corroborate a judgment.[67] The difference between opinion and judgment is that opinion frequently
errs, whereas judgment always approximates the truth.[68] Such is the
case provided we choose our words correctly; for, in practice, we
often misuse certain words by employing them where we should use
others. Even sophistry is rational; and although it is deceptive, it still
vindicates its right to a place among the various branches of philosophy. For sophistry introduces its own reasons [or rational methods].
At one time it disguises itself as demonstrative logic; at another it
pretends to be dialectic. Never does it announce its own identity, but
always it puts on a false front. For it [sophistry] is only "seeming
wisdom." [69] It often brings about acceptance of an opinion, which
is not actually true or probable, but only seems to be so. Sometimes
it even uses true and probable arguments. It is a shrewd deceiver,
and often sweeps one along, by means of detailed interrogations and
other tricks, from the evident and true to the doubtful and false. "It
transforms itself into a minister of light," [70] and like Neptune,[71]
exposes anyone it can lead astray to shoals and shame.[72] A philosopher who uses demonstrative logic is endeavoring to determine the
truth, whereas one who employs dialectic contents himself with
probability, and is trying to establish an opinion. But the sophist is
satisfied with the mere appearance of probability. [At the same
time] I am loath to brand knowledge of sophistry as useless. For
the latter provides considerable mental exercise, while it does most

---

[66] *opinionem.*
[67] *sententiam* (stronger than mere opinion) a judgment, authoritative opinion, or decision.
[68] *sententia semper assidet ueritati,* judgment always (or ever) is on the side of (or approximates) the truth.
[69] Cf. Aristotle, *Soph. El.,* c. 1 (165a, 21).
[70] II Corinthians, xi, 14.
[71] This seems to refer to the story of Hippolytus. Cf. Cicero, *De Off.,* i, 10, § 32.
[72] Literally: to perils and laughter.

harm to ignoramuses who are unable to recognize it. "One who knows [what is going on] cannot be deceived." [73] And one who takes no steps to avoid a fall which he foresees makes himself responsible. In conclusion, one who will not embrace demonstrative and probable logic is no lover of the truth; nor is he even trying to know what is probable. Furthermore, since it is clear that virtue necessitates knowledge of the truth, one who despises such knowledge is reprobate.

CHAPTER 6.   *That all seek after logic, yet not all are successful in their quest.*

From what has been said, it can be seen that logic gives great promise. For it provides a mastery of invention and judgment, as well as supplies ability to divide, define, and prove with conviction. It is such an important part of philosophy that it serves the other parts in much the same way as the soul does the body. On the other hand, all philosophy that lacks the vital organizing principle of logic is lifeless and helpless. It is no more than just that this art should, as it does, attract such tremendous crowds from every quarter that more men are occupied in the study of logic alone than in all the other branches of that science which regulates human acts, words, and even thoughts, if they are to be as they should be. I refer to philosophy, without which everything is bereft of sense and savor, as well as false and immoral. All are shouting to one another: "Let him who is last catch the itch"; [74] and let him who does not come to logic, be plagued by continuous, everlasting filth. Therefore: "I hate to be left behind," [75]—a plight that is also embarrassing and dangerous. I crave to behold the light, revealed only to these public criers of logic. I approach, and with

[73] *Dolus scienti non infertur,* an established legal principle that if one recognizes deceit, he cannot be deceived.
[74] Horace, *A.P.,* 417.
[75] *Ibid.*

humble supplication, beseech them to teach me, and if [at all] possible, to make me like themselves. They promise great things, but meanwhile they command me to observe a Pythagorean silence,[76] for they are disclosing the secrets of Minerva,[77] of which, according to their boasts, they are custodians. However, they permit and even require that I converse with them in childish prattle, which for their kind is to dispute.[78] When, after long association, I come to know them better, so that they will finally deign to heed me, I ask more firmly, knock more insistently, and implore more ardently that the door of the art be opened to me. At long last [they comply, and] we begin with definition. They tell me to define in a few words whatever I have in mind. First I must give the genus of the subject, and then add the latter's substantial differences until I have enough of these to be able to convert the proposition.[79] Highest and lowest concepts[80] cannot be defined: the former because they are without genus, the latter because they lack differences. Such are, nonetheless, described by their properties, the same aggregate of which is not found elsewhere. There cannot be, however, any definition of a substance, unless we state its genus and enumerate some substantial differences. Behold, I have so been taught the art of defining; and I am directed to go ahead and adequately define, or at least describe, whatever is proposed. We move on to treat the science of division. I am [similarly] admonished to apportion a genus adequately into its species by means of differences, or by affirmation and negation. The whole should be entirely resolved into its parts, the universal into its subjects, the virtual into its powers. When we want to divide a word, we should enumerate either its meanings or its forms. I am instructed to divide an accident according to its subjects, and to show what subjects can possess this accident. Conversely, I am directed to divide a subject according to its accidents, as it is pertinent to point out the various acci-

[76] See Gellius, *Noct. Att.*, i, 9. It was said that Pythagoras required of his disciples an initial silence of two years, during which they listened rather than talked.

[77] Ovid, *Met.*, ii, 749, 755.

[78] Namely, which is all that disputation means with them.

[79] Conversion is an interchange of places between the subject and predicate terms of a proposition, after which the transposed form is equally true.

[80] Namely, the most general and most particular ideas or things.

dents that a subject is capable of possessing. I am even told to divide according to the coaccidents of accidents, since for a variety of subjects these are shown to be numerous or even excessive. I have thus been rapidly conducted through two-thirds of the course. There still remains the final third, whose mastery is even more essential for the aspirant [to logic], and which it takes longer to explain. This [last] is the art of drawing inferences,[81] useful for defeating an opponent in argument, or for demonstrating philosophical truth without regard to what one's listeners may think. A few precepts for this are presented, and these I still further synopsize for brevity's sake. We are to take careful note that, if we wish to win assent to a given proposition, we must first posit something from which it may be inferred as probable or necessary. Thus we may posit a genus in order to establish its species; or eliminate one of two contraries in order to posit the other. I proceed accordingly, for I have a rather dull mind,[82] and am one for whom "belief comes through hearing,"[83] and who [alas] all too often fails to comprehend what I hear or read. Since therefore the rules are being brought out into the light, I beseech my very learned teachers, who will never admit ignorance of anything, to take sample passages[84] found in books, and demonstrate the application of the rules. For it is no great matter for one who has mastered this art to review the findings of others in definitions composed at an earlier date. If logic is definitive because it possesses a certain number of definitions, other disciplines are still more so, since they have a still greater number of them. These unadulterated philosophers, who despise everything save logic, and are ignorant of grammar, physics, and ethics alike, grow furious. They accuse me of being a reprobate, a dullard, a blockhead,[85] a stone. What they have told me [they insist] should adequately take care of the three functions of the art. They demand that I [now] pay them their stipulated fee. If I take exception, and object, quoting the moralist:[86] "What is this talk

---

[81] *colligendi,* of drawing inferences, of arriving at a conclusion by means of reasoning.
[82] Cf. Gellius, *Noct. Att.,* xiii, 25, § 21.
[83] Romans, x, 17.
[84] *exemplis,* examples or instances [in] or perhaps copies [of].
[85] *caudicem;* cf. Terence, *Hauton.,* v, 1, 4.
[86] Juvenal, *Sat.,* vii, 158–160.

about payment? What have I learned?" Immediately they rejoin, in the words of the same moralist:

> The teacher is blamed, forsooth,
> For the lack of wit[87]
> In the boorish[88] youth.

"That's just it," they taunt: "Everyone desires knowledge, but no one is willing to pay the price." [89] Since I blush at the thought of being branded an ingrate, I decide to repay them [in full measure]: doctrine for doctrine, the essential for the essential. I present them [in return] with a compendium of rules, instructing them how to apply the latter. Since they have taught me three useful arts, I will also teach them three other arts, still more useful. One should know the arts of military science, medicine, and law, both civil and canon.[90] Thus one will become a master of moral philosophy.[91] [I therefore proceed:] Whenever you have to fight an enemy, your primary precaution should be not to let him wound you in any way. At the very outset, while you are as yet uninjured, charge in upon him, and wound him, until either your vanquished opponent himself acknowledges defeat, or onlookers acclaim you as the victor over your breathless adversary. In medicine,[92] first ascertain the cause of the sickness, then cure and eliminate it. Subsequently, restore and build up the health of your patient by remedial and preventive medicine until he has fully recuperated. In cases involving civil law,[93] always make justice your object, and be affable with everyone. Then, as the comic poet says: "Praise free of envy will be yours, and many will be your friends." [94] What further? In all things "be clothed with charity." [95] Note that I have ready the keys to these

[87] *in leua parte mamille nil salit:* literally: there is no perception or response in the left part of the breast, that is, in the heart as the seat of intellect and will.

[88] *Archadio iuueni,* the Arcadian youth: the Arcadians were noted for their simplicity. Hence, the boorish youth.

[89] Juvenal, *Sat.,* vii, 157.

[90] *iuris ciuilis et decretorum,* literally of civil and decretal law.

[91] *ethice,* ethical or moral philosophy: evidently taken here in a wide mediaeval sense, as comprising all organized directive knowledge concerning human action, practical as well as ethical.

[92] *physica.*

[93] *ciuilibus,* evidently refers to "cases of civil law," in view of what John has said above. It also may mean "in politics."

[94] Terence, *Andr.,* i, 1, 39.

[95] Colossians, iii, 12, 14.

latter arts,[96] in the same way that they had the rules for the aforesaid ones.[97] Alas, they are the more to be pitied in that they are
blind to their own want.[98] They deceive themselves, with the consequence that, in their very quest of the truth, they come to know
nothing. The only sure road to truth is humility. Pilate, for example, on hearing the word "truth," asked: "What is truth?" But
his incredulity prompted the proud man to turn away from the
master before he could be enlightened by the revelation of the
sacred reply.[99]

CHAPTER 7.   *That those who are verbal jugglers of irrelevant*
nonsense[100] *must first be disabused of their erring*
ways[101] *before they can come to know anything.*

It has not been my purpose in the foregoing to belittle logic
(which is both a fortunate and useful science). I have rather
wanted to show that those who are haranguing at the crossroads,
and teaching in public pleaces,[102] and who have worn away, not
merely ten or twenty years, but their whole life with logic as their
sole concern, do not really possess what they are pretending to
teach. Even as old age descends upon them, enfeebling their bodies,
dulling their perceptions, and subduing their passions, logic alone
still remains the exclusive topic of their conversation, monopolizes
their thought, and usurps the place of every other branch of knowledge. As these Academicians age and gray, they remain preoccupied
with the concerns of boyhood. They meticulously sift every syllable,
yea every letter, of what has been said and written, doubting

[96] That is, the three arts of warfare, medicine, and law, just mentioned.
[97] That is, the "logical" arts of definition, division, and inference, above discussed.
[98] Apocalypse (or Book of Revelation), iii, 17.
[99] See John, xviii, 37–38.
[100] *nugiloquos uentilatores*, jugglers of senseless prattle.
[101] *dedoceri*, literally: "be untaught."
[102] Cf. Jerome, *Ep.*, i, 1 (in Migne, *P.L.*, XXII, 512).

everything, "forever studying, but never acquiring knowledge." [103]
At length "they turn to babbling utter nonsense," [104] and, at a loss
as to what to say, or out of lack of a thesis, relieve their embarrassment by proposing new errors. They are either unfamiliar with or
contemptuous of the [long-accepted] views [105] of the ancient authorities. They make compilations of what everybody has ever
thought on the subject. Lacking judgment, they [laboriously]
copy and [tediously] quote all that has ever been said or written
[on their subject], even by the most obscure. They cannot omit
anything because they lack the knowledge to discriminate as to
what is better. So towering does this mixed-up heap of opinions
and counteropinions become that even the compiler himself can
hardly keep track of all it contains. One is reminded of a story told
of Didymus, [106] the number of whose writings has never been ex-
ceeded. Once, after he had taken exception to a certain tale because
of its lack of credibility, one of his own books containing the same
was adduced. Today many such Didymuses are to be found. Their
commentaries are not only filled, but even stuffed with encum-
brances which have been spun by logicians, and which [counter-
propositions] are rightly called "oppositions," [107] for they detain
one from going on to better studies, [108] and constitute impediments
to progress. They do not even pay attention to Aristotle, the only
authority whom these verbal jugglers of empty nonsense [109] will
condescend to recognize. For he [Aristotle] says, with good taste
and accuracy, that it is foolish to be bothered about everyone who
brings up objections to [generally accepted] opinions. [110] Quintilian
relates that a certain Timothy, who was famous as a master of the
art of flute-playing, used to require of those who had previously
been instructed by some other teacher twice the fee that he charged

---

[103] Cf. II Timothy, iii,
[104] See I Timothy, i, 6, 7.
[105] *sententias*, opinions, views, authoritative judgments.
[106] Quintilian, *Inst. Or.*, i, 8, §
[107] *oppositiones*, counterpropositions, objections.
[108] *studiis*, studies or pursuit
[109] Cf. Quintilian, *Inst. Or.*, x, 7, § 11.
[110] Aristotle, *Top.*, i, 11 (104 b, 23).

those who came to him as complete novices.[111] For in such a case, the teacher has a double job: the first to erase the [effects of] previous faulty instruction, the second to give the student true and correct training. Nor is it an easy matter to reduce one who is already reputed to possess an art to the study of its elementary principles, which are, however, prerequisites for his progress. Timothy accordingly was wise [and knew what he was doing], since:

> The earthen jug long will harbor
> The scent of the wine with which it once was filled.[112]

Likewise, everyone, on coming of age,[113]

> . . . scurries back to that fare,
> He first tasted on breaking the egg.[114]

CHAPTER 8.   *If they had but heeded Aristotle, he would have prevented them from going to extremes.*

This evil [of immoderate disputation] sometimes has a certain [incidental] utility. Those who are made accustomed to frequent disputation on all sorts of topics, provided this training is kept within bounds, may thus obtain a well-stocked vocabulary, fluent speech, and retentive memory, in addition to mental subtlety. For the mind is improved by consistent exercise. However, once we go beyond the proper limits, everything works in reverse, and excessive subtlety devours utility. As Seneca notes in his first *Disputation*,[115] "Nothing is more disgusting than subtlety by [itself] and for itself." In his *Letter to Lucilius,* Seneca[116] further observes: "An awn of grain[117]

---

[111] Quintilian, *Inst. Or.,* ii, 3, §§ 3, 4.

[112] Horace, *Ep.,* i, 2, 69, 70.

[113] *sui iuris effectus,* also "on becoming his own master."

[114] *rupto . . . ouo,* literally: on breaking the egg, as a new-born babe or infant.

[115] *in primo Declamationum,* in his first *Discourse, Disputation,* or *Controversy;* see Seneca the Elder, *Controv.,* i, praef., § 21.

[116] John quotes the *Controversies* of Seneca the Elder and the *Letters to Lucilius* of Seneca the Younger without distinguishing the two authors.

[117] *arista,* the bristle-like appendage of certain grasses; the beard, as of wheat or rye.

is the most subtle of all things," [118] but for what is it good? The
same may be said of a mind which, at the sacrifice of both seriousness and depth, has abandoned itself [entirely] to subtlety. In the
book *On the Education of the Orator,*[119] this is termed "blossoming
before the proper time," [120] and we are warned that this type of
mentality "rarely bears sound fruit." Such subtlety, while admirable
in boys, is despicable and culpable in mature men. By means of it,
"youths perform small tasks with ease. Thus emboldened, they
proceed to display the full limit of their ability, which, in fine,
does not proceed beyond doing what is obvious and easy. They
unblushingly harness words together and [121] trot them out, without
being deterred by the slightest embarrassment or as much as batting
an eye. They talk at a break-neck pace, but without saying much.
Their statements lack solid basis and deep roots. It is as when we
sow seed on top of the soil. It sprouts up instantly, and the small
blades, in [pathetic] imitation of spikes of grain, yellow with their
useless awns long before the harvest." So it is with minds that
affect to be subtle and productive, yet lack [real] depth. "Such ex-
hibitions evoke our applause, in view of the youth of the principals,
but as progress comes to a halt, admiration also fades." [122] In the
case of Nisius Flavius,[123] who declaimed before Arellius,[124] as
Seneca recounts, it was not merely his eloquence which commended him, but his eloquence coupled with his youth. It was the
age at which the talent was displayed that excited admiration.[125]
Fluency does not always merit praise. "To have held one's tongue
when one did not know, is just as creditable as to have spoken when
one knew," observes Sidonius.[126] Even Cicero[127] condemns useless
words, which are uttered without conferring advantage or pleasure

[118] Seneca, *Ep.,* 82, § 24.
[119] Quintilian, *Inst. Or.*
[120] *precoquum,* blossoming before the usual time, precocity.
[121] The two words *concinnant et* here translated: "they harness words together . . . and,"
are not found in Quintilian.
[122] Quintilian, *Inst. Or.,* i, 3, §§ 3–5.
[123] That is, Alfius Flavius.
[124] Cestius in Seneca, although elsewhere in the *Controversiae* there is frequent mention
of Arellius.
[125] See Seneca the Elder, *Controv.,* i, 1, § 22.
[126] Sidonius, *Ep.,* vii, 9, § 5.
[127] Or: Cicero too.

either to the speaker or to the listener.[128] How true is the poetic
principle that:

> The poet's purpose is either to enlighten or to please,
> And sometimes both of these together.
> He who instructs while he entertains wins the crown.[129]

It is also true that "Sin consorts with loquacity." [130] Fluency is
advantageous only when it is oriented to [the acquisition of] wisdom. The tongue of man is, so to speak, "in liquid," [131] and easily
slips. While "but a small member of the body," [132] it "sets aflame
the whole orbit of human existence." [133] It throws our life into
confusion, and, unless it is checked by the reins of moderation, it
hurls our entire person into the abyss. Of what worth is it to have
things that we will never use stuffed away in the [musty] archives
of our memory? Even as it is pointless "to wrangle over the question of goats' wool," [134] so it is both inappropriate and ill-advised to
cram our memory with passages that are useless. What man, determined to acquire riches, has ever set himself to gathering valueless
leaves and the awns of grasses in order to become wealthy? The
excesses of those who think dialectical discussion consists in un-
bridled loquacity should have been restrained by Aristotle. Verily
he would have silenced them, had they but heeded him. "It is not
fitting," Aristotle says, "to consider every problem and thesis.[135]
We should concern ourselves with what may seem dubious to one
who wants [to know] the reason ⟨rather than⟩ [136] with what is con-
tested by one who needs discipline or lacks sense. Those who question the principles that the gods should be reverenced and our
parents honored really need punishment; but those who call into

---

[128] This apparently refers to pseudo-Cicero, *Ad Herennium*, iv, 3, § 4.

[129] Literally, "has carried every point." See Horace, *A.P.*, 333, 334, 343.

[130] Proverbs, x, 19.

[131] *in udo;* see Persius, *Sat.*, i, 105.

[132] See James, iii, 5, 6.

[133] *rotam humane natiuitatis*, the wheel, whole course, orb, or orbit of human nativity
or existence.

[134] *de lana caprina;* the proverbial question on whether goats' hair could be called
"wool." See Horace, *Ep.*, i, 18, 15.

[135] *positionem.*

[136] Webb has here inserted [*non*] in his edition of the *Metalogicon*. This corresponds
better with the Greek of Aristotle and the Boethian translation. I have similarly inserted
[rather than].

doubt the whiteness of snow, actually lack the use of their senses. There is no point in demonstrating things that are immediately evident, any more than there is any sense in trying to demonstrate things whose proof is too far-fetched. The former do not admit of doubt; the latter are so questionable that it is beyond our power to solve them." So says Aristotle.[137] But our over-loquacious logicians, without consulting him, and even against his prohibition, are always disputing, at all times, in all places, and on all topics—perhaps because they have equal knowledge of all things.[138]

CHAPTER 9.   *That dialectic is ineffective when it is divorced from other studies.*

It is a well known fact that "Eloquence without wisdom is futile." [139] Whence it is clear that eloquence derives its efficacy from wisdom. The utility of eloquence is, in fact, directly in proportion to the measure[140] of wisdom a person may have attained. On the other hand, eloquence becomes positively harmful when it departs from wisdom. It is accordingly evident that dialectic, the highly efficient and ever-ready servant of eloquence, is useful to anyone in proportion to the degree of knowledge he possesses.[141] It is of greatest advantage to a person who knows much; and of least use to one who knows little. In the [puny] hand of a pigmy or dwarf, the sword of Hercules is worthless; but in the [mighty] grasp of an Achilles or a Hector, it becomes a veritable thunderbolt, which levels everything in its way.[142] So also, if it is bereft of the strength which is communicated by the other disciplines, dialectic is in a way maimed and practically helpless; but if it derives life and vigor

[137] Aristotle, *Top.*, i, 11 (105 a, 2 ff.).

[138] John's humorous sarcasm here evidently refers to supposed equality of knowledge with Aristotle, or perhaps to equality of knowledge (or ignorance) concerning all things.

[139] Cicero, *Orat.*, 4, § 14.

[140] Literally: according to the small measure.

[141] Cicero, *Part. Or.*, 23, § 78.

[142] Cf. Quintilian, *Inst. Or.*, vi, 1, § 36, and viii, 6, § 71.

from other studies, it can destroy all falsehood, and at least enables
one to dispute with probability concerning all subjects. Dialectic,
however, is not great, if, as our contemporaries treat it, it remains
forever engrossed in itself, walking 'round about and surveying
itself, ransacking [over and over] its own depths and secrets: limit-
ing itself to things that are of no use whatsoever in a domestic or
military, commercial or religious, civil or ecclesiastical way, and
that are appropriate only in school.[143] For in school and during
youth, many things are permitted within certain limits, and for
the time being, which are to be speedily sloughed off when one
advances to a more serious study of philosophy. Indeed, when one
has become intellectually or physically mature, the treatment of
philosophy becomes more earnest. It not only divests itself of
puerile expressions and speech that were [formerly] permitted by
indulgent concession, but even frequently discards all books. This
is the lesson contained, 'neath a veil of poetic fiction, in the Marriage of Mercury [Eloquence] and Philology, contracted with the
approval of all the gods, and useful for all men who observe[144] it.
According to this [allegory], Philology, on ascending to the
heavenly temples and attaining the freedom of a purer state, relieved herself[145] of the numerous books with which she had been
burdened.[146] It is easy for an artisan to talk about his art, but it is
much more difficult to put the art into practice. What physician
does not often discourse at length on elements, humors,[147] com-
plexions,[148] maladies, and other things pertaining to medicine?
But the patient who recovers as a result of hearing this jargon
might just as well have been sickened by it. What moral philosopher
does not fairly bubble over with laws of ethics, so long as these
remain merely verbal? But it is a far different matter to exemplify
these in his own life. Those who have manual skills find no dif-

[143] Literally: of no use at home or in war, in the market place or in the cloister, at
court or in church: in fact nowhere except in school.
[144] Literally: embrace, or correspond to [it].
[145] Literally: vomited.
[146] Martianus Capella, *De Nupt.*, ii, § 136.
[147] *humoribus*, the "humors," consisting of blood, phlegm, yellow bile, and black bile,
which were supposed to determine the temperament of a person.
[148] *complexionibus*, combinations of certain assumed qualities in definite proportions,
supposed to control the nature of plants, bodies, and so on.

ficulty in discussing their arts, but none of them can erect a building or fight a boxing match with as little exertion. The like holds
true of other arts. It is a simple matter, indeed, to talk about definitions, arguments, genera, and the like; but it is a far more difficult
feat to put the art [of logic] into effect by finding the aforesaid
in each of the several branches of knowledge.[149] One who has the
sad misfortune of being in want of the other disciplines, cannot
possess the riches that are promised and provided by dialectic.

CHAPTER 10.   *On whose authority the foregoing and following are based.*

When, still but a youth, I first journeyed to Gaul for the sake of
study, in the year following the death of the illustrious King of
the English, Henry [I],[150] "the Lion of Justice," [151] I betook myself
to the Peripatetic of Pallet, who was then teaching[152] at Mont Ste.
Geneviève. The latter was a famed and learned master, admired
by all. At his feet I learned the elementary principles of this art,[153]
drinking in, with consuming avidity, and to the full extent of my
limited talents, every word that fell from his lips. After his departure,[154] which seemed to me all too soon, I became the disciple of
Master Alberic,[155] who had a very high reputation as the best of the
other dialecticians. Alberic was in fact a most bitter[156] opponent of

[149] *in singulis facultatibus.*

[150] Henry I of England died on December 1, 1135, and John went to study in France
in 1136.

[151] *Leo iustitie;* Galfridus Monumetensis (Geoffrey of Monmouth), *Hist. Brit.,* vii, 3,
in the prophecy of Merlin.

[152] Literally: who then presided.

[153] Of dialectic or logic.

[154] Abelard apparently left Paris in 1137; see R. L. Poole in his preface to John's *Hist.
Pont.,* p. lxi.

[155] What John relates later, in this same chapter, concerning the transfer of the present
Alberic to Bologna, hardly fits the Alberic mentioned in *Met.,* i, 5. Perhaps John here
refers to that Alberic of Rheims, "whom," as he says in his *Ep.* 143, written to Henry,
Count of Champagne, "they call *'de Porta Veneris,'* which is popularly known as
'Valesia.'"

[156] *acerrimus,* very acute, penetrating, zealous, or bitter.

the Nominalist sect. After thus passing[157] almost two full years at
the Mont, I had, as instructors in this art, Alberic and also Master
Robert of Melun[158] (the latter being the cognomen he had attained
in the scholastic regime,[159] although he belonged to the English
nation[160] by birth). Alberic was always most meticulous, and
everywhere found something to question. For him, not even a plain
surface that was polished smooth could be entirely free from objec-
tionable roughness. According to the saying, for him "the very
bulrush[161] would not be free of nodes."[162] For, even in the bulrush, he would be sure to discover knots in need of untying. Conversely, Robert of Melun was ever ready with the answers.[163] For
purposes of subterfuge, he would never complete his discussion[164]
of a proposed point without [first] choosing to take up the contradictory side,[165] or showing with deliberate variety of speech[166]
that there was more than one answer.[167] In short, while Alberic[168]
was full of subtle questions, Robert was penetrating, concise, and
to-the-point in his replies. If anyone were to have the qualities of
Alberic and Robert combined, in the degree that they possessed
them separately, it would be impossible in our age to find his
match as a disputant. Both [Alberic and Robert] had keen minds
and were diligent scholars. I am confident that each of them would
have been outstanding as great and illustrious students of nature,[169]
had they but possessed a broad foundation of literary learning, and
kept to the footsteps of their predecessors as much as they took
delight in their own inventions. Such was the case during the

[157] Or: having thus passed.
[158] Robert of Melun was consecrated Bishop of Hereford in 1163, and died in 1167.
[159] *in scolarum regimine*, in the administration or system of the Parisian schools of the
day.
[160] Note this use of the word "nation" (*natio*) in the mid-twelfth century.
[161] *cirpus*, that is, *scirpus*.
[162] That is, difficulties would be conjured up where they did not actually exist. See
Isidore, *Etym.*, xvii, 9, § 97.
[163] *in responsione promptissimus*, most ready with answers.
[164] *subterfugii causa . . . numquam declinauit.*
[165] *alteram contradictionis partem*, the opposite side of the contradiction.
[166] *determinata multiplicitate sermonis*, with a fixed multiplicity of speech.
[167] This may be translated: He would never, in order to conceal evasion . . . ; or: In order
to conceal evasion, he would never . . .
[168] Literally: the former.
[169] *in phisicis studiis*, in the study of physical things, of nature or of natural philosophy.

period when I was their disciple. Afterwards Alberic departed for
Bologna, where he "unlearned" what he had formerly taught; and
subsequently, on returning, "untaught" it. Let them judge who
heard his lectures both before his departure and after his return.
But Robert became proficient in divine learning,[170] and acquired
the glory of a still higher philosophy and greater renown. After
working with the aforesaid masters for two full years, I became
so accustomed to pointing out the topics, rules, and other elementary principles, with which teachers stock youthful minds, and of
which the aforesaid doctors were skilled masters, that these seemed
as familiar to me as my own nails and fingers.[171] For I had learned
the subject [dialectic] so thoroughly that, with youthful lack of
reflection, I unduly exaggerated my own knowledge. I took myself
to be a young sage, inasmuch as I knew the answers to what I had
been taught. However, I recovered my senses, and took stock of my
powers. I then transferred, after deliberation and consultation, and
with the approval of my instructors, to the grammarian of Conches.[172] I studied under the latter for three years,[173] during which
I learned much. Nor will I ever regret the time thus spent. Following this I became a disciple of Richard, known as "the Bishop." [174]
Richard is familiar with practically every branch of knowledge. His
breast[175] is larger than his mouth, and his [scientific] knowledge
exceeds his eloquence. He is honest rather than vain, virtuous
rather than ostentatious. With Richard, I reviewed all that I had
studied under the others, as well as learned certain additional points
concerning the Quadrivium, to which I had been previously introduced by Hardewin the German.[176] I also reviewed rhetoric, of
which, together with certain other subjects, I had already learned

[170] *in diuinis . . . litteris,* in divine letters, writings, or learning, in theology and the
sacred scriptures.
[171] Cf. Juvenal, *Sat.,* vii, 231–232.
[172] That is, William of Conches; see *Met.,* i, 5, p. 21, n. 65. John now transferred from
Paris to Chartres, where he studied under William.
[173] From the winter of 1137/38 to 1140/41, according to R. L. Poole in *English Historical
Review,* XXV (1920), 322.
[174] Richard l'Evêque, cf. *Met.,* i, 24, p. 71, n. 370.
[175] *pectoris,* the breast was considered the seat of intelligence as well as of emotion.
Hence John means here Richard's understanding and appreciation.
[176] *Teutonicum . . . Hardewinum.*

a little in previous studies under Master Theodoric,[177] but of which, as of these, I did not understand a great deal. Later, however, I learned more rhetoric from Peter Helias.[178] Meanwhile I took as pupils the children of nobles, who in return provided for my material necessities.[179] For I lacked the help of friends and relatives, and God thus aided me and relieved my poverty. In this capacity, because of my duties and the insistent questions raised by the youths, I was forced frequently to recall what I had previously heard.[180] Consequently I had recourse to Master Adam,[181] with whom I became very intimate. Adam is a man of very keen intellect, and also, regardless of what others may think, a person of wide learning. He was especially devoted to the study of Aristotle. Even though I was not one of his own disciples, he would graciously share with me his goods [of knowledge],[182] and very clearly explained to me his doctrines: something he never or rarely did with outsiders. He was [in fact] reputed to suffer from the affliction of jealousy. Meanwhile I taught the first principles of logic to William of Soissons. William later, according to his followers, invented a device[183] to revolutionize the old logic by constructing unacceptable conclusions and demolishing the authoritative opinions of the ancients. After instructing William, I sent him on to the aforesaid teacher.[184] Perhaps it was there that he learned

---

[177] Theodoric or Thierry of Chartres; see *Met.*, i, 5, p. 21, n. 64.

[178] *Petro Helia;* the *Menkonis Chronicon* (*Monumenta Germaniae historica, . . . Scriptorum*, XXIII, 524), indicates that Peter Helias was a famous grammarian. It says of Emo, Abbot of Wierum (or Wittewierum), who died in 1237: ". . . he wrote on all the authors, including . . . the greater and lesser Priscian and Peter Helias, as well as on other books and *Summae* of the Art of grammar."

[179] *alimenta*, food, support, material necessities.

[180] John thus confirms the old saying that one really learns a thing when he teaches it.

[181] Concerning Adam, see *Met.*, iii, 3, as well as iii, Prologue. He was called "Adam of the Little Bridge" or "du Petit Pont" (*de Parvo Ponte*) from the location near a little bridge over the Seine where he taught. Otto of Friesing (in *Gest. Frid.*, i, 53), relates that Adam appeared against Gilbert of Poitiers in the consistory held by Pope Eugenius III at Paris in 1147. Adam was consecrated Bishop of St. Asaph in Wales in 1175. He wrote a book (as John says *Met.*, iv, 3), entitled *Ars disserendi*, or the *Art of Reasoning*, from which some extracts have been edited by Victor Cousin (*Fragments philosophiques. Philosophie scholastique*, pp. 419 ff.).

[182] *sua benigne communicaret*, he shared his own possessions: that is, his knowledge.

[183] *machinam*, an artificial method of argumentation or reasoning, called a "machine" because it was devised to construct and to demolish, as above stated; a device, system, or [reasoning] process.

[184] To Adam du Petit Pont.

that the same conclusion may be inferred from either of two contradictories,[185] although Aristotle teaches the contrary, saying: "It
is impossible that both the existence and the non-existence of something should [each] alike necessitate the existence of something else
[i.e., one and the same other thing];"[186] and again "It is impossible
that the existence of something [one thing] should necessitate both
the existence and the non-existence of something else [i.e., one
(same) other thing]."[187] Nothing can eventuate from [both sides
of] a contradiction, and it is impossible for [both sides of] a contradiction to eventuate from something. Not even by the [reason-
ing] process devised by a friend could I be brought to believe that,
because one thing is inconceivable, all things become inconceivable.
My pinched finances, the entreaties of my associates, and the advice of friends [had] induced me to assume the office of teacher.[188]
At the end of three years I returned[189] and sought out Master Gilbert,[190] whose disciple I became in dialectical and theological subjects. But all too soon Gilbert was transferred.[191] His successor was
Robert Pullen,[192] a man commendable alike for his virtue[193] and
his knowledge. Next, Simon of Poissy,[194] a dependable lecturer,
but rather dull in disputes, took me as his student. The last-men-
tioned two [Robert and Simon] only instructed me in theology.
I [had] thus spent almost twelve years[195] engaged in various studies.
Accordingly, I felt that it would be pleasant to revisit my old

[185] That is, that the same thing can be the necessary consequent of both sides of a
contradiction.
[186] Cf. Aristotle, *An. Prior.,* ii, 4, 57 b, 2, 3.
[187] Cf. *ibid.,* ii, 4, 57b, for the sense of this intended quotation, although the exact words
John uses are not found there.
[188] *Officium docentis.* Very likely "had," with reference to what precedes, is to be understood here, as later, where John speaks of passing twelve years in study, and also uses
the perfect instead of the pluperfect.
[189] Apparently to Paris.
[190] Gilbert of Poitiers; see *Met.,* i, 5, p. 21, n. 61.
[191] To become Bishop of Poitiers in 1142. Cf. Poole, *op. cit.,* p. 322.
[192] See *Met.,* i, 5, p. 23, n. 83.
[193] Literally: life.
[194] Simon of Poissy may be the same teacher whom John (*Met.,* i, 5), calls "Simon of
Paris."
[195] *duodennium,* namely 1136–1148, according to R. L. Poole in his preface to John's
Hist. Pont., p. lxxii. For this chapter, cf. Poole's article on "The Masters of the Schools at
Paris and Chartres in John of Salisbury's Time," *English Historical Review,* XXV (1920),
321–342.

associates, whom I had previously left behind, and whom dialectic still detained at the Mont. I wanted to confer with them concerning matters that had previously appeared ambiguous to us, and to estimate our progress by mutual comparison. I found them just as, and where, they were when I had left them. They did not seem to have progressed as much as a hand's span. Not a single tiny [new] proposition had they added toward the solution of the old problems. They themselves remained involved in and occupied with the same questions whereby they used to stir their students.[196] They had changed in but one regard: they had unlearned moderation: they no longer knew restraint. And this to such an extent that their recovery was a matter of despair. I was accordingly convinced by experience of something which can easily be inferred [by reason]: that just as dialectic expedites other studies, so, if left alone by itself, it lies powerless and sterile. For if it is to fecundate the soul to bear the fruits of philosophy, logic must conceive from an external source.

CHAPTER 11.   *The limited extent of the efficacy of dialectic by itself.*

There is something, however, which dialectic itself, with the assistance of grammar alone, does promise and provide. Although it does not rise to other problems, dialectic resolves questions relative to itself. Thus it supplies the answers to such problems as: "Is affirmation also enuntiation?" and "Can two contradictory propositions be simultaneously true?" But anyone can see what [little] practical utility such information has in itself, apart from its application to particular cases. Dialectic, pure and simple, hardly ever investigates such questions as: "Is pleasure good?" "Should virtue be preferred to aught else?" "Do good habits[197] exist in the highest

---

[196] With the same stimuli whereby they spurred on their students.
[197] *bone habitudines.*

state?" [198] and "Should one labor when one is in need?" But upon the answer to problems such as these, depends whether or not our life will result in the attainment of happiness and salvation.[199] Although logic may expedite its own investigations, such is not its primary purpose. The [vital] spirit of animals constitutes the source of their organic structure and vegetative processes. It regulates and quickens the humors [necessary] for their animate life, although it originally took birth from these same humors. With its subtle energy it vivifies and systematizes a large mass of matter according to its own form, except so far as it may be hindered by poisonous bodies.[200] In almost the same way, logic has come into existence as a consequence of other studies, and these it subsequently organizes and vivifies, except so far as it may be deterred by the noxious impediments of inertia and ignorance. This is obvious to those who are familiar with other branches of knowledge besides the art of argumentative reasoning.[201]

CHAPTER 12.   *The subject matter of dialectic, and the means it uses.*

Dialectic comes into play in all studies, since its subject matter consists in questions. The dialectician leaves what is known as the "hypothesis," [202] namely, that which is involved in circumstances, to the orator. Such circumstances, as enumerated by Boethius in his fourth book on *Topics,* are: "Who, what, where, by what means, why, how, and when." [203] Dialectic, however, reserves to itself the

---

[198] *in summo* may mean in the highest place (on high), the highest state, or even the highest or best person or being. The sense here is apparently: "Are good habits a part of perfection?"

[199] *incolumitatem,* security, soundness, salvation.

[200] See Vergil's *Aen.,* vi, 726, 731; where, however, the poet is speaking of the spirit which "inwardly nourishes" the whole world.

[201] *disserendi,* discussion, argumentative reasoning.

[202] *ypotesis,* the hypothesis, assumption, supposition.

[203] For the content and differences of dialectic and rhetoric here discussed, see Boethius, *De Diff. Top.,* iv (in Migne, *P.L.,* LXIV, 1205 ff.).

"thesis," [204] that is, the question considered apart from the above-mentioned circumstances. For dialectic is concerned with reasoning of a more general nature, and does not of its own right descend to particulars. When, on occasion, it does so, it is in the position of a guest utilizing the property of others. Speech is an instrument used in common by both dialectic and rhetoric. Rhetoric, which aims to sway the judgment of persons other than the contestants, usually employs prolonged oration and induction,[205] owing to the fact that it is addressed to a larger number of people and generally solicits the assent of the crowd. Dialectic, on the contrary, expresses itself succinctly, and generally in the form of syllogisms,[206] for it has one judge alone: an opponent, to convince whom is its sole goal and purpose. For dialectic neither addresses itself to the crowd, nor seeks to win a legal judgment. The reasoning itself, which is clothed in speech, and which moves the mind after entering [it] through the ears with the aid of words, is likewise an instrument. Indeed the reasoning is what makes the speech itself an instrument. For the real force of speech derives from the thoughts or judgments it expresses, without which it would be dead and powerless. Since the subject matter of dialectic consists in questions, and has reasoning or speech as its instrument, the main task of the [dialectical] art is to forge a strong, versatile, and efficacious instrument, and to provide instruction for its use. The material [to work on] is ordinarily furnished by the other disciplines. Of a truth, there is no dearth of questions, which present themselves everywhere, although they are by no means everywhere solved.

[204] *Thesim,* the thesis or proposition.
[205] The above-quoted passage in Boethius contains no mention of induction; see, however, Cicero, *De Inv.,* i, 31, § 51.
[206] That is, with deductive reasoning.

CHAPTER 13. *The tremendous value of a scientific knowledge of probable principles; and the difficulties involved in determining what principles are absolutely necessary.*

The three fields of philosophy:[207] natural, moral, and rational, all provide material for dialectic. Each presents its own special problems. Ethics investigates [such questions as] whether it is better to obey one's parents or the laws when they disagree. Physics inquires [into matters such as] whether the world is eternal,[208] or perpetual,[209] or had a beginning and will have an end in time, or whether none of these alternatives is accurate. Logic considers [such problems as] whether contraries belong to the same branch of study, inasmuch as they involve the same terms. Every branch of philosophy therefore has its own questions. But while each study is fortified by its own particular principles, logic is their common servant, and supplies them all with its "methods" [210] or principles of expeditious reasoning.[211] Hence logic is most valuable, not merely to provide exercise [for our faculties], but also as a tool in argumentative reasoning and the various branches of learning that pertain to philosophy. One who has command of a method for so doing, can proceed with ease in argumentative reasoning. And one who, while cognizant of the existence of numerous diverse opinions on a subject, does not merely parrot the arguments of others, but develops his own, is a capable disputant, and modifies whatever does not seem well said.[212]

---

[207] Literally: faculties. Concerning the following division of the faculties, or parts of philosophy or learning, see Seneca, *Ep.*, 89, § 9; Apuleius, *De Dogm. Plat.*, i, 3; Augustine, *De C.D.*, viii, 4; and John's *Policraticus*, vii, 5.

[208] Without beginning or end.

[209] Having a beginning, but without end.

[210] *metodos.*

[211] *compendii . . . rationes*, its rational principles to expedite [their investigations], its system, reasons, or rational plans for the accomplishment [of expeditious or compendious proof].

[212] That is, appropriate, correct, or well stated.

Furthermore, one who takes account of attendant reasons, more easily discriminates between the true and the false in all instances, and is in a better position to understand and to teach, which constitute the object and office of the philosopher. Since dialectic is the science of [rational] investigation, it has [ready] access to the principles underlying all methods. But every art has its own special methods, which we may figuratively characterize as its "approaches" or "keys."[213] Seeking is a necessary preliminary to finding,[214] and one who cannot endure the hardship of inquiry cannot expect to harvest the fruit of knowledge. Demonstrative logic, however, seeks methods [of proof] involving necessity,[215] and arguments which establish the essential identification[216] of terms that cannot be thrust asunder.[217] Only that which cannot possibly be otherwise is necessary. Since no one, or hardly anyone, ever fully comprehends natural forces,[218] and since God alone knows the limits of possibility, it is frequently both dubious and presumptuous to assert[219] that a thing is necessary. For who has ever been absolutely sure about where to draw the line between possibility and impossibility? Many ages took the following principle: "If a woman gives birth to a child, she must have had previous sexual intercourse, whether voluntary or involuntary, with someone," to be a necessary axiom. But finally, in the fulness of time,[220] it has been shown that it is not such, by the fact that a most pure and incorrupt virgin has given birth to a child. Something that is absolutely necessary cannot possibly be otherwise. But something that is conditionally[221] necessary may be modified. Victorinus, in his work on rhetoric, explains this when he discusses necessity. He tells us that, while previous sexual intercourse may be inferred with probability, it cannot be deduced as absolutely necessary from the fact of childbirth.[222]

[213] Literally: entrances or entrance-ways.
[214] Cf. Matthew, vii, 7; Luke, xi, 9.
[215] *necessarias metodos.*
[216] *inherentiam.*
[217] Mark, x, 9.
[218] Literally: the forces, powers, or laws of nature.
[219] Literally: to judge.
[220] *in fine temporum.*
[221] Literally: by determination.
[222] Cf. Victorinus, *In Cic. de Inv.,* i, 29.

Augustine asserts that necessary reasons are everlasting, and cannot in any way be gainsaid.[223] It is clear, however, that the reasons[224] of probable things are subject to change, since they are not necessary. The great difficulty with [absolute] demonstration is apparent, as the demonstrator is always [and solely] engaged in the quest of necessity, and cannot admit of any exception to the principles of truth he professes.[225] If it is a difficult matter to perceive the truth, which (as our Academicians say) is as indefinite in outline as though it lay at the bottom of a well;[226] how much energy is not required to discern, in addition to the truth, the hidden secrets of necessity itself? Is it not easier to recognize what exists than to decide what is possible? The method of demonstration is therefore generally feeble and ineffective with regard to facts of nature (I refer to corporeal and changeable things). But it quickly recovers its strength when applied to the field of mathematics. For whatever it concludes in regard to such things as numbers, proportions and figures is indubitably true, and cannot be otherwise. One who wishes to become a master of the science of demonstration should first obtain a good grasp of probabilities. Whereas the principles of demonstrative logic are necessary; those of dialectic are probable. The dialectician, for his part, will shun theses which seem likely to no one, lest he become suspected of insanity. On the other hand, he will refrain from disputing about principles that are already self-evident, lest he seem to be "groping in the dark." [227] He will limit himself to the discussion of propositions which are [well] known to all, or to many, or to the leaders in each field.[228]

---

[223] See Augustine, De Div. Quaest., lxxxiii, 46, § 2 (in Migne, P.L., XL, 30), a passage frequently cited by scholastic writers of the Middle Ages in reference to the doctrine of ideas.

[224] rationes, here used in a broad sense. Cf. Met., ii, 5.

[225] See Boethius, De Diff. Top., near the end of Book I (in Migne, P.L., LXIV, 1182).

[226] Cf. Cicero, Acad. Post., i, 12, § 44.

[227] Job, xii, 25.

[228] Or: in each department of knowledge. See Aristotle, Top., i, 11, 105 a–b, 2–38; and also i, 1, 100 a, 30–100 b, 23. Cf. likewise Boethius, De Diff. Top., i.

CHAPTER 14.   *More on the same subject.*

Dialectical principles are accordingly probable, while those of demonstration are necessary.[229] If something involves both probability
and necessity, it may pertain to both dialectic and demonstration;
but if this is not the case, it belongs either to one or to the other.
Probability alone is sufficient for dialectic. Whence Cicero, in the
second of his *Tusculan Disputations,* says: "We, who take probability as our guide, cannot do more than assent or affirm that a
thing seems true, and are prepared both to argue against the views
of others without becoming angry, and to be ourselves corrected
without obstinacy." [230] Cicero also says elsewhere: "According to
our Academy, we have a right to defend any proposition that seems
probable." [231] A proposition is probable if it seems obvious to a
person of [good] judgment,[232] and if it occurs thus in all instances
and at all times, or [at least] is otherwise only in exceptional cases
and on rare occasions. Something that is always or usually so, either
is, or [at least] seems probable, even though it could possibly be
otherwise. And its probability is increased in proportion as it is
more easily and surely known by one who has [good] judgment.
There are some things whose probability is so lucidly apparent
that they come to be considered necessary; whereas there are others
which are so unfamiliar to us that we would be reluctant to include
them in a list of probabilities. If an opinion is weak, it wavers with
uncertainty; whereas if an opinion is strong, it may wax to the
point of being transformed into faith and approximate[233] certitude.
If its strength grows to the degree that it can admit of no or hardly
any further increase, even though it is [really] less than [scientific]

[229] Boethius, *De Diff. Top.,* i.
[230] Cicero, *Tusc. Disp.,* ii, 2, § 5.
[231] Cicero, *De Off.,* iii, 4, § 20.
[232] Literally: if it becomes apparent to one who has judgment, even on superficial consideration.
[233] *aspirat,* aspire to, approach.

knowledge, it comes to be [deemed] equivalent to the latter so far as our certainty of judgment is concerned. This is apparent, as Aristotle observes,[234] in matters which we perceive only by our senses, and which can be otherwise. Thus when the sun has set, we do not [really] know with certainty that it will continue its course over the earth[235] and return to our hemisphere. For the sensory perception whereby we were apprised of the course of the sun has ceased. Nevertheless our confidence concerning its course and return is so great that it seems, in a way, equivalent to [scientific] knowledge. However, when sensation leads to a [scientific] knowledge of something that cannot be otherwise, as when our eyes show us that a line has length and a surface color, such knowledge does not terminate when we no longer perceive the object. The reason is that these are necessary facts. When something is found to hold true in all or in most examples of a given kind, we should either conclude that it is thus universally in such, or should allege an instance[236] to the contrary. Such a contrary instance is an evidently true thesis prejudicial to the assumed universality. [From what has been said, it is consequently apparent that:] A wide knowledge of probabilities constitutes a master key whose use is universal.[237]

CHAPTER 15.   *What is a dialectical proposition, and what is a dialectical problem.*

"A dialectical proposition is one that holds true in several cases, and against which there is no objection," that is to say, no argument appealing to a thesis.[238] One who is cognizant of such propositions, and is also aware whether there are any contrary objections resting

---

[234] Aristotle, *Top.*, v, 2, 131 b, 19 ff.

[235] Literally: whether it continues on above the earth.

[236] *instantia.*

[237] Literally: prepares expeditious access to all things. Cf. the concluding sentence of the following chapter.

[238] *positionem,* a thesis, position, affirmation, assumption, postulate, hypothesis, or premise, as explained later in this same chapter. Cf. Aristotle, *Top.*, viii, 2, 157 b, 32. The Greek *thesis* and the Latin *positio* are equivalents.

on theses, will truly be well prepared for an opponent in all kinds
of disputations. Furthermore, if he sincerely devotes himself to
philosophy,[239] he will be happy in no small degree. He is in a position to discuss with probability every kind of question, whether it
be ethical, physical, or logical. "A dialectical problem consists in
reasoning about a question which, either in itself or as subsidiary to
something else, tends to acceptance or rejection,[240] or to the estab-
lishment of truth and knowledge, a question concerning which
either there is no [definite] opinion, or most people think differently
from those who are wise, or [vice versa] wise men disagree with
the crowd, or [finally] both wise men and the masses are at log-
gerheads among themselves [namely, each in his own number.]" [241]
The style discloses the author of this definition, and both the words
and the thought reveal that Aristotle composed it. For Aristotle did
not consider each and every speculation that leads to affirmation or
negation a dialectical problem. Nor did he believe that a skilled
craftsman in his art [of logic] should waste time discussing things
that are useful to no one, whether in themselves or by way of any
of the aforesaid disciplines. For although there are some who hold
that what Aristotle says about "tending to acceptance or rejection"
refers solely to ethical questions, I believe that it also includes physical [242] problems. However, I think that it has absolutely or practically no reference to questions of logic. In ethics, materials for
selection or rejection are provided by virtue, vice, and the like. In
physical science, health and sickness, causes and symptoms, and the
circumstances of each case serve a like purpose. At the same time,
questions treated by all three disciplines [ethics, physics, and logic]
tend equally to [establish] scientific knowledge and truth. Whether
or not pleasure[243] should be chosen is an ethical speculation, useful
in itself. Whether or not the world is eternal is a philosophical speculation, which contributes to knowledge and truth, as well as perhaps
to additional ends. Thus if we recognize that the world has been

---

[239] *si philosophice secum exerceatur*, literally: if he exercises philosophically with himself.
[240] Literally: to choice or flight, to affirmative or negative choice.
[241] Aristotle, *Top.*, i, 11, 104 b, 1.
[242] *phisicas,* physical or natural, including medical.
[243] *uoluptas.*

created, we will reverence the author of this stupendous work.
And as we become aware that the world is transitory, it cheapens
in our estimation in comparison with piety,[244] for the world with
everything in it "is subject to vanity." [245] Logic inquires into [such
questions as] whether one of two contradictory propositions must
always be true. To have a knowledge of the answer to the latter
question is helpful in other connections. But those who dispute
with each other about whether or not goats have wool are not
really discussing dialectical problems. They have strayed far afield
from both the subject matter and the purpose of the [logical] art.
For the subject matter of logic is what is called a "thesis" or "position." The latter is an opinion of some learned authority,[246] which
[opinion] is not commonly accepted. Examples include the proposition of Heraclitus that all things are in motion, and the tenet of
Melissus that [all] being is one." [247] Anyone who is in possession of
his senses will not posit something which either seems plausible
to no one, or is apparent to everyone or [at least] to those whose
judgment is sought.[248] The latter sort of premise does not admit of
any doubt, while no one would advance the former. I am convinced
that none of the liberal disciplines has greater utility than this one
[dialectic], which serves as an easy and pleasant pathway into all
parts of philosophy, for one who understands probabilities[249] will
not be at a loss in any department of learning.

CHAPTER 16.   *That all other teachers of this art [of dialectic]
acknowledge Aristotle as their master.*

To detract from this discipline [of logic] which builds up and
organizes all other branches of learning, and is a prerequisite if one
is to proceed correctly in philosophical investigations, seems mani-

[244] *moribus piis,* pious morals.
[245] Romans, viii, 20.
[246] Literally: someone noted in philosophy.
[247] Aristotle, *Top.,* i, 11, 104 b, 19 ff.
[248] *Ibid.,* i, 11, 105 a, 3 ff.
[249] *probabilia,* probabilities, probable things, what is probable.

fest insanity. Since a great number of authors, including the keenest
and the most assiduous philosophers, have written about logic, those
who condemn it are evidently criticizing all of the former. For there
can be no doubt that to arraign a study is also to indict its author.
Of one thing I am certain: that posterity will by no means regard
Cornificius more highly than these authors. For Aristotle, Apuleius,
Cicero, Porphyry, Boethius, and Augustine, as well as Eudemus,
Alexander, and Theophrastus, not to mention many more [of its]
exponents, whose names I need not bother to enumerate (although
they are likewise famous), have all, with enthusiastic praise, raised
the banner of logic as, so to speak, supreme among the arts. While
each of these authors is illustrious by his own right, all of them
take pride in treading carefully in the footsteps[250] of Aristotle. So
true is this that the common noun "philosopher" has, with a certain
preëminence, come to be preserved for Aristotle. For Aristotle is
called by *antonomasia*[251] or *par excellence* "the Philosopher." It is
he who has reduced methods of probable proof [252] to an art. Building up, as it were, from what is most elementary, he has kept on
until he has successfully completed his proposed structure. This is
apparent to those who study and discuss his works. Taking words
in their primary senses,[253] that is uncombined [254] words, from the
hand of the grammarian, he has carefully explained their differences and implications,[255] to the end that they may more effectively
contribute to the formation of propositions, and to the sciences of
invention[256] and judgment.[257] But since, as an aid to understanding
Aristotle's elementary book,[258] Porphyry wrote another [book] in
a way still more elementary, the ancients believed that [this work
of] Porphyry should be studied as an introduction to Aristotle. And
right they were, provided that Porphyry's book is properly treated.

[250] *adorare uestigia,* literally: to adore the traces or footprints; to follow carefully in
the footsteps of. This may be influenced by Statius, *Theb.,* xii, 817.
[251] *antonomasia,* a form of trope by which a common noun replaces a proper one.
[252] *probabilium rationes,* methods of probable things, or of proving things with probability.
[253] *Uoces enim primo significatiuas.*
[254] Incomplex, uncombined, simple.
[255] Literally: forces. John states above that a word's force is in its meaning, so that he
obviously means here: [possible] meanings.
[256] *inueniendi.*
[257] Aristotle does this in his book the *Categoriae.*
[258] The *Categoriae* (*The Categories* or *Predicaments*).

For the latter should not be taught in such a way as to confuse and
obfuscate those being instructed, or monopolize all their time. It
is not right that one should spend his life studying the five categoricals,[259] with the consequence that no time remains to learn those
things for which these are taught as preparatory in the first place.
Because of its introductory nature, Porphyry's work is entitled the
Isagoge.[260] But its very name is contradicted by those who become
so engrossed in it that they leave no time for the principal essentials,
on which the whole significance of the introductory work depends.

CHAPTER 17.   *In what a pernicious manner logic is sometimes
                taught; and the ideas of moderns about [the
                nature of] genera and species.*[261]

To show off their knowledge, our contemporaries dispense their
instruction in such a way that their listeners are at a loss to understand them. They seem to have the impression that every letter
of the alphabet is pregnant with the secrets of Minerva.[262] They
analyze and press upon tender ears everything that anyone has ever
said or done. Falling into the error condemned by Cicero, they
frequently come to be unintelligible to their hearers more because of
the multiplicity than the profundity of their statements. "It is
indeed useful and advantageous for disputants," as Aristotle observes,[263] "to take cognizance of several opinions on a topic." From
the mutual disagreement thus brought into relief, what is seen to

---

[259] *quinque uoculis,* the five categoricals, generally called the "predicables": genus, species,
difference, property, and accident.

[260] That is, *Guide* or *Introduction*.

[261] Compare, with the present chapter, Abelard's *Fragm. Sangermanense de generibus et
speciebus* (in *Ouvr. Inédit. d'Abelard,* ed. V. Cousin, pp. 507–550).

[262] *secretis Minerue* here evidently means hidden gems of wisdom, although it refers to
Ovid, *Met.,* ii, 749.

[263] Reference may be made to Aristotle, *Top.,* i, 2, 101 a, 30 ff., where Aristotle, however, does not use the exact equivalent of John's present wording. Neither does the translation which goes under the name of Boethius. John may here be following a version other
than the latter.

be poorly stated may be disproved or modified. Instruction in elementary logic does not, however, constitute the proper occasion for such procedure. Simplicity, brevity, and easy subject matter are, so far as is possible, appropriate in introductory studies. This is so true that it is permissible to expound many difficult points in a simpler way than their nature strictly requires. Thus, much that we have learned in our youth must later be amended in more advanced philosophical studies. Nevertheless, at present, all are here [in introductory logical studies] declaiming on the nature of universals, and attempting to explain, contrary to the intention of the author,[264] what is really a most profound question, and a matter [that should be reserved] for more advanced studies. One holds that universals are merely word sounds,[265] although this opinion, along with its author Roscelin, has already almost completely passed into oblivion.[266] Another maintains that universals are word concepts,[267] and twists to support his thesis everything that he can remember to have ever been written on the subject.[268] Our Peripatetic of Pallet, Abelard, was ensnared in this opinion. He left many, and still has, to this day, some followers and proponents of his doctrine. They are friends of mine, although they often so torture the helpless[269] letter that even the hardest heart is filled with compassion for the latter. They hold that it is preposterous to predicate a thing concerning a thing, although Aristotle is author of this monstrosity. For Aristotle frequently asserts that a thing is predicated concerning a thing,[270] as is evident to anyone who is really familiar with his teaching. Another is wrapped up in a consideration of acts of the [intuitive] understanding,[271] and says that genera and species are

---

[264] Aristotle.
[265] *uocibus*, physical, spoken, or audible word sounds.
[266] Cf. *Policraticus*, vii, 12.
[267] *sermones*, words as predicated or as signifying concepts, word concepts. This distinction between *uoces* and *sermones* John probably obtained from Abelard. Cf. J. G. Sikes, *Peter Abailard* (Cambridge, England, 1932), pp. 104, 88–112 *passim*, in addition to the references there cited by Sikes. According to Abelard, *uox* is the mere physical, audible, spoken word; *sermo*, the word considered in relation to its meaning as a mental concept.
[268] Cf. *Policraticus*, vii, 12.
[269] Literally: captive.
[270] See Boethius, *Comm. II in Arist. de Interpr.*, v, 11 (in Migne, *P.L.*, LXIV, 568, and ed. Meiser, II, 352).
[271] *intellectibus*.

nothing more than the latter.[272] Proponents of this view take their cue[273] from Cicero[274] and Boethius,[275] who cite Aristotle as saying that universals should be regarded as and called "notions." [276] "A notion," they tell us, "is the cognition of something, derived from its previously perceived form, and in need of unravelment." [277] Or again [they say]: "A notion is an act of the [intuitive] understanding, a simple mental comprehension." [278] They accordingly distort everything written, with an eye to making acts of [intuitive] understanding or "notions" include the universality of universals. Those who adhere to the view that universals are things,[279] have various and sundry opinions. One, reasoning from the fact that everything which exists is singular in number,[280] concludes that either the universal is numerically one, or it is non-existent. But since it is impossible for things that are substantial [281] to be non-existent, if those things for which they are substantial exist, they further conclude that universals must be essentially one with particular things. Accordingly, following Walter of Mortagne,[282] they distinguish [various] states [of existence],[283] and say that Plato is an individual in so far as he is Plato; a species in so far as he is a man; a genus of a subaltern [subordinate] kind in so far as he is an animal; and a most general genus in so far as he is a substance. Although this opinion formerly had some proponents, it has been a long time since anyone has asserted it. Walter[284] now upholds [the doctrine of] ideas, emulating Plato and imitating Bernard of Chartres,[285] and maintains that genus and species are nothing more nor less than

---

[272] Cf. *Policraticus*, vii, 12.

[273] Literally: take occasion from.

[274] Cicero, *Top.*, 7, § 31.

[275] Boethius, *Comm. in Top. Cic.*, iii (in Migne, *P.L.*, LXIV, 1105–1106).

[276] *notiones.*

[277] Cicero, *Top.*, 7, § 31.

[278] Boethius, *op. cit.*, iii.

[279] *qui rebus inherent;* again cf. *Policraticus*, vii, 12.

[280] Cf. Boethius, *Comm. in Porph.*, iii (in Migne, *P.L.*, LXIV, 110).

[281] Or essential.

[282] Concerning *Gauterus de Mauritania*, see *Gallia Christiana*, IX, 533. Walter was consecrated Bishop of Laon in 1155, and died in 1174.

[283] *status.*

[284] Literally: "that one," evidently Walter of Mortagne, who apparently was subsequently converted to the opinion of Plato and Bernard of Chartres.

[285] See *Met.*, i, 24, and note.

these, namely, ideas. "An idea," according to Seneca's definition,[286] "is an eternal exemplar of those things which come to be as a result of [287] nature." And since universals are not subject to corruption, and are not altered by the changes[288] that transform particular things and cause them to come and go, succeeding one another almost momentarily, ideas are properly and correctly called "universals." Indeed, particular things are deemed incapable of supporting the substantive verb,[289] [i.e., of being said "to be"], since they are not at all stable, and disappear without even waiting to receive names. For they vary so much in their qualities, time, location, and numerous different properties, that their whole existence seems to be more a mutable transition than a stable status. In contrast, Boethius declares:[290] "We say that things 'are' when they may neither be increased nor diminished, but always continue as they are, firmly sustained by the foundations of their own nature." These [foundations] include their quantities, qualities, relations, places, times, conditions, and whatever is found in a way united with bodies. Although these adjuncts of bodies may seem to be changed, they remain immutable in their own nature. In like manner, although individuals [of species] may change, species remain the same. The waves of a stream wash on, yet the same flow of water continues, and we refer to the stream as the same river. Whence the statement of Seneca,[291] which, in fact, he has borrowed from another:[292] "In one sense it is true that we may descend twice into the same river, although in another sense this is not so." [293] These "ideas," or "exemplary forms," are the original plans[294] of all things. They may neither be decreased nor augmented; and they are so permanent and perpetual, that even if the whole world were to come to an end, they could not perish. They include all things,

---

[286] Seneca, *Ep.*, 58, § 19.
[287] Or: by.
[288] *motibus*, movements, forces, changes.
[289] *uerbi substantiui*, the substantive verb: *esse*, to be.
[290] Boethius, *Arithm.*, i, 1 (p. 8, lines 1–4, in Friedlein's edition).
[291] Seneca, *Ep.*, 58, § 23.
[292] Heraclitus.
[293] Literally: go down twice into the same river, yet into a different river.
[294] *rationes*.

and, as Augustine seems to maintain in his book *On Free Will*,[295] their number neither increases nor diminishes, because the ideas always continue on, even when it happens that [particular] temporal things cease to exist. What these men promise is wonderful, and familiar to philosophers who rise to the contemplation of higher things. But, as Boethius[296] and numerous other authors testify, it is utterly foreign to the mind of Aristotle. For Aristotle very frequently opposes this view, as is clear from his books. Bernard of Chartres and his followers[297] labored strenuously to compose the differences between Aristotle and Plato.[298] But I opine that they arrived on the scene too late, so that their efforts to reconcile two dead men, who disagree as long as they were alive and could do so, were in vain. Still another, in his endeavor to explain Aristotle, places universality in "native forms," [299] as does Gilbert, Bishop of Poitiers,[300] who labors to prove that "native forms" and universals are identical.[301] A "native form" is an example of an original [exemplar].[302] It [the native form, unlike the original] inheres in created things, instead of subsisting in the divine mind. In Greek it is called the *idos*,[303] since it stands in relation to the idea as the example does to its exemplar. The native form is sensible in things that are perceptible by the senses; but insensible as conceived in the mind. It is singular in individuals, but universal in all [of a kind]. Another, with Joscelin, Bishop of Soissons,[304] attributes universality to collections of things,[305] while denying it to things as

---

[295] Augustine, *De Lib. Arbit.*, ii, 17 (in Migne, *P.L.*, LXIV, 1106).

[296] Boethius, for example, in his *Comm. in Top. Cic.*, iii (in Migne, *P.L.*, LXIV, 1106).

[297] Literally: his hearers.

[298] Boethius also declares that he himself tried "to reconcile the opinions of Aristotle and Plato in some way": see Boethius, *Comm. II in Arist. de Interpr.*, ii, 3 (ed. Meiser, II, 79, and in Migne, *P.L.*, LXIV, 79–80).

[299] *formis natiuis;* see Gilbert of Poitiers, *In Boeth. de Trin. Comm.*, and his *Comm. in Boeth. lib. de Duabus Naturis* (in Migne, *P.L.*, LXIV, 1267 and 1366).

[300] Gilbert became Bishop of Poitiers in 1142, and died in 1154. Commentaries written by him on the theological works of Boethius, and his famous *De Sex principiis*, which editors used to append to Aristotle's *Organon*, are extant.

[301] *in earum conformitate laborat.*

[302] *originalis*, namely, of the original exemplar in the mind of God.

[303] See Seneca, *Ep.*, 58, § 20.

[304] *Gausleno*, Joscelin; also called *Joslenus*, *Johelinus*, and *Jocelinus*. He was Bishop of Soissons 1126–1152. Some small extant works of his are to be found in Migne's *P.L.*, CLXXVI, but there is nothing in them about universals.

[305] Literally: to things collected together.

individuals. When Joscelin tries to explain the authorities, he has his troubles and is hard put, for in many places he cannot bear the gaping astonishment[306] of the indignant letter.[307] Still another takes refuge in a new tongue, since he does not have sufficient command of Latin. When he hears the words "genus" and "species," at one time he says they should be understood as universals, and at another that they refer to the *maneries*[308] of things. I know not in which of the authors he has found this term or this distinction, unless perhaps he has dug it out of lists of abstruse and obsolete words,[309] or it is an item of jargon [in the baggage] of present-day[310] doctors. I am further at a loss to see what it can mean here, unless it refers to collections of things, which would be the same as Joscelin's view, or to a universal thing, which, however, could hardly be called a *maneries*. For a *maneries* may be interpreted as referring to both [collections and universals], since a number of things, or the status[311] in which a thing of such and such a type continues to exist[312] may be called a *maneries*. Finally, there are some who fix their attention on the status of things, and say that genera and species consist in the latter.

CHAPTER 18.   *That men always alter the opinions of their predecessors.*

It would take too long, and [also] be entirely foreign to my purpose, to propound the opinions and errors of everyone. The saying of the comic poet that "There are as many opinions as heads," [313] has almost come to hold true. Rarely, if ever, do we find a teacher who is content to follow in the footsteps of his master. Each, to

---

[306] *rictum*, literally: the opening of the mouth.

[307] That is, the letter or writing which is opposed to his view, and is, as it were, violated.

[308] *maneries*, ways, modes, manners, ways of handling.

[309] *in glosematibus.*

[310] *modernorum*, modern or present-day.

[311] *status.*

[312] *permanet*, as though *maneries* would be said to be derived from *manendum*, "remaining."

[313] Terence in his *Phorm.*, ii, 4, 14.

make a name for himself, coins his own special error. Wherewith, while promising to correct his master, he sets himself up as a target for correction and condemnation by his own disciples as well as by posterity. I recognize that the same rule threatens to apply in my own case. By disagreeing with others and committing my dissent to writing, I am, in fact, laying myself open to be criticized by many. He who speaks is judged merely by one or a few persons; whereas he who writes thereby exposes himself to criticism by all, and appears before the tribunal of the whole world and every age. However, not to be overly harsh with the doctors, I must observe that, very often, many of them seem to be wrangling over words, rather than disputing about facts. Nonetheless there is nothing that is less appropriate for a professor of this art [of logic], since such procedure ill befits a serious man. As Aristotle declares, "To dispute in this wise over a word is utterly abhorrent in dialectic, unless it be the sole possible way in which a proposition may be discussed." [314] Of a truth, on points where they seem to be in profound disagreement, such [professors of logic] admit one another's interpretations, even though they may maintain that the latter are inadequate. They are mutually condemning, not the meaning, but the words of one another's statements.

CHAPTER 19. *Wherein teachers of this kind are not to be forgiven.*

I do not criticize their opinions, which [probably] do not actually disagree, as would be shown if it were possible to compare their meanings.[315] Still, they are guilty of certain offenses which, in my opinion, should not be overlooked. In the first place, they load "insupportable burdens" on the frail shoulders of their students.[316]

[314] Aristotle, *Top.,* i, 18, 108 a, 35.

[315] Literally: were it possible to superimpose them [their opinions], one on another, for comparison.

[316] Cf. Matthew, xxiii, 4.

Second, they pay no attention to proper order in teaching, and
diligently take care lest "All things be suitably arranged, each in
its own place."[317] Thus they, so to speak, read[318] the whole art[319]
into its title. With them, Porphyry practically teaches beforehand the
contents of the *Topics,* the *Analytics,* and the *Elenchi.*[320] Finally,
they go against the mind of the author, and comb, as it were, in
the wrong direction. For the [supposed] purpose of simplifying
Aristotle, they teach the doctrine of Plato, or [perhaps even] some
false opinion, which differs with equal error from the views[321] of
both Aristotle and Plato. At the same time, they all profess to be
followers of Aristotle.

CHAPTER 20.   *Aristotle's opinion concerning genera and species, supported by numerous confirmatory rea-
sons and references to written works.*

Aristotle stated that genera and species do not exist [as such], but
are only understood.[322] What is the point, then, in inquiring as to
what genus is, when Aristotle has definitely asserted that it does not
exist? Is it not inane to try to determine the nature, quantity, and
quality of something that has no existence? If substance be lacking,
then none of these other attributes can be present. If Aristotle, who
says that genera and species do not exist [as such], is right, then the
labors of the foregoing inquiry as to their substance, quantity,
quality, or origin, are futile. We cannot describe the quality or
quantity of something that lacks substance. Neither can we give the
reason why something that does not exist is one thing or another,
and of this or that size or kind. Wherefore, unless one wants to
break with Aristotle, by granting that universals exist, he must

[317] Horace, *A.P.,* 92.
[318] *legunt,* they read, or perhaps they lecture or teach.
[319] *finem . . . artis,* the end or completion of an art [namely, this art of logic].
[320] Of Aristotle.
[321] *sententia,* judgment, authoritative opinion, view.
[322] See Boethius, *Comm. in Porph.,* i (in Migne, *P.L.,* LXIV, 82–86).

reject opinions which would identify universals with word sounds,[323] word concepts,[324] sensible things,[325] ideas,[326] native forms,[327] or collections.[328] For all of the latter doubtless exist. In short, one who maintains that universals exist,[329] contradicts Aristotle. We should not, however, fear that our understanding[330] is empty when it perceives universals as abstracted from particular things, although the former have no [actual] existence apart from the latter. Our understanding [has two different modes of operation:] at times [it] looks directly at the simple essence of things, apart from composition,[331] as when it conceives of "man" *per se,* or "stone" *per se,*[332] in which operation it is simple. But at times it proceeds gradually, step by step,[333] as when it considers a man as white, or a horse as running,[334] in which case its operation is composite. A simple act of the understanding at times considers a thing as it is, as when it considers Plato; but at other times it conceives of a thing as otherwise. Sometimes it combines things that are [in actual life] uncombined, at other times it separates things that cannot [in reality] be dissociated. One who imagines a goat-stag[335] or a centaur,[336] conceives of a combination of man and beast that is alien to nature, or a combination of two species of animals. On the other hand, one who considers line or surface apart from a given mass, dissociates form from matter by the keen blade of his contemplative insight,[337] although, actually, it is impossible for them to exist apart from each other. However, the abstracting intellect does not in this case con-

---

[323] *uocibus;* with Roscelin, as explained above (ii, 17).

[324] *sermonibus;* with Abelard, *ibid.*

[325] *sensibilibus rebus;* with Walter of Mortagne, *ibid.*

[326] *ideis;* with Walter, after his conversion to the view of Plato and Bernard of Chartres, *ibid.*

[327] *formis natiuis;* with Gilbert of Poitiers, *ibid.*

[328] *collectionibus;* with Joscelin of Soissons, *ibid.*

[329] Or: that universals are these things.

[330] *intellectus,* our [intuitive] understanding, intellect, or mind, or the mental concept or idea conceived by the former.

[331] *simpliciter,* simply, without admixture.

[332] *per se,* of or in himself or itself.

[333] *gradatim suis incedit passibus.*

[334] See Aristotle, *De Interpr.,* i, as well as the commentary thereon by Boethius.

[335] *hircoceruum,* a fabled combination of goat and stag: from Aristotle, *De Interpr.,* i, 16 a, 16.

[336] *centaurum,* an imaginary monster half man and half horse.

[337] Literally: by the eye of his contemplation.

ceive of form as existing apart from matter. If it did, its operation
would be composite. Rather, it simply contemplates the form, without considering the matter, even though in fact the former cannot
exist apart from the latter. Such an operation agrees with the intellect's simplicity, which comes into sharper relief in proportion
as it considers simpler things in themselves, namely, apart from
composition with other things. Nor is this procedure contrary to
the order of nature, which has bestowed on the [human] intellect
this faculty of distinguishing things that are combined, and putting
together things that exist separately, in order to facilitate its investigation of nature itself. The combining process of the intellect,
whereby things that are not united are copulated, lacks objec-
tivity;[338] but its abstracting process is both accurate and true to
reality. The latter constitutes, as it were, the common factory of all
the arts. While things possess but one manner of existence which
they have received from nature, they may nevertheless be understood or signified in more than one way. Although a man who is
not a specific man cannot exist, "man" may still be conceived
mentally and represented in such a way that no given individual
man is thought of or denoted. Therefore genera and species may be
conceived by the abstracting intellect in order to signify things [as
considered] apart from composition.[339] But if one were, ever so
diligently, to search for the latter in nature, dissociated from sensible
things, he would be wasting his time, and laboring in vain, as
nature does not count anything of the sort among her brood.
Reason, on considering the substantial mutual resemblances of
certain individual things, has discerned genera and species. Thus it
has, as Boethius tells us,[340] defined the general concept: "Rational
mortal animal," which it has, on reflection, concluded from the
mutual conformity existing among men, even though such a "rational mortal animal" [actually] exists only in individual cases.
Consequently, genera and species are not things that are really and
by their nature unrelated to individual things. Rather, they are

---

[338] Literally: is empty.

[339] ad significationem incomplexorum.

[340] Boethius, Comm. in Arist. de Interpr., I, i, 5 (ed. Meiser, pp. 72, 26 ff.); cf. I, i, 2
(54, 16) and II, ii, 5 (101, 15).

mental representations[341] of actual, natural things, intellectual images of the mutual likenesses of real things, reflected, as it were, in
the mirror of the soul's native purity.[342] These concepts the Greek
call *ennoyas*[343] or *yconoyfanas*,[344] that is to say images of things
clearly discernible by the mind. For the soul, as it were by the
reflected ray[345] of its own contemplation, finds in itself what it
defines. The exemplar[346] of what is defined exists in the mind,
while the example[347] exists among actual things. A similar condition maintains when we say in grammar: "Names which have such
and such an ending are feminine or neuter."[348] A general rule is
laid down, which provides, so to speak, an exemplar for many
declinable words. The examples, in turn, are to be found in all the
words with a given termination. In like manner, certain exemplars
are mentally conceived after their examples have been formed and
presented to the senses by nature. According to Aristotle, these exemplars are conceptual, and are, as it were, images and shadows of
things that really exist. But if one attempts to lay hold of them,
supposing them to have an existence of their own, apart from
particular things, they vanish [into thin air] as do dreams. "For
they are representations,"[349] apparent only to the intellect. When
universals are said to be substantial for individual things, reference
is made to causality in the cognitive order, and to the nature of individual things. It is clear in particular cases that subordinate

[341] *notiones*, concepts, ideas, semblances.

[342] The comma in the Webb text between *speculo* and *natiue* should be omitted. Cf. MSS
A, B, and C, and the sense.

[343] *ennoyas;* see Cicero, *Top.*, 7, § 31; cf. *Tusc. Disp.*, i, 24, § 57.

[344] *yconoyfanas:* MSS C, B, and A have in their margin the gloss: "*ykos: imago; nois:
mens; phanos: apparens,*" indicating the etymology of the word as "image appearing to
the mind."

[345] *reuerberata acie.*

[346] *exemplar*, the image, exemplar.

[347] *exemplum*, the instance, example.

[348] Cf. Priscian, *Inst. Gram.*, v, 3 ff. (Keil, *G.L.*, II, 142 ff.).

[349] *monstra.* This may also be translated, monstrosities, things out of the ordinary course
of nature, marvels. I have translated it as "representations," in view of John's later discussion of *monstra* in this chapter: cf. below. Here John follows the translation of Aristotle's
An. Post., i, 22, 83 a, 33, concerning Platonic ideas, which is attributed to Boethius,
Post. Anal. Interpr., chap. 18 (in Migne, *P.L.*, LXIV, 733). See below concerning the
"new translation," which more correctly gave *cicadationes*, chatter, or mere sounds without
sense. See in this chapter, nn. 436, 437.

things[350] cannot exist or be understood without superior ones.[351] Thus the non-existence of animals would preclude the existence of man [a particular kind of animal]. And we must understand what an "animal" is, in order to understand what "man" is. For man is a certain kind of animal. In the same way "man" is in Plato, as Plato both exists and is understood, though Plato actually is a particular given man. While the idea and existence of animal are postulated by the idea and existence of man, this proposition is not convertible, as the concept and existence of man are not postulated by those of animal. For although the concept of man includes that of animal, the concept of animal does not include that of man. Since, therefore, both essentially and in the order of cognition, a species requires its genus, but is not itself required by its genus, the latter [genus] is said to be substantial for the former [species]. The same [general principle] holds true for individual things, which require [their] species and genus, but are not themselves necessitated by their species and genus. A particular thing cannot possess substance or be known by us, unless it is a [certain] species or genus, that is unless it is some [sort of] thing, or is known as this or that. Despite the fact that universals are called things, and are frequently spoken of as existing, without [any] qualification, neither the physical mass of bodies, nor the tenuity of spirits, nor the distinct essence of particular things is for this reason to be found in them. In a similar way, although matters that are the subject of affirmation or negation are called "things," and we very often say that what is true "is," still we do not classify such as substances or accidents. Neither do we refer to them as "Creator" or "creature." In the mart of the various branches of knowledge, free mutual exchange of words between one discipline and another ought to prevail, as observes Ulger, venerable Bishop of Angers.[352]

[350] *inferiora*, subordinate, of less wide application.

[351] *superioribus*, superior: of wider application.

[352] *Ulgerius* or Ulger was consecrated Bishop of Angers in 1125, and died in 1149. No writings of his are known to be extant, save certain testaments and letters (in Migne, *P.L.*, CLXXX, 1641 ff.). Concerning Ulger, cf. St. Bernard's *Ep.*, 200 to the former, where he says: "the great name of master Ulger"; as also Bernard's *Ep.*, 340 to Pope Innocent II, on behalf of Ulger, "whose old age is made venerable both by his life and his knowledge." Also cf. Sikes, *Peter Abailard*, p. 265; and J. F. E. Raby, *Secular Latin Poetry* (Oxford, 1934), ii, 42.

Liberality reigns in the market place of philosophers,[353] where words may be borrowed without restriction or charge.[354] Accordingly, even if it were granted that universals "exist" and are "things," to please the obstinate, still it would not, on this account, follow that the [total] number of things would be increased or diminished by adding or subtracting universals. If one examines universals, he will find that, while they can be numbered, this number cannot be added to the number of individual things. As with corporate colleges or other bodies, the number of heads cannot be added to that of the bodies, or vice versa, so with universals and particular things, the number of universals cannot be added to that of particular things, or vice versa. Only things of the same sort, which are by nature distinct in each given kind of things, can be numbered together with one another. Nothing can be universal unless it is found in particular things. Despite this, many have sought to find the universal, in itself, apart from individual things. But at the end of their search, they have all come out empty-handed. For the universal, apart from particular things, is not an entity, unless perhaps in the sense that truths and like meanings of combined words are entities. It does not make any difference that particular material things are examples of universal immaterial things, as every mode of activity (according to Augustine) is immaterial and insensible, although what is done, together with the act whereby it is done,[355] is generally perceptible by the senses. That which is understood in a general way by the mind, as pertaining equally to many particular things, and that which is signified in a general way by a word,[356] as referring equally to several beings, is beyond doubt universal. But even the terms "that which is understood," and "that which is signified," must be accepted in a broad manner, and cannot be subjected either to the narrow straits of disputation or to the subtle analysis of the grammatical art. The latter, of its nature, does not allow demonstrative expressions to be

[353] *philosophantium*, those philosophizing, those who seek wisdom.
[354] *distrahuntur ad gratiam.*
[355] *illud . . . quod geritur et actus quo geritur*, the thing done and the act of doing, the object of the activity and the activity itself. Thus the food I eat and the eating of it can be seen; but "eating," as a kind of behavior, is a universal, neither material nor sensible.
[356] For example, a common noun.

unlimited in application, except after one has sought and obtained such permission. Neither does it tolerate relative expressions that are vague. It requires, rather, that the meaning of such expressions be fixed by determining the person, or [his] act, or the action of another. A relative expression is, in fact, one which designates something as the subject of foregoing speech or thought. In the saying: "Wise and happy is the man who has recognized goodness,[357] and has faithfully conformed his actions to this," the relative words "who" and "this," [358] even though they do not designate the specific person [and act], are nevertheless in a way limited, and freed of their indefiniteness, by specification as to how they are to be recognized. There must be someone who corresponds to the statement, someone who, recognizing what is right, has acted accordingly, and is consequently happy. Only in cases where there is a mistake or a figure does it happen that there is nothing sure and definite to which a relative expression refers. Whence if a horse in general [in a generic manner] is promised, and the one to whom the promise was made says: "The horse which is promised to me is either healthy or sickly,[359] since every horse is either healthy or sickly," he is clearly quibbling. For there is no horse that was promised to him. I do not say "There is no horse" because the horse does not or will not exist. Even that which does not exist, such as Arethusa's giving birth to child,[360] may be the subject of a very definite promissory obligation. Rather, I say, "There is no horse," because the promise of a general kind of thing [a generic promise] does not involve the promise of the specific, that is a distinct thing. For when I say "That which is promised," "That which is signified," "That which is understood," and the like, some definite thing is promised or meant if the relation is proper.[361] However, there are also relations that are general [generic], which, if they are to remain true and are to be properly understood, cannot be tied down to some particular subject [the specific]. Examples of such are provided by the sayings: "A woman, both saved [us],

---

[357] Literally: good things.
[358] qui et ea.
[359] The semicolon after est in Webb's edition should evidently be changed to a comma.
[360] partus Arethuse; see Ovid, Met., v, 577 ff.
[361] Proper, particular, special.

and damned [us]"; "A tree both bore the cause of our death, and
that of our life"; "The green leaves, which the freezing north wind
bears off, the mild west wind restores." [362] In the instances which I
have just mentioned, I believe that these relative expressions should
not be conceived as descending to the specific, and pointing out
some particular person or thing, but rather that they should be
understood as remaining general [generic]. In brief, what is signified by the noun "man" is a species, because man is signified, and
man is a special kind [363] of animal. What is signified by the word
"animal" is a genus, as an animal is signified, and an animal is
a general [generic] kind of thing. [364] For what is signified by a
word is that to which it directly refers, or that which the mind
reasonably conceives on hearing the word. When one hears the
word "man," one does not mentally run through all men, for this
would be a task both endless and impossible. Neither does he
restrict his concept to one particular man, for this would be inadequate, and would not really correspond to the meaning of the
term. [365] Likewise, when one defines an animal as a substance possessing life and the power of sensation, one is not simply describing
a single particular animal, lest his definition be incomplete. Neither
is he trying to give a description of every animal, lest his labor be
endless. Each of these universals signifies or defines, not merely
"what," [366] but rather "what kind of what," [367] not merely a given
[particular] thing, [368] but rather a certain kind of thing. [369] Thus
Galen, in his *Techne*, [370] defines medicine as "the science of health-
ful, unhealthful, and intermediate [371] things." He does not say "the

---

[362] A woman, namely, Mary, brought about human salvation, but another, namely, Eve,
occasioned human damnation. A tree, namely, the tree of knowledge, gave us the cause of
death, yet another, the cross of Christ, bore for us the source of life. The cold north wind
takes away green leaves in winter, the warm west wind restores green leaves in the
springtime.

[363] Literally: a species.

[364] Literally: a genus of things.

[365] *doctrinam*, the teaching, meaning, sense, or message intended; the instruction.

[366] *non simpliciter quid.*

[367] *quale quid.*

[368] *non simpliciter hoc.*

[369] *quid tale.*

[370] *Galienus in Tegni*, namely, Galen in his Τέχνη ἰατρική or *Ars Medica*. See Galen, *Ars
medica*, chaps. 1–2 (ed. Kuhn, *Med. graec. op.*, I, 307–313).

[371] *neutroum*, neutral, intermediate, neither healthy nor unhealthy.

science of everything," since this would be infinite. Neither does
he say "the science of certain [particular] things," since this would
be inadequate for the definition of an art. Rather, he defines medicine as the science of a given kind of things.[372] Aristotle tells us:[373]
"Genera and species determine the kind[374] of a substance. They
do not merely designate 'what,' but, in a way, 'what kind of a
thing.'" In like vein, Aristotle declares in his *Elenchi:*[375] "General
terms, such as 'man,' do not denote some particular thing, but
rather a certain kind of thing, or [a thing in] some sort of relation
to something, or something like this."[376] A little further on he says:
"It is evident that a general, universal predication [concerning
things of a class] is not to be understood as referring to some particular thing, but rather as signifying quality, relation, quantity, or
something of the sort."[377] In fact, what is not a particular thing
cannot be described in detail.[378] Real things[379] have from nature
certain limitations, and are distinguished from one another by their
properties, even though frequently our knowledge of them is not
very definite, and our concept of them rather vague. The well-
known principle that what common names mean and what they
name are not identical, does not militate against what has just been
said. For their meaning is universal, even though they name particular things. Evidently, if one looks only for a simple general relationship, he will have no trouble understanding the foregoing, but
if he insists on trying to find the precise determination of some
individual thing, he may well be at a loss to put his finger on anything of the sort. There is a rule that[380] "Demonstrative expressions provide primary cognition, relative expressions knowledge of
a secondary kind."[381] In fact [our] cognition, in apprehending

[372] *quorum qualium.*
[373] Aristotle, *Cat.,* 5, 3 b, 20.
[374] *qualitatem,* quality, kind, or nature.
[375] Aristotle, *Soph. El.,* chap. 22, 178 b, 37 ff.
[376] Webb's text should here read: *sed quale quid, uel ad aliquid aliquo modo uel huiusmodi quid significat.* Cf. MSS C, B, and A.
[377] Aristotle, *Soph. El.,* chap. 22, 179 a, 8 ff.
[378] Literally: cannot be explained by express signification.
[379] Literally: existing things.
[380] *Regulariter proditum est,* It is stated as a rule (of grammar); it is a (grammatical) rule.
[381] Priscian, *Inst.,* xii, 4 (Keil, *G.L.,* II, 579). *secundam . . . cognitionem,* secondary cognition, knowledge of a secondary or indirect kind.

something, circumscribes and defines the latter for itself by a certain [comprehensive] capacity of the mind, so that if a thing presents itself to the mind as absolutely unlimited in every respect, neither primary nor secondary cognition can proceed. All knowledge or cognition possessed by creatures is limited. Infinite knowledge belongs solely to God, because of His infinite nature.[382] However limitless things may be, they are at the same time most certainly circumscribed by His infinite immensity, and defined by His boundless knowledge and wisdom, which cannot be counted and have no limit.[383] But we are imprisoned within the petty dimensions of our human capacity, wherefore we attain neither primary, nor secondary, nor tertiary, nor any distinction of knowledge of what is infinite, save the realization that it is unknown because it is infinite. Accordingly, all demonstrative and relative expressions must refer to a specific, definite subject if they are correctly posited. Otherwise they will miss their mark. For cognition naturally seeks or possesses certitude as its object. However, language is often conscripted to serve in extraordinary senses,[384] and frequently incorrect expressions are used as a matter of convenience. Thus the axiom that "All men love themselves," [385] is generally accepted, not merely to provide material for the pedantic bickering of those who are content to chatter on any sort of topic that permits disputation, but also to convey knowledge of a truth to hearers who are in good faith. However, if one analyzes this principle according to the strict and proper meaning of a relative expression, one will perhaps charge that it is improperly stated and false. For it is evident that all men do not love all men. Neither do all men love any given man. So whether the expression: "all men," be understood collectively or distributively, the relative pronoun "themselves," which follows, cannot correctly be understood as referring either to every man or to any one man. The relation [here] is accordingly not a strict one. Begging, as it were, indulgent forgiveness from its own

[382] Cf. Augustine, *De C.D.*, xii, 19.
[383] See Psalms, cxlvi, 5.
[384] *Frequens tamen est usurpatio*, There is frequent abuse, misuse, or forcible conscription of language . . .
[385] *omnis homo diliget se.*

rule, it refutes the reliability of the universal with reference to the truth of particular things. While it is true in individual cases that everyone loves himself, and this is affirmed of all men in general in a distributive sense by the saying that "all men love themselves," the relation is to be understood in a broad and free way. It should not be taken in a narrow, grammatical sense, whereby it would either compass all men, or single out some particular individual from this universality. Hence, according to those who always seize upon difficulties and subtleties, and decline to use good faith as their principle in [interpreting] conversation or reading, this is "a form of statement" rather than "a statement of regular form." They also assert the same whenever a pronoun refers to a common noun, since a pronoun, which is always demonstrative or relative, stands in the place of a proper noun, at least when it correctly fulfils the purpose for which it was originally invented. For occasionally, by indulgence, pronouns have a wider meaning.[386] Thus, when it is said that "If a being is a man, it[387] is also an animal," we have not so much a consequence in a hypothetical statement, as a form of a consequence when something is expressed in a hypothetical manner. For the word "it," according to the strict laws of disputation,[388] does not refer to a man. Nor can we see any definite thing to which it may be referred. Whence come many meaningless and vexatious objections, raised by such as delight in harassing the ignorant and those of a more liberal and less petty disposition. Such tireless wranglers, who refuse to desist from their stubborn objections [must] do so out of either ignorance, or perversity, or greed. Just as cognition seeks certitude, so demonstrative and relative expressions, which convey either primary or other cognition, depend on certain and definite subjects, which such expressions, when they are properly employed, present to our mind as particular things. Let us suppose that common names signify some general status (for I have already declared [389] that I side with the Academicians in regard to things that are doubtful to a wise man, and that I do not

---

[386] Priscian, Inst., xii, 3 (Keil, *G.L.*, II, 578).
[387] *illud*, that.
[388] *ex angustia disputandi.*
[389] In *Policraticus*, vii, 2.

care for contentious argumentation). Although I can somehow dream of a status wherein particular things are united, yet [wherein] no particular thing exists, I am still at a loss to see how this can be reconciled with the opinion of Aristotle, who contends that universals do not exist. Even the designations "incorporeal" and "insensible," which, as I have previously mentioned, are appropriate for universals, are only privative[390] with reference to them. They do not attribute to universals any properties whereby the nature of the latter may be ascertained. For a universal is not an incorporeal or insensible thing. Something that is incorporeal is either a spirit or the property of a body or spirit. As universals are neither of these, they cannot strictly be called incorporeal. What incorporeal thing is not a substance created by God, or something united with a substance created by God? If universals were incorporeal [things], they would either be substances, that is, bodies or spirits, or things in composition with the same. They would depend on the Creator as the cause of their existence and the originator and support[391] of their substance. For they would bid farewell and vanish, were they not subject to Him. "By Him, all things were made"[392] to be what they are called from their qualities or effects, whether they are the subjects of forms or the forms of subjects. If a substance is a substance made by the Creator, it must have a certain size, kind, and existence relative to something else, in a given place at a specific time. It must also possess, do, or undergo something, with Him as author through Whom exists every substance and property of a substance, every part or combination of parts. Substantial and accidental forms alike receive from Him their existence and power to produce certain effects in their subjects. If anything exists, it is [necessarily] dependent on Him. The Stoics suppose that matter is coeternal with God, and maintain that form had no beginning. They posit three principles: matter, form, and God, saying that the latter is not indeed the Creator, but only the conciliator of the aforesaid.[393] Others, who, although they profess and affect to be

---

[390] *priuatiua*, privative, negative.
[391] *quodam . . . contactu.*
[392] John, i, 3.
[393] See Seneca, *Ep.*, 65.

philosophers, by no means attain full cognition of the truth, falsely maintain that there are even more principles. Notwithstanding, there is but one principle of all things, from Whom has proceeded everything that is correctly considered and called something. As Augustine says,[394] "God has created matter possessing [given] form."[395] Although matter is sometimes spoken of as "formless,"[396] it has never existed utterly destitute of form. Reason is subservient to inquiry rather than to actuality. Ylen,[397] which neither exists, nor can exist, nor can be fully understood without form, is, by our intellect, relentlessly divested, so to speak, of the forms wherewith it is attired, and stripped down to its own particular nudity and deficiency. But the strength of reason seemingly melts when confronted by the [first] principles of things.[398] Hence it is that Boethius, defining "nature" in his book *Against Nestorius and Eutyches,* says that it "pertains to things, which, since they exist, may, at least in some way, be understood by the intellect."[399] Explaining the force of the expression "at least in some way,"[400] used in his definition, Boethius states that this qualification is included because of God and matter, since in the investigation of the latter the human intellect is deficient. Indeed, God made matter from nothing, while form, likewise simultaneously created from nothing, is united[401] with this matter, in such a way that, just as the privilege of determination is granted to the form, so that of existence is accorded to the matter. Thus, in a way, the form exists through the matter, while conversely the matter is determined by the form. Neither does the form exist of itself,[402] nor would the matter be determinate without the form. Chaos would reign, or rather the sensible world would come to an end, if nature did not compose the figures of things by means of forms. To the point here is what Boethius says

[394] See Augustine, *De Gen. ad Litt.,* i, 15 (in Migne, *P.L.,* XXXIV, 257).
[395] *informatam,* having form.
[396] *informis,* lacking form, without form. Cf. Wisdom, xi, 18.
[397] *ylen* (from the Greek ὕλη), matter, prime matter.
[398] *rerum principia.*
[399] Boethius, *Lib. contra Nestorium et Euticen,* chap. i (ed. Peiper, p. 189).
[400] *quoquo modo.*
[401] *concreta,* grown together, joined, united.
[402] *per se.*

in the first part of his work *On the Trinity:*[403] "Every existence is the result of a form." This proposition he clarifies by examples. "A statue," he points out, "is so called, not because of the bronze,[404] the matter whereof it is made, but because of the form of Hector or Achilles, into which the bronze has been molded. The bronze itself is called bronze, not from the earth, which is its matter, but from the forms allotted it by nature. Even earth itself obtains its name, not from *poutou yle,* its matter, but from dryness and weight, its forms." To its form everything, accordingly, owes the fact that it is what it is, possesses such and such qualities, and has this or that quantity. Just as matter has the potentiality of becoming something of a certain size and kind, so forms have from their Creator the power of making this or that, for example, an animal or a tree, or something of a given size and kind. It is true that mathematics, which deals theoretically[405] with abstractions, and in its subtle analysis separates things that are united in nature, treats matter and form apart from one another, so that the nature of what is composite may be more accurately and definitely understood. Still, the one cannot exist apart from the other, as [in this case] either matter would be without form, or form would lack a subject and hence be ineffective. "Even so the one requires the assistance of the other, and they work together in friendly fashion." [406] It is recorded [407] that in[408] the beginning, heaven and earth were created, and then their[409] various embellishments were created and interposed between the fire and water, which God had, so to speak, established as the first foundations of the world's body. In this account, reference is made to species. I do not refer here to the sort of "species" which logicians have dreamt of as being independent of the Creator. I speak rather of the forms in which things have been born,

---

[403] Boethius, *De Trin.,* chap. 2 (ed. Peiper, pp. 152, 153).

[404] *ere: aere,* bronze, or copper; here apparently bronze.

[405] *doctrinaliter,* in doctrine, teaching, or theory. Isidore in his *Etym.,* ii, 24, § 14, says: "A science which considers abstract quantity is called doctrinal," and lists Arithmetic, Geometry, Astronomy; and Music, namely, the Quadrivium, as the *doctrinales scientie.*

[406] Horace, *A.P.,* 410, 411.

[407] Genesis, i.

[408] Literally: from.

[409] *tam eorum quam illorum,* literally: both of these and of those.

first in their own essence, and subsequently in our human understanding. The very fact that we call something "heaven" or
"earth" [410] is due to its form. It is likewise said that "The earth
brought forth the green grass and the various kinds of trees." [411]
This shows that forms are united to matter, and also teaches that
God is the author, not only of the grass, but also of its greenness.
"Without Him, nothing was made." [412] And verily whatever comes
from the one principle, not only is one in number, but also is itself
good, yea, "exceedingly good." [413] For it proceeds from the supreme
good. God willed to make all things similar to Himself, so far as
the nature of each was, by His divinely established order, receptive
of goodness. [414] And so, in the approving judgment of the Divine
Artisan, all the things which He had made were "exceedingly
good." [415] If genera and species do not proceed from God, they are
nothing. But if each of them does proceed from Him, it is certainly
one, and likewise good. And if a thing is numerically one, it is
forthwith singular. The fact that some people call a thing "one"
simply because it unites several things by expressing their conformity, although it is not one in itself, does not contradict our
point. In the latter case, what is called "one" is neither immediately
nor adequately one. If it were, it would be singular. However
similar God's works may be, they are singular and distinct, one
from another. Such is the arrangement decreed by Him, Who has
created all things in number for their differentiation, in "weight" [416]
for their generic value, [417] and in measure for their quantitative
determination, [418] all the while reserving to Himself universal
authority. All things other than God are finite. Every substance is
subject to number because it has just so many, and no more accidents. Every accident and every form is likewise subject to number,

[410] *aliquid celum aut terra.*
[411] Genesis, i, 12; cf. Augustine, *De Gen. ad Litt.*, ii, 12, for wording (*protulit, produxit*).
[412] John, i, 3.
[413] Genesis, i, 31.
[414] Cf. Plato, *Tim.*, 29 E, in the version of Chalcidius.
[415] Genesis, i, 31.
[416] *pondere*, weight, force, value. From what is said later, John seems to regard
pondus or weight in its more general sense, including value.
[417] *ad generis dignitatem,* for the dignity or value of their kind or genus.
[418] Cf. Wisdom, xi, 21.

although in this case because of the singular nature of its subject, rather than a participation of accidents or forms. Everything also has its own "weight," either according to the respect due its form, if it is a substance, or according to the worth of its effects, if it is a form. Hence it is that, in comparing substances, we place man above the brute animals, out of esteem for his form, which is rational, as we deem external appearance[419] less important than rationality, which provides the ability to reason. Measure, for its part, consists in the fact that everything has no more than a certain quantity. An accident or form cannot exceed the limits of its subject, and the subject itself cannot be greater than its accidents or form allow. The "color" of a body is both diffused throughout the whole body, and bounded by the external surfaces of the latter. On the other hand, the body itself extends only as far as its "color," neither going beyond, nor stopping short of the latter. In like manner, every subject is considered to extend as far as its accidents, while every accident which pertains to an entire subject exists complete throughout its whole subject, or if it pertains only to a part of the subject, it exists solely in that part. I do not hesitate to affirm that either genera and species are from God, or they are nothing at all; and I would do so even if the whole world were to hold the opposite. Dionysius the Areopagite makes clear that he holds the same view, and says that the number whereby all things are distinguished, the "weight" wherein they are established, and the measure wherewith they are limited, image God.[420] For, of a truth, God is number innumerable, weight incalculable, and measure inestimable. And in Him alone all things that have been made in number, in "weight," and in measure, have been created.[421] Whence Augustine says: "The invisible differences of invisible things are determinable only by Him, Who has ordained all things in [their] number, weight, and measure, and in Him, Who is measure, fixing the extent of all things; number, giving everything its specific existence;[422] and "weight," drawing each entity to a

[419] *colori*, color, complexion, general aspect.
[420] *Dionisius Ariopagita;* see *De Div. Nomin.*, chap. 4, § 4, in the version of John Scotus.
[421] Cf. Augustine, *De Gen. ad Litt.*, iv, 3, 4, 5 (in Migne, *P.L.*, XXXIV, 299, 300).
[422] *speciem*, species, individual existence.

stable existence, or, in other words, delimiting, forming, and ordering all things.[423] In the account of the works of the six days [of creation], although we read that all good things were created, each according to its own kind, we find no allusion whatsoever to universals.[424] Nor could there properly be such, if universals are essentially united with particular things, or [even] if the Platonic doctrine[425] is correct. Furthermore, I cannot remember ever having read anywhere whence universals have derived existence, or when they have originated. According to Aristotle, universals are only understood, and there is no actual thing that is universal. These representations[426] have licitly, and for instructional purposes,[427] been given names that denote the way in which they are understood. It is true that every man is this or that [particular] man, that is to say, an individual. But "man" can be understood in such a way that neither this nor that [given] man, nor any being that is one in the singularity of its essence, is understood. And by means of this concept we can reason about man in general,[428] that is man in general can be actually represented because of the general nature of the intellect. Accordingly, something that can be so understood, even though it may not be [at a given time actually] understood by anyone, is said to be general.[429] For [certain] things resemble one another, and our intellect, abstracting from consideration of the [particular] things themselves, considers this conformity. One man has the same form as another, inasmuch as they are both men, even though they [assuredly] differ in their personal qualities. Man also has in common with the horse (from which he differs completely in species, that is, in the whole form of his nature, and so to speak, in his entire appearance) [430] that they both live and have sensation, or, in other words, that they are both animals. That in which men, who are alike in the form of their nature, and distinct only in number (whereby so and so is one, and so and so another man),

[423] Cf. Augustine, *loc. cit.*
[424] Cf. Genesis, i.
[425] According to which universals are eternal.
[426] *figuralia.*
[427] *doctrinaliter,* in the interests of teaching and learning.
[428] Literally: "the subject," which in view of the foregoing, is man in general.
[429] *communis,* general, common, universal.
[430] *facie.*

correspond, is called their "species." And that which is, so to speak, a general image of various forms, is known as "genus." Therefore, in Aristotle's judgment,[431] genera and species are not merely "what" [things are], but also are, in a way, conceptions of "what kind of what" [432] [they are]. They are, as it were, fictions, employed by [human] reason as it delves deeper[433] in its investigation and explanation of things. Reason does this validly, for, whenever there is need, it can point to a manifest example in the world of reality to substantiate its concepts. Civil law does likewise, and has its own fictions. So, in fact, do all branches of learning, which unhesitatingly devise fictions to expedite their investigations. Each of them even, in a way, prides itself on its own special figments. "We may dispense with forms," [434] says Aristotle[435] "for they are representations (or, according to a new translation:[436] chatter[437]) and even if they did exist, they would have no bearing on our discussion." Although Aristotle may be understood as referring here to Platonic ideas, genera and species may still both, not without reason, be said to "exist," if one bears in mind the diverse meanings of which "being" and "existence" are susceptible when applied to various subjects. For our reason prompts us to say that things exist, when we can see that they are exemplified by particular instances, of whose existence no one can doubt. It is not because genera and species are exemplary forms in the Platonic sense, "and existed as concepts in the Divine mind before they emanated into entities of the external physical world," [438] that they are said to be exemplars of particular things. It is rather because, when one looks for an example of what is represented in a general way by [e.g.] the

---

[431] Aristotle, *Cat.*, 5, 3 b, 20.

[432] *non omnino quid sit, sed quale quid.*

[433] *subtilius.*

[434] *species*, forms: said of the Platonic forms or ideas: *species* and *forma* are renderings of the same Greek word, *eidos.*

[435] Aristotle, *An. Post.*, i, 22, 83 a, 33.

[436] *nouam translationem;* see Webb's Prolegomena to his edition of the *Policraticus*, pp. xxiii–xxvii. Cf. V. Rose, "Die Lücke im Diogenes Laertius und der alte Uebersetzer," *Hermes*, i, p. 383; C. H. Haskins, *Mediaeval Science*, p. 236.

[437] *cicadationes*, literally: the shrill noises of the cicadae (large insects common in southern countries); hence, chatter or sounds without sense.

[438] Priscian, *Inst. Gram.*, xvii, § 44 (Keil, *G.L.*, III, 135). Cf. Abelard, *Introd. ad Theol.*, ii (in *Opp.*, ed. Cousin, II, p. 109; cf. II, p. 14).

word "man," and what is defined when we say [e.g.] that "man is a mortal rational animal," forthwith Plato or some other particular man can be pointed out, in order firmly to establish the general meaning or definition. Genera and species may be called "representations," because on the one hand they represent particular things, and, on the other, they are represented by the latter. Things are made manifest sometimes by what is prior, sometimes by what is posterior. More general things are, in themselves, prior, for they are also understood in other things; while particular things are posterior. Frequently, however, things which are naturally prior, and of themselves more properly objects of knowledge, are actually less known by us. The more solidly substantial things are, the more readily we can recognize them with our senses; the more subtile they become, the more difficult it is to perceive them. As Aristotle observes, "The point is prior to, and in itself more evident than the line. The same may be said of the line relative to the plane surface, and of the plane surface with reference to the solid. It is likewise true of unity in relation to plurality, for which unity is the principle. This also holds in regard to the letter relative to the syllable." The foregoing list could be extended. [Aristotle continues:] "The reverse, however, sometimes occurs in the case of our knowledge. Generally the average mind more readily perceives what is posterior, whereas the comprehension of what is prior is reserved to the more profound and learned intellect."[439] Whence, even though it is true that what is posterior is best defined by what is prior, and this is always more scientific,[440] still, frequently, of necessity, and to provide subject matter within the ken of our senses,[441] what is prior is actually explained by what is posterior. A point is thus said to be the end of a line; a line, the edge of a surface; a surface, the side of a solid. In like manner, unity is said to be the elementary principle of number, the moment that of time, the letter that of speech. Genera and species are accordingly exemplars of particular things, but rather as instruments of learning[442] than as essential

[439] Aristotle, *Top.*, vi, 4, 141b, 5 ff.
[440] *disciplinabilius.*
[441] Literally: because of the impotence of our senses.
[442] Literally: for "doctrinal purposes."

causes of particular things. And this representative[443] (to use the
term with considerable license) contemplation of fictions even goes
to the extent of completely dispensing with[444] the consideration of
individual things. Since every substance is comprised of its own
properties, the same collection of which is not found in any other
substance, the abstracting intellect proceeds to consider each thing
as it is in itself.[445] Although Plato could not exist without form,
and divorced from place or time, reason regards him as, so to
speak, "nude," stripped of his quantity, quality, and other accidents.
It thus gives the individual a [common] name.[446] This, it must be
admitted, is a fiction, designed to expedite learning and deeper
inquiry.[447] No such thing [as "man" in general] can actually be
found. Still, the concept of "man" in general is a valid act of
understanding. This is perhaps why, in the *Analytics,* we find the
statement: "Aristomenes is always intelligible, even though Aristomenes does not always exist, as he must one day disintegrate." [448]
What is uniquely individual can only, according to some, be predicated of a certain subject.[449] Plato, [as] the son of Aristides,[450] is
individual neither in quantity, as an atom, nor by solidity, as a
diamond, nor even, so they say, by predication. I, personally, neither
strongly oppose nor sponsor this opinion. Nor do I think that it is
a matter of moment, since I advocate recognition of the fact that
words may be used in various senses.[451] This is, I believe, an indispensable condition, if one is accurately to understand what authors
mean. What is there to forbid lest, just as a genus may, with truth,
be predicated of its species, so this particular Plato, perceptible by
the senses, may, with truth, be predicated of the son of Aristides,
if he is Aristides' only son. Then, just as man is an animal, so the

---

[443] *monstruosa,* see *monstra* (n. 349, above), to which reference is evidently made.
[444] *uentilationem,* literally airing, winnowing, minute analysis, elimination.
[445] This may also be translated: The activity of the abstracting intellect contemplates each
thing in general, namely, the essences of things.
[446] Namely, in the case of Plato, the name "man."
[447] *subtilioris agitationis,* of more subtle or intensive (mental) application or investigation.
[448] In other words, Aristomenes, as an object of thought, is eternal; but Aristomenes
himself is not eternal, since he is perishable. Aristotle, *An. Prior.,* i, 33, 47 b, 21 ff.
[449] *Et hoc quidem est singulariter indiuiduum, quod solum quidam aiunt posse de aliquo
predicari.* The translator is not absolutely certain of the sense of this.
[450] This should be Ariston (*Aristonis*).
[451] *indifferentiam in uicissitudine sermonum.*

son of Aristides[452] is Plato. Some believe that this was what Aristotle meant when he said in his *Analytics:* "Of all the things that exist, some[453] are such that they cannot be predicated of anything else with true universality. Such is the case, for example, with Cleon and Callias, as well as with whatever is singular and perceptible by the senses. However, other things may be predicated of them, as each [Cleon, Callias] is both a man and an animal. Some things are themselves predicated of other things, but other things that are prior are not predicated of them. With certain things, however, it is true that both they themselves are predicated of other things, and other things are predicated of them. Thus, for example, man is predicated of Callias, while, in turn, animal is predicated of man. Certain things which exist are clearly fated by their nature not to be predicated of anything. Almost all sensible things fall in this category, and cannot be predicated of anything save as accidents, as when we say, 'That white figure is Socrates'; and 'That object approaching [in the distance] is Callias.' "[454] This distribution would seem entirely out of place if a sensible thing could not be predicated. But while the latter is predicated of something else, it is predicated only as an accident. If it could not be predicated as an accident concerning itself or something else, what Aristotle says would be false, and his example would be pointless. And if a sensible thing could not be made the subject of a predication, then, doubtless, Aristotle would be either lying or talking nonsense. Here, as elsewhere, Aristotle has proceeded in the manner which one should use in teaching the liberal arts, and has discussed his subject in a greatly simplified fashion,[455] so that he may [more easily] be understood. Accordingly, he has not introduced into genera and species a difficulty which the doctors themselves are unable to understand, much less to explain to others. The statement found in the *Topics* that "In the case of animals, all differences must be either species or individuals, since every animal is either a species

---

[452] Literally: that man (the son of Aristides, or Ariston).

[453] Literally: these.

[454] Aristotle, *An. Prior.,* i, 27, 43 a, 25 ff.

[455] *Minerua pinguiora,* literally: Minerva being lazy, wisdom lagging; hence, with simplicity, without subtlety; cf. Cicero, *De Amic.,* 5, § 19.

or an individual," [456] exemplifies the sovereignty of this principle of simplicity. Similar simplification is found in the statement of Boethius that "Every species is its own genus." [457] For every man is an animal, and all whiteness is color. By the same token, what prevents sensible things being predicated, or made the subject of predications, in like extended sense? I do not believe that the authors have so done violence to words as to tie them down to a single meaning in all contexts. Rather, I am confident that they express their teachings so as always to serve understanding, which is highly adaptable [to varying meanings], and which reason requires should be here the first and foremost consideration. Predication has several different meanings, which vary according to the context. Still it probably everywhere denotes some sort of conformity or intrinsic connection. For when a word shows an aptness to be joined with another word in the terms of a true affirmation, and when a word is said to be predicated of a thing, it is evident that such an appellation must suit it. At times, to predicate something about a thing denotes that the latter is such and such, as when we say that Plato is a man. At other times, such predication denotes that the subject partakes of something, as for instance that a subject has a certain accident. I do not have any misgivings about declaring that a thing may be predicated of a thing in a proposition, even though the thing is not [explicitly stated] in the proposition. For a thing may be signified by the predicate term of a true affirmation, in whose subject some [given] thing is involved or signified. In fine, instead of fighting against what is written, [458] I believe that we should accept [and try to understand] it in a friendly manner. Our policy should be to admit the liberal interpretation of words that are susceptible of more than one meaning. [459] It is unbefitting a reader or listener to snap like a dog [460] at every figure of speech, [461]

---

[456] Aristotle, *Top.*, vi, 6, 144b, 1 ff.

[457] Boethius frequently teaches this; e.g., *In Porph. Dial.*, i (in Migne, *P.L.*, LXIV, 39).

[458] *littere*, the letter, things written.

[459] *licentioris uerbi indifferentia.*

[460] *dentem exercere caninum;* cf. Jerome, *Ep.*, I, § I. This may also be translated: to gnash his teeth.

[461] *translationem*, transfer (of meaning), figure of speech, metaphor.

or employment[462] of what is deemed poor diction.[463] "Become used to what is hard to bear, and you will bear it." [464] Certainly one is rash, ungrateful, and imprudent if he contradicts his teacher at every turn, and refuses to agree with him on any point. Let us fall [gracefully] into step, therefore, with the figurative speech used by the authors, and let us weigh whatever they say in the light of the causes behind their saying it.[465] In this way we will arrive at an accurate understanding of what they have written. Thus the word "thing" may admit of a wider extension, whereby it may apply to universals, even though Aristotle says that the latter are to be understood as abstracted from particular things in such a way that they would have no existence in the absence of the aforesaid. But those who maintain that genus is numerically one assert the independent existence of universals, according to Aristotle.[466] This they do who suppose the [separate] existence of forms, that is to say "ideas." Aristotle vigorously opposed this doctrine, together with its author, Plato, whenever he had the opportunity. It is true that a great host of philosophers, including not only Augustine,[467] but also several of our contemporaries,[468] have [adopted and] championed Plato's doctrine of ideas. Still we by no means follow Plato in his analysis of the nature of universals. On this question we acknowledge Aristotle, the prince of the Peripatetics,[469] as the master. To judge between the opinions of such great men is a tremendous matter, a task which Boethius in his second commentary on Porphyry,[470] declares to be beyond his abilities.[471] But one embarking upon a study of the works of the Peripatetics, should accept the judgment of Aristotle, if not because it is truer, then certainly because it will serve him better in his studies. Those who

[462] *usurpationem.*
[463] *discole.*
[464] Ovid, *Art. Am.,* ii, 647.
[465] Cf. Hilary, *De Trin.,* iv, 14. Also see *Met.,* i, 19 (47, 8); and iii, 2 (125, 16).
[466] John may here be confusing Aristotle with Boethius, *Comm. in Porph.,* i (in Migne, *P.L.,* LXIV, 83).
[467] Augustine, *De Div. Quaest.,* lxxxiii, 46 (in Migne, *P.L.,* XL, 29 ff.).
[468] *nostrorum,* of ours: of our contemporaries, or of our fellow Christians.
[469] *Peripateticorum principem Aristotilem,* Aristotle is so called by Boethius, *Comm. in Arist. de Interpr.,* iii, 9 (ed. Meiser, p. 193).
[470] Namely, toward the end of the first book (Migne, *P.L.,* LXIV, 86).
[471] Literally: too difficult or trying.

declare that genera and species are merely word sounds or word concepts, as well as those who are led astray by other of the aforesaid opinions in their investigations, have all alike obviously strayed far afield from Aristotle's teaching. Indeed, they diverge from his views even more childishly and stupidly than do the followers of Plato, whose opinion[472] they will not even deign to recognize. I believe that what we have said should suffice to show that those who review every opinion that has ever been advanced concerning genera and species, in order to disagree with all of them, and at length establish some plausibility for their own [pet] notion, are neither [really] trying to explain Porphyry with accuracy, nor treating what is introductory in a suitable manner. Such a procedure, entirely foreign to the mind of the author, dulls the mental faculties of students, and usurps time that ought to be given to the study of other points whose knowledge is equally necessary.

END OF BOOK TWO

[472] That is, the opinion of Plato, as above.

ßooĸ Tʜʀєє

[PROLOGUE]

Almost twenty years have elapsed[1] since I was forced to forsake the workshop and gymnasium [or school] of the logicians because of straitened circumstances, and the advice of friends whom I could not disregard. Since then, to confess the truth as I myself know it,[2] not once have I consulted the writings of the dialecticians. Not even in passing have I glanced at their treatises on the arts, or commentaries, or glossaries, wherein this science [of logic] is begotten, preserved, and revised. Meanwhile, I have been preoccupied with other concerns, which have been, not merely diverse from, but even well nigh diametrically opposed to dialectic. I have hardly been able to find time to philosophize even an hour, and then only by dint of snatching [occasional] moments like a thief. Leaving England,[3] I have crossed the Alps [no less than] ten times,[4] journeyed to Apulia twice, and repeatedly handled negotiations with the Roman Church for my superiors and friends. I have, also, on numerous occasions, traveled about Gaul as well as England, in connection with various cases which have arisen. A host of business concerns, numerous responsibilities, and the pressure of work that had to be done have consumed all my attention, and have left me no time for learning. Hence I hope that my reader will see fit to pardon me for parts of this work that may seem somewhat dull or crude. The dryness of my tongue and the slowness of my wits are due partly to the facts I have mentioned

[1] Namely, by 1159. John apparently left Paris and went to Chartres about 1139. Cf. *Met.*, ii, 10.

[2] *ut ex animi mei sententia uerum fatear.*

[3] Or: After I left England [the first time], according to Webb, *ad loc.*

[4] John evidently made "round trips" to Italy five times: in 1146–1147, 1148–1153, 1155–1156, and 1158–1159. See R. L. Poole, "The Early Correspondence of John of Salisbury," *Proceedings of the British Academy*, XI (1924–1925), 50 and 51; and *idem*, "John of Salisbury at the Papal Court," *English Historical Review*, XXXVIII (1923), 321 ff.

above, partly to my responsibilities in the court, partly to the deceit and effrontery of my adversary,[5] who has goaded and provoked me, unarmed and reluctant though I am, to make some sort of rebuttal. The saying of the moral poet has been fulfilled in me:

> Age makes off with everything, even one's mind:
> I remember how, as a boy, I used to sing the whole day through;
> But today I can no longer recall the many songs I once knew,
> And even his voice itself now fails Moeris.[6]

Would it not, therefore, be unjust to expect of me the mental spryness of youth, the quick comprehension of glowing natural talent, and an exact memory, always sure of itself? Immersed in a busy turmoil of affairs, I have reached an age at which one is occupied only with more serious things, except so far as this seriousness may be diminished or extinguished by the infirmity of the flesh or the negligence of the spirit, or[7] the malice which has flamed up from these as a result of the smoldering fire of sin.[8] Just as that virtue which is out of proportion to tender youth is acknowledged, so that virtue which does not desert those who are becoming feeble with age is also acceptable. Ascanius won renown because, while yet a mere boy, he overcame Numanus.[9] On the other hand, the veteran[10] Entellus, as an old man, increased his repute by vanquishing Dares, who was famous for many victories.[11] It is a wonderful thing to see virtue victorious over nature. But although I am already a deserving veteran, who should rightfully be exempt from attack, because of both my age and my state of life, I am in a way dragged into the arena, and forced to engage again in combats, which I had [long ago] set aside, and to which I am no longer used. I find myself confronted with the dire and harsh alternative of either fighting, inexpedient as this may be, or

---

[5] The adversary John has already discussed under the name of "Cornificius" in Book I.

[6] Vergil, *Ecl.*, ix, 51–54.

[7] *aut* should be here inserted, between *spiritus* and *ex*, in the Webb edition of the *Metalogicon* (118, 5). Cf. MSS A, B, and C.

[8] *fomitem peccati* is a technical phrase hard to translate precisely, though "smoldering fire of sin" gives the idea.

[9] Vergil, *Aen.*, ix, 590 ff.

[10] *emerito*, a veteran (like a professor emeritus).

[11] Vergil, *Aen.*, v, 362 ff.

surrendering, and, by so doing, acquiescing to foul falsehood.
The second possibility is utterly abhorrent. I have refused to become an accomplice in evil, to which alone, or above all else, philosophizing is opposed. Because I lack sufficient weapons[12] of my
own, I make use of those of all my friends without distinction. I
am not, as [some of] our contemporaries, contemptuous of the
means that are here and now at hand.[13] Rather I employ the latter
with greater confidence, so far as I am more certain that they are
the gifts of faithful friends. The truth of things endures, impervious to corruption. Something that is true in itself does not melt
into thin air, simply because it is stated by a new author. Who,
indeed, except someone who is foolish or perverse, would consider an opinion authoritative, merely because it was stated by
Coriscus,[14] Bryso,[15] or Melissus?[16] All of the latter are alike obscure,
except so far as Aristotle has used their names in his examples.
And who, except the same sort of person, will reject a proposition
simply because it has been advanced by Gilbert,[17] Abelard,[18] or
our own Adam?[19] I do not agree with those who spurn the good
things of their own day, and begrudge recommending their contemporaries to posterity. None of the latter [none of our contem-
poraries] has, so far as I know, held that there is no such thing
as a contradiction.[20] None of them has denied the existence of
movement and asserted that the stadium is not traversed.[21] None
of them has maintained that the earth moves[22] because all things
are in motion, as did Heraclitus,[23] who, as Martianus puns, is red
hot, because he is all afire, since he maintains that everything was

[12] *iaculis,* literally: darts.
[13] *domestica . . . instrumenta.*
[14] Aristotle frequently uses the name of Coriscus, his fellow disciple in the school of Plato, to signify "a certain man."
[15] Brisso: Bryso, who tried to construct a square circle, concerning whom see Aristotle, *An. Post.,* i, 9, 75 b, 40 ff.
[16] Melissus, an Eleatic philosopher who is referred to in Aristotle, *Top.,* i, 11, 104 b, 22; *Soph. El.,* 5, 167 b, 13, 6; 168 b, 35, 30; 181 a, 27.
[17] Gilbert de la Porrée. See *Met.,* ii, 17.
[18] Peter Abelard. See *Met.,* ii, 10.
[19] Adam du Petit Pont. See *Met.,* ii, 10.
[20] As did Antisthenes, according to Aristotle in his *Top.,* i, 11.
[21] As did Zeno; cf. Aristotle, *Top.,* viii, 8, 160 b, 8.
[22] Literally: is moved.
[23] See Aristotle, *Top.,* i, 11, 104 b, 21.

originally composed of fire.[24] But these opinions of the ancients are admitted, simply because of their antiquity, while the far more probable and correct opinions of our contemporaries are, on the other hand, rejected merely because they have been proposed by men of our own time. Everyone can say what he thinks: I believe that such procedure frequently springs from envy. Each jealously imagines that his own opinion is belittled to the degree in which the slightest praise is conceded to that of anyone else. For my part, I seek not my own glory, but only that of Him from Whom proceeds everything that is good, whether it be in myself or in others.[25] And I also desire that credit be given those to whom I owe what little I know or think. For I am an Academician, and am not ashamed to acknowledge the authors of my own progress. As Pliny says: "It is the laudable sign of good character to admit the author of one's progress." [26] Even those who at present criticize my viewpoint on this, will, one day, God being the source, be praised for their worthwhile contributions. While the envy of their contemporaries will melt away with the passage of time, the glory of their virtues will endure untarnished. Let us now proceed with our discussion. I will briefly summarize what I can recall at an advanced age concerning what I studied in my youth. Happy days are brought back to mind, as I reminisce with pleasure as to what books should be read in preference to others, and how they should be studied. If I overlook anything, or make any mistakes in what I say, this should be attributed to the limitations of my memory, the lapse of time, and my [many] occupations.

[24] Martianus Capella, *De Nupt.*, ii, § 213.

[25] Reference is of course here made to God.

[26] Cf. Pliny, *Nat. Hist.*, praef., § 21. This is not a direct quotation, though John evidently intends it as such.

CHAPTER 1.   *How one should lecture on²⁷ Porphyry and other books.*

It is my conviction that one should lecture on any book in such a way as to make the comprehension of its contents as easy as possible. Instead of searching for loopholes, whereby we may introduce difficulties, we should everywhere endeavor to facilitate understanding. Such was, as I recollect, the practice of the Peripatetic of Pallet. I believe that this was why, if I may so speak with the indulgence of his followers, he [Abelard] favored a somewhat childish opinion concerning genera and species. For he preferred to instruct his disciples and expedite their progress by more elementary explanations, rather than to lose them by diving too deep into this question. He very carefully tried to observe what Augustine laid down as a universal rule: he concentrated on explaining things so that they could be easily understood.²⁸ According to this principle [the *Isagoge* of] Porphyry should be taught in such a way that the author's meaning is always preserved, and his words accepted on their face value. If this rule be followed, Porphyry's work will remain the right kind of introduction, remarkable for easy brevity. It thus suffices for introductory purposes to know that the word ²⁹ "genus" has several meanings. In its original sense, "genus" refers to the principle of generation, that is one's parentage or birthplace.³⁰ Polynices,³¹ when asked his "genus" by Adrastus, included both these elements in his reply: "Cadmus³² was my fore-

²⁷ *legi,* read, interpret, explain, lecture on, teach. The same word occurs in the immediately preceding sentence, where it is translated "read" and "studied."

²⁸ Augustine teaches this in his *De Magistro.*

²⁹ Literally: the name, noun.

³⁰ Porphyry teaches this in his *Introductio in Arist. Cat.* (or *Isagoge*), translated by Boethius (ed. Busse, p. 26).

³¹ Polynices: son of Oedipus, and later son-in-law of Adrastus, who contended with his brother Eteocles for the kingdom of Thebes.

³² Cadmus: son of Agenor, king of the Phoenicians, and founder of Thebes.

bear, and my fatherland warlike[33] Thebes."[34] Subsequently the word "genus" was transferred from its primary meaning to signify that which is predicated in answer to the question "What is it?"[35] concerning [a number of] things that differ in species.[36] The word "species" likewise has several senses. Originally it meant "form,"[37] which consists in the general lineaments of constituent parts.[38] Hence *speciosus*[39] and *formosus*[40] mean the same.[41] Later [the word] "species" came to be employed to signify what is predicated in answer to the question "What is it?" concerning things that are numerically distinct. It is clear that these names [genus and species] are not of secondary imposition,[42] but that, while of primary origin, they have been transferred to new meanings.[43] Since this is done out of necessity rather than merely for ornamentation, it is comparable to equivocal usage.[44] Boethius ascribes a third meaning to species, when he says that the substantial form of a species is referred to as a species, as when humanity is called the species of man.[45] But Boethius also says that this [use of] species is rather abstruse, and remarks that Porphyry purposely omitted mention of it so as not to retard the minds [of students] by over-complicating [his] introductory explanations. What, then, are they about,[46] who add, against the author's judgment, not only this

---

[33] *Mauortia*, belonging to Mars; warlike.

[34] Statius, *Theb.*, i, 680.

[35] *in quid*, in answer to the question "what is it?" or in the category of substance.

[36] Porphyry, *Introd.*, translated by Boethius (ed. Busse, p. 27).

[37] *formam*, form, figure.

[38] See Boethius, *In Porph. Dial.*, i (in Migne, *P.L.*, LXIV, 37 ff.).

[39] *speciosus*, having a good appearance; beautiful.

[40] *formosus*, having a good form; beautiful.

[41] Cf. the version of Porphyry by Victorinus, employed by Boethius in *In Porph. Dial.* (in Migne, *P.L.*, LXIV, 37).

[42] *impositionis*, imposition, application, intention.

[43] It is evident that John was familiar with the doctrine of primary and secondary imposition or application or intention, a distinction which afterwards became widespread, but for which Prantl, *Geschichte der Logik*, III, p. 91, does not cite any author earlier than Albertus Magnus (who, according to him, owed it to Avicenna). John apparently obtained this from Boethius, *In Cat. Arist.*, i.

[44] *equiuocationi*. Cf. *Met.*, i, 15. The doctrine of primary and secondary imposition seems to be from Boethius, *In Cat. Arist.*, i, praef. (in Migne, *P.L.*, LXIV, 159). On equivocal use of words, see *Met.*, iii, 2.

[45] See Boethius, *Comm. in Porph.*, iii (in Migne, *P.L.*, LXIV, 99).

[46] *uoluit* in the Webb text is a misprint for *uolunt*. Cf. MSS A, B, and C.

sense of species, but also every possible one of which they can
think? It seems to me that they are trying to appear very learned
and eloquent by talking in such a way that they cannot be understood. The same method [which I have recommended for the discussion of genus and species] should also be followed in discussing
differences, properties, and accidents. What the words mean
should be explained in a simple way. Terms that are pertinent
should be pinned down by very definite descriptions, and their
divisions given in each case. Finally, the differences between words,
as they occur, should be designated in a clear manner. With this,
one has completed his treatment of Porphyry. That which is
written should be studied with sympathetic mildness, and not
tortured on the rack, like a helpless prisoner, until it renders what
it never received. One who withdraws what he never deposited,
and harvests what he never sowed,[47] is far too severe and harsh
a master, as also is one who forces [poor] Porphyry to cough up
the opinions of all philosophers, and will not rest content until
the latter's short treatise teaches everything that has ever been
written. Plainly, "Truth is the bosom companion of simplicity,"
while "One who tries to extort what is not his due, very frequently
comes off in the end without even that which was rightfully his."
A trustworthy and prudent lecturer[48] will respect as inviolable
the evident literal meaning of what is written, until he obtains
a fuller and surer grasp of the truth by further reading or by
divine revelation. As it is, what one claims to teach with accuracy
and utility, another claims to unteach with equal accuracy and
utility. On the contrary, a good teacher dispenses his instruction
in a way that is suited to the time and adapted to his students.
Porphyry asserts that body is the genus of man, inasmuch as it is
also [the genus] of animal.[49] Aristotle, however, unteaches this,[50]
and corrects the error of those who are of the opinion that genus is
predicated of species in some particular respect.[51] For genus is not

[47] Cf. Luke, xix, 21.
[48] *lector;* cf. *legi* above: lecturer, reader, teacher.
[49] See Porphyry, *Introd.,* translated by Boethius (ed. Busse, p. 29).
[50] Aristotle, *Top.,* iv, 5, 126 a, 17 ff.
[51] *secundum quid,* according to something, in a particular respect.

predicated of species in any such way. Clearly the genus of animal
does not consist in visibility or sensibility. For these characteristics
are predicated only in a certain particular respect, that is, concerning the body, but not the soul. And, as Aristotle says, the body
is not the genus of animal, since it is only a part.[52] The part may
by no means be predicated of the whole, strictly[53] speaking, although there is nothing against the part being predicated of the
whole in figurative speech. Grammarians accept and explain the
figure of speech called "synecdoche," [54] whereby the name of a
whole is attributed to a part, or vice versa, and a thing is frequently
referred to by the name of its more excellent or better known part.
Man, who is composed of both soul and body, is commonly
referred to as "a body" by popular usage. For man's body is more
evident and apparent to our senses, even though man is no more
a body than he is a soul, and is rather, in a way, less a body than
he is a soul, as is maintained by Cicero[55] and Apuleius,[56] and,
what is more, by Jerome[57] and Augustine,[58] as well as by many
others, both Christians[59] and non-Christians. It is equally true
that man is "a soul," though this is recognized only by philosophers.
Nor does it follow [from the fact that he is a soul] that man is
"incorporeal." For, as Abelard used to say, negation is stronger
[than affirmation].[60] Abelard used also to discourage the extension
of figurative speech, for it is not permissible to stretch figures,
which are themselves only accepted as a matter of expedience. No
genus is predicated of its species figuratively or metaphorically,
for it always holds true in a direct and proper sense in regard to
everything of which it is the genus. Finally, if a lecturer or student[61] encounters something very difficult to understand in Porphyry or any of the books, let him not be therewith deterred.

[52] Aristotle, *Top.*, iv, 5, 126 a, 28.
[53] Properly, literally, in its ordinary sense.
[54] *sinedoche,* that is, synecdoche; cf. Donatus, *Art. Gramm.*, iii, 6.
[55] Cicero, *De Fin.*, iv, 10, § 25; v, 12, § 34.
[56] Apuleius, *De Dogm. Plat.*, i, 13.
[57] Jerome, *Adv. Jovin.*, ii, 10 (in Migne, *P.L.*, XXIII, 299).
[58] Augustine, *De C.D.*, x, 6; *Ep.*, iii, § 4 (in Migne, *P.L.*, XXXIII, 65).
[59] Literally: those of our own number.
[60] Thus to affirm "Man is a soul," does not go so far as to say "Man does not have a
body."
[61] *audientem,* a listener or student.

Rather, let him go on, as authors mutually explain one another, and all things help in turn to explain other things. For which reason there is little or nothing that lies concealed from one who is well read.

CHAPTER 2.   *The utility of the* Categories,[62] *[some remarks concerning] their instruments.*

Aristotle's book of the *Categories* is elementary [or alphabetical].[63] Taking a student as, so to speak, a helpless and speechless infant in regard to logic, it instructs him in the ABC's of this science.[64] For it treats of uncombined [65] words and how they signify things, which, after all, is the primary consideration of the dialectician. Aristotle prefaces his discussion by observations concerning equivocal, univocal, and derivative[66] terms, for a knowledge of this distinction is essential for one who wishes to define, divide, and draw inferences.[67] Undetected ambiguity may easily lead one into many errors, and persons can hardly do business together if they do not understand each other. "But once it has been made clear," as Aristotle observes, "how many meanings a word may have, and in what sense it is actually being used, the questioner [in a disputation] [68] will appear ridiculous if he does not direct his argument to the latter.[69] This certainly both helps us to avoid being misled by fallacious reasoning, and empowers us to deceive others by the

[62] Aristotle's *Book of the Categories.*
[63] *elementarius,* alphabetical, elementary.
[64] It accepts the weakness and practical speechlessness (*infantiam*) of one beginning the study of logic as a novice.
[65] *incomplexis,* simple [terms], apart from their use in propositions. See Aristotle, *Cat.,* 2, 1 a, 16; Boethius, *In Cat. Arist.,* i (in Migne, *P.L.,* LXIV, 168).
[66] *denominatiuis.*
[67] See Aristotle, Cat., i, 1 a, 1 ff., where Aristotle explains ὁμώνυμα, συνώνυμα, παρώνυμα. Cf. Boethius, *In Cat. Arist.,* i (in Migne, *P.L.,* LXIV, 163 ff.).
[68] *interrogans,* the questioner. Reference is here made to the logical dialogue in which there were two parties: one the questioner (which Socrates affected), the other the respondent (or answerer).
[69] That is, to the sense in which his interlocutor is using the word.

same.[70] If we are cognizant of the various meanings of a given term, we will not be duped, but will know when one who presents a question[71] is not talking about the same meaning. Also we will be in a position to elude questioners by fallacious reasoning, provided that in some of the various senses in which a term may be used, the statement is true, while in others it is false; unless of course, the answerer also recognizes the several meanings of the term."[72] So necessary is the knowledge of univocal and derivative terms that Isidore maintains that these three, that is, equivocal, univocal, and derivative terms, comprise the instruments of the categories.[73] For whatever is predicated is ascribed to its subject in either an equivocal, a univocal, or a derivative manner. Things are predicated equivocally if they are not ascribed in one and the same sense. They are predicated univocally if they are ascribed neither precisely in one and the same sense, nor exactly in another sense, but with a certain approximation of meaning that corresponds to the similarity in the sound of the words. Thus "good [man]" comes from "goodness,"[74] and "courageous [man]" from "courage."[75] Their closely similar meaning is, in a way, suggested by the very form of the words. Whence many say that while derivative words and the words from which they stem, signify fundamentally the same thing, they differ in their simultaneous secondary meanings.[76] Bernard of Chartres used to say[77] that "whiteness"[78] represents an undefiled virgin; "is white"[79] the virgin entering the bed chamber, or lying on the couch; and "white"[80] the girl after she has lost

[70] *paralogizari* . . . *paralogizare,* to paralogize is "to deceive under the appearance of truth," according to Boethius.

[71] *qui interrogat.*

[72] Aristotle, *Top.,* i, 18, 108 a, 24 ff. Cf. the Boethian translation (in Migne, *P.L.,* LXIV, 922), which is different from John's.

[73] Isidore, *Etym.,* ii, 26, § 2.

[74] *a bonitate bonus.*

[75] *a fortitudine fortis.* This is an example given by Aristotle, *Cat.,* i, 1 a, 14 (in Migne, *P.L.,* LXIV, 167).

[76] *consignificatione,* simultaneous or connected secondary meaning or connotation. For Boethius *consignificatio* is the same as Aristotle's προσσημαίνειν or connotation. Cf. n. 90.

[77] See *Met.,* i, 24; ii, 17. Also cf. R. W. Hunt, "Studies on Priscian," in *Mediaeval and Renaissance Studies,* I, No. 2, pp. 218–220.

[78] *albedo.*

[79] *albet.*

[80] *album.*

her virginity. He used this illustration because, according to him, "whiteness" denotes the quality itself simply, without any participation of a subject, that is [it denotes] merely a certain kind of color, which pierces one's vision.[81] "Is white" basically denotes the same quality, but admits of some participation by a person. For if one inquires as to what this verb denotes relative to a substance, the answer is the quality of whiteness, but in the accidents of the verb one will also discover a person. "White" signifies the same quality [of whiteness], but as infused into and mixed with a substance, and in a way still more impure. Indeed the word "white," when used as a substantive denotes the subject of whiteness, and when used adjectivally denotes the color of a subject that is white. Bernard felt he was backed by Aristotle, as well as several other authorities. For does not Aristotle say: " 'White' signifies nothing more than a quality." [82] Bernard advanced several other reasons, quarried from every side, whereby he strove to prove that things are predicated at times absolutely,[83] and at other times in an approximate manner.[84] He further asserted that a knowledge of derivative words is very useful in this latter connection. This opinion has its opponents, as well as its proponents. I am not interested in verbal hair-splitting[85] in such matters, since I realize that "What is said is to be interpreted in the light of the causes for which it has been said." [86] I do not believe that the writings of Aristotle mentioned above, or those of other authorities should be so interpreted that everything that is stated anywhere at all is dragged into the discussion. Aristotle[87] is taken to have predicated movement of animals, wakefulness[88] of bipeds, and several things of

---

[81] *disgregatiuam uisus,* διακριτικὸν ὄψεως. Cf. Aristotle, *Top.,* iii, 5, 119 a, 30; vii, 3, 148 a, 38 (also cf. Migne, *P.L.,* LXIV, 939, 990).

[82] Cf. Aristotle, *Cat.,* 5, 3 b, 19; and Boethius, *In Cat. Arist.,* i (in Migne, *P.L.,* LXIV, 180). I have been unable to find this exact passage in Aristotle, although John evidently considers it a direct quotation.

[83] *pure,* simply, absolutely, directly and without qualification.

[84] *adiacenter.*

[85] Literally: disputing over a name, quibbling over a word.

[86] See Hilary, *De Trin.,* iv, 14 (in Migne, *P.L.,* X, 14). Cf. *Met.,* i, 19, and ii, 20 (47, 8 and 115, 17 in the Webb edition).

[87] Namely, Aristotle: *An. Prior.,* i, 9, 11, 30 b, 6, 31 b, 28 (cf. Migne, *P.L.,* LXIV, 649, 651).

[88] *uigilatio.*

the sort. Otherwise his examples in the *Analytics* would not hold.
But if "blindness" and "to be blind" [89] were the same, they would
be predicated of the same thing. While a man may be called
"blind," he is never called "blindness." The meaning an author
has in mind, which is ascertainable from the circumstances of
his statement, should not be discarded by quibbling over a word.
We may convey the same thought in various ways, and it is not
necessary always to use the same form of expression. Clearly
derivative words do not have the same [identical] meaning as the
words from which they come, nor do they produce the same concept in our mind. Neither do they, as names, stand for the same
things. Rather, they frequently differ so widely in meaning that
they are in effect contradictory. Occasionally, however, words that
are related derivatively can tolerate one another, and may be
simultaneously predicated of the same thing, or mutually predicated
of one another. Thus "goodness is called "good," and "unity" is
said to be "one." As a rule, however, when words related by derivation are predicated of one another, a contradication results. We are
told that this is due more to their consignification[90] than to their
[fundamental] meaning. Which is probably so, though we will let
the experts decide whether it is sufficiently proved. With things
which signify the same thing, a contradiction can result only because of their consignification. When we posit a name in the singular number, this excludes its plural. If something is "a man," it
cannot be "men." It does not matter why this is so. Dialectic accomplishes its entire purpose so long as it determines the force of
words and acquires a scientific knowledge of how to investigate
and establish the truth by verbal predication. This is what dialectic
is doing, whether it is dividing, defining, inferring, or analyzing
things previously inferred. Derivative words in a way signify what
kind of things come from certain things,[91] while those words from

[89] *"cecitas"* et *"cecum esse."* Cf. Aristotle, *Cat.*, 10, 12 a, 39 ff.; Boethius, *In Cat. Arist.*,
iv (in Migne, *P.L.*, LXIV, 271).

[90] *consignificationis,* consignification: this may mean either their simultaneous secondary
or acquired meaning or connotation, or perhaps their corresponding meaning (their identity of reference). It probably means the former. Thus "whiteness" cannot be said to
be "white," since "whiteness" is an abstract quality, whereas "white" is the epithet of a
body, and connotes or consignifies a body which possesses this color. Cf. above, n. 76.

[91] *qualia ex aliquibus.*

which they are derived denote whence such kinds of things come.[92] "Courage" refers to what makes one "courageous"; "courageous" denotes of what sort one is when one has "courage." [93] The word "courage" designates not "what," [94] but rather "from what," [95] and thus indicates the cause. Hence Gregory says: " 'Angel' [or messenger] is the name of an office, rather than of a nature." [96] For the word derives from an office, even though the latter is the office of a person. In a way, it signifies, as has been said, what kind of service one renders by the office. There are many similar instances. "Consul" is the name of an official dignity, "studious" [97] the name of a virtue, "Platonist" and "Socratic" the names of [philosophical] professions,[98] and they each respectively signify the aforesaid.[99] From what has been said, it is apparent that [the words] "to signify" and "to predicate" may be used in several different senses. But it is easy to determine which sense is the most suitable.[100] Thus "just," [101] and like words found throughout the works of the authors, are at one time said to signify or predicate "[a] just [person]," and at another "justice." But the reverse never, or, at most, rarely occurs. Thus "justice" never or hardly ever signifies or predicates "[a] just [person]." Boethius in his work *On the Trinity,* declares: "When I say 'God is just,' although I apparently [only] predicate a quality, I actually predicate a substance, and in fact more than [an ordinary] substance." [102] How, I ask, could he seem to predicate a quality, if the word "just" did not predicate such? Aristotle substantiates this, saying: "Expressions

[92] *a quibus qualia.*

[93] *fortitudo . . . fortis,* here translated "courage" and "courageous," as sufficiently close, and better adapted to English.

[94] *cuius.* Or of whom.

[95] *ex quo.*

[96] Gregory, *Hom. in Evang.,* xxxiv, § 8 (in Migne, *P.L.,* LXXVI, 1250). Gregory here apparently follows Hilary, *De Trin.,* v, 11, 22 (in Migne, *P.L.,* X, 136, 143), Jerome, *Contra Ioann. Hieros.,* § 17 (in Migne, *P.L.,* XXIII, 369), etc.

[97] Or serious or earnest.

[98] *professionum.*

[99] Namely, an official dignity, a virtue, and a [philosophical] profession.

[100] *familiarissimus.*

[101] *iustus.*

[102] Boethius, *De Trin.,* chap. 4 (ed. Peiper, p. 156). In other words, although "just," when applied to a person, such as Aristides, predicates the quality of justice, when applied to God, it does not predicate a quality, since God is substantially justice itself.

may signify a quality, as 'white,' or a quantity, as 'two cubits long.' "[103] Since such terms originate from a quality or quantity, they accordingly predicate the quality, which, when they are ascribed, they indicate to be present in their subjects. They are sometimes said to signify what kind of things, since when used with reference to anything, they point out what kind of a thing it is. But derivative words and the words from which they are derived have closely related meanings, even though on hearing the word "white," one thinks of whiteness in some subject, whereas on hearing the word "whiteness," one thinks not of a white subject, but rather of the color [itself] that makes a subject white. What our understanding conceives on hearing a word is its most familiar[104] meaning.

CHAPTER 3.   *What is the scope of the predicaments,[105] and with what the prudent moderation of those who philosophize should rest content.*

Since all terms are predicated either equivocally, univocally, or derivatively, in accordance with the principle of indifference [relative to possible variations in the meanings of words];[106] and since this very predication is in a way the [basic] material of reasoning, these instruments[107] of the predicaments[108] are discussed at the outset. For they either deter and impede, or foster and expedite the work of those who are endeavoring to proceed [109] according to the

[103] John here evidently intends to quote directly from Aristotle, *Cat.,* 4, 1 b, 28, 29; Boethius, *In Cat. Arist.,* i (in Migne, *P.L.,* LXIV, 180).

[104] *familiarissima,* most familiar, suitable, commonly accepted. Cf. n. 100.

[105] *predicamentorum,* the predicaments or categories.

[106] *indifferentie rationem,* a plan, method, or principle of indifference, neutrality, or impartiality. Evidently John here means the liberal principle of impartiality or indifference, which would allow for and accept a variety of meanings in the interpretation of an author's words, so that, e.g., the same word could be used by the same author in various different senses. Cf. also later, in this same chapter, and *Met.,* iii, 5.

[107] *instrumenta,* namely, equivocal, univocal, and derivative expressions. They are also so-called by Isidore, *Etym.,* ii, 26, § 2.

[108] Or categories.

[109] *negotiantium.*

art [of logic]. The classifications "multivocal"[110] and "diversivocal"[111] [terms], added by Boethius,[112] belong more to grammar.
In the case of "multivocal" terms, several words, such as *ensis,*
mucro, and *gladius,*[113] all mean and name the same thing [sword].
In that of "diversivocal" terms, the words differ both in sound
and in meaning, an example of such being "man" and "stone." This
book,[114] more than the others, commends adherence to a principle
of "indifference" [relative to variations in the meanings of words],
which we always favor, and whose application is everywhere manifest to a careful student. While at one time the book is treating of
things that signify, and at another of things signified, it uses their
names interchangeably. There are some who assert that because
it is elementary,[115] this book is therefore practically useless. They
imagine that the fact that they have despised or ignored those
things which Boethius, in his first commentary on Porphyry,[116]
teaches should be studied before one can attain anything of the
[logical] art, is proof that they are therefore masters of dialectical
and demonstrative logic.[117] I strongly disagree. I fail to see how
anyone can become a logician without studying the predicaments,[118]
any easier than one can be "lettered"[119] without "letters."[120] This
work explains clearly what things are universal and what ones
singular, what ones substances and what ones accidents, as well
as what words may be predicated equivocally, what ones univocally,
and what ones in a derivative manner. It discloses the meanings of
uncombined terms, provides a most correct system of [scientific]
research, and opens up a primary and evident highway for the
perfection of knowledge. These seem to be the principal means of
affording a complete knowledge of everything pertaining to the

[110] *multiuoca,* having many names or meanings.
[111] *diuersiuoca,* having different names or meanings.
[112] Boethius, *In Cat. Arist.,* i (in Migne, *P.L.,* LXIV, 168).
[113] Each of these three words means "sword."
[114] Aristotle's *Categories.*
[115] Or alphabetical. Cf. *Met.,* iii, 2 and n. 63.
[116] In his *In Porphyrium Dialogi.*
[117] *in dialectica et apodictica disciplina;* see Boethius, *In Porph. Dial.,* i (in Migne,
P.L., LXIV, 14).
[118] Literally, this: Aristotle's book on the *Categories* or *Predicaments.*
[119] *litteratus,* lettered, learned..
[120] *litteris,* letters, literature (recorded) learning.

Peripatetic discipline, which is concerned with investigating the truth. The first item of information we want concerning anything is whether or not it exists. Next we need to know what, of what kind, and how great it is, as well as its relation to other things, where and when it exists, its position (or posture),[121] and its state (or condition),[122] what it does,[123] and what it undergoes.[124] The final question about a thing is why it is so, in which speculation we not only draw nigh to the perfection of the angels, but even approach the special prerogatives of the divine majesty. For the reasons of all things are known only to Him, Whose will constitutes the original cause of all, and Who has willed, to the degree in which it has pleased Him, to reveal to each [of His creatures] why things are as they are. While divine perfection involves complete knowledge of all things, and angelic perfection implies freedom from [all] error, human perfection consists in having a good concept[125] of many things.[126] The answers to the aforesaid twelve questions comprise all [scientific] knowledge. Philosophical investigation modestly contents itself with eleven of these questions, and when it goes beyond this limit, ascribes its progress largely to [divine] grace. The latter opens [the door] to [all] those who knock,[127] while the Lord discloses His will, the original cause of everything, to all who seek it[128] with their whole heart.[129] The logician deals with the ten elements [namely, the categories] that pertain to his own branch of study. After he is fully trained in these, he proceeds to take up the opposite side of an argument with the object of fully vanquishing his opponent. First come those questions which are called "natural,"[130] and which are in a way [more] elementary, namely,

[121] *quomodo situm,* its position, posture, or attitude.
[122] *quid habeat,* its state, condition, circumstances, or properties.
[123] *quid . . . faciat,* what it does, its activity.
[124] *quid . . . paciatur,* what it undergoes or suffers, its passivity.
[125] *bene sentire,* to have or in having a good or reasonably correct concept, notion, or judgment.
[126] *plurimis,* most, very many, a great number of things.
[127] Cf. Matthew, vii, 8.
[128] His will.
[129] Cf. Deuteronomy, iv, 29, and Jeremiah, xxix, 13.
[130] Seneca wrote seven books on "Natural Questions," that is, questions relative to things of nature. A copy of this work of Seneca's was bequeathed to the church of Chartres by John.

"what," "how great," "of what kind," and the rest. After these "nude philosophers" [131] have been grounded in the predicaments, they align themselves on the opposite sides of a question, and, as the saying goes, proceed to tear it apart in the arena.[132] Both strive to force each other back with the sharp points of their reasoning, as each tries to disprove the other's thesis. Since the things of nature provide the initial subject matter of our investigations, the ten categories were originally formulated for these, and words were thought up, whereby the substance, quantity, and quality of those things which first present themselves to our senses or understanding, such as bodies or spirits, might be expressed or might be explained in answer to other questions that could naturally arise. The name "predicaments" was given, for words and things alike, to these ten kinds of predicables, which could thus be referred to particular individual substances, and which indicate concerning their subjects what, how great, and of what kind they are, as well as their relation to other things, where and when they exist, their position (or posture) and state (or condition), what they do, and what they undergo. The first predicament comprises those things that state what a substance is; the second those that indicate how great it is. The third predicament explains its relations; the fourth of what kind it is; the fifth where it is; the sixth when it is; the seventh its position (or posture); the eighth its state (or condition); the ninth what it does; and the tenth what it undergoes. We have this number of predicaments because philosophical speculation used to be primarily concerned with material [133] things. Before Zeno, no one or very few persons had any correct concept of the soul or incorporeal spirits. Zeno it was who, according to Jerome,[134] taught the immortality of the soul. As a result, position (or posture) and certain other categories are hardly suitable to spirits, since they

---

[131] *gimnosophiste,* nude or pure philosophers. John here possibly compares dialecticians to athletes since, just as the latter discard their garments when competing in the gymnasium, so the former rid themselves of superfluous and accidental handicaps when engaging in disputations. Historically the term refers to the naked sages and ascetics of India.

[132] Literally: in the narrow field.

[133] Literally: corporeal.

[134] See Jerome, *Comm. in Dan.,* i, 2 (in Migne, *P.L.,* XXV, 495–496).

primarily refer to bodies. The first consideration, and one which in a way belongs to those who philosophize about nature,[135] concerns substances. The second is mathematical and imitates nature, for which reason the ancients[136] were wont to characterize the mathematician as "an ape[137] of natural philosophers." Just as one who investigates nature inquires concerning a subject, such as Cleon or Callias, as to what, of what kind, or how great it is, so the mathematician, after abstracting the substance of the subject, inquires, relative to the latter [the substance], what, of what kind, or how great it is, and subsequently, like the natural philosopher, proceeds to further questions. But those whose minds are vigorous with the penetrating discernment of purer philosophy,[138] have long since agreed that there is no room for secondary mathematics.[139] Otherwise the labor of philosophy would have no end, and investigation would wander on interminably, despite the fact that it always tends to arrive at some conclusion. One who is already stripped absolutely bare cannot be further denuded. After form has been abstracted from matter, or matter from form, it is futile to try to attire form with circumstances or properties which it cannot bear, or to divest matter of clothing that it does not possess. Anyone who presumes to exceed this limitation is no longer considering the constitution of nature. He is rather dealing with the figments of a mind that is involved in mathematical subtleties. For after the question: "What is 'whiteness'?" is asked, and the reply that "It is such and such a color" has been made, whatever is added in order to determine a subsistence, either smacks of an effect, and is thus dependent on a substance, or scents of a power, which is perhaps not yet in operation. And if investigation persists to the point of inquiring as to "how great" or "where" whiteness is, one is compelled to digress to corporeal things. Whence I am inclined to impute error

[135] *naturaliter philosophantium,* that which belongs to philosophizing about nature or pertains to natural philosophers.
[136] To whom John refers here we do not know; cf., however, Seneca, *Ep.,* 88, §§ 26 ff.
[137] Namely, an imitator.
[138] See Boethius, *Arithm.,* i, 1 (in Migne, *P.L.,* LXIII, 1079 ff.).
[139] Secondary mathematics would inquire in an abstract manner about the properties of substances, just as mathematics proper inquires in an abstract manner about substances.

to that minority of philosophers, who hold that a mathematician proceeds in the same way as a judge of nature[140] in all respects, and opine that the same kinds of predicaments that are evident in corporeal and spiritual substances, also apply to other things. They force all genera and species not only of substances, but also of qualities and other things, into the first category. The first question is thus answered, and what a thing is, is stated by an apposition of genus and species. The following [predicaments] are then disposed according to the kinds of questions. Such a procedure is apparently contrary to Aristotle, who says: "It is clear that when something is said to be, reference is sometimes made to substance, but at other times to quality or to some other category."[141] Thus, when, in the case of a man, we say that he is "man" or "animal," we both say "what" he is, and denote his substance. But when, in the case of the color white, we say that it is a color, although we say "what" it is, we denote "what kind of a thing" [it is]. Likewise, in the case of a size in cubits, when we say that it is a certain quantity, while we say "what" it is, we also denote "how great" it is. The same holds true in other [similar] cases. In all such instances, whenever the same thing [its species] or its genus is predicated of a thing, this denotes what it is;[142] but when it is predicated about something else, it denotes not what, but how great or of what kind it is, or one of the other predicaments. Certainly our author does not here mean that all genera are in one and the same category, even though they may be predicated in the same manner. Neither does he mean that the nine kinds of accidental things may not be predicated concerning substances, nor that they may be predicated in the same way about subjects and their attributes.[143] Isidore,[144] Alcuin,[145] and other wise men tell us that all the remaining categories are predicated of primary substances, and, to illustrate their

---

[140] *nature arbitro*, a judge of nature, or a natural philosopher, to whom John above refers as, "one who investigates nature."

[141] Aristotle, *Cat.*, 4, 1 b, 25 ff. (cf. Migne, *P.L.*, LXIV, 180) John's wording here is very approximate, though he apparently intends a direct quotation.

[142] Thus when Socrates is said to be a man (his species) or an animal (his genus) reference is made to what he is (namely, to his substance).

[143] *contentis suis*, their contents, constituents, or attributes.

[144] Isidore, *Etym.*, ii, 26, § 11.

[145] Alcuin, *De Dialectica*, chap. 3 (in Migne, *P.L.*, CI, 954–955).

point, give the following very full sentence, which includes all ten predicaments: "Augustine, a great orator,[146] the son of so and so, today stands in the church, clothed in his [sacred] vestments,[147] exhausted by disputing." [148] The foregoing is [indeed] a full sentence, and indicates the substance, quality, quantity, and other predicables of the subject concerning whom it speaks, although perhaps its [proposed] example of quantity is not quite adequate. Just as nature, the mother of all [that exists], has created primary substances possessing form[149] with given accidents; it has also created, together with particular substances, each and every accident which pertains to its form. But those things, such as secondary substances, which are understood as abstracted from particular substances, are, as already observed, mental fictions devised for a [good and] sufficient reason.[150] Those substances which are actually such, and with their individual essences underlie accidents, are called "primary," whereas those which are concepts abstracted by the operation of the intellect from the mutual conformity of individual things are called "secondary." In like manner, and with due proportion, those quantities and qualities which are individually present in primary substances may also be called "primary"; while those quantities which are abstracted from particular things by an analogous process[151] may be termed "secondary." The same holds true with the other predicaments. "It is certain," as Isidore observes, "that the 'categories' are so called from the fact that they can only be known from their subjects." [152] For the same reason, they are also properly termed "predicaments," inasmuch as they are *dicata* [dedicated, predicated, or attributed], that is *addicta* [addicted, dedicated, or

---

[146] *magnus orator* or *magnus, orator*. This may mean "great [in stature or historical importance, etc.] and an orator," or it may mean "the great orator." "Great" is taken to illustrate the category of quantity.

[147] *infulatus*, wearing his chasuble or official insignia.

[148] Isidore has this sentence in his *Etym.*, ii, 26, § 11. Inclusion of the ten predicaments or categories is evident: "Augustine (substance), who is tall or great (quantity), an orator (quality), the son of so and so (relation), is standing (posture), in the church (place), today (time), attired in his sacred vestments (state), exhausted (affection) by disputation (action)."

[149] *informatam*, given or possessing form.

[150] *ex ratione probabili*, for a probable or sufficient reason.

[151] *quadam ratione similitudinis*, by a certain plan of likeness, by an analogous process, or by reason of a certain resemblance.

[152] Isidore, *Etym.*, ii, 26, § 14.

assigned], to things that are present,[153] manifest in the constitution of nature. Indeed *dicare* [to dedicate or attribute] is the same as *addicere* [to assign or dedicate], as is exemplified in Vergil's statement:

> I will unite you together in lasting wedlock,
> and will dedicate[154] her to thee as thy very own.[155]

In fact, the predicaments are so dedicated[156] to things other than themselves that they cannot be known independently of the latter. For, as we have already remarked, if we are unable to find examples of our mental concepts among actually existing things, our ideas are empty. A [scientific] account[157] of nature includes all particular things, but excludes anything that is actually never found existing. Since they are known from their subjects, things that are predicated are, as observes Boethius, "such as their subjects permit."[158] The great efficacy of the categories with regard to the works of nature melts away when confronted with the divine essence, as words applied to the latter are either completely transformed [in meaning] or false. Those who erroneously extend the [full] force of the predicaments to all things, are causing themselves much [needless] work, and are also storing up trouble. By disregarding the limitations of natural things, they are undermining the integrity of the art [of logic], whose rules they will not suffer to remain within the bounds of their own genera. Every rule and every universality refers to some genus [some certain kind of things]. Accordingly, if, with wanton abandon, it refuses to abide within the scope of the same, it becomes vitiated on the spot. Truly, a knowledge of the predicaments, both things and words, is very useful. This [science] is clearly explained and taught by Aristotle. The latter [master] classifies and divides all things.[159] He teaches what terms may be compared, what ones admit of contraries, what are their contraries,

---

[153] *presentibus.*
[154] *dicabo.*
[155] Vergil, *Aen.*, i, 73.
[156] *addicta.*
[157] *historia*, a history [scientific] account, inventory.
[158] Boethius, *De Trin.* (ed. Peiper, p. 156).
[159] Literally: He describes and divides the universality of things.

and what terms have no contraries. He has bequeathed to posterity a way whereby it may obtain knowledge of the truth in a most direct and expeditious fashion. And since the multifarious meanings of words frequently becloud our understanding, Aristotle further teaches that we should investigate the number of different senses in which each word [160] may be predicated. In this connection, he has devoted the remainder of his book [on the *Categories*] to a discussion of opposites, priority, and simultaneity of predication, the various kinds of motion, and the several senses of the term "to have." [161] For nothing contributes more to [scientific] knowledge, or to vanquishing an opponent,[162] than to distinguish [the varying meanings of] things said in several different senses. As time passes, with the acquiescence of their users, many [new] words are born, while, on the other hand, many [old ones] expire. Whereas with Aristotle,[163] "a sharp[164] knife" meant that the knife's edge was an acute[165] angle, at present it seems rather to signify the keenness of something that cuts with ease. We thus speak of "a sword doubly sharp," [166] meaning that either side of the sword's blade cuts readily, although if one reflects, he will realize that this is due to the acuteness of the angles. A body is sharpest where its sides [surfaces] converge in the most acute angle, whereas if the angle where the sides come together is obtuse,[167] the body is accordingly blunt.[168] The expression "to be in something" is likewise used in more different senses today than it would have been in Aristotle's time.[169] Moreover, words which then meant something, have perchance come to be meaningless. How true is it that:

[160] Literally: the multiplicity of words . . . how many times each [word].
[161] The foregoing is a synopsis of Aristotle's book of the *Categories*.
[162] Literally: victory; evidently in disputation.
[163] Aristotle, *Top.*, i, 15, 107 a, 17 (cf. Migne, *P.L.*, LXIV, 920).
[164] *acutus*, sharp or acute.
[165] *acuti*, acute or sharp. Throughout the present discussion the word John uses is *acutus*, which may mean either sharp or acute.
[166] *gladius bis acutus*. His point is that, whereas, formerly the word *acutus* referred primarily to the angle of the edge, it now refers primarily to the readiness with which it cuts.
[167] *obtusus*.
[168] *obtusum*.
[169] See Boethius, *In Cat. Arist.*, i (in Migne, *P.L.*, LXIV, 172). Boethius observes that the expression in his own day had nine different senses, whereas Aristotle had only pointed out three.

Many a word, which has fallen into disuse, will be resurrected,
While others, now highly esteemed, will sink into oblivion,
If usage, the judge, the law, and the norm of speech, but so ordains.[170]

At the same time, those who [try to] read everything into this little book,[171] and refuse to allow it to rest content with its own brevity, evidently "unteach" [172] rather than instruct. Such [teachers], who would sooner ignore than admit the truth,[173] cram into[174] their commentary on this book every possible sort of discussion. That English Peripatetic, our Adam,[175] who has many followers, although few will admit it, because they are deterred by envy, was wont to make fun of such [logicians]. He used to declare that if he himself were to teach logic with the simplicity of words and clear statement of opinions that it deserves, he would have no or few listeners. I became very intimate with Adam, and we had many conversations, mutually exchanged books, and made it a practice to confer almost daily on problems as they arose, although I was not his disciple for a single day. I am grateful, because I learned a great deal from his explanations, although, as he will witness, I disagree with many of his opinions, simply because on grounds of reason I preferred others. Here [in treating the *Categories*], as everywhere, I believe that one should aim at facilitating comprehension. I have not brought up these matters because I feel that they are all essential,[176] but lest that which should somewhere be said be everywhere omitted.[177] I have recommended this book and will continue to do so, because it is truly laudable. If I have [praised it too highly and] been overindulgent out of charity, which strives particularly to attract the uneducated and scoffers to study the elements of the [logical] art, even so:

[170] Horace, *A.P.*, 70–72.
[171] Aristotle's *Categories*.
[172] *dedocent.*
[173] Literally: to whom admission of the truth seems more of a hardship than does ignorance of the truth.
[174] *hic congerunt,* literally: they gather together here; namely, in their commentaries on the *Categories*.
[175] See *Met.*, ii, 10.
[176] Literally: that they may be said everywhere.
[177] The Webb text here should be corrected to read *expedit. Librum* (134, 25). Cf. MSS A, B, and C.

Persuasive masters sometimes give sweet cookies to boys,
To prevail upon them to learn their ABCs.[178]

And since the book has been greatly disparaged by numerous as-
sailants, it should be the more vigorously defended. For, as Aristotle
tells us: "One who is a universal objector should be opposed without qualification, measure for measure." [179]

CHAPTER 4.   *The scope and usefulness of the* Periermenie
              [Interpretation],[180] *or more correctly of the* Per-
              iermenias.

Just as the book of the *Categories* is proportionately "alphabetical,"
that of the *Periermenie* [*Interpretation*], or rather the *Periermenias*
[*Periermeneias*], is comparatively "syllabic." The [constituent] elements of reasoning, which, in the book of the *Categories,* are
presented separately, as uncombined words,[181] are, in the book *On
Interpretation,* assembled, much as letters are put together to make
syllables, and thus presented in combination to designate what is
true and what false. The ancients considered this book so subtle
that, as Isidore, in praising it, relates,[182] there was a saying to the
effect that "When Aristotle wrote the *Periermenie,* he dipped his
pen [directly] in his mind." [183] On the other hand, if I may say so,
begging leave of all, any one of the doctors could (as many of them
in fact do) more concisely and lucidly provide everything that is
taught in this book in the elementary lessons which they call
Introductions. The only thing lacking would be the respected authority of the [author's] words. There is hardly any one [of the

---

[178] Horace, *Sat.,* i, 1, 25, 26: *"elementa . . . prima,"* literally "the first elements."

[179] Aristotle, *Top.,* v, 4, 134a, 3, 4 (cf. Migne, *P.L.,* LXIV, 961).

[180] Aristotle's Περὶ ἑρμηνείας (etymologically: about interpretation), known as the *De
Interpretatione* or *Interpretation.*

[181] *sermonibus incomplexis;* cf. John's *Hist. Pont.,* chap. 13, p. 35 (1, 16).

[182] Isidore, *Etym.,* ii, 27, § 1.

[183] *calamum in mente tinguebat,* he dipped or moistened his pen in his mind, he
wrote directly from his mind, as though using it as his inkwell.

doctors] who would not, in addition to teaching what is contained
in this book, also add other things equally necessary, without which
a knowledge of the art cannot be acquired. They run through and
inquire into the questions as to what is a name, what a verb, and
what a sentence.[184] They discuss the different kinds of sentences
and the varying force of propositions. They also treat what propositions may obtain[185] from quantity or quality, as well as what propositions are definitely true or false, what ones are equivalent to one
another, what ones agree or disagree, what ones that are predicated
separately may also be predicated jointly or conversely,[186] or may
not be so predicated. They further discuss the nature of modal
propositions,[187] and point out their contradictories. The foregoing
constitutes a summary of the main contents of this work, whose
thoughts are very subtle, and whose wording is very difficult to
understand. However, we should be thankful for both of these
features, for while the thoughts instruct, the words exercise our
minds. Besides, we should reverence the words of the [great]
authors, whose expressions we should not only hold in high esteem,
but should also employ with assiduity. Not only do these words
possess a certain majesty or prestige from the great names of antiquity [with whom they are associated], but also anyone who is
ignorant of them is handicapped, since they are very effective when
used for proof or refutation. Like a whirlwind, they snatch up
those who are ignorant of them, and violently lash such persons about
or dash them to the ground, stunning them with fear. For words of
the philosophers, with which one is not familiar, are veritable
thunderbolts. While the sense of the words that were used by the
ancients and those that are used by moderns may be the same,
their greater age has made the former more venerable. I recollect
that the Peripatetic of Pallet made the observation, which I believe
was correct, that it would be easy for one of our own contempo-

---

[184] *oratio*, a sentence. Cf. Boethius, *Comm. I in Arist. de Interpr.*, i (ed. Meiser, and in
Migne, *P.L.*, LXIV, 301–312).

[185] *quid . . . sortiantur*, what they may derive. Apparently the subject is *enuntiationes*
(understood).

[186] *conuersim*, in a turned-about manner, in which the parts are interchanged.

[187] *modalium*, the possibility, impossibility, necessity, or contingent nature of propositions.

raries to compose a book about this art,[188] which would be at least the equal of any of those written [on the subject] by the ancients, in both its apprehension of the truth and the aptness of its wording, but [at the same time] it would be impossible or extremely difficult for such a book to gain acceptance as an authority. He also used to assert that recognition as authorities should be conceded to these earlier authors, whose natural talent and originality flourished in fertile luxuriance, and who bequeathed to [an indebted] posterity the fruits of their labors, with the consequence that the very things which several men have expended their whole lives in investigating, and which they have labored and sweated [189] in discovering, can now be quickly and easily learned by one person. Our own generation enjoys the legacy bequeathed to it by that which preceded it. We frequently know more, not because we have moved ahead by our own natural ability, but because we are supported by the [mental] strength of others, and possess riches that we have inherited from our forefathers. Bernard of Chartres used to compare us to [puny] dwarfs perched on the shoulders of giants. He pointed out that we see more and farther than our predecessors, not because we have keener vision or greater height, but because we are lifted up and borne aloft on their gigantic stature.[190] I readily agree with the foregoing. Teachers of the arts, even in their *Introductions*,[191] explain the basic elements[192] of the art and many truths of the science[193] equally as well as, and perhaps even better than do the ancients. Who is content even with what Aristotle gives in his [book] *On Interpretation?* Who does not add points obtained from other sources? All are gathering together everything [they can]

---

[188] Of interpretation, or of logic.

[189] Literally: have sweated profusely.

[190] Bernard of Chartres, see *Met.*, i, 24. Alexander Neckam (1157–1217), in his *De Naturis Rerum*, c. 78 (ed. Wright, p. 123), also quotes this saying. Cf. R. Klibansky, "Standing on the Shoulders of Giants," *Isis*, no. 71, XXVI, i (Dec., 1936), 147–149.

[191] John seems to refer to works such as Abelard's *Introductiones;* concerning which, see Abelard himself in his *Anal. Prior.*, ii (*Ouvr. Inéd.*, pp. 254, 305, 332, 366, 440).

[192] *preparatitia*, literally "preparatory things," or elements. This Latin word, whose meaning is evident, is not found in lexicons.

[193] *artis . . . ueritatis*, may mean of the logical art and truth relative to it; or of skilled or artful accomplishment of purpose and speculative truth in general, as of the arts and sciences.

that pertains to the whole art, and explaining it in terms that may be easily understood. They, so to speak, dress the message of the authors in modern style, which becomes in a way even more splendescent when it is more brilliantly adorned with the jewels[194] of antiquity. Accordingly the words of the authors should not be lost or forgotten, especially those which give [their] full opinions,[195] and have wide applicability. Such words preserve scientific knowledge in its entirety, and contain tremendous hidden as well as apparent power.[196] Many words, however, when torn from their context, make little or no sense to one who hears them. Such is the case with most of the examples in the *Analytics,* where letters stand for terms. Although these examples help explain the doctrine [contained in the *Analytics*], they wilt when they are transplanted. While rules may have great force because of the truth of what they teach, they have very little control over changing verbal usage[197] [which may modify the meaning of the words in which they are expressed]. To say that a thing "wholly pertains" to something else, or "does not pertain to it in any way," [198] and that something "is predicated in a universal way" of something else, or "is completely alien to it" [199] amount to the same thing.[200] Nevertheless, while one form of expression is [now] in frequent use, the other has become practically obsolete, except so far as it may occasionally be admitted through mutual agreement.[201] In Aristotle's day it was perhaps customary to use both of these forms of expression, but now one has replaced the other [simply] because usage has so decreed.[202] Similarly, the word "contingent" [203] today has a somewhat

---

[194] *grauitate,* gravity, dignity, prestige, jewels (to fit the figure).

[195] *plenas sententias explent;* cf. Cicero, *De Fin.,* iv, 14, § 36.

[196] Cf. Jerome, *Ep.,* liii, § 2 (in Migne, *P.L.,* XXII, 541).

[197] *in commercio uerbi,* in verbal commerce, traffic, or intercourse. John apparently means here that the important thing is accuracy in the matter taught, while the verbal expression, which is less subject to strict rules, admits of wide variation. It evidently is at least one explanation of his *ratio indifferentie,* or "principle of indifference" relative to varying meanings of words.

[198] *quod dicitur in toto esse alterum alteri uel in toto non esse.*

[199] Or: is in every way distinct from it.

[200] What John means to say is that "wholly pertains" is the same as "is predicated universally," and "does not in any way pertain" the same as "is entirely alien or foreign."

[201] *ex condicto,* by mutual agreement, or perhaps, in view of the context.

[202] *uult usus,* usage so wills it. Cf. Horace, *A.P.,* 71.

[203] *contingens.*

different sense from that in which Aristotle employed it. At present, we by no means consider "contingent" equivalent to "possible," although this is the meaning Aristotle seems to have attributed to it in his treaties on modals.[204] While it is "possible" for the Ethiopian race to become white, and the species we know as swans to become black, neither of these [alternatives] is "contingent."[205] If one were to assume that these things are contingent,[206] simply because they are possible, and were publicly to assert this, on the authority of Aristotle, but in opposition to the evident[207] way in which the public use the terms, he would evidently be out of his head, or at least a bit tipsy. And if we take a further sense of the word, wherein "contingent," though not considered equivalent to "possible," is circumscribed by the latter, than which it has a lesser extension, we will find here, also, evident deviation from former usage. Aristotle says in his *Analytics:* " 'To be contingent' and 'contingent'[208] mean that, although something does not necessarily exist, no impossibility would result if it did exist."[209] While this meaning excludes all that is necessary from the comprehension of "contingent," it otherwise equates the latter to the "possible." But not even this still holds. It is not necessary for Hodge[210] to reign, and no impossibility would eventuate if he did reign. Still, if one were to declare that Hodge's reigning at Winchester[211] is "contingent," no one would readily assent to his proposition. To demonstrate even more conclusively how far earlier usage of the term has been abrogated, the word in question ["contingent"] no longer fully holds in any of the senses ascribed to it by Aristotle. The latter declared: "We say that the expression 'to be contingent' is used in two ways. In its first sense, it refers to something that often happens, yet falls short of necessity, as for instance that a man grays or

---

[204] *in Tractatu modalium;* see Aristotle's *De Interpr.,* chaps. 12 and 13, esp. 13, 22 a, 15.
[205] According to Porphyry, black color is an inseparable attribute of Ethiopians, and white color is an inseparable attribute of swans.
[206] *contingere.*
[207] The comma after *plane* in the Webb text should be omitted. Cf. MSS A, B, and C.
[208] *Contingere et contingens est.*
[209] Aristotle, *An. Prior.,* i, 13, 32 a, 18 ff. (cf. Migne, *P.L.,* LXIV, 651).
[210] *Hobinellus,* Hodge; a rustic.
[211] *Wintonie,* Winton or Winchester; the early capital of Wessex, and subsequently of all England.

grows larger or smaller, or in general that what is natural comes to pass. Such things are not continually necessary, since there is not always a man [to grow gray, etc.], although when man exists, these things either necessarily or usually occur. The second way in which the expression [to be contingent] is used is with reference to something that is indeterminate, and may either be or not be so, as that an animal may walk, or that, as the animal walks, an earthquake may occur, or in general that something may possibly happen. In the latter case, nothing of the kind is naturally more one way than the other." [212] But at present, if we follow usage, "In whose keeping is the judgment, the law, and the norm of speech," [213] the word "contingent" is used only with reference to something that happens from time to time.[214] Something that never occurs is not today called "contingent" simply because of the absence of necessity or the presence of possibility. It is accordingly clear that usage prevails over Aristotle when it comes to derogating from or abrogating the meaning of words. But the actual truth itself cannot be changed by man's will, since it was not established by man. We may therefore conclude that, if possible, both the words of the arts and their sense should be preserved; but that if we cannot save them both, the words should be dropped without losing their sense. Knowing the arts does not consist in merely repeating [parrotlike] the words of the authors. On the contrary, it involves comprehending their meaning and understanding the thoughts they present.

CHAPTER 5.   *What constitutes the body of the art, and [some remarks on] the utility of the Book of the* Topics.

Up to this point we have discussed the introductory elements of the logical art, whose founder and virtual legislator[215] did not feel that novices should be admitted to it entirely without instruction or

[212] Aristotle, *An. Prior.,* i, 13, 32 b, 4 ff. (cf. Migne, *P.L., LXIV,* 652).
[213] Horace, *A.P.,* 72.
[214] Or sometimes.
[215] Namely, Aristotle.

proper reverence, and, as they say, "with unwashed hands." [216] In
the art of warfare, preparation of the weapons which are its means,
precedes [practice of] the art. So with those who take up the sacred
cult of logic, certain elements are first provided as instruments,
whereby those entering upon this study may more easily and effectively progress into the body of the art and more readily accomplish their profession. These introductory elements are extremely
useful. While they may not be exactly classified as "of the art," [217]
they may be correctly enough characterized as "for the art," [218] so
that it does not matter much which way we put it. If we do
not include these preparatory elements, what we may call "the body
of the art" consists chiefly in knowledge of three things: the *Topics,*
the *Analytics,* and the *Refutations.* If the last three are thoroughly
mastered, and the habit of employing them is firmly fixed by
practice and exercise, then one who applies them in demonstration,
dialectic, or sophistry will have a wide command of invention[219]
and judgment in every branch of learning.[220] Of the aforesaid three,
the most necessary is knowledge of the *Topics,* especially for those
whose aim is [to prove with] probability. While the science of the
Topics chiefly builds up our power of invention, it also assists our
judgment in no small measure. And although many are of the
opinion that it is of greatest service to the dialectician and the
orator,[221] I believe that it is almost equally helpful to those who are
engaged in the weighty labors of demonstration, or involved in
sophistic fallacy and strife. All things have a way of adding up
together, so that one will become more proficient in any proposed
branch of learning to the extent that he has mastered neighboring
and related departments of knowledge. The *Analytics* and the
Sophistics are also useful in invention;[222] while the *Topics,* on their
part, likewise aid in judgment. At the same time, I readily grant
that each is supreme in its own domain, and that the advantage

[216] Cf. *Corp. Iur. Civ., Dig.,* i, 2, § 1.

[217] *de arte.*

[218] *ad artem.*

[219] *inuentionis,* invention; the discovery of arguments; cf. Cicero, *De Inv.,* i, 7, § 9.

[220] *in omni facultate,* in every branch of learning or philosophy.

[221] Cf. Boethius, *De Diff. Top.,* i, *ad fin.* (in Migne, *P.L.,* LXIV, 1182).

[222] *inuentori,* literally: to one engaged in invention.

conferred by the others is in this respect supplemental. Since the *Topics* have such evident utility, it surprises me that this book of Aristotle was neglected by our fathers for so long that it had completely, or almost entirely, fallen into disuse. At length, however, in our own day, through the insistent researches of diligent geniuses,[223] it has, as it were, been raised from the dead, or aroused from sleep, so that it may summon back to their senses those who have been wandering, and make plain the way of truth to those who have been seeking it. The wording and contents of the *Topics* are not so difficult that they cannot be understood by one who carefully applies himself; and, at the same time, their value is so tremendous that they are more worth knowing than are any of the other books. In comparison with various other treatises that have been translated from Greek [to Latin] according to a very strict plan of translation,[224] this book is sufficiently clear. At the same time, there is no mistaking the style of its author. Accordingly the work can be rightly understood only by one who observes the principle of indifference [relative to varying meanings of words],[225] without which no one among us, or even among the Greeks themselves, has ever really comprehended Aristotle (as a Greek interpreter,[226] who was by native citizenship a Severitan,[227] used to say). Its author [himself] has clearly shown how highly useful he considers this work by the very number of books into which he has divided it,[228] apparently thereby presaging its perfection. In it, he has, as it were, sowed the seeds of all those things which antiquity subsequently expanded into many volumes. Everything in the work, both rules and examples, can usefully be applied, not only to logic,

[223] John may be here referring to such scholars as Thierry of Chartres, in whose *Heptateuchon* Aristotle's eight books of the *Topics* are discussed.

[224] Or: in very literal translation.

[225] *indifferentie rationem*, a plan or method of indifference or impartiality relative to (the admission of) varying meanings of words [i.e., of the same word].

[226] *Grecus interpres*. H. Rose (in *Hermes*, I [1866], 379 ff.) has conjectured that this was Evericus Aristippus, translator of Plato; cf. Webb's Prolegomena to his edition of the *Policraticus*, I, pp. xxv, xxvi. Against this view, cf. O. Hartwig: "Re Guglielmo," in *Archivo storico per la provincie napoletane*, VIII (1883), 432 ff.; and L. Labowsky, in his preface to the edition of Aristippus' translation of Plato's *Meno*, in *Corpus Platonicum Medii Aevi* (London, 1940), p. x.

[227] *natione Seueritanus*, by birth or native citizenship a Severitan; perhaps from the city of St. Severino in Calabria; see Rose, *loc. cit.*

[228] The *Topics* consists of eight books.

but also to practically all branches of learning. The work comprises eight volumes, each of which surpasses in cogency the one that precedes it.[229] The first book lays down beforehand, as it were, the subject matter of all the following ones, and establishes certain foundations for the whole [edifice] of logic. It teaches[230] what are syllogisms, the nature and sources of demonstration, the fundamental principles[231] of the arts, and the bases of the confidence[232] the latter provide. It explains the nature of dialectical and contentious syllogisms, what is probable,[233] and what the mistake of those who use fallacious reasoning or draw false figures.[234] It also expounds the nature of propositions and problems.[235] And since the discussion of problems and the proof of propositions[236] must be taken up, it goes on to treat whence we derive problems, that is what propositions may, according to the art, be brought into question,[237] taking into consideration the difference between the various predicaments which condition the nature[238] of questions.[239] It does not indiscriminately apply its forms to all questions that may be asked, since to inquire into everything indicates a lack of discretion. Rather, it reserves them for matters that are deserving of study and worth knowing. There is no point in bothering about everyone who advances propositions contrary to the [generally accepted] opinions, nor with one who quibbles about trifling details in contemptible fashion. Since it is the nature of predicaments to predicate greater or equal things about subjects, Aristotle teaches that dialectical problems may be divided into four classes.[240] According to him (although this, together with certain other points in his treatise,

[229] Cf. Matthew, xii, 45.
[230] See Aristotle, *Top.*, i, 1 ff.; and the Boethian translation (in Migne, *P.L.*, LXIV, 909 ff.).
[231] *principia*, the principles, bases, preliminary suppositions.
[232] *fidei*, confidence, credibility, certitude.
[233] *quid probabile.*
[234] *falsigrafus*, one who writes incorrectly or falsely, according to Baxter and Johnson, *Medieval Latin Word List*: evidently, from the present context, one who draws false figures, as discussed by Aristotle in *Top.*, i, 1, 101 a.
[235] Aristotle, *Top.*, i, 10.
[236] *positionum*, positions, arguments, propositions.
[237] *ex arte deducantur in questionem.*
[238] *ratio*, reason, plan, nature, make-up.
[239] Aristotle, *Top.*, i, 11.
[240] *Ibid.*, i, 4, 5, 6.

is open to question) where the inquiry concerns what is greater and substantial, it is a question of genus, but where it relates to what is equal and substantial, it is one of definition. Likewise, when the inquiry concerns what is greater and accidental, there is a question of an accident, whereas when it concerns what is equal and accidental there is a question of a property. But since, when someone asks what, or how great, or of what kind, something is, our answer, if correct, cannot be less than the subject, it is clear that what is less may neither be predicated nor be the subject of a question. Aristotle explains the nature of genus, definition, accident, and property, far more aptly than those who have filled up numerous bulky volumes trying to elucidate on Porphyry or the *Categories*. "Let not my soul enter into their council," [241] and I hope that none of my friends will [be so unfortunate as to] have any of them as their teachers! Aristotle also explains the nature of induction, as well as in what cases the latter may be employed with greatest profit.[242] He discusses in how many senses[243] contraries may be predicated, and how things which have several different meanings are to be divided.[244] Indeed, it is very helpful just to know that ambiguous terms[245] admit neither of mutual comparison nor of combination into plural number, and consequently that they cannot be jointly inferred after they have been separately posited. Although a voice[246] and an angle or knife may each by themselves be called "sharp," [247] they may not by any means be called "sharp" together without [any] distinction. Neither can one of them be said to be "sharper" than the other. This consideration of the various senses of terms also frequently helps us to estimate the force of contraries from [that of] their contraries. If one of two contraries is used [either] equivocally or univocally with reference to several things, the other is also generally, or at least very often, employed

---

[241] Genesis, xlix, 6, that is, I do not want to join them.

[242] Aristotle, *Top.*, i, 12.

[243] *quotiens,* literally: how often.

[244] Aristotle, *Top.*, i, 15.

[245] *equiuocatio,* equivocation, ambiguity, using a single term with more than one meaning.

[246] *uox,* a voice, vocal sound, spoken word.

[247] *acutum,* sharp or acute. In this passage applied to both sound and angle or knife.

in like manner. As "heavy" [248] is the contrary of "sharp" in sounds, whereas it is the contrary of "light" [249] in mass, it is evident that both "light" and "heavy" may be used equivocally with respect to various things. One who wishes to know what is being discussed, must shake out the [full] force of words; for, unless he comprehends the latter, he cannot be confident that he understands what is said. Pertinent [here] is a statement of Augustine,[250] traceable to Aristotle,[251] from whom, as from a fountain, all have drunk. Augustine says that there are three things to be considered in every proposition: the expression [of the concept],[252] the concept [expressed],[253] and the reality [itself].[254] The reality is the thing concerning which the statement is made; the concept [expressed] is what is predicated of the thing; the expression [of the concept] is the way in which the predication is made. Occasionally, however, it happens that the expression is the thing [concerning which the statement is made], as when a word is employed with reference to itself. This occurs in what our teachers used to call "materially attributed concepts," [255] as when we say that: " 'Man' is a noun," and " 'Runs' is a verb." [256] The realities [themselves] and the concepts [expressed] generally pertain to nature, whereas their expression [is arbitrary, and] depends on man's free will. Consequently, when we investigate the truth, it is necessary that the reality [in question] be not entirely beyond our knowledge; that the concept [expressed] conform to the reality which is its subject, namely, to what is being discussed; and, finally, that the expression [or diction] be in conformity with both of the foregoing, in order that all occasion for criticism may be effectively precluded.

[248] *graue*, heavy or flat.
[249] *leui*.
[250] Cf. pseudo-Augustine, *De Dialectica*, chap. 5 (in Migne, *P.L.*, XXXII, 1411).
[251] Or rather, according to several scholars, from Varro's *De Lingua Latina*.
[252] *dictio*, the diction, the expression of a concept.
[253] *dicibile*, literally: the sayable; the concept expressed.
[254] *res*, the thing [itself], the fact, the reality.
[255] *materialiter . . . imposita et dicibilia*, materially attributed [or imposed] concepts [expressed].
[256] " 'Homo est nomen' . . . 'Currit est uerbum.' "

CHAPTER 6.   *The utility and scope of the [first] three books*
                          of the Topics.

Just as the treatise on the *Categories* is, so to speak, "alphabetical"
and that *On Interpretation* "syllabic," [257] so that on the *Topics* is
in a way "verbal" [of the nature of words].[258] While the work
On Interpretation treats of simple propositions, that is of true or
false statements,[259] it does not go to the extent of discussing the
force of inferences, and hence does not arrive at the chief concern
of the dialectician. The *Topics* is the first work which [really]
explains reasons.[260] It teaches argumentation from commonplaces[261]
and explains the sources of the conclusions that follow [from
them].[262] In much the same manner as, according to the moralist,[263]
"Everyday is the teacher of that which comes after it," [264] the first
book of the *Topics* serves as a preceptor for those which follow.
It makes manifest the topics[265] from which problems are derived,
while succeeding books explain whence and how proofs may be
constructed, and what propositions are more or are less arguable,
as well as why this is so. In giving due credit to this work, I do not,
however, exaggerate its efficacy to the point of considering the
labors of moderns useless. Scholars of our own day, drawing in-

[257] See *Met.*, iii, 4.
[258] *dictionalis,* dictional, verbal, like a word, as compared to a letter or syllable. The
nature of *dictio* is explained by Priscian, *Inst.*, ii, 14 (Keil, *G.L.*, II, 53); cf. Boethius,
Comm. II in Arist. de Interpr., ii, 4 (ed. Meiser, pp. 80–82). According to Priscian, a
dictio is an element of speech, intermediate between the syllable and the sentence, and
conveying an idea, although not a complete judgment.
[259] *dictio,* diction, expression, saying.
[260] *primus est in rationibus explicandis,* is first in explaining reasons or reasonings.
[261] *localium,* that is, τοπικῶν topical things, things relating to places or commonplaces
whence arguments may be drawn. Cf. Boethius, *De Diff. Top.*, i (in Migne, *P.L.*, LXIV,
1173).
[262] *sequentium complexionum,* the inferential complexes or conclusions that follow.
[263] *ethicum,* the moralist: in this case Publilius Syrus.
[264] Publilius Syrus, *Sent.* (ed. G. Meyer), p. 36. Codices B and A have "Seneca" in
the margin, for the proverb which today is recognized as coming from Publilius Syrus,
was formerly thought to be from Seneca. See Meyer's edition, pp. 6 ff.
[265] *locis.*

spiration and strength from Aristotle, are adding to the latter's findings many new reasons, and rules equally as certain as those he himself enunciated. Which are all ultimately traceable to Aristotle, for he who taught that the whole may be proved from a part, also showed that inferences may be drawn from two or three or more[266] parts. The same holds true in other cases. We are indebted, not only to Themistius, Cicero,[267] Apuleius,[268] and Boethius,[269] for their contributions, but also to the Peripatetic of Pallet, and to others of our teachers, who have striven to promote our progress by developing new doctrines as well as by elucidating old ones. I find it hard to understand, however, why the Peripatetic of Pallet restricted admissible hypothetical propositions exclusively to those whose consequent is included in its antecedent, or whose antecedent is voided if its consequent be disproved.[270] Indeed, while he [Abelard] used to be quite liberal about accepting arguments, he would refuse to admit hypothetical propositions, unless forced to do so by manifest necessity. Perhaps it was because, as Boethius observes,[271] "All men desire necessity in their inferences." [272] This is their wish, which they profess [even] when a condition is added. At the same time, however, certain things are admissible because of their evident probability, which often borders on necessity. Just as probable arguments suffice for the dialectician, so also he is satisfied with probable consequents. But both of these lose their convincing force if necessity is [clearly] lacking, as happens when a contrary instance wherein the proposition does not hold is alleged. Aristotle, however, posits consequents almost everywhere, whether he teaches that what has been proposed is to be proved, or that it is to be disproved. And since many things follow from any given proposition,

[266] *aut amplius*, literally: or from a greater number of parts.

[267] Boethius, in his *De Diff. Top.* (in Migne, *P.L.*, LXIV, 1200 ff.), tells us that Themistius and Cicero made some additions to the doctrine of the *Topics*.

[268] Apuleius, namely, in his book, which, as Cassiodorus says in his *De Art. ac Disc. Lib. Litt.*, chap. 3 (in Migne, *P.L.*, LXX, 1173) "is entitled the *Perihermeniae* of Apuleius." P. Thomas has added this treatise in Volume III of his edition of the *Opera* of Apuleius, in the Teubnerian series, 1908.

[269] Boethius, both in his *Comm. in Top. Cic.*, and in his *De Diff. Top.*

[270] See Abelard, *An. Post.*, i (*Ouvr. inéd.*, pp. 441, 442); ii (*ibid.*, pp. 446, 447). A hypothetical proposition consists of an "antecedent" and a "consequent."

[271] Boethius, *De Syllogismo Hypothetico*, i (in Migne, *P.L.*, LXIV, 843).

[272] *consequentiam*, consequence, sequence, inference.

we should take into consideration whence several conclusions may result whenever we prove or disprove something. As he [Aristotle] [273] observes: "Whenever one says anything, he in a way says several things. For any statement necessarily involves several consequences. One who has said that man exists, has also said that an animal, and a being which possesses activity, and a biped, and a being that is capable of thinking and learning exists." [274] [Aristotle also says that] "A problem that is suitable for argumentative reasoning[275] is one for which there are numerous and good arguments." [276] In view of the foregoing, the whole second book [of the *Topics*] is devoted to a discussion of accidents. Since it explains the nature of accidents in superb fashion, with convincing reasons and well-chosen examples, it can serve many purposes. As only accidents admit of comparison, the third book [of the *Topics*] discusses the [relative] values[277] of things that may be compared. Dwelling on the nature of accidents, it shows, by rules, reasons for selection or rejection. It also manifests, in similar manner, which are more preferable among preferable things, and which are least desirable among undesirable things. It is accordingly evident how helpful this particular branch of knowledge[278] can be in [the study of] physics and ethics.[279] Since this subdivision of the discipline is so valuable in instances where positive or negative choice is necessary, and in all cases where things are to be compared, certainly it has much to commend it. And clearly our predecessors made a mistake when they neglected this work, disregarding its outstanding utility and its very readable style, as well as its great contributions to ethics and physics.

---

[273] *Aristotiles* (Aristotle) is here apparently an addition from the margin to the text since, although MS A includes it in the text, MSS C and B have it only in the margin.

[274] Aristotle, *Top.*, ii, 5, 112 a, 16 ff. (cf. Migne, *P.L.*, LXIV, 928).

[275] *rationabile*, reasonable, capable of being argued, arguable.

[276] Aristotle, *Top.*, v, 1, 129 a, 30, 31 (cf. Migne, *P.L.*, LXIV, 955).

[277] *uim*, force, import, value.

[278] *disciplina*.

[279] *phisice et ethice*, for physics and ethics in their broader, earlier sense, namely, for natural and moral philosophy as then conceived.

CHAPTER 7.   *A brief account of the fourth and fifth books*
              [of the Topics*].*

The fourth book [of the *Topics*] treats of problems that concern
genus. It explains the agreement[280] of genus and species with each
other, as well as with other things. Whence all may readily see
how much time has been lost because our teachers have neglected
it. I do not deem it necessary to tarry long discussing genera, since
we have already said a good deal about them,[281] and it is not our
object to write a detailed commentary on the work. However, I do
believe that I should call attention to one point that is made by
Aristotle (as Porphyry, whom the little ones follow, teaches otherwise).[282] For Aristotle says that, just as genus is predicated in a
univocal, rather than a derivative sense, so also it is not predicated
merely in a particular respect.[283] Thus, undoubtedly, body is not the
genus of animal. He [Aristotle] says: "It should be carefully observed whether or not some things partake of a genus merely in
some particular respect, as would be the case if an animal were said
to be 'an object that may be sensed,' or 'an object that can be seen.'
An animal is perceptible by the senses or visible only in a certain
respect: so far as its body is concerned, but not with regard to its
soul. Wherefore it is impossible that 'an object that can be sensed,'
or 'an object that can be seen' should be the genus of animal. Those
who put the whole in a part, as do those who define an animal as
'a body possessing sensation,'[284] sometimes escape detection.[285] But

[280] *coherentiam,* coherence, agreement.
[281] Literally: genera of things.
[282] Porphyry teaches that body is the genus of animal. See Porphyry, *Isag.,* 2 a, 20
(*Comm. in Ar. Gr.,* IV, 4, 29; in Migne, *P.L.,* LXIV, 102).
[283] *secundum quid,* according to something, or in some particular respect. See Aristotle,
Top., iv, 6, 127 b, 6, 5; 126 a, 18.
[284] *sensibile,* sensible: may mean either perceptible by the senses, or capable of sensation. A correct translation of Aristotle's ἔμψυχον would rather be *animatum,* animated or
possessing movement.
[285] *Latent,* are hidden, escape observation.

a part may not in any sense be predicated of the whole. Wherefore 'body' cannot be the genus of animal, since it is only a part [of animal]." [286] Every genus holds true of the species and individuals in that genus in a direct, rather than a metaphorical [287] or figurative sense. It is never predicated otherwise than properly (speaking), as the most intimate of all attributions is that of substance, which is most correctly indicated by genus and species. When one predicates "body" with reference to man [that is, speaks of man as "a body"], this is done by synecdoche,[288] that is, in a figurative manner. It is obvious that the same person who, because of the evidence of one of his parts, may be called "a body," may likewise, because of the dignity of his other part, be called "a soul." But philosophers of lesser caliber,[289] such as Porphyry, follow the crowd, and generally accept practically nothing beyond what is apparent to their senses. Plato, however, as well as the Stoics and the Peripatetics, teaches that man is more correctly called "a soul" than "a body." Marcus Tullius [Cicero] agrees, and says in his book on *The Commonwealth:* "Look for yourself, not in the body delineated by your external form, but in the thinking soul,[290] which is everyone's real self." [291] The Doctors of the Church, as, for example, Augustine,[292] held the same view. If anyone still has any doubt concerning this, let him consult the Scriptures, which attribute to the soul a certain dominion[293] over the [human] person, and compare man's body to a temporary lodging[294] or garment.[295] The fifth book [of *Topics*] gives a very full explanation of the different senses in which a thing may be said to be a property. It teaches what is attributed as a property in a strict sense, and [what] in various

[286] Aristotle, *Top.,* iv, 5, 126 a, 20–29 (cf. Migne, *P.L.,* LXIV, 950).

[287] *translatione,* by transfer, trope, or metaphor.

[288] According to Isidore, *Etym.,* i, 37, § 13, "synecdoche" is "a conception whereby the whole is signified by a part, or a part by the whole." The comma after *scilicet* in the text of Webb's edition should apparently be transferred to before *scilicet.* Cf. MSS A, B, C, and the sense.

[289] *minutiores philosophi,* lesser or more mediocre philosophers; cf. Cicero, *De Senect.,* 23, § 85; *De Divin.,* i, 30, § 62.

[290] *mens,* mind, thinking soul, conscious soul, soul.

[291] Cicero, *De Republica,* vi, 24, § 26; *Somn. Scipionis,* 8, § 2.

[292] Cf. Augustine, *De Moribus Eccl. Cath.,* i, 4 (in Migne, *P.L.,* XXXII, 1313).

[293] *principatum,* preëminence, government, dominion.

[294] *hospitio,* a hospice, an inn; see II Corinthians, v, 1 ff.

[295] *indumento;* see II Corinthians, v, 2; and II Peter, i, 13, 14.

senses, as well as when a property is correctly or wrongly predicated. These considerations are very useful in proof and refutation, since a property, strictly so called, and its subject define[296] each other by mutual predication.

CHAPTER 8.   *Of definition, the subject of the sixth book [of the Topics].*

Definition is discussed in the sixth book [of the *Topics*], which lucidly teaches the art of defining. One who has mastered the contents of this book need not be hesitant about establishing or refuting definitions. The rules for definitions it lays down are very strict, and are never or hardly ever fully observed. Aristotle would outshine all others by his treatment of definitions, as well as by the rest of his discussion concerning argumentative reasoning, had he only as clearly built up his own contentions as he has effectively demolished those of others. But just as Aristotle has here been more successful with his refutations than with his affirmations,[297] so there are many others who are better at establishing than at disproving. Each of us cannot do everything,[298] although anyone who cooperates with the efficacy of grace is distinguished by his own special gift.[299] Not to mention Christians,[300] Naso [Ovid] composed [charming] lyrics, Cicero was a [very] successful advocate, Pythagoras plumbed the depths of nature, Socrates laid down a norm of ethics, Plato wrote convincingly concerning all sorts of topics, and Aristotle attained acute discernment.[301] While Marius Victorinus,[302]

[296] *concludunt,* define, circumscribe, complement, fill out.
[297] *ualidior hic expugnator extitit quam assertor.*
[298] Cf. Vergil, *Ecl.,* viii, 63.
[299] Cf. I Corinthians, vii, 7.
[300] *fidelibus,* the faithful, Christians, Christian writers.
[301] *argutias.*
[302] *Marius Victorinus:* the book *De Diffinitione,* commonly attributed to Boethius (in Migne, *P.L.,* LXIV, 891 ff.) seems to be by Marius Victorinus. See Boethius, *Comm. in Top. Cic.,* iii (in Migne, *P.L.,* LXIV, 1098 ff.); and Isidore, *Etym.,* ii, 29, an abridgment of the foregoing.

Boethius, and Cicero,[303] all of whom published books on definitions, each drew the basic principles of his doctrines from Aristotle, they widened the extension of the word "definition" to cover
fifteen kinds[304] [of so called "definitions"], including forms of
description. Aristotle's[305] primary concern is with substantial definitions, which should so comprise genus and substantial differences
that they are equivalent to their subject. Such definitions are
correctly posited when they are equivalent to what is defined, taken
in its broadest sense. In a substantial definition, we must not only
eliminate what is equivocal, but must also shun the indefiniteness
of things that are uncertain, since something provided to make
something else clear should itself be evident. Consequently, we
must avoid transfers [of meaning],[306] and whatever is predicated
in other than its proper sense, as when it is said that "Law is the
'measure' or 'image' of things that are naturally just."[307] As Aristotle says, "Such [statements] are worse than metaphor. Metaphors
do somehow make known what they mean by the comparison
they involve. Whenever we use them, we transfer meaning according to some similarity. But statements such as the aforesaid do not
make anything known. There is no inherent resemblance to justify
calling law 'a measure' or 'an image,' nor is it customary to refer
to it as such. If one says that law is literally 'a measure' or 'an
image,' he is either deceiving or being deceived.[308] An image is
something fashioned in the likeness of something else, but such is
not an inherent characteristic of law. If, on the other hand, the
statement is not made in a literal sense, it is evident that it is
obscure, and worse than any metaphorical expression." Characteristics should be selected that are readily recognizable to anyone
who is well disposed. Unless what is posited is something that is
in itself more intelligible,[309] or [at least] more intelligible to us,

---

[303] See Cicero, *Top.*, chaps. 5–7, which Boethius treats in Book III of his commentary.
[304] Fifteen kinds of definitions are enumerated by Victorinus, according to the above-
quoted passages in Boethius, *Comm. in Top. Cic.*, and Isidore, *Etym.*
[305] *huic*, Aristotle or his book.
[306] *translationes*, transfers [of meaning], metaphors.
[307] This, together with the following quotation, is from Aristotle, *Top.*, vi, 2, 140 a,
7 ff. (cf. Migne, *P.L.*, LXIV, 971).
[308] *mentitur.*
[309] *notioribus*, more known, better known, more intelligible.

it does not help define.[310] A definition should also be "equivalent in parts," [311] that is "equivalent in members," [312] to what it defines. If, for example, we are asked "What is speculative science?" then neither "speculative" nor "science" should be left ambiguous.[313] Moreover, in substantial definitions,[314] nothing should be stated that would approximate a state of being the recipient of action.[315] As Aristotle says, "Every state of being acted upon[316] detracts proportionately from a substance. It is otherwise, however, with differences, which seem rather to conserve their subject. It is an absolute impossibility for anything to exist without its own specific differentiation. 'Man' does not exist if 'a being that has the power to walk' [317] does not exist. We may say, without qualification, that any quality which alters a subject possessing it cannot be a difference of this subject. For all such [qualities] detract from a substance in proportion as they are increased. If anyone attributes a difference of this kind, he is making a mistake.[318] Indeed, we undergo absolutely no alternation as a consequence of our differences." [319] Plato lays himself open to criticism when he includes "mortal" in the definition of animal.[320] Although mortality may not become greater, or be predicated in greater measure, so far as things of this sort do not admit of greater or lesser degree, still it is not a difference. Perhaps it would be more correct to say that mortality denotes a disposition[321] and a capacity, or rather a necessity, to undergo something. It is easy to persuade a Christian to accept this proposition, since, looking forward to immortality, he does not believe that his nature will dissolve in corruption, but rather that his condition of living will be transformed into a better one. Our

---

[310] Aristotle, *Top.*, vi, 4, 141 a, 26 ff.

[311] *Equicolam;* ἰσόκωλον; see Aristotle, *Top.*, vi, 11, 148 b, 33, 34. The Boethian translation has *aequimembris* (in Migne, *P.L.*, LXIV, 983).

[312] *equimembris.*

[313] Cf. Aristotle, *Top.*, vi, 11, 149 a, 9 ff.

[314] *substantialibus diffinitiuis,* substantial definitives, terms defining substances.

[315] *passionem.*

[316] *passio,* state of being acted upon, state of receptivity of action, affection.

[317] *gressibile.*

[318] *peccauit,* literally: he has sinned, that is, he has erred, is mistaken, is at fault.

[319] Aristotle, *Top.*, vi, 6, 145 a, 3 ff. (cf. Migne, *P.L.*, LXIV, 978, and note differences).

[320] See *ibid.*, vi, 10, 148 a, 15, 16 (cf. Migne, *P.L.*, LXIV, 982).

[321] *habitum,* a condition, circumstance, habit, disposition.

substance will be glorified, and instead of decomposing, will be
exempted from the necessity of suffering. Even the capacity for
suffering will disappear, when, "death being swallowed up, what
is mortal puts on immortality, and what is corruptible attains in-
corruptibility." [322] It is not surprising that mortality is classed as a
capacity of being the recipient of action,[323] since immortality itself,
according to Aristotle, should be described as "a state of being acted
on [by an external cause]." For he says: "Immortality seems to
be a receptive and accidental condition of life.[324] The truth of this
becomes apparent when one grants that man passes from a state of
being mortal to a state of being immortal. No one says that man has
taken on another life. Rather, we say that a certain 'accidental
condition,' [325] or 'passive receptivity' has been generated with
regard to[326] his original life.[327] So then 'life' is not the genus of
immortality." [328] From the foregoing it is clear that mortal and immortal are not species or differences of living things, but rather
indicate manners of living, or the condition of a nature. There is
nothing evil in substance, as "the substance of anything especially
includes what is best about it." [329] It is, however, difficult, save for
one who possesses most extensive knowledge, to define substances
according to the rules.[330] What is substantial is frequently uncertain,
owing either to the difficulty involved in investigating it, or to our
ignorance of it, or to the ambiguity of words [when applied to it].
There are, furthermore, several things which, by their very nature,
lack definitions strictly so called.[331] Thus principles do not have
definitions proper. With regard to things of this type that rise to
a higher plane,[332] no genera can be found, since they have none.
Individual entities likewise lack definitions properly so called, since

[322] See I Corinthians, xv, 53.
[323] *passibilitati,* capacity for passivity, affectibility.
[324] *passio uite et casus.*
[325] *casum.*
[326] *adgenerari.*
[327] *eidem,* to the same; to this same life.
[328] Aristotle, *Top.,* iv, 5, 126 b, 36 ff. (cf. Migne, *P.L.,* LXIV, 951). For *casus* Aristotle
has σύμπτωμα or incident, and Boethius *accidens* or accident.
[329] *Ibid.,* vi, 12, 149 b, 37 (cf. Migne, *P.L.,* LXIV, 985).
[330] *regulariter,* by rule, regularly, properly.
[331] See Boethius, *In Cat. Arist.,* i (in Migne, *P.L.,* LXIV, 166).
[332] *sursum pergentibus,* rising to a higher level, themselves more general.

they are not distinguished from one another by substantial differences. In the latter case, descriptions serve in lieu of definitions,
and are the more plausible the more closely they resemble definitions.
Descriptions are judged much more leniently than are definitions.[333]
It is easier to do something than to do it well; and virtue always
involves difficulty.[334] But once a definition is firmly established, it
serves as a most efficacious instrument for proving or refuting
propositions. For the strength or weakness of a proposition is
directly dependent on the definition of its terms.[335]

CHAPTER 9. *The problem of identity and diversity, which is
treated in the seventh book; together with some
general observations concerning the* Topics.

The seventh book [of the *Topics*] depends on definitions, and discusses problems relative to identity and diversity. This involves
considerable difficulty, for a [swirling] confluence[336] of contrary
considerations[337] provides subject matter for doubt. Things are said
to be "different" and "the same" in several different senses. Both
identity and diversity are generic, specific, and numerical.[338] If
things differ in genus, we may at once say that they also differ in
species and number. On the other hand, if things are numerically
identical, we may forthwith declare that they are identical in other
respects.[339] "Especially indubitable is it that what is numerically
one and identical with something is seen to be called 'the same' by
everyone, for it is absolutely such. Even this identity, however, is
likely to be referred to in more than one sense. The primary and

---

[333] *earum.*

[334] Cf. Ovid, *Art. Am.,* ii, 537.

[335] *qui* in the Webb edition (150, 19) should be corrected to read *quia.* Cf. MSS A, B,
and C.

[336] *concursus,* a confluence, a meeting as on a field of battle.

[337] *rationum,* reasons or points of view, ways of looking at a question, manners of interpretation, considerations.

[338] Cf. Boethius, *De Trin.,* c. i (ed. Peiper, p. 15).

[339] Namely, in genera and species.

literal sense occurs when the identity is designated by an alternative
name or definition, as when a 'tunic' is referred to as a 'garment,'[340] or a 'man' as a 'two-footed animal able to walk.' The
second sense occurs when the identity has reference to a property,
as when 'man' is alluded to as '[a being] capable of being educated,'
and 'fire' as 'something that rises upwards by its nature.'[341] The
third sense is found when identity is attributed accidentally, as
when Socrates is spoken of as 'the one who is sitting' or 'the
learned one.'[342] Each of these [three types of] expressions is employed to designate numerical identity. Anyone may see that what
we had just said holds true, from the fact that one appellation
may be substituted for another. Thus, frequently, when we direct
someone to call a person who is seated, and only mention the latter
by name, if the one whom we have so instructed does not understand to whom we refer, we change our directions and tell him to
summon 'the man who is seated' or 'the fellow who is engaged
in disputation,' since he is likely to recognize the person more
easily from an accident. It is clear that, in so doing, we are intend-
ing to designate the same individual, independently of whether
we refer to him by name or by accident. Therefore identity (as we
have stated) may be divided into three types."[343] A knowledge of
genus, property, and accident, as well as of definitions, is necessary
for both proof and refutation in questions of identity and diversity.
Nothing, however, is more useful for both of these projects than
definition, since nothing is more efficacious, or more understand-
able. Because of the abundance of commonplaces [from which
arguments may be drawn[344]] that are therein contained, it is very
properly said that the sum of the *Topics* is found in the seven
volumes we have just discussed. They have been, as Isidore says,
entitled *Topics,* because they contain *topos,*[345] that is "common-

[340] *uestis tunice.*

[341] Namely, rather than being pulled down to earth, as are other things.

[342] *musicum,* the musical, poetical, or learned one.

[343] Aristotle, *Top.,* i, 7, 103 a, 23–103 b, i (cf. Migne, *P.L.,* LXIV, 914, 915, and note differences).

[344] *locorum,* places, commonplaces, maxims, principles, sources.

[345] *topos,* that is, τόπους. Note that John here, as elsewhere, substitutes Latin for Greek characters.

places,"[346] which are "foundations[347] of arguments, fountainheads of meanings, and sources of expressions."[348] The branch of study itself is also called *Topice,* because it deals with these commonplaces. One who carefully studies this work [of Aristotle] will discover that from these seven volumes have come, not only the *Topics* of Cicero and Boethius, but also Boethius' book of *Divisions,*[349] which, owing to its succinct wording and judicious insight,[350] has acquired special favor among the latter's logical treatises. Nevertheless, I do not believe that all topics are included in this work, as such would, indeed, be impossible. I observe that other equally necessary topics are, every day, even more clearly explained by moderns who have the benefit of the foregoing [*Topics* of Aristotle]. There is involved in these [topics] the subject matter of invention.[351] The latter is defined, if imperfectly, by William of Champeaux, subsequently Bishop of Chalons-sur-Marne, of happy memory, as the science of finding a middle term, and of thence constructing an argument.[352] When inherent agreement[353] is doubted, it is necessary to search for some middle term whereby extremes may be copulated. It is hard for me to see how any other speculation could be more subtle or efficacious for this purpose than the present one. A middle term is necessary where the force of the inference[354] is involved in the terms. But if the force of the inference lies between whole propositions, so that it depends rather on a combination of parts than on the parts combined, then the bond[355] of the middle term ceases.[356] In such inferences as derive their proving force from terms or parts of terms, the "topic" proceeds from the relationship[357] existing between the

---

[346] *locos,* topics, subjects, places from which arguments may be drawn, commonplaces.
[347] *sedes.*
[348] Isidore, *Etym.,* ii, 29, § 16.
[349] *librum Diuisionum* (in Migne, *P.L.,* LXIV, 875 ff.).
[350] *elegantia sensuum,* elegance, taste, propriety, or apt selection of meanings, senses, or thought.
[351] *inuentionis,* the discovery or thinking up of proofs. Cf. Cicero, *De Inv.,* i, 7, § 9.
[352] *argumentum.* John (*Met.,* iii, 10 [160, 7]), defines an "argument" as "a dialectical syllogism."
[353] *inherentia,* inherent or fundamental connection or agreement.
[354] *inferentie;* this word, whence comes our modern English and French "inference," is employed by Abelard in his *Topics* (*Ouvr. Inéd.,* pp. 278, 325, 328).
[355] *nexus,* bond, connection.
[356] Cf. Abelard, *Top.* (*Ouvr. Inéd.,* p. 407).
[357] *habitudine.*

term that is eliminated in the conclusion[358] and the term that replaces it, as consequents are established by their antecedents. But that term which is unmodified in both instances, neither experiences the force of proving, nor participates in the certitude established by the proof. And just as from their meanings terms come to be called "universal" or "particular," so also conformity or disagreement of meanings causes one term to follow from or be incompatible with another. Unless the things that terms signify agree or disagree with one another, there is no reason for looking for friendship or hostility between the terms. It is not always easy in particular cases to determine the [precise] strength of the connection between things, or the [exact] amount of their mutual repugnance. For the same reason, it is occasionally very difficult to judge what is absolutely necessary or what very probable.[359] However, what is generally so is probable; what is never otherwise is very probable; and what we believe must be so[360] is termed "necessary." The [final] determination as to what is necessary and what probable lies concealed in nature's bosom, and nature alone [really] knows her own forces. For a long time, men thought that it was impossible to cut diamonds, since the latter were unaffected by the sharpness of either iron or steel. But when, at length, the diamond was finally cut by means of lead with goat's blood, it was seen that what had formerly been considered impossible was really quite easy.[361] Accordingly, the wonted chain of events[362] should be carefully observed, and the contents of nature's bosom should be, so to speak, thoroughly examined,[363] so that what is necessary and what probable may become clear. There is nothing that helps more [than does this scrutiny of nature] to provide a knowledge of topics, to beget fuller understanding of the truth,

---

[358] *id quod demitur conclusioni,* the minor term of the preceding syllogism, which is the middle term of the subsequent syllogism, and is not expressed in its conclusion.

[359] *magis probabile,* more probable, very probable.

[360] Literally: cannot be otherwise.

[361] Cf. Pliny, *Hist. Nat.,* xxxvii, §§ 59, 60; cf. xx, § 2; Augustine, *De C.D.,* xxi, 4; Isidore, *Etym.,* xvi, 13, § 2. However, neither Pliny, Augustine, nor Isidore makes any reference to lead in this connection.

[362] *solitus rerum cursus.* This savors of Augustine, who everywhere teaches that miracles are not contrary to nature, but rather are simply outside of nature's customary and usual course. Cf. *Contra Faust.,* xxvi, 3 (in Migne, *P.L.,* XLIII, 481), where Augustine says: "We also call nature's familiar and customary course 'nature.' "

[363] *excutiendus,* explored, ransacked, shaken out.

to teach and to persuade, and to develop a happy faculty of dealing
with every kind of subject.[364]

CHAPTER 10.   *The utility of the eighth book
[of the* Topics].

It is a well-known fact that all experts make ready their instruments before they attempt to accomplish anything by means of their
art, lest their particular competence be nullified by the lack of suitable implementation. In military matters,[365] a commanding officer
must first see that his army is properly supplied with arms and
other military equipment. The architect-builder with his tools first
determines and obtains the materials he will use in his construction. The mariner makes ready his rudder, ropes, oars, anchors, and
other nautical equipment, whereby he may expedite his voyage,
and may the better make his way over the water.[366] In like manner,
the contriver of the science of reasoning,[367] the drill-master[368] of
those who profess to be logicians, has in the foregoing books, as it
were, provided the means of disputation, and stacked in the arena
arms for the use of his students. This he has done by explaining
the meanings of uncombined words and clarifying the nature of
propositions and topics. His next step is to show his disciples how
they may use these instruments, and somehow to teach them the
art of engaging in [argumentative] combat. As if to set the members of the contestants in motion, he shows them how to propose
and answer questions,[369] as well as how to prove and evade. By his
precepts, he gives form to the faculty[370] for the sake of which the

---

[364] *omnium dicendorum.*
[365] *re militari,* in military affairs, military science or tactics, or warfare.
[366] Literally: that he may the more expediently obtain the object of his art.
[367] Namely, Aristotle.
[368] *campidoctor,* drill-master or field-instructor: Vegetius frequently uses this term in
his *De Re militari.*
[369] *proponendi et respondendi.*
[370] That is, the faculty of argumentative reasoning.

contents of the foregoing books have been taught. To extend our previous analogy, just as the *Categories* are "alphabetical," the *On Interpretation* "syllabic," and the aforesaid [seven] books of the *Topics* "verbal," so the eighth book of the *Topics* "constructs[371] reasoning," whose component parts or topics have been explained in the foregoing books. This [eighth] book alone discusses the [practical] rules which constitute the art. If what it teaches is both borne in mind and correctly observed, it contributes more to the science of argumentative reasoning than practically all the works on dialectic that our modern predecessors[372] were accustomed to teach[373] in the schools.[374] Without this book, one depends on chance, rather than on art, in disputation.[375] On the other hand, this book cannot attain its full efficacy unless one also understands the preceding ones, which, although they contain but few rules, nevertheless teach numerous very useful facts concerning both things and words. Since dialectic is carried on between two persons,[376] this book teaches the matched contestants[377] whom it trains and provides with reasons and topics, to handle their [proper] weapons and engage in verbal,[378] rather than physical conflict. It instills into its disciples such astute skill that one may clearly see that it is the principal source of the rules of all eloquence, for which it serves as a sort of primary fountainhead. It is undoubtedly true, as Cicero[379] and Quintilian[380] acknowledge, that this work has not merely been helpful to rhetoricians, but has also, for both them and writers on the arts,[381] even served as the initial starting point

---

[371] *constructorius;* lexicons do not give *constructorius,* whose meaning, however, is evident.

[372] *moderni patres nostri,* literally: "our modern [or recent] fathers."

[373] *legere.*

[374] That is, before Aristotle's *Topics* was, as John says (*Met.,* iii, 5), ". . . in our own time . . . as it were resurrected from death or sleep . . ."

[375] Although John did not have access to Plato's *Gorgias,* either in the original or in translation, this may be a reflection of the same (line 448). What John means here is that anyone disputing without Aristotle's *Topics* proceeds only by chance, rather than by the rules of the logical art.

[376] *ad alterum est,* is directed or addressed to another, or to an interlocutor.

[377] *pares.*

[378] *sermones . . . conserere,* to duel with words, to weave words.

[379] Cicero, *Orat.,* 32, §§ 113 ff.; cf. *De Fin.,* ii, 6, § 17.

[380] Quintilian, *Inst. Or.,* xii, 2; §§ 12, 13.

[381] *scriptores artium;* cf. Quintilian, *Inst. Or.,* iii, 1, § 1.

for the study of rhetoric, which subsequently expanded and acquired its own particular rules. Dialectic consists entirely in a discussion carried on between a questioner and an answerer,[382] to whom it is limited, since each is the other's judge. Either of these [disputants] may attain his object by not omitting anything that is relevant,[383] and by adhering to his proposition in such a way that he maintains both himself and his statements invulnerable. Occasion for adverse criticism is not always the same: often it is a consequence of what is proposed and often the fault of the one who has proposed it.[384] As Aristotle observes, "it does not lie in the power of one person, by himself, to bring a joint enterprise to a satisfactory conclusion. . . ."[385] "In a dispute, both he who questions[386] in a contentious fashion, and he who, in answering, refuses to grant what is evident, and declines to meet the real issue the questioner raises,[387] are at fault. At the same time, it is clear that we should not necessarily criticize the argument and the one who advances it in the same way. There is no reason why a questioner cannot be disputing very well against an answerer, even though his [the questioner's] speech is poor. Against those who are ill-tempered,[388] it may not be possible immediately to construct the kind of syllogisms that we might desire, and in this case we must be content with what is practicable under the circumstances.[389] "One who impedes a work that has been undertaken together is certainly a poor partner."[390] I cannot say [precisely] how adverse criticism of one's opponent is to be expressed or avoided, since I am not sure whether Aristotle would say that we should lay greater stress on utility or on subtlety and strictness. "It is the object of a good questioner to get the answerer both to make very unlikely statements, and to

---

[382] *inter opponentem et respondentem.*

[383] *ex contingentibus.*

[384] See Aristotle, *Top.,* viii, 11, 161 a, 16. Cf. Boethius' translation (in Migne, *P.L.,* LXIV, 1002–1003).

[385] *commune opus,* a common or coöperative project: Aristotle, *Top.,* vii, 11, 161 a, 19 ff.

[386] *interrogat,* questions, presents an argument.

[387] Literally: wishes to ask, intends to ask.

[388] *discolos,* δυσκολαίνοντας in Aristotle, the bad-tempered or perverse, those who lose their temper.

[389] Aristotle, *Top.,* viii, 11, 161 b, 2 ff.

[390] *Ibid.,* viii, 11, 161 a, 37.

say more than his thesis[391] really requires. On the other hand, it is the answerer's business to make it seem that not he [himself], but his thesis is responsible for whatever seems impossible or contrary to commonly accepted opinions.[392] One may perhaps distinguish between the fault of proposing something that is unfitting, and that of failing adequately[393] to maintain what has been proposed." [394] But an opponent, although he occasionally directs his efforts "to establishing a universal by induction, or giving greater weight to his argument, or clarifying what he says," deems that always the most effective stratagem is "to conceal the conclusion," so that, when he finishes his speech, one may ask: "What is the point?" [395] Whence, in *The Marriage of Mercury and Philology,* Dialectic[396] carries both a serpent and rules, so that [either] the uncautious and unlearned may be bitten by the wily and secretive serpent, which creeps up on and surprises its victims, or the malicious[397] may be instructed or corrected by the rules of reasoning.[398] Caution[399] [in dialectic] consists in accomplishing one's object in an orderly, expeditious manner, whether one is dividing, defining, or drawing inferences. This caution ordinarily proceeds from a previous knowledge of topics and argumentation, and other forms of speech whereby divisions and definitions may be explained. While the topics for arguments, divisions, and definitions are frequently the same, the art flourishes most in argumentation. This art is also most cogent in syllogisms, whether it is complete in its entirety in the latter, or hastens on to the conclusion by suppressing the middle proposition in the fashion of an enthymeme.[400] Therefore this art is

---

[391] *positionem.*

[392] *preter opinionem,* apart from, beside, not in conformity with the [generally accepted] opinion.

[393] *secundum modum,* κατὰ τρόπον in Aristotle.

[394] Aristotle, *Top.,* viii, 4, 159 a, 18–24 (cf. Migne, *P.L.,* LXIV, 999).

[395] *Ibid.,* viii, 1, 155 b, 22 ff.; 156 b, 14, 15.

[396] *Dialectica,* dialectic or dialectics, personified.

[397] *improbi,* the malicious or perhaps the erring.

[398] See Martianus Capella, *De Nupt.,* iv, § 328.

[399] *cautela,* caution, care, diligence, prudence, astuteness.

[400] *enthimematis,* the enthymeme is here understood, not according to Aristotle, but according to Boethius, *Comm. in Top. Cic.,* i (in Migne, *P.L.,* LXIV, 1050): "An enthymeme is an imperfect syllogism, some of whose parts have been omitted, either for the sake of brevity, or because they are well known."

most effective in disputation.[401] Induction, on the contrary, is more gentle.[402] Which is the case, regardless of whether it advances deliberately from several instances to a universal or particular [proposition], or leaps across by inference from one thing, introduced by way of example,[403] to another. This method is more suitable for orators, although from time to time the dialectician [also] employs it for ornamentation or explanation. For it serves more to persuade than to convince. Socrates generally used this kind of argumentation, as Marcus Tullius testifies in his treatise on Rhetoric.[404] When examples are adduced to prove something, whether there are several such [examples], or only one, "they should be relevant, and drawn from things with which we are well acquainted. They should be the sort [of examples] that Homer uses, and not the kind that Choerillus gives."[405] If examples are taken from the [classical] authors, a Greek should quote Homer, a Latin, Vergil and Lucan. Familiar examples have greater cogency, whereas strange ones lend no conviction concerning what is doubtful. Unsophisticated[406] and straightforward ways of putting things[407] are very useful, both to help conceal what is proposed, and to assist either of the contestants[408] in his efforts to attain his objective. For they so disguise one's art that one is thought either to be without it, or to have decided not to use it. Showing off one's art always excites suspicion. On the other hand, those who approach in an unassuming manner are more readily received. First, and above all else, both of the disputants must correctly understand the issue under discussion. If the proposition in question is not [entirely] clear, it is very difficult to carry on an argument. For then

---

[401] Cf. Aristotle, *Top.*, i, 12, 105 a, 18 ff.

[402] *lenior*, more gentle, mild, or indulgent.

[403] See Aristotle, *An. Prior.*, ii, 24.

[404] Cicero, *De Invent.*, i, 31, § 53.

[405] Aristotle, *Top.*, viii, 1, 157 a, 14 ff. (cf. Migne, *P.L.*, LXIV, 996). Concerning Choerillus, see Horace, *A.P.*, 357.

[406] *idiotismus*, a vulgar, common, or popular way of speaking, such as one would not expect of a learned man; cf. Seneca, *Controv.*, vii, praef., § 5.

[407] *ortonismus*, apparently a manner of speaking such as is used by a man who is free from deceit; straightforwardness. Whence John has obtained the word is uncertain.

[408] *gignadiorum*, the contestants; that is, the disputants. In *Policraticus*, i, 8, John uses this term to refer to those who exercise in the gymnasiums proper. Here he employs it metaphorically, with reference to those who train in the schools. Cf. also *Met.*, iii, 3.

we are likely to descend to quibbling over words, or, as is often the case, to lack any real disputation. Argumentative reasoning is impossible if the minds of the disputants do not meet and agree upon some particular proposition.[409] If two persons are to come together, they must travel on the same road. Either there should be only one question, or [if there is more than one ⟨question⟩, then] the various questions involved should be properly distinguished. This is why Aristotle says: "Since it is permissible for an answerer who does not understand a question to say 'I do not understand,' and he is under no compulsion either to grant or to deny what has been said in several senses, it is evident that, if what is said is not clear, we should not hesitate to declare at the outset that we do not understand it. Often some difficulty later ensues from the fact that assent was [originally] given to a question that was not clearly stated. If, despite the fact that a question has several senses, it is understood, and is consistently true or false in all these senses, it should be granted or denied universally and without qualification.[410] But if the [proposition in] question is false in one sense although true in another, we should point out that it has several senses, and that it is in one way false, but in another true. If this distinction were to be held back till later, uncertainty might well arise whether the question was considered ambiguous in the beginning. If, however, without foreseeing the doubt, we earlier assented to a question, having in mind an alternative sense of the words, we should say to him who has subsequently taken the words in a different sense: 'I admitted the question having in mind, not this, but its other meaning.' For when a word [411] or statement[412] has several different senses, doubt very easily arises. If, however, the question is plain and simple, one should reply either 'Yes' or 'No.' " [413] For, as Agellius[414] says, one who in such cases answers more or less than what he has been asked, either does not understand or violates the proper proce-

---

[409] *articulo*, article, proposition, point.
[410] *simpliciter*
[411] *nomine*, a name or word.
[412] *oratione*, a speech, expression, sentence, or statement.
[413] Aristotle, *Top.*, viii, 7, 160 a, 18 ff. (cf. Migne, *P.L.*, LXIV, 1001).
[414] That is, Gellius.

dure in disputation.[415] One who impedes his colleague by excessive verbosity, or by distortion in his response, not only is a poor partner, but also is clearly perverse.[416] Especially is this so, if, without having a negative instance,[417] one contradicts a universal after having admitted the particular instances that support it. "To bring an argument to a halt without a negative instance, real or apparent, is a mark of perversity. If therefore, one, despite the fact that he cannot allege such [a negative instance], refuses to grant the universality of something that is manifest in many instances, he shows a perverse disposition, unless perhaps he has a contrary argument to disprove the validity of the inference."[418] There can be no doubt that "If a conclusion is false, it evidently does not follow from true premises." Falsehood is never the offspring of truth, whose chaste womb neither conceives nor harbors error.[419] "Nevertheless, it is not enough to bring up an argument to the contrary. Frequently propositions which differ from the [commonly accepted, authoritative] opinions are not easily dispensed with, since there are conflicting arguments on both sides.[420] Zeno[421] maintained that 'movement and traversing the stadium do not take place,'"[422] but Empedocles,[423] on the contrary, asserted that "everything is in motion."[424] The opinion of a few, especially if it lacks the solid support of very good reasons, does not detract from an equally firm and more general opinion. "Consequently one is guilty of perversity if, in such cases, he [refuses to grant a proposition, but] neither cites a negative instance nor advances counterarguments. For, in disputation, to answer in other ways than those that have been enumerated, and thereby to wreck a syllogism, is perversity."[425] This is true of

---

[415] Gellius, xvi, 2, § 1.

[416] *proteruus,* bold, impudent, shameless, ill-tempered, wanton, or perverse.

[417] A negative instance or argument.

[418] Aristotle, *Top.,* viii, 10, 160 b, 2 ff. (cf. Migne, *P.L.,* LXIV, 1001–1002).

[419] *Ibid.,* viii, 11, 162 a, 8 ff.; *idem, An. Prior,* ii, 2, 53 b, 11 ff.

[420] Aristotle, *Top.,* viii, 10, 160 b, 6 ff.

[421] Zeno; see *ibid.,* viii, 8, 160 b, 8.

[422] *Ibid.,* viii, 10, 160 b, 6 ff.

[423] Empedocles, rather Heraclitus; see *ibid.,* i, 10, 104 b, 21, 22. Shortly afterwards Aristotle refers to the opinion of Empedocles concerning the four elements (105 b, 16).

[424] *omnia moueri;* see *ibid.,* viii, 9, 160 b, 19.

[425] See *ibid.,* viii, 10, 160 b, 10 ff.

the answerer. The questioner, on his part, is perverse,[426] if, after
what was granted has been made clear, he takes unfair advantage
of the words, twists them around to the contrary, and refusing to
accept their intended meaning, seizes upon syllables,[427] so that he
disputes like a madman over a word. The more obstinately one
insists, the more reprehensible is his perversity. Each of the disputants may, however, impede what the other proposes without becoming guilty of perversity, provided that he observes propriety, and
does not overstep the [rightful] bounds of his function[428] in proof
and rebuttal. One may speed up another who is naturally or habitually
sluggish. On the contrary, one may slow down, with the measured
pace of gravity,[429] one who is overhasty owing to his natural disposition or assiduous practice. One may also hide what he proposes,
in order to mislead the other by his art. Or, for purposes of prudent
evasion, one may unveil something that has been concealed. There
are, indeed, several such alternatives. But if it seems that something
false follows from what is true, we may rest assured that either
the reasoning is sophistical, or is some other variety of fallacious,
unreliable argumentation, which does not deserve our assent, even
though we may not be able to put our finger directly on the fallacy.[430] This is more useful in contentious argumentation[431] than in
demonstration or dialectical exercises. "A sophism is a contentious
syllogism," "a philosopheme[432] is a demonstrative syllogism"; "an
argument is a dialectical syllogism"; "an aporeme[433] is a dialectical
syllogism that reasons to a contradiction." [434] A knowledge of all
these [kinds of] syllogisms is necessary, and they are employed with
great utility in every branch of study.[435] Accordingly, one should
become well versed in disputation. First principles should be

[426] proteruia is here understood. Literally: the same [perversity] would exist in the
questioner.
[427] aucupans sillabas; see Jerome, Ep., lvii, 6 (in Migne, P.L., XXII, 572).
[428] officii sui partibus.
[429] grauitatis mora.
[430] See Aristotle, Top., viii, 11, 162 a, 8 ff.
[431] litigiis, contests, disputes, litigations.
[432] philosofima.
[433] aporisma, that is, ἀπόρημα.
[434] Aristotle, Top., viii, 11, 162 a, 15 ff.
[435] facultatibus.

reviewed in one's mind. Things that are necessary and probable should be distinguished from their opposites, and also from each other. The meanings of words should be carefully determined, since a person who has this knowledge can see that a single statement may readily imply several propositions, whereas, on the other hand, several statements may be reduced to a single proposition. Extreme care should be observed in establishing or eliminating universals, for it is quite evident that these constitute both the greatest secrets of success and the chief obstacles to progress. "It is impossible to reason without a universal." [436] Although brevity is the prime virtue in all speech, [437] its efficacy and worth shine most brilliantly and are most welcome in arguments addressed to a fellow disputant. [438] Excessive verbosity is the greatest wastrel of all. If a question cannot be [directly] speeded up, it should at least be purged of the delay occasioned by new [and extraneous] considerations, even though these may not seem beside the point. As Aristotle says, "Anyone who keeps on asking the same question for a long time is a poor questioner. If the answerer is replying to the questions, it becomes evident either that the questioner is asking several questions, or that he is repeating the same one over and over. In such a case, the questioner is either babbling, [439] or lacks a syllogism, since every syllogism is composed of a few elements. If, on the other hand, the one interrogated is not replying to the question, it is evident that the questioner [is also at fault, because he] is neither taking him to task nor breaking off the discussion. [440] It [sometimes] happens, however, that questions are multiplied in order to afford opportunities for reproof, and to supply abundant and ready handles [441] for just criticism. This is generally to be approved, although sometimes when one keeps retracing his steps and going round in circles, [442] and is continually in motion without making

[436] . . . *non est sine uniuersali sillogizare;* see Aristotle, *Top.,* viii, 14, 164 a, 10, 11.

[437] As in the speech of Thucydides, according to Seneca the rhetorician, *Controu.,* ix, 1, § 13.

[438] Literally: addressed to another.

[439] *iuuenatur,* ἀδολέσχει (in Aristotle), which the translation used by John seems to have taken as derived from *adolescens.*

[440] Aristotle, *Top.,* viii, 2, 158 a, 25 ff.

[441] *ansas,* handles. Cf. Cicero, *De Amic.,* 16, § 59.

[442] *auras easdem circinat;* see Ovid, *Metam.,* ii, 721.

any forward progress,[443] this indicates a deficiency. Thus the question proposed may be indefinite, or the way for proceeding with it may be blocked. Hescelin, the artisan, according to Master William, used to do as those who have no definite objective in disputation, and practiced his craft in the same fashion as they carry on dialectic.[444] He would not count on his art, but would trust in chance to determine the outcome of his work. If, as he turned a heated mass [of metal] on the anvil, and shaped it with his hammer, he was asked what he was making, he would answer, not something definite, but a list of several things disjunctively, as: a knife,[445] a sickle, a ploughshare, or whatever else might happen to result from his forging of the material. The nature of the issue of his labors would be determined by mere possibility rather than by his own will. Nothing, however, is less becoming a craftsman than to let the whims of [blind] chance replace the [enlightened] decision of reason as his guide. We should search everywhere to find abundant reasons whereby we may [convincingly] establish or overthrow a thesis, and thus we will become masters of proof and refutation. If an opponent is not available, let everyone consider in his own mind what, how many, and how strong are the arguments for or against a particular thesis. In this way, everyone will easily be able to establish the affirmative or negative side of a proposition. And whether there be need of contending,[446] or persuading, or philosophizing, one will have strong arguments pro and con, and will either win out over his opponent, or will come off the field with glory, or, even if defeated, will emerge without dishonor and ignominy. In the ancient Roman military system, men were trained to become soldiers by being habituated to make-believe warfare from their earliest youth. Boys at play were familiarized with the

---

[443] Cf. Terence, *Eun.*, v, 3, 5.

[444] *Hescelinus,* Hescelin. Webb surmises that this is *Ascelinus,* which name, as *Gallia Christiana,* XI, 652, testifies, existed in the thirteenth century in the diocese of Evreux, wherein Conches was situated. As J. A. Giles notes in his edition of John's works, a manuscript codex of the fourteenth century, preserved in the public library of the University of Cambridge (II, ii, 31), has after *faber* ("the artificer"), *Conches* ("of Conches"). It is likely that the "master William" here is the grammarian, William of Conches, referred to in *Met.,* i, 24, and ii, 9.

[445] *cultrum,* a knife or the coulter of a plow.

[446] *agonizandum,* ἀγωνίζεσθαι, ἀγών, competing, contending; Aristotle, *Top.,* viii, 5, 159 a, 27, 30, 33.

skills whereby they would later successfully triumph, when the commonwealth was in need of their [military] prowess.[447] Each was trained in the use of weapons, and learned ahead of time, at home,[448] when to attack or retreat from a horseman or a foot soldier, as well as when to strike with the edge or thrust with the point of his sword. In the same way the logician must become a skilled master[449] of the instruments of his art, so that he is familiar with its principles, is amply provided with likely proofs,[450] and is ready with all the methods of deductive and inductive reasoning.[451] He should also carefully estimate the strength of his opponent, since the issue frequently depends on an accurate appraisal of this. "It does not lie within the power of one person alone to bring to a successful conclusion, by himself, a joint enterprise, which requires the coöperation of another."[452] One who is proceeding according to the art [of logic] is very often impeded by the slowness of his hearer, or the difficulty of the subject matter, as well as by a lack of skill on the part of his questioner or the one who is doing the explaining. "It is no small part of prudence," as observes Palladius, "to take into account the kind of person with whom we are dealing."[453] In law, it is a principle that: "No one should be ignorant of the status[454] of one with whom he makes a contract."[455] We should deal with a learned man in one way, but with an illiterate person in another. The former is to be convinced by syllogisms,[456] whereas the latter's assent must be won by inductive reasoning.[457] For progress, two things are necessary: studious practice and a supporting vein of good natural talent.[458] A good intellect readily assents to what is true, and rejects what is false. Such mental

---

[447] See Vegetius, *De Re Mil.*, i, 4, 11, 12.
[448] *domi prediscebatur;* cf. Cicero, *De Orat.*, i, 32, § 147.
[449] *expeditam habere facultatem,* to have a ready faculty, be a skilled master or expert.
[450] *probabilibus,* probable or likely proofs or arguments.
[451] *sillogizandi et inducendi,* of reasoning by syllogisms and of building up inferences, that is, of deduction and induction.
[452] Aristotle, *Top.*, viii, 11, 161 a, 19 ff.
[453] Palladius, *Agric.*, i, 1, at the beginning.
[454] *conditionis,* status, condition.
[455] See *Corpus Juris Civilis, Dig.*, 1, 17, § 19.
[456] That is, by deductive reasoning.
[457] See Aristotle, *Top.*, viii, 14, 164 a, 12, 13.
[458] Cf. Quintilian, *Inst. Or.*, vi, 2, § 3.

capacity is originally a gift of nature, and is fostered by our inborn reason. It rapidly waxes in strength as a combined result of affection for what is good and exercise. "Practice makes perfect," and begets a skill in proving and investigating the truth. But it does the latter even more readily and expeditiously when it is founded on the essential principles[459] of the art [of logic] and its rules. Although one may sometimes profitably exercise [his reason] alone, just as he does with a partner,[460] still [mutual] discussion[461] is evidently more profitable than [solitary] meditation.[462] "Iron is sharpened by iron,"[463] and one's mind is more cogently and effectively stimulated by the sound of the words of another, particularly if the other person is wise or modest. At the same time, the fool's mouth, "babbling nonsense," and the wanton one, heedless of modesty,[464] are more likely to pervert, than to instruct the natural talents of the young, who are much inclined to become like others by imitation. Foolish or wanton speech serves neither to fit the young for life, nor to equip them with scientific knowledge. On the contrary, it infatuates the mind and poisons the tongue. Despite the fact that nothing helps us more than to talk things over with others, we should not indiscriminately argue and practice with everyone. "It is inevitable," as Aristotle observes, "that against some [persons] our speech will surely degenerate.[465] When our opponent tries by every means [fair and foul] to seem to escape unbeaten, it is likewise permissible for us to attempt to construct a syllogism in any way we can. But this is not in good taste, for it is both unbecoming and inappropriate immediately to contest anyone and everyone. An irksome discussion[466] will necessarily result, as those who [thus] practice together cannot refrain from engaging in contentious disputation."[467] We should not dispute everywhere, and always, and

[459] *compendio,* a short cut, compendium, summary, the essential principles.
[460] *ad alterum.*
[461] *collatio,* conference, colloquy, talking together, mutual discussion.
[462] *meditatione,* thinking by one's self (alone), reflection.
[463] Proverbs, xxvii, 17.
[464] Proverbs, xv, 2.
[465] *prauas fieri orationes,* speeches or arguments are certain to become bad or degenerate.
[466] *laboriosum sermonem.*
[467] Aristotle, *Top.,* vii, 14, 164 b, 9.

on all sorts of topics. Many subjects do not admit of disputation. Some transcend human reasoning, and are consecrated entirely to faith. Some, on the other hand, appear unworthy of the attention of the questioner and answerer, and serve only to demonstrate that those disputing about them have either lost their minds, or never did have any sense. We gain nothing by knowing the answers to this latter type of questions; and, conversely, we lose nothing by being ignorant of them. If we devote our energies to them, we are building, not so much an approach to philosophy, as a departure therefrom; we are displaying, not intellectual progress, but mental deterioration. Blessed Ambrose summarized this very well when he said: "I am willing to admit my ignorance of what I do not know, and of what, furthermore, there is no point in knowing." [468] The investigation of probabilities, which [probabilities, after all] comprise most [of our] human knowledge, flows, in a way, from the *Topics* as its fountainhead. Accounting for the mutual connection of things and words, the *Topics* provide us with an abundance of reasons. Hence one who has been adequately trained in them will come to see the truth of the Pythagorean *dictum* that "One can argue with probability on either side of any given subject." [469] To grasp the truth as it actually is, belongs to divine and angelic perfection, to which one approaches more closely in proportion as he more earnestly seeks, ardently loves, accurately investigates, and happily contemplates reality. [470] In answer to the provocations of my challenger, I have here given a brief, selective summary [of the *Topics*], not with a view to furnishing a full account of the utility and contents of the books I have discussed (something beyond my power, and foreign to my purpose), but rather to prove and establish the real value of those parts [of the *Topics*] which my opponent has indicted and condemned as useless. [471] I intend to continue this same policy in what I have yet to say. Thus I propose to

---

[468] Ambrose, *Hexaemer.*, vi, 2, § 7 (in Migne, *P.L.*, XIV, 244).

[469] Seneca, *Ep.*, 88, § 43. John had obviously read or understood what Seneca wrote of Protagoras as referring to Pythagoras.

[470] Cf. *Met.*, iii, 3.

[471] Cf. *Met.*, iv, 24, and i, note 64 on Theodoric of Chartres.

parry and counter the thrusts of my opponent, rather than to compose commentaries on the arts, which all are teaching or learning. And I [sincerely] invite anyone who is dissatisfied with the present treatment of the subject,[472] to present a better one.

END OF BOOK THREE

[472] *ista*, these things.

ᴃoo𝕂 𝔽oᴜ𝕣

[PROLOGUE]

I am constrained [in the present treatise] to return to subject matter with which I have lost contact,[1] and which should [by rights] have been a [mere] prelude to more serious studies.[2] My advancing years, the dignity of my order,[3] and the nature of my position,[4] to omit mentioning, for the present, the pressure of impending cases and the burdens of administrative responsibilities,[5] have made it necessary that I devote my time to other concerns. But since the presumptuous impudence of my opponent[6] has refused to give quarter [subside], and as you,[7] whose wishes deserve compliance, have so requested, I quickly and succinctly summarize my opinion on the matter,[8] as far as time allows. "To revive golden yesterdays and return to happier years," would, as Seneca muses, be "most pleasant,"[9] if only one were not oppressed by a bitter sadness, owing partly to the realization that the good old days have gone, and partly to other disturbing thoughts. Since you have deigned to investigate the dispute between myself and Cornificius, I descend, though unwilling, and in a way [forcibly] dragged thither, into

[1] *intermissam*, left off, dropped, interrupted.

[2] Or occupations: evidently on the part of Cornificius and his followers.

[3] *gradus ordinis*, grade or dignity of order, rank in orders, or ecclesiastical state of life. John may here be referring to his rank in holy orders: to his priesthood, or simply to his membership in the clergy.

[4] *conditionis forma.* John may here refer to his position as secretary to Archbishop Theobald, or to his general circumstances: financial or otherwise.

[5] Evidently reference is here made to John's responsibilities as secretary to the Archbishop of Canterbury, which were particularly weighty at this time, owing to Theobald's illness; cf. *Met.*, iv, 42.

[6] *emuli.* "Cornificius."

[7] Namely, Thomas Becket, the royal chancellor.

[8] *opinionis mee sententiam*, literally, the judgment of my opinion.

[9] Seneca, *Controv.*, i, praef., § 1. Seneca has *studia*, studies, where John has *tempora*, times or days.

this arena of combat. But enough of such musings: let us proceed with our discussion.

CHAPTER 1.   *The book of the* Analytics[10] *examines*[11] *reasoning.*

The drillmaster[12] of the Peripatetic discipline,[13] which is the branch of learning most concerned with inquiry into the truth, was dissatisfied with the inadequate general condition of his enterprise. Prompted by this deficiency, as well as by the confidence that every art sings the praises of its author, he organized the whole into a science. After he had procured the instruments of invention and mastered their use, he set himself, as it were, to the forge,[14] and worked away at hammering out a crucible to serve in his scientific analysis of reasoning. The product was the book of the *Analytics.* The latter chiefly concerns judgment, although it is also helpful in invention. For the principles of all branches of learning are interwoven, and each requires the aid of the others in order to attain its own perfection. Few if any disciplines can achieve their full development without help from the outside. If you would fully understand my view, bear briefly with what I have to say concerning this work.

[10] Aristotle's *Prior Analytics.*
[11] *est . . . examinatorius,* examines, tests, analyzes, is a crucible for.
[12] *Campidoctor,* namely, Aristotle; cf. *Met.,* iii, 10.
[13] That is, logic.
[14] *conflatorio,* place for heating and forging metals, forge; cf. Proverbs, xxvii, 21.

CHAPTER 2.   *The universal utility of this science [of the*
             Analytics], *and the etymology of its title.*

The science of the *Analytics* is so useful that anyone who would
profess to be a logician without it, is ridiculous. The meaning of
its title becomes clear when we consider that the Greek word *Ana-*
leticen[15] means "Resolvent." [16] And its name becomes still more
intelligible when we translate *Analyticen* as "equivalent expression." [17] For *ana* may be translated as "equal," and *lexim* as
"speech." Thus, oftentimes, when the meaning of an expression is
not evident, and we would like to have it resolved equivalently
into something that is easier to understand, we request that it be
"analyzed." When my [Greek] interpreter would hear a term
with which he was not familiar, especially if it was a compound
word, he would say to me: "Analyze this," [18] signifying that he
would like to have it explained in equivalent terms. Such analysis
into component parts is a very great aid to our intellect in the
acquisition of [scientific] knowledge. Although what it teaches is
necessary, the book [of the *Analytics*] is not itself equally necessary.
For everything the work contains is elsewhere explained in an
easier and more satisfactory manner, though certainly nowhere
with more precise accuracy or more forceful cogency, since, even
from the unwilling, this book extorts assent. The work conducts a
vigorous offensive, and, like Caesar, allows no alternative save
that of surrender;[19] nor does it put any value on merely winning
friendly favor. Such a plan of procedure is well suited to the function of judgment, since affection for a friend, or aversion to an

---

[15] *Analeticen,* a Latin translation of the Greek.
[16] *Resolutoriam,* analytical, resolving, or breaking down a thing into its components or
constituent parts. Cf. Boethius, *Comm. I in Arist. de Interpr.,* ii, 10; *II,* iv, 10 (ed.
Meiser, pp. 135, 293).
[17] *equam locutionem.*
[18] *Analetiza hoc.*
[19] Cf. Lucan, *Phars.,* ii, 439 ff.

enemy, is likely to pervert the [impartial] integrity of a judge. But the book is so confusing because of its intricately involved examples, and its transference of letters, which are used in the interests of meticulous exactness and brevity, as well as to prevent its examples being anywhere subjected to refutation, that it teaches with great difficulty what could otherwise be very easily explained. In fact, often, owing to its overweaning concern with the avoidance of falsehood, it becomes, as a result, neither true nor false, or perhaps [one would even say that it] deceives, if petulance[20] would lead [one] to calumny.[21]

CHAPTER 3.   *The book's utility does not include the provision of rhetorical expression.*

Although its rules are not only useful, but even an indispensable prerequisite for [the] science [it teaches], this book is practically worthless for providing rhetorical expression.[22] The latter may be explained as "a clothing with words," and consists in the ability to express oneself easily and adequately in a given language. The scientific knowledge [contained in this book] should be fixed in our mind, and we should even often excerpt [for memorization and use] its very wording. For it should be the precaution of one who philosophizes, first to take care to understand the meaning of what is taught, and then to select for retention terms susceptible of wider application and more frequent use. What remains after this may be compared to foliage without fruit, and consequently it may be either left on the tree or trampled under foot. Those who follow Aristotle [down to the last iota] in a confusing babel of names

---

[20] *proteruia*, that is, δυσκολία, perversity, ill-temper; cf. *Met.*, *passim*, and Aristotle, *Top.*, viii, 8, 160 b, 3 ff.

[21] *calumnian faciat*, makes or leads to calumny or slander.

[22] *frasim*, concerning *phrasim*, see Quintilian, *Inst. Or.*, viii, 1: "What the Greeks call 'Φράσις' we in Latin call *'elocutio'* [style]." Style is revealed in individual words and combinations of words. I have translated it "rhetorical expression."

and verbs[23] and subtle intricacies,[24] blunt the mental faculties of
others in their effort to show off their own intellectual capacity,
and, to me, seem to have chosen the worse part. It is my belief that
our own English Adam, especially, fell into this vice, in the book
which he entitled *The Art of Reasoning*.[25] Would that he had expressed well the good things that he has said! Although his friends
and followers attribute his obscurity to subtlety, many [critics] have
judged that it stems from the folly or envy of vanity. For Adam
has presented Aristotle in such involved language that a judicious
listener may well comment:

> Is not this as frothy, with thick and puffed up bark,
> As the shrivelled old branch of a superannuated cork tree? [26]

Nevertheless we should be grateful to the authors, for their works
are a fountain from which we may drink, and thus be enriched
by the labors of others.

CHAPTER 4.   *The scope of the first book [of the* Analytics].

Despite its [stylistic] shortcomings, this work teaches what must
necessarily be known, and does so with exceeding accuracy and
certainty. It explains the nature of dialectical, demonstrative,
universal, particular, and indefinite propositions; as well as of
terms, namely, predicates and subjects; and of perfect and imperfect syllogisms. It sheds light on the meaning of being [included] [27]
in a whole,[28] and, vice versa, not being [included] in a whole. It
makes clear what propositions are convertible for use in syllogistic

[23] *uerborum*, verbs or words
[24] See Boethius, *De Syll. Categ.*, i (in Migne, *P.L.*, LXIV, 793).
[25] See *Met.*, ii, 10, and ii, n. 181, concerning Adam and his *Art of Reasoning*.
[26] Persius, *Sat.*, i, 96, 97. Jahn, in his edition of Persius' *Satires* (1868), has argued that the reading here should be *vegrandi* instead of *pregrandi*. The translation of Persius would then be "dwarfed" instead of "overgrown" or "superannuated."
[27] That is, of being predicated.
[28] *in toto*, as in a whole.

reasoning, and what propositions are not so convertible; and what
holds for propositions which, according to present-day practice, are
said to concern what is necessary,[29] contingent, or privative.[30] Next
the [first] book analyzes the three figures. After giving definitions
of the extremes and the middle [term], it explains how many and
what modes may be constructed in each of the figures by varying
the arrangement of the extremes,[31] thus sowing the seed for those
things which were later added by Theophrastus and Eudemus,
according to Boethius.[32] Next, focusing attention on the nature of
modals, it discusses combinations of necessary and contingent
[premisses] with those [premisses] that "belong," [33] so as to show
what results in each of the figures.[34] Notwithstanding, I would not
say that even Aristotle has anywhere, so far as I have been able
to determine in my reading,[35] adequately treated modals, except
perhaps to the extent that was necessary for his own purpose.
Nevertheless, he has given us a most reliable scientific method of
dealing with all modes. Those who expound the Divine Scriptures
say that it is very necessary to take modes into consideration, and
that a great deal of attention must be paid to them, whether they be
explicitly expressed or only understood. In the Scriptural passage:
"That which you had perfected, they have destroyed," [36] the mode
is tacit[37] and implied. In reality, it is as though the qualification
"in their will" [38] were added [to "they have destroyed"], just as
when it is said: "He devours the tender lamb in expectation." [39]
They tell us that a mode is, so to speak, "a certain relationship be-

---

[29] *naturali,* natural or necessary.

[30] *remota,* remote or privative. See Aristotle, *An. Prior.,* i, 1–3.

[31] Aristotle, *An. Prior.,* i, 4–7.

[32] Boethius, *De Syllogismo Hypothetico,* i (in Migne, *P.L.,* LXIV, 831).

[33] *que sunt de inesse,* which are from belonging or being inherent, pure.

[34] Aristotle, *An. Prior.,* i, 8–26.

[35] *quod legerim.*

[36] Psalms, x, 4. Cf. Augustine's *Enarr. in Ps.* (in Migne, *P.L.,* XXXVI, 135): "For all
of them [the heretics] have, as far as they could, destroyed the praise which God has
perfected [receives] from the very mouths of speechless babes before they are even
weaned from the breast.

[37] *subticetur,* is tacit or lies hidden.

[38] Or, as Augustine: "so far as lies in their power."

[39] *Tenerum spe deuorat agnum.*

tween terms." [40] It is impossible for anyone to enumerate separately
all the modes whence statements are said to have [different shades
of] modality, which indeed the art does not require. Still the
masters in the schools discuss[41] modes well enough, and, if I may
say so, begging leave of the multitude, do it even more aptly than
does Aristotle himself. In my opinion, independently of whether
modals are so called because of the actual presence of true modes,
or simply because of their forms, it is still frequently necessary to
recognize them, if we are to obtain the correct meaning of many
passages in the Scriptures. I also believe that the supreme authority
in such cases is usage, which can extend, constrict, change, and
even cancel the meanings of words. A clear example is found in
the term "contingent," whose broadest usage, in which it is considered equivalent to the possible, never emerges beyond the
walls of the schools in modern parlance. This book next discusses
how one may become skilled in syllogistic reasoning,[42] since it is
of little use to have a [theoretical] knowledge of the formation of
syllogisms, and yet remain unable to construct them. How syllogisms may be reduced to modes of the first figure follows,[43] and
concludes the contents of the first book.

CHAPTER 5.   *The scope of the second book [of the* Analytics].

The second book [of the *Analytics*] proceeds to discuss the process
of drawing the inferences that are apparent in the form of a given
conclusion.[44] It remarks on how truths may be concluded from
false premises in the second and third figures: something possibly

[40] *medius habitus terminorum,* a middle, mean, or intermediate condition, state, disposition, or relationship of or between terms.
[41] Literally: dispute concerning.
[42] Aristotle, *An. Prior.,* i, 27–44.
[43] *Ibid.,* i, 45–46.
[44] *que in formam conclusionis patet.* The word *formam* in Webb's text should be
corrected to read *forma;* cf. MSS A, B, and C.

overlooked by those[45] who contend that nothing can follow from
what is false.[46] Next it discusses circular syllogisms, which it pursues
through all figures. Then it takes up the conversion of syllogisms
in each of the figures.[47] It does this so that imperfect syllogisms
may be reduced to perfect ones, and the dependability of all
syllogisms may be made similarly apparent. This [the resultant
syllogism] is a form of direct reasoning. The [syllogistic] "hypothesis," [48] which attains its object because of the necessity of an
impossible or improbable consequence, is its next topic.[49] In such a
"hypothesis," if one refuses to consent to its conclusion, the contradictory of this conclusion and something that was granted are
taken and arranged according to the first figure, in such a way
that the opposite of something [already] conceded may be therefrom concluded. How to do this in each figure is shown, the
truth of all modes being demonstrated by some impossible consequence. The book accurately explains by what means, and in
what figure, one may reason syllogistically from opposite propositions.[50] It adds rules on "begging the question," [51] which are well
worth the attention of both of the demonstrator and the dialectician, even though [the latter differ in that] the dialectician is
content with probability, whereas the demonstrator will accept
only [incontrovertible] truth. Instances where something that
is not a cause[52] is posited as a cause are also discussed. Thus it is
possible to allege that one is led to an impossible conclusion, not
because of the inferential complex as such,[53] but rather because
something false was assumed.[54] The book next explains the causes

<hr/>

[45] Those whom Jocelin de Brakelond calls "men of Melun," in his *Chron.*, chap. 25
(*Memorials of St. Edmund's Abbey*, ed. Arnold, I, 240).
[46] Aristotle, *An. Prior.*, ii, 1–4.
[47] *Ibid.*, ii, 4–10.
[48] *hipoteseos, ὑποθέσεως*, the [syllogistic] hypothesis or syllogism *per impossibile*, which
proceeds by reduction to an impossibility.
[49] Aristotle, *An. Prior.*, ii, 11.
[50] *Ibid.*, ii, 12–15.
[51] *petitio principii.* Aristotle, *op. cit.*, ii, 16.
[52] A cause or reason.
[53] *ratione complexionis*, the nature of the inferential complex or inference, the structure
of the syllogism, the way the propositions are combined.
[54] Aristotle, *op. cit.*, ii, 17.

of false conclusions as well as of countersyllogisms,[55] and refutations;[56] and discusses erroneous opinions,[57] as well as the conversion of means and extremes.[58] All the practical aspects of the foregoing could, however, be far more aptly explained. How to analyze both induction,[59] herein called a rhetorical syllogism, and examples, follows. Deduction[60] is also discussed.[61] Next the work explains the nature of objections,[62] as well as what is probability,[63] which it characterizes as a proposition that is likely, even though it is possible that there be an instance to the contrary: that is, the proposition may happen not to hold true in all cases. An illustration of the latter is [the adage] that "Mothers love, but stepmothers envy." [64] The book goes on to explain signs,[65] and shows how enthymemes consist of probabilities and signs.[66] Finally the recognition of natures[67] is discussed. The last is a tremendous chapter. But, even though it achieves its purpose to a certain degree, it by no means fully measures up to what its promise would lead one to expect. One thing I do know is that I have never known anyone who became a master at recognizing natures as a consequence of [studying] this chapter.

[55] catasillogismi, κατασυλλογίζεσθαι, a catasyllogism, countersyllogism or "boomerang-syllogism," wherein the premises of an opponent's syllogism are used to draw a conclusion contrary to his own.
[56] elenchi, ἔλεγχος, a refutation.
[57] fallaciam secundum opinionem, a fallacious or erroneous opinion, error.
[58] Aristotle, op. cit., ii, 17–22.
[59] ratio reducende inductionis, that is, the method of reducing or analyzing induction into quasi-syllogistic form.
[60] deductione, ἀπαγωγή. Aristotle here discusses reduction, rather that deduction.
[61] Aristotle, op. cit., ii, 23–25.
[62] instantia, ἐνστᾰσις, a proposition contrary to a proposition, an objection.
[63] icos, εἰκός, likelihood or probability.
[64] Aristotle, An. Prior., ii, 26–27.
[65] signum, Σημεῖον, a sign: a demonstrative proposition that is either necessary or generally approved.
[66] Aristotle, op. cit.
[67] cognitione naturarum, that is, τοῦφυσιογνωμονεῖν, the recognition or judging of natures or natural resources or dispositions; ibid.

CHAPTER 6.   *The difficulty of the* Posterior Analytics, *and*
               whence this difficulty proceeds.

The science of the *Posterior Analytics* is extremely subtle, and one
with which but few mentalities can make much headway. This fact
is evidently due to several reasons. In the first place, the work discusses the art of demonstration, which is the most demanding of
all forms of reasoning. Secondly, the aforesaid art has, by now,
practically fallen into disuse.[68] At present demonstration is employed by practically no one except mathematicians, and even
among the latter has come to be almost exclusively reserved to
geometricians. The study of geometry is, however, not well known
among us, although this science is perhaps in greater use in the
region of Iberia and the confines of Africa.[69] For the peoples of
Iberia and Africa employ geometry more than do any others; they
use it as a tool in astronomy. The like is true of the Egyptians, as
well as some of the peoples of Arabia. The present book, which
teaches demonstrative logic, is even more perplexing than the rest.
This is partly a result of its complicated transposition of words and
letters, as well as its out-moded examples, borrowed from various
branches of study. Finally, though this is not the fault of the
author, the book has been so mutilated by the bungling mistakes
of scribes[70] that it contains almost as many stumbling blocks as
subjects. Indeed, we feel fortunate when we find that these stumbling blocks do not outnumber the book's chapters. Whence many
assert that the latter has not been correctly rendered [into Latin] for
us, and throw the blame for its difficulty upon the translator.

----

[68] Note that Aristotle's *Posterior Analytics* is not discussed in the *Heptateuchon* of
Theodoric of Chartres. Cf. Clerval, *Les Écoles de Chartres,* pp. 222, 245; and *Met.,*
iii, 5, n. 223.
[69] *in tractu Hibero uel confinio Affrice;* cf. C. H. Haskins, *Studies in the History of
Mediæval Science,* pp. 4 ff. John is apparently referring to old Roman Africa, rather than
to the whole continent; cf. later, in this same chapter.
[70] *scriptorum,* writers or scribes, probably copyists.

CHAPTER 7.   *Why Aristotle has come to be called*[71] *"the philosopher" par excellence.*

So highly was the science of demonstration esteemed by the Peripatetics that Aristotle, who also excelled practically all other philosophers in nearly every regard, established his right to the [otherwise] common name of "philosopher," as in a way his own special prerogative, by giving us this branch of knowledge [namely, demonstration]. For it was because of this, we are told, that Aristotle came to be called "the philosopher." If anyone does not believe me, let him at least heed Burgundio the Pisan,[72] who is my source for this statement. Since this science[73] both dispels the shadows of ignorance, and illumines its possessor with the privilege of foreknowledge,[74] it has frequently served [as a lamp] to guide from darkness to light the school of the Academicians, with whom we [frankly] profess our agreement on questions that remain doubtful to a wise man. And just as, at the outset, Aristotle, by forging a crucible [or method] for analysis [of arguments],[75] made ready the judge, so here he now advances his client to the authoritative position of teacher. Which is in well-chosen order, since one who has creditably fulfilled the function of judge deserves to be elevated to the master's chair.

[71] Literally: has merited the title of.
[72] Burgundio the Pisan was one of the chief translators of works from Greek to Latin in John's day. He held the office of judge at Pisa, and died in 1193. Cf. Haskins, *Studies in Mediæval Science,* pp. 206 ff.
[73] *hec,* the science of demonstration.
[74] *prenoscendi,* of prior knowledge, either in the sense of foreknowledge, or more fundamental knowledge, such as that of general principles.
[75] *examinatorium cudens;* cf. *Met.,* iv, 1.

CHAPTER 8.   *The [proper] function of demonstrative logic, as
well as the sources and techniques of demonstration. Also the fact that sensation is the basis[76] of
science, and how this is true.*

But who is equal to this discipline?[77] Even though one may be able
to master it in some field, no one can do so in very many branches
of study. In demonstration, it is first of all necessary to know (beforehand) the principles of the various departments of learning,
and thence, by reasoning, to infer conclusions based on the necessity
of incontrovertible truths. In so doing, one must, as it were, use
every effort to fortify and consolidate his proofs,[78] lest there seem
to be, as if through lack of necessity, some gap, which would
jeopardize [the strict proving force of] demonstrative science. By
no means all science, but only that which is based on truths that are
primary and immediate, is demonstrative.[79] Not every syllogism
provides demonstration, strictly so called, although every real demonstration consists in a syllogism. It is the inherent nature of science
to strive for demonstration. First come universal concepts of the
mind,[80] and then things that are known *per se,* as the fundamental
bases of demonstrative logic. It is important to distinguish, in
things known, whether they are better known by their [own] nature,
or merely better known to us. What is more immediate to sense experience is better known to us, whereas what is more remote from
it, as with the universal, is better known in itself and of its [own]
nature.[81] One who demonstrates can accordingly attain his project by

---

[76] *principium,* the principle, beginning, foundation.

[77] Namely, demonstration. For this passage, cf. II Corinthians, ii, 16.

[78] *calcatius urgendo,* by pressing or urging very emphatically; cf. Boethius, *De Syll.
Categ.,* ii (in Migne, *P.L.,* LXIV, 830).

[79] John continues to describe the contents of Aristotle's *An. Post.,* i, although he does
not always follow Aristotle's order.

[80] *communes . . . conceptiones animi,* common or universal or general concepts or conceptions of the mind.

[81] *simpliciter et naturaliter.*

using propositions which are immediately evident and require no proof. Although the science of demonstration may be said to relate chiefly to judgment, it also contributes considerably to invention. For it explains from what and whereby one may effect demonstration, as well as when and how materials that are special [e.g. proper to a given science] or general [e.g. common to more than one science] are to be used. For the sciences mutually aid one another. And because not all topics are suitable for use in demonstration (such as a topic [derived] from an accident, since, strictly speaking, there can be no necessary proof or scientific knowledge of what is corruptible), the demonstrator successfully asserts his claim to those topics that are necessary, and leaves all remaining topics to the dialectician and the orator, who are satisfied if their syllogisms simply possess considerable likelihood [or probability]. Demonstrative logic also explains what syllogisms and propositions should be employed, as well as what influence the quantity and quality of syllogisms, carefully considered, have on the force of proof or refutation. It further answers the questions as to what is a syllogism, what is called into question, and what figure is suitable for the syllogism? It so establishes the science of demonstration, that we may be as certain of things which our reason proves to be indubitably true as if we held them in our hands. Universal concepts derive their credibility from the fact that they are inductively inferred from particular things. As Aristotle says, "The only possible way to conceive universals is by induction, since we come to know abstractions by induction. But unless we have sense experience, we cannot make inductions. Even though sense perception relates to particular things, scientific knowledge concerning such can only be constructed by the successive steps of sense perception, induction, and formulation of universals." [82] [Aristotle also says:] "Sense perception is a prerequisite for memory; the memory of frequently repeated sense perceptions results in experimental proof;[83] experimental proofs provide the materials for a science or an art." [84] And the art, which becomes firmly established by use

[82] Aristotle, *An. Post.*, i, 13, 81 b, 2 ff.
[83] *experimentum*, experience, experimental proof.
[84] Aristotle, *op. cit.*, ii, 19, 100 a, 3 ff.

and practice, yields a faculty of accomplishing those things that
are proper to it. Accordingly, bodily sensation, which is the
primary power[85] or initial operation[86] of our conscious soul,
constitutes the basis for all the arts, and forms the initial knowledge which both clears and makes ready the way for first principles.

CHAPTER 9.   *What sensation is,[87] and how it, together with
              imagination, is the foundation of every branch of
              philosophy.*

The truth of what we have just said should be quite clear to
anyone who carefully considers particular instances. As sensation
is, according to Aristotle,[88] "an innate power that discriminates
things," [89] no or very little knowledge can exist independently of
it. If one, with the scientist,[90] studies the works of nature, which
are made up of elements or matter and form, his reasoning[91] is
dependent on the data provided by sense-experience.[92] And if one,
with the mathematician, abstracts figures[93] or calculates numerically, he must, in order to gain assent, accurately adduce many
examples of both differentiated plurality and quantitative extension. The like holds true of the philosopher, whose domain is
[abstract] reasoning, and who is the client of both the scientist and
the mathematician. For the philosopher, too, begins with those
things which are based on the evidence of the senses and contribute

---

[85] *uis,* force or power.
[86] *excercitium,* exercise, activity, or operation.
[87] *sensus,* sense, sensation, or sense perception.
[88] Aristotle, *op. cit.,* ii, 19, 99 b, 35.
[89] *naturalis potentia indicatiua rerum,* a natural, congenital, or innate power or faculty,
that indicates, perceives, or discriminates things. MS C has *iudicatiua,* or "discriminatory,"
namely, "that discriminates," which is a more natural rendering of Aristotle's εδιτικήν,
than is the *indicatiua* or "indicative," namely, "that indicates," found in MSS A and B.
[90] *phisico,* physicist, scientist, natural philosopher.
[91] Literally: one's way or course of ratiocination.
[92] Aristotle, *An. Post.,* i, 13, 81 a, 38 ff.
[93] *figuras,* forms, shapes, figures.

to the knowledge of immaterial intelligibles. According to Chalcidius, sensation is "a bodily state of being affected by action,[94] a state which is induced by things that are extrinsic and that make an impression on the body in various ways, a state which makes its way even to the conscious soul." Unless the bodily condition has some impetus, it neither reaches the conscious soul, nor develops into the form of a sensation. If this state of being acted on is bland and agreeable, it begets pleasure,[95] and if the latter is increased, it comes to be called joy.[96] But if this state is harsh and irritating, pain results.[97] [Such is the doctrine of Chalcidius.] But Aristotle asserts[98] that sensation is a power[99] of the soul, rather than a [mere] bodily state of passive receptivity. However, Aristotle admits that in order for this power to form an estimation of things, "it must be excited by a [bodily] state of being affected by action." [100] As it perceives things, our soul stores up their images within itself, and in the process of retaining and often recalling them [to mind], builds up for itself a sort of treasury of the memory. And as it mentally revolves the images of [these] things, there arises imagination, which proceeds beyond the [mere] recollection of previous perceptions,[101] to fashion, by its own [creative] activity, other representations similar to these. The question has been raised whether imagination is really distinct from sensation in nature, or is only a different mode of perception. There have been, I recollect, philosophers who believed that, just as the soul's substance is immaterial, simple, and individual, so also the soul has only one power,[102] which it exercises in various ways according to varying circumstances. The view of such philosophers is that the same power at one time senses, at another remembers, at another

[94] *passio,* a state of being acted on by, or of being susceptible to the action of external forces, as well as the feeling arising from this state.

[95] *uoluptatem.*

[96] *gaudium.*

[97] Chalcidius, *Comm. in Tim. Plat.,* §§ 193, 194.

[98] Aristotle, *An. Post.,* ii, 19; and *Top.,* iv, 5, 125 b, 15–18.

[99] *uim,* force, power.

[100] Chalcidius, *op. cit.,* § 191.

[101] The Webb text should be corrected to read *perceptorum,* instead of *preceptorum;* cf. MSS A, B, and C.

[102] *potentiam.*

imagines, at still another discriminates as it investigates, and finally comprehends by the [intuitive] understanding what it investigates.[103] There are, on the contrary, many who believe that the soul, although quantitatively simple, is qualitatively composite. They would say that, just as the soul can, on the one hand, be affected by many types of external action, so, on the other, it has at its disposal several sorts of powers. To me it seems easy to conceive of the soul as having even more powers than those that are enumerated in the books of the above authors. For during its journey as "a wayfarer apart from its Lord,"[104] our soul not only knows little concerning its own origin, but hardly even recognizes its own capabilities.

CHAPTER 10.   *The imagination, and the fact that it is the source of affections that either compose and order, or disturb and deform the soul.*

Imagination, accordingly, is the offspring of sensation. And it is nourished and fostered by memory. Through a kind of *simplasis*,[105] or "conformation,"[106] it beholds not only things that are present, but also those which are absent in place or time. Imagination's operation is exemplified in the passage [from Ovid]:

> She sat, was dressed, and even spun her thread in this very way,
> While her pretty tresses fell[107] in the same fashion when she bent her
> head.[108]

[103] Cf. Isidore, *Diff.*, ii, 29 (in Migne, *P.L.*, LXXXIII, 84).

[104] Cf. II Corinthians, v, 6.

[105] *simplasim*, σύμπλασις, a fashioning together or fabricating, a molding or conforming.

[106] *conformationem;* cf. Cicero, *De Orat.*, ii, 87, § 357. Obviously John here partly refers back to *conformanda* in the preceding chapter with reference to fashioning similar examples or patterns.

[107] John has *decuere*, were becoming, for Ovid's *iacuere*, hung. I have tried to incorporate both meanings.

[108] Ovid, *Fast.*, ii, 771, 772.

That the imagination is "abstractive,"[109] Vergil[110] indicates, when Andromache[111] attests that she has, in recollection, abstracted[112] an image of her Astyanax:

> Oh, sole surviving image of my Astyanax!
> His eyes, his hands, and his face were just like thine,
> And he would be a youth of the same age as thyself.[113]

And since, as Plato observes in his *Republic*,[114] "It is easy to discover nature's secrets from what happens again and again," our imagination conceives of the future[115] in terms of present or past perceptions.[116] If it visualizes our future state as dire,[117] fear arises; but if it paints a bright picture of a future brimful with profit and pleasure, hope springs in the breast. Numbered among imagination's offspring is carnal lust,[118] a poisonous pest, extremely opposed to the project of philosophizing. It is impossible to surrender oneself to the lusts of the flesh, and at the same time to dedicate oneself to philosophy. Imagination is indeed a composite of contraries. "The expectation of enjoying something gives birth to pleasure, whereas postponement of its realization engenders sadness and sorrow." And if the sadness and sorrow grow so violent that they disorder[119] and upset the soul, anger flares from the friction.[120] As a result, and to repress evil impulses, imagination develops caution, whereby it comes to shun whatever is noxious, such as images that encourage melancholy,[121] anger, and lust,

[109] *abstractiua,* abstractive, capable of and actually abstracting or mentally withdrawing from material reality or corporeal embodiment.

[110] *Maro,* Publius Vergilius Maro: Vergil.

[111] The wife of Hector.

[112] *abstraxisse,* has abstracted, has mentally withdrawn or detached from corporeal embodiment.

[113] Vergil, *Aen.,* iii, 489–491.

[114] *Politia,* Plato's *Republic.*

[115] *future* in the Webb text should be corrected to read *futura;* cf. MSS A, B, and C.

[116] See Chalcidius, *Comm. in Tim. Plat.,* § 231. However, the words: "as the same Plato taught in his *Politia*" in Chalcidius, refer to what precedes, namely, to: "From conjecture arises opinion, and from opinion understanding . . . ," from Plato's Rep., vi, 509 ff., rather than to what follows, as John took them to refer.

[117] *passionem asperam;* cf. Augustine, *De C.D.,* xiv, 15.

[118] *cupiditas,* carnal passion or lust.

[119] *exordinent.* Lexicons do not give this word (at least not in this sense), but *exordinatio* is found in the *Regulae* of St. Benedict, chap. 65 (ed. Woeffl, p. 64).

[120] Cf. Chalcidius, *Comm. in Tim. Plat.,* § 194.

[121] *dolor,* sorrow, dejection, melancholy.

or their daughters, envy, hate, calumny, carnal wantonness,[122] and
vanity.[123] If our imagination becomes overly cautious, it risks
becoming timid, whereas if it grows too uncautious, it is in peril
of becoming foolhardy. In like manner [our] other emotions all
proceed from sensation, through the activity of the imagination.
Which also holds true of love, which contributes greatly to the
care[124] of the body, the conservation of what is useful, and the
provision of succession.[125]

CHAPTER 11.   *The nature of imagination, together with remarks on opinion. Also how opinion or sensa-
tion may be deceived, and the origin of* fronesis,
which we call "prudence."

Imagination is accordingly the first activity [movement] of the
soul after it is subjected to external stimulation.[126] Imagination
either formulates second judgment,[127] or brings back first judgment by recollection. It is sensation which [originally] makes first
judgment when it pronounces, for example, that something is
white or black, warm or cold. Second judgment, however, is reserved to imagination, which, for example, on the basis of an
image that has been retained, affirms that something perceived
is this or that, [thus] judging concerning something that is in
the future or absent. The judgments of sensation and imagination are classed as "opinion." The latter [opinion] is trustworthy[128]
when it judges things to be as they really are, but unreliable when
it judges them to be otherwise than they actually are. Aristotle

[122] *luxuria*, wanton sensual indulgence, carnal dissipation.
[123] Cf. Chalcidius, *op. cit.*, § 195.
[124] *tutelam*, care, protection, safeguarding.
[125] Cf. Chalcidius, *op. cit.*, § 194. *procurandam successionem*, procuring or providing
succession or the continuation of the [human] species.
[126] *extrinsecus pulsate*, knocked on or aroused by some impulse from the outside.
[127] *iudicium*, judgment, discernment, discrimination.
[128] *certa*, certain or reliable.

asserts that opinion is "a state of the conscious soul wherein it is the recipient of action."[129] This he says in view of the fact that when our imagination operates, the images of things are [so to speak] impressed on the soul. If one image is impressed instead of another, by a mistake whereby our act of judgment is deceived, the resultant opinion is called "fallacious" or "erroneous."[130] For often our senses are duped. This not only happens with children, who are considered as not yet possessing the use of reason, but it also even befalls those of more advanced years. Explaining his doctrine, Aristotle observes that infants regard all men as fathers, and all women as mothers.[131] Sensation deceives the untutored, and cannot pronounce sure judgment. A stick in the water seems bent, even to the most keen sighted. Since our mind[132] perceives how we may be deceived by our senses,[133] it strives to obtain knowledge which it can be sure is correct, and on which it can rely with confidence. It is this concern which gives birth to that virtue the Greeks term *fronesis,* and the Latins "prudence."[134]

CHAPTER 12. *The nature, subject matter, and activities of prudence; and how science[135] originates from sensation.*

Prudence, according to Cicero, is a virtue of the conscious soul, a virtue whose object is the investigation, perception, and skillful utilization of the truth.[136] Whereas the other virtues relate to certain requirements of everyday life,[137] the subject matter of this

---

[129] Aristotle, *De Interpr.,* i, 16 a, 3, 7.
[130] *fallax aut falsa.*
[131] Aristotle, in *Phys.,* A, 1, 184 b, 12 ff.; see Chalcidius, *Comm. in Tim. Plat.,* § 208.
[132] Literally: "it." The subject is not expressed here. This may possibly refer back to "reason" or to "opinion.
[133] Literally: perceives the fallacy of the senses.
[134] *prudentia.*
[135] *scientia,* science or scientific knowledge.
[136] Cf. Cicero, *De Off.,* i, 5, §§ 15 ff.
[137] *domestice quedam necessitates,* certain familiar or everyday necessities or requirements.

virtue is truth. Taking care to avoid deception from any and every
quarter, prudence looks to the future, and forms providence; re-
calls what has happened in the past, and accumulates a treasury
of memories;[138] shrewdly appraises[139] what is present, and begets
astuteness or discernment; or takes full cognizance of everything
[whether past, present, or future], and constitutes circumspection.
And when it has ascertained the truth, prudence develops into a
form of scientific knowledge. Since sensation gives birth to imagination, and these two to opinion, and opinion to prudence, which
grows to the maturity of scientific knowledge, it is evident that
sensation is the progenitor of science. Or, as we put it above,[140]
many sensations, or sometimes even only one, result in a memory,
many memories in an experimental proof,[141] many experimental
proofs in a rule, and many rules in an art, which provides scientific
skill.[142]

CHAPTER 13.   *The difference between "science" and "wisdom," and what is "faith."* [143]

In view of the aforesaid, our forefathers used the words "prudence" and "science" with reference to temporal sensible things,
but reserved the terms "understanding"[144] and "wisdom"[145] for
knowledge of spiritual things. Thus it is customary to speak of
"science" relative to human things, but of "wisdom" with regard
to divine things. Science is so dependent on sensation that we
would have no science concerning things we know by our senses,

[138] *thezaurizat memorie;* cf. Cicero, *De Orat.,* i, 5, § 18.
[139] *callet.*
[140] *Met.,* iv, 8, from Aristotle's *An. Post.,* ii, 19.
[141] *experimentum,* experience or experimental proof.
[142] *facultatem,* literally: a faculty, ability or skill, art or science, or scientific adroitness.
[143] *scientie . . . sapientie . . . fides.*
[144] *intellectum,* understanding or rational intuition; cf. Cicero, *De Off.,* i, 153; Augustine,
De Trin., xii, 15, § 25; xiii, 1, § 1; xiv, 1, § 3; Chalcidius, *Comm. in Tim. Plat.,* § 178.
It is to be noted, however, that, with Cicero, "knowledge" (*scientia*) is related to "wisdom" (*sapientia*), not as a coördinate species, but as its genus.
[145] *sapientia.*

if these things were not subject to sense perception. This is
clear from Aristotle.[146] Despite what I have said above, opinion
can be reliable. Such is our opinion that after the night has run
its course, the sun will return. But since human affairs are transitory, only rarely can we be sure that our opinion about them is
correct. If, nevertheless, we posit as a certainty something that is
not in all respects certain, then we approach the domain of faith,
which Aristotle defines as "exceedingly strong opinion." [147] Faith
is, indeed, most necessary in human affairs, as well as in religion.
Without faith, no contracts could be concluded, nor could any
business be transacted. And without faith, where would be the
basis for the divine reward of human merit? As it is, that faith
which embraces the truths of religion deserves reward. Such faith
is, according to the Apostle, "a substantiation of things to be hoped
for, a testimonial to things that appear not." [148] Faith is intermediate between opinion and science. Although it strongly affirms the certainty of something, it has not arrived at this certainty
by science. Master Hugh[149] says: "Faith is a voluntary certitude
concerning something that is not present, a certitude which is
greater than opinion, but which falls short of science." [150] Here,
by the way, the word "science" is used in an extended sense, as
including the comprehension of divine things.[151]

---

[146] Aristotle, *An. Post.,* i, 13, 81 a, 38 ff.

[147] Aristotle, *Top.,* iv, 5, 126 b, 18. Cf. the translation of Boethius (in Migne, *P.L.,*
LXIV, 950). Aristotle says that conviction is a vehement conception, but John is apparently following the Boethian translation.

[148] Hebrews, xi, 1.

[149] Hugh of St. Victor.

[150] Hugh of St. Victor, *Summ. Sent.,* i, 1; *De Sacram. Leg. Nat. et Script.;* and *De
Sacramentis,* i, 10, c. 1 (in Migne, *P.L.,* CLXXVI, 43, 35, and 330).

[151] Augustine had distinguished "wisdom," the comprehension of divine things, from
"science.

CHAPTER 14.   *The relationship of prudence and truth, the*
origins of prudence, and the nature of reason.

Since the subject matter of prudence is truth (for prudence is
concerned with comprehending the truth), the ancients[152] conceived of Prudence[153] and Truth[154] as sisters, related by a divine
consanguinity. Thus perfect prudence needs must contemplate
the truth, from which nothing can separate it. But as this[155] is
not the privilege of man, we weak humans[156] avidly seek to discover the hidden truth. In fact, handicapped as it is by errors
begotten by sense perceptions and opinions, human prudence can
hardly proceed with [entire] confidence in its investigation of
the truth, and can scarcely be [completely] sure as to when it has
comprehended the latter. It realizes [all too well] that, having been
deceived before, it can be deceived again. Accordingly, it bends
every effort to secure that valid perception and unwavering judgment, which may be called "reason." [157] For reason's estimate is
sure and reliable. Prudence therefore begets Philology.[158] This love
of the truth in turn importunes prudence for a knowledge of
things concerning which it desires genuine, sure judgment.[159]
"Philology," like "philosophy," is a modest[160] appellation. Just as
it is more within one's power to love wisdom than to attain it, so
too it is easier to love reason than to possess it. "To have reason,"

---

[152] *antiqui;* cf. Theodulus, *Eclog.,* v, 335 (ed. Osternacher, p. 53); cf. *Met.,* ii, 3.

[153] *Fronesis,* Φρόνησις, prudence.

[154] *Aliciam,* ’Αλήθειαν, truth.

[155] *hoc,* this; that is, the possession of perfect prudence.

[156] *infirma conditio,* literally: our infirm condition, we in our weakness.

[157] *ratio.*

[158] *Philologia,* philology: the love or study of words, literature, and reasoning; the love or study of the logical arts of the Trivium or of learning in general.

[159] See Martianus Capella, *De Nupt.,* ii, § 114.

[160] *temperatum,* moderate, mild, or "mixed." Philology, like philosophy, means a love of, striving after, or study of its objective.

that is, to possess genuine certitude of judgment, is the lot of few.[161]

CHAPTER 15. *More about what reason is, as well as the fact that the word "reason" has several different meanings, and that reasons are everlasting.*

Stimulated by sense perceptions,[162] and keyed up by the solicitude of prudence, the conscious soul exerts itself. Summoning its strength, it endeavors strenuously to avoid errors arising from sense perceptions and opinions. By dint of its intensified effort, it sees with greater clarity, holds with greater security, and judges with greater accuracy.[163] This more perspicacious force is called "reason," which is a spiritual nature's power to discriminate and distinguish material and immaterial entities, in order to examine things with sure, unvitiated judgment.[164] The latter, this judgment of reason, is also referred to as "reason." Furthermore, the very things concerning which reason alone judges, and whose essence is distinct from the nature of sensible and individual things, are likewise called "reasons." Father Augustine and many others state that the latter "reasons" are everlasting.[165] In such, original reason, which we may properly identify as the wisdom of God, has from the beginning, and in fact without beginning, established and decreed the divine eternal plan and the order in which it was to be unfolded.[166] It is quite evident that some truths[167] are infinite

[161] Plato, *Tim.*, 51 E, in the translation of Chalcidius. Also cf. *Met.*, iv, 18, and n. 211.

[162] *pulsata sensibus*, knocked on or aroused by sense perceptions; cf. Plato, *Tim.*, 44 A, in the translation of Chalcidius.

[163] *sincerius*, more sincerely, truly, or accurately.

[164] Cf. the pseudo-Augustinian *De Spiritu et anima*, chap. 38 (in Migne, *P.L.*, XL, 809).

[165] See Augustine, *De Div. Quaest.*, 83, xlvi; *De Trin.*, xii, 2, § 2 (in Migne, *P.L.*, XL, 30–31; and XLII, 999).

[166] *eterne constitutionis decretum et sue dispositionis seriem sanxit*, sanctioned the decree of the eternal constitution and the order of the divine arrangement: authoritatively approved of and established the provisions of His divine plan, and the order in which it was to be realized.

[167] *in ipsis ueris*, John apparently refers here to divine truths.

realities of this kind. That God is God, that the Father has a Son, and that the Holy Spirit has the same substance as both [Father and Son], are not merely statements. They have been eternally true, and are firmly founded in the divine judgment. In addition to such truths, there are also other infinite realities.[168] The ratios[169] of two to three, and three to two, and several such things are likewise everlasting, according to Augustine.[170] If anyone thinks that this is absurd, let him read Augustine's book concerning *Free Will*,[171] which should be sufficient to convince him.

CHAPTER 16.   *A distinction of various meanings [of the word "reason"], and the fact that brute animals do not possess reason, even though they may seem to have discernment.[172] Also the origin of human reason according to the Hebrews.*

Cassiodorus, in his book on *The Soul*, gives the following definition of reason: "By the term 'reason,' I mean that admirable[173] activity of the rational soul[174] whereby, through what is already granted and known, it concludes something that was formerly unknown, and thereby gains access to hidden truth."[175] Hence we see that reason is defined as both a power and the activity of a power. Plato asserts, in his work on *The State*,[176] that this activity is "a deliberative faculty[177] of the soul," which, after having

---

[168] *non modo in ueris, sed in aliis*, literally: not only in truths, but in other things or (others); obviously, from the context: not only in such truths, but in other cases: not only in truths concerning the divine nature, but also in mathematical truths.

[169] *ratio.*

[170] Augustine, *De Lib. Arbit.*, ii, 8 (in Migne, *P.L.*, XXXII, 1252–1253).

[171] *de Libero Arbitrio.*

[172] *discernere*, to discern, to exercise [a sort of] judgment, to discriminate.

[173] *probabilem*, admirable, commendable, excellent, or perhaps even capable of proving.

[174] *animi*, of the rational soul or human mind.

[175] See Cassiodorus, *De Anima*, chap. 2 (in Migne, *P.L.*, LXX, 1284).

[176] That is, in his *Republic*.

[177] *uim*, force, activity, faculty.

studied the outward forms[178] of things and the causes thereof, investigates, with reliable judgment, questions concerning what is right or useful, and what should be sought after or shunned.[179] Although brute animals have a certain power of discernment, whereby they select their food, shun snares, leap across precipitous places, and recognize relationship,[180] still, they do not reason, but are rather moved by their natural instincts.[181] Although they have mental images of many things, they are by no means able to reason concerning causes. The Hebrews say[182] that this is due to the fact that when, in the beginning of creation, by the divine disposition, other creatures were formed, and with the fomentation of warmth and moisture,[183] acquired that natural, animate, sentient form, which is the vital principle of appetite and imagination, and which is possessed by brute animals, to man alone was given the more efficacious and objectively truthful power of argumentative reasoning.[184] For God, breathing life into man, willed that he partake of the divine reason. The soul of man, which comes from, and will return to God, alone contemplates divine truths. This prerogative is, in fact, almost man's sole claim to preëminence over other animals.[185] Material entities are perceived by both imagination and sensation, which also even partly discern the forms of corporeal things, and their true agreement or disagreement.[186] For sense perception sees a man, and accordingly a corporeal object; it perceives color and movement, and consequently the forms of material things; it even recognizes that a man is moving his hand, which is more than to see a man moving [his hand], that is [a man] who moves his hand. If anyone wonders about this, let him at least believe Augustine.[187] Reason,

---

[178] *species,* species, outward forms, appearances.

[179] Cf. Chalcidius, *Comm. in Tim. Plat.,* § 230 (ed. Wrobel, p. 267).

[180] *necessitudinem.* This may mean necessity, need, dependence, friendship, or relationship by blood or mating.

[181] Literally: by their natural appetite.

[182] Cf. Chalcidius, *op. cit.,* § 300.

[183] *fotu caloris et humoris.*

[184] *disserendi.*

[185] Ecclesiastes, xii, 7.

[186] The comma after *formas* in the Webb edition (182, 7) should probably be a semicolon. Cf. MSS A, B, C, and the sense.

[187] Cf. Augustine, *De Lib. Arbit.,* ii, 3, 4, 5 (in Migne, *P.L.,* XXXII, 1245 ff.); and *De C.D.,* xi, 27.

on the other hand, transcends all sense perception, and judges concerning spiritual as well as material realities. Not only does it consider all things found here [on earth] below, but it also rises to the contemplation of heavenly things. Seneca's definition of reason fits in with the Hebraic concept, although his opinion was not really exactly the same. Seneca says:[188] "Reason is a certain part of the Divine Spirit, immersed in human bodies." [189] Seneca's definition may be understood as indicating that he agrees with the error of the Gentiles,[190] who believed that a World Soul was divided into individual souls, and mistakenly identified this with the Holy Spirit. On the other hand, Seneca's definition may be more liberally interpreted, and taken as meaning that reason is a virtual rather than quantitative part of the Divine Spirit. For Seneca added "a certain" to show he was using a figure of speech.[191] At any rate while reason is, in a way, a divine faculty,[192] it is by no means a part of Him whose simplicity is absolute.[193]

CHAPTER 17.   *Reason's function; why sensation,[194] which reason supervises, is situated in the head; and who are philology's servants.*

Since our reason is ennobled by its divine origin, and powerful with a divine activity, all philosophy agrees that the cultivation of reason should be our primary concern. For reason curbs unruly impulses, and brings everything into conformity with the norms of goodness. Nothing that agrees with reason is out of harmony with God's plan. In obedience to the Divine mind, one will move

---

[188] Webb's text should have a colon, rather than a semicolon here (after *enim*).

[189] Seneca, *Ep.*, 66, § 12.

[190] Cf. Plato, *Tim.*, 35 A; Macrobius, *Comm. de Somn. Scip.*, i, 14.

[191] Reference is made to Seneca's use of the qualifying *quedam* in the passage above. This can also mean a "sort of" or "a kind of."

[192] *uirtus*, power, virtue, faculty.

[193] Literally: most absolute; better translated simply as "absolute" in English.

[194] *sensus*, sensation or the senses.

BOOK IV

through his allotted span of life making happy progress. But if
one tries to oppose it, he, according to Plato in his *Timaeus,* "re-
sembles a hobbling, mangled [195] cripple, trying to edge himself
tortuously along the way of life, until he is finally recalled, in
company with his inveterate folly,[196] to the infernal regions." [197]
Reason watches out for both our body and soul, and serves as a
moderator to bring them into [felicitous] coöperation. One who
is contemptuous of both his body and his soul, is crippled and
weak, while he who slights either is [thereby] lamed. Since reason
examines our sensations, which, because they are wont to deceive
us, are subject to suspicion, mother nature, the very considerate
parent of all [that exists], has made our head the seat of all sensation, in which citadel she has enthroned reason as queen. In
other words, reason serves as a sort of supreme senate in the soul's
Capitoline Hill,[198] where it is centrally situated between the
chambers of imagination and memory, so that from its watch-
tower, it may pass upon the judgments of sensation and imagination.[199] Reason, although divine, is, as it were, set into motion
by the winnowing fan[200] of sensory perceptions and acts of the
imagination. And since prudence, in her inquiry into the truth,
has need of reason's unvitiated examination, she [prudence] begets
for reason "Philology." The latter is constantly attended by two
handmaids, "Carefulness" [201] and "Vigilance." [202] "Carefulness"
concentrates on the labors of learning,[203] while "Vigilance" diligently supervises these activities and moderates them lest anything become excessive. For love[204] is not lazy. Although Philology
has a terrestrial origin, and is in itself mortal, still, when it rises

---

[195] *claudum . . . et mancum,* literally: lamed and maimed. The words *et mancum* have
been added to Plato's text.
[196] *familiari stultitia,* with his familiar or accustomed folly, foolishness, or vice.
[197] See Plato, *Tim.,* 44 C, in the translation of Chalcidius.
[198] *Capitolio.*
[199] Cf. Chalcidius, *Comm. in Tim. Plat.,* § 231.
[200] *uentilabro,* winnowing fan, fork, or bellows.
[201] *Periergia,* περιεργία, periergy: extreme exactness or carefulness.
[202] *Agrimnia,* Αγρυπνία, Agrypnia: vigilance, sleeplessness, watchfulness. For this passage,
cf. Martianus Capella, *De Nupt.,* ii, §§ 111 ff.
[203] *laborem circuit operis,* literally: "goes about the work of the undertaking."
[204] This is evidently a reference to the *philos,* or loving, in "Philology." Cf. what follows.

to [contemplate] divine truths, it is deified by a certain immortality. Thus when love of reason, which concerns earthly things, ascends with prudence to the hidden secrets of eternal and divine truths, it becomes transformed into wisdom, which is in a way exempt from mortal limitations.

CHAPTER 18.   *The distinction between reason and [intuitive]*
understanding,[205] *and the nature of the latter.*

Just as reason transcends sense perception, so it, in turn, is surpassed by [intuitive] understanding, as Plato observes in his *Republic.*[206] For [intuitive] understanding actually attains what reason investigates. [Intuitive] Understanding enters into the very labors of reason,[207] and treasures up the preparatory gains of reason unto wisdom.[208] It is, in fact, the highest power of a spiritual nature. Besides comprehending what is human, it also contemplates the divine causes behind all reasons within the natural powers of its perception. For there are some divine reasons[209] which utterly exceed, not merely human, but even angelic comprehension.[210] And there are some divine truths, in like manner, which become either more fully or less fully known to us, according to the decree of the divine dispensation. [Intuitive] Understanding, according to Plato, "is possessed only by God and a few select individuals." [211]

[205] *intellectus, vovs,* rational intuition; the understanding or intuitive faculty, as opposed to *ratio,* reason; the discursive or reasoning faculty. Where John speaks of *rationem,* Chalcidius has *deliberatio.*

[206] Plato, *Republic,* vi, 544, D, ff. See Chalcidius, *Comm. in Tim. Plat.,* § 231, with which John's passage here corresponds in sense, except for the direct reference to Plato.

[207] Cf. John, iv, 38.

[208] Cf. Ecclesiasticus, iv, 21.

[209] *rationes,* reasons or fundamental truths.

[210] Philippians, iv, 7.

[211] *selectorum.* Chalcidius has *lectorum;* both words mean "chosen," "favored," "select." See Plato, *Tim.,* 51 E; which passage is also cited by John in his *Historia Pontificalis,* chap. 14 (ed. Poole, p. 33); cf. *Met.,* iv, 14, toward the end; cf. also Chalcidius, *Comm. in Tim. Plat.,* § 340; and the passage attributed to Augustine, *Met.,* iv, 30. Cf. Abelard, *Log. Ingred.*

CHAPTER 19. *The nature of wisdom, and the fact that, with the help of grace, wisdom derives [originally] from sense perception.*

From [intuitive] understanding proceeds wisdom. For from reason's disquisitions [intuitive] understanding excerpts divine truths. And the latter [truths] have a delicious savor, which engenders an affection for them in intelligent souls. In this connection, I believe that wisdom[212] derives its name from the fact that good men have a discerning taste[213] for the things of God.[214] The Fathers[215] associated [scientific] knowledge[216] with action, and wisdom with contemplation. To one who reflects on the aforesaid steps, it becomes clear that wisdom itself [also] flows originally from the same fountainhead of the senses, with grace both preparing the way and providing assistance. The prophets testify that even fear, which is "the beginning of wisdom," [217] is a result of the sensory experience or mental image of pain.[218] On the one hand, when we are tempted, the thought of punishment restrains us from giving offense to Him who will chastise us; while, on the other [hand], the sense perception or imagination of rewards stimulates us to serve Him who is able to make us happy, as well as to punish. By refraining from offense, one practices piety, and by exercising[219] obedience, one acquires [scientific] knowledge, which relates to action. If one becomes accustomed to the practice of obedience, this habit develops into [the

[212] *sapientia.*
[213] *saporem.*
[214] Namely, for divine truths. See Isidore, *Etym.,* x, § 240.
[215] Cf. Augustine, *De Trin.,* xii, 14, § 22, 15, § 25, xiii, 1, § 1 (in Migne, *P.L.,* XLII, 1009, 1012, 1013); and Isidore, *Diff.,* ii, 147 (in Migne, *P.L.,* LXXXIII, 93).
[216] *scientiam,* knowledge, science, scientific knowledge.
[217] Psalms, cx, 10; Ecclesiasticus, i, 16.
[218] *pene,* that is, *poenae,* pain or suffering. Here is an instance of John's habitual use of *e* for *ae* and *oe.*
[219] *experientiam,* experience, experimental knowledge, practice, exercise.

virtue of] fortitude. And so that one may offer that "rational
submission"[220] which is the most acceptable, there arises reflective
deliberation[221] concerning action.[222] [Intuitive] Understanding is
consequent upon deliberation, and firmly embraces the better part.
For [intuitive] understanding concerns itself with divine truths,
and the relish, love, and observance[223] of the latter constitutes true
wisdom. Rather than being the [mere] product of nature, these
successive steps are the result of grace. The latter, according to its
own free determination, derives the various rivulets of the sciences
and wisdom from the fountainhead of sense perception. Grace
reveals hidden divine truths by means of those things which have
been made,[224] and by that unity which belongs to love, communi-
cates what it has made manifest, thus uniting man to God.[225]

CHAPTER 20.   *The cognition, simplicity, and immortality of
the soul, according to Cicero.*

Certain lesser philosophers,[226] reasoning from the fact that from
sense perceptions our mind proceeds to scientific knowledge, argue
that we can have [scientific] knowledge only of those things that
are perceived by our senses. It is evident how lethal admission of
such a proposition would be to philosophy. Reason's activity,
whereby it seeks and finds in its processes[227] the ideas[228] of things,
which the Greeks call *ennoias*,[229] would be futile if the aforesaid
assumption were true.[230] But without reasoning, not even a [com-
mon] name can have a solid foundation. "It is the mark," as

[220] *obsequium rationale*, rational compliance or reasonable service; cf. Romans, xii, 1.
[221] *consilium deliberationis*, the counsel or reflection of deliberation, judicious consideration.
[222] Literally: concerning acts and what is done.
[223] *inherentia*, inherence, faithful observance, persevering devotion.
[224] Namely, visible creation.
[225] Cf. Romans, i, 20.
[226] *quidam minuti philosophi*; cf. Cicero, *De Sen.*, 23, § 85.
[227] *apud se.*
[228] *notiones*, notions, concepts, ideas.
[229] *ennoias*, ἔννοίας, notions or mental concepts, ideas or intuitions.
[230] Cf. Cicero, *Tusc. Disp.*, i, 24, § 57.

Cicero observes in his *Tusculan Disputations*,[231] "of great natural
intelligence to withdraw the mind from sensation, and to extricate thought from the rut of habit." [232] "The only possible explanation of our knowledge of God, whom we do know, is that
our mind is unfettered, free, and exempt from [essential unity
with] what is mortal and material." [233] "The [thinking] soul's
nature and powers are unique, they are distinct from and independent of the ordinary natures with which we are familiar.
Whatever it may be, the [thinking] soul is truly divine." "The
[thinking] soul cannot fully know itself. Still, like the eye, it
beholds other things without seeing itself. Perhaps it is true that
it does not see its own form, which is not an important defect.
Although possibly it even sees this.[234] But whatever the case,
the [thinking] soul certainly perceives its own force, sagacity,
memory, activity, and quickness. These are great, divine [and]
everlasting. There is no need of inquiring about what the [think-
ing] soul looks like, or where it is situated. . . ."[235] Although one
cannot see the human mind,[236] any more than one can see God, still,
just as one knows God from his works, one may recognize the divine
force of the [human] mind from its powers of memory and invention, and from its swift apprehension, and beauteous virtue. . . .
When one considers the soul's knowledge, he cannot doubt, unless
he is a stupid ignoramus[237] as far as natural science is concerned,
that, in the soul, there is nothing mixed, nothing composite, nothing
copulated, nothing added, nothing twofold. This being the case, cer-

[231] *in Tusculanis*. What follows is from Cicero, *Tusc. Disp.*, i, 16, and 27–29, 38, 66–67, 70–71.

[232] Cicero, *op. cit.*, i, 16, § 38. In John *reuocare* is probably *seuocare* in Cicero, to abstract. Cf. T. W. Dougan's edition of the *Tusculan Disputations* (Cambridge, England,
1905).

[233] *segregata ab omni concretione mortali*, that is, free from any mortal concretion or
essential unity with the mortal and material or with perishable matter.

[234] In Cicero this passage reads: *Quam quam fortasse* (or *Fortasse quamquam*), rather
than: *fortasse. Quamquam* as in the Webb text. Consequently the translation of Cicero
would here read: ". . . its own form. And yet perhaps also; . . ." The Webb text
should apparently be corrected to read: *fortasse; quamquam* or perhaps even *fortasse
quamquam*. Cf. MSS A, B, C. In the A text it would read as I have translated it in
the text; in the C text as I have translated Cicero above.

[235] The foregoing is from Cicero, *Tusc. Disp.*, i, 27, §§ 66, 67.

[236] *mentem*, mind or soul.

[237] *plumbei*, leaden, heavy and dull, stupid ignoramuses.

tainly the [thinking] soul can be neither cut nor divided, neither chopped into pieces nor torn asunder. Hence it is imperishable."[238] Cicero makes these observations in his *Tusculan Disputations* to show that our deliberative power, that is to say our reason, is indeed divine, and that human souls are immortal. In the foregoing discussion, we have briefly summarized the power of the senses to receive external impressions,[239] and the faculties and dignity of the [conscious] soul, to establish [and explain] the fact that, as Aristotle says, the arts and sciences derive originally from sensory perceptions.[240] If anyone cares to investigate the powers of the [conscious] soul further, he will find that this a subject of great subtlety, requiring a keen and gifted mind, a retentive and ready memory, uninterrupted leisure, and the diligent study of numerous large works. Those who wish to study the nature of the soul in more precise detail may consult not only the writings of Plato, Aristotle, Cicero, and [other] ancient philosophers, but also those of the [Christian] Fathers, who have more correctly stated the truth. For the doctors of the Church, as well as Claudianus,[241] and other still more recent authors,[242] have written much about the soul. If it is impossible for one to peruse[243] the aforesaid works, he should at least read the *Phrenonphysicon*.[244] The latter [book] discusses the soul at considerable length, although I do not mean to say that I consider it the best of all treatises on the subject. But enough of this; now let us return to our subject.

[238] The foregoing is from Cicero, *Tusc. Disp.*, i, 28–29, §§ 70–71.
[239] *passione sensuum*, the feeling or receptive power of the senses.
[240] Aristotle, *An. Post.*, ii, 19, 100 a, 6 ff.
[241] Claudianus Mamertus, *De Statu Animae.*
[242] *moderniores*, more modern or more recent [authors].
[243] Literally: roll out, roll [unroll] and read, peruse.
[244] *Phrenonphisicon*, as if it were Περὶ φρενῶν φύσεῶς. Apparently John refers here to the *Phremnon Physicon*, a translation by Alfano, Archbishop of Salerno of the περὶ φύσεῶς ανθρώπου of Nemesius (ed. C. Burkhard, Leipzig, 1917). The same treatise was also translated by Burgundio the Pisan, whom John mentions earlier. (*Met.*, iv, 7).

CHAPTER 21.   *Although Aristotle has not sufficiently discussed*
hypothetical [conditional] reasoning[245] *in the*
foregoing books, he has, at it were, sowed seed
for such a treatment.

Although the foregoing books [of Aristotle] explain both dialectical
and apodictical logic, which latter is called by us "demonstrative"
[logic], they contain no or very little discussion of hypothetical
[conditional] reasoning.[246] However, Aristotle as it were sowed the
seed, which subsequent authors could develop into a scientific treatment of the subject. When the topics of probable and necessary arguments were pointed out, what follows probably or necessarily from
what also was shown. The establishing of consequences is, in my
opinion, chiefly dependent on the evidence[247] of hypothetical [condi-
tional] reasoning. Boethius tells us that Aristotle's statement in his
Analytics to the effect that "If a given thing can both be and not be,
then the existence of the thing in question is not necessary," [248] has
been taken as a seed for subsequent findings.[249] While Boethius and
others[250] have somewhat supplied for Aristotle's deficiency in this
respect [i.e., in the treatment of hypothetical reasoning], it seems to
me that their treatises are also inadequate. In regard to hypothetical
reasoning, we are shown what syllogisms may be made in the prior
form by establishing the antecedent, and what ones in the posterior
form by eliminating the consequent.[251] We are also instructed as to
what figures or modes consist of composite conditionals, or of equi-

[245] *hypotheticarum*, hypothetical or conditional reasoning or syllogisms.
[246] Cf. Boethius, *De Syll. Hypoth.*, i (in Migne, *P.L.*, LXIV, 831).
[247] *indicium*, evidence, proof, indication.
[248] Aristotle, *An. Post.*, ii, 4, 57 b, 3, 4. John has: *Idem cum sit et non sit, non necesse
est idem esse*, as has Boethius in his (quotation of Aristotle) *De Syll. Hypoth.*, i (in
Migne, *P.L.*, LXIV, 836).
[249] Boethius, *op. cit.*, i.
[250] Theophrastus and Eudemus; cf. Boethius, *ibid.*
[251] Boethius tells us that the consequences in hypothetical syllogisms are two: if the
antecedent exists, the consequent exists; and if the consequent exists, the antecedent exists.
Cf. Boethius, *ibid.* (in Migne, *P.L.*, LXIV, 836–837).

modal or non-equimodal propositions.[252] The nature of those hypothetical syllogisms that are made up of disjunctive propositions[253] is
also explained.[254] Perhaps Aristotle avoided this subject and left this
labor to others on purpose. For the book of the author who has
most carefully written on hypothetical syllogisms[255] seems to contain
even greater difficulty than utility. And if Aristotle himself had written on this topic in his wonted style,[256] it is likely that the resulting
work would be so difficult that no one except the Sybil[257] would be
capable of understanding it. I do not, however, believe that hypothetical reasoning is sufficiently explained in the works I have mentioned,[258] and hence I consider the supplements of the schools
exceedingly useful and [even] necessary.

CHAPTER 22.   *Sophistry and its utility.*

That [logic] which makes a pretext of being dialectical and demonstrative [logic] with a flourish of hollow imitation, and strives more
to acquire the [external] semblance than the [true] virtue of
wisdom, is known as "sophistry."[259] Lest his followers become ensnared by this artifice, Aristotle rightly appends a treatment of the
latter. The resultant treatise is worthy of him. I would be reluctant
to say that any other study could be more beneficial for the young.
Since they cannot really obtain true wisdom in all matters, the young
strive to obtain a name for being wise, and endeavor to win esteem,

[252] *equimodis et non equimodis*, equimodal or regular, and non-equimodal or irregular.
Boethius gives as an example of an equimodal proposition: "If *a* is, *b* is; and if *a* is,
c is not"; and of a non-equimodal proposition: "If *a* is, *b* is; if *a* is not, *b* is not." In
the first case, the form or mode of the condition is the same, in the second case it is different. Boethius, *op. cit.*, ii (in Migne, *P.L.*, LXIV, 859 ff.).
[253] *disiunctiuis*.
[254] Cf. Boethius, *op. cit.*, ii (in Migne, *P.L.*, LXIV, 873 ff.).
[255] Apparently reference is here made to Boethius.
[256] Cf. Boethius, *De Syll. Categ.*, i (in Migne, *P.L.*, LXIV, 793).
[257] Cf. Plautus, *Pseudol.*, i, 25, 26, as also William of Malmesbury, *De Gestis Pontificum*,
i, 15 (ed. N. E. S. Hamilton, Rolls Series, LII, p. 22). Concerning Plautus in the Middle
Ages, see J. E. Sandys, *History of Classical Scholarship*, I, 607.
[258] *hic*, here. John evidently means in the works he has mentioned earlier.
[259] See *Met.*, ii, 3.

which is the very thing that sophistry promises. For sophistry affects
the appearance of wisdom, rather than its reality, while the sophist
bubbles over with simulated, rather than actual wisdom.[260] Sophistry
disguises itself as all the disciplines, and masked, now as one, now as
another of the various branches of knowledge, lays its traps for
everyone, and catches the unwary. If one lacks [a knowledge of]
sophistical logic, in vain does he claim to be a philosopher. For,
without this, he can neither avoid falsehood, nor unmask one who is
lying. There is need for this knowledge of sophistry in every branch
of learning. You may see those who know nothing about sophistry,
when they find themselves deceived by fallacious reasoning,[261]
whether their own or someone else's, exclaiming in astonishment,
with puzzled Nicodemus: "But Lord, how could this happen?"[262]
Nothing less becomes one who is striving to win distinction or gain
a victory [in disputation]. A person who is contending[263] is trying to
win out over an opponent, and a person who is using sophistry is
aiming to achieve a reputation. Their objects are, in each case, quite
satisfactory for disputes and contests. Exercising in sophistical argumentation is very advantageous, both for the development of skillful
oratorical expression,[264] and for the facilitation of all philosophical
investigations. This is [of course] provided that truth, and not verbosity, is the [ultimate] fruit of this exercise. In which case, sophistry
can serve as the handmaid of truth and wisdom. Otherwise it will
play the adulteress, who betrays her blinded lovers by exposing them
to errors and leading them to the precipice.[265] Wisdom says: "One
who speaks sophistically is odious."[266] But surely more loathsome
is one whose manner of living is sophistical. An erroneous life is
more pernicious than faulty speech. However, there is hardly anyone, who, in his actual way of living, does not take after the sophists.
Those who are bad, long to appear good, and strive in every [pos-
sible] way to acquire a respectable reputation. On the other hand,

---

[260] Aristotle, *Soph. El.*, 1, 165 a, 21 ff.
[261] *paralogizentur.*
[262] John, iii, 9.
[263] *litigiosus*, contending or contentious. Cf. Met., iv, 23.
[264] *frasim.*
[265] To destruction.
[266] Ecclesiasticus, xxxvii, 23.

those who are good often try to conceal their defects from others,[267] so that they may seem to be better than they actually are. To act thus is to become a sophist in one's way of life. At least this is so if one tries to seem good or better for one's own [personal] glory. For if one is endeavoring to enhance the glory of God, and this in an enlightened manner,[268] he may perhaps be excused.

CHAPTER 23.   *The* Sophistical Refutations.[269]

Aristotle accordingly introduces [the study of] sophistry[270] into the Peripatetic discipline. Dispersing the fog[271] of fallacies, he explains how sophistry is to be admitted or avoided. He also discloses the full extent of sophistry's possibilities, together with the means it employs.[272] Just as dialectic[273] uses the *elenchus,*[274] which we call a refutatory[275] syllogism, because it argues to the contrary, so sophistry uses the sophistical *elenchus,* which is only a fictitious [refutatory] syllogism. In place of really presenting a counterargument, the latter only seems to do so. For a sophistical *elenchus* consists in [nothing more than] a paralogism, that is a pseudo[276] syllogism. Aristotle also distinguishes the various general kinds of disputations[277] in order to reveal how the sophist, who, as I say, in competing, uses contentious[278] argumentation, now imitates the demonstrator teaching from principles,[279] now the dialectician concluding from probabilities, now

[267] Literally: to circumvent (or elude) the judgment of others.
[268] *ex scientia,* from scientific or enlightened knowledge, with enlightened purpose.
[269] *De Sophisticis Elenchis,* the *Sophistical Refutations.*
[270] *hanc,* literally: "this."
[271] *nube,* cloud or fog.
[272] Aristotle, *Soph. El.,* chap. 1.
[273] Literally: the dialectician.
[274] *elenchus,* a refutation, a refutatory syllogism or reasoning.
[275] *eluctatorium,* contentious, struggling, refutatory; a word possibly coined by John from *eluctor,* because of its resemblance in sound and meaning to *elenchi.*
[276] *umbratilis,* merely shadowy or imaginary, unsubstantial.
[277] Arguments in dialogue form.
[278] *litigiosam.*
[279] *ex principiis,* that is, from the principles of the various branches of knowledge.

the investigator[280] arguing to probabilities from things that are not [entirely] evident. Aristotle next enumerates the five aims of sophists: namely, to contrive to trap an adversary into either a self-refutation, a fallacy, a paradox, a solecism, or babbling. A quibbling, sophistical objector[281] is satisfied even if he only seems to accomplish one of these aims.[282] Aristotle subjoins a list of the forms of [refutatory] argumentation that depend on wording. These include ambiguity, amphibology, combination, division, accent, and figurative speech. He further explains those [forms] that do not depend on wording,[283] but rather on (1) an accident, (2) whether or not an expression is used absolutely,[284] (3) ignorance of [the nature of] refutation, (4) the consequent, (5) taking for granted the original point in question, (6) positing as a cause something that is not a cause, and (7) reducing several questions to a single question.[285] How a questioner or answerer should be trained in these various forms is carefully pursued through several chapters. Excellent drillmaster that he is, Aristotle coaches the questioner to be aggressive, the answerer to be wary.[286]

In the books we have discussed, what is desirable and what undesirable [in reasoning] are made evident. The topics of probable reasons, which are the only ones we weak humans can fully comprehend, are also exposed. The composition of demonstration or proof of necessity is disclosed. The methods and ways of teaching[287] are explained. Finally, the possible stumbling blocks of fallacies are removed. Consequently it becomes clearer than day that these books provide a full account of argumentative reasoning,[288] together with its limits and its parts.

---

[280] See Aristotle, *Soph. El.*, chap. 2, wherein he contrasts didactic, dialectical, examinatory, and contentious argumentation.

[281] *cauillatori*, a caviller, one who raises captious or frivolous objections, a sophist.

[282] Aristotle, *op. cit.*, chap. 3.

[283] *extra dictionem.*

[284] *simpliciter*, absolutely, unreservedly, without qualification.

[285] Aristotle, *op. cit.*, chaps. 4–14. I have inserted the numbers (1–7) here for purposes of clarity.

[286] *Ibid.*, chaps. 15 ff.

[287] *docendi*, of teaching, proving, or demonstrating.

[288] *rationem disserendi*, an account, method, or system of reasoned discussion, or argumentative reasoning.

CHAPTER 24.   *A word about those who disparage the works*
of Aristotle.

I will never cease to wonder how much sense those who rail against
these works of Aristotle can possess (if indeed they have any at all).
Accordingly, it has been my object [in the present treatise] to commend rather than to expound these works. Master Theodoric,[289] as
I recollect, derided the *Topics* of Drogo of Troyes rather than of
Aristotle,[290] although he sometimes taught these *Topics*.[291] Some of
the disciples of Robert of Melun unjustly criticize the *Topics*[292] as
practically useless. Others try to tear down the *Categories*. It is for
this reason that I have devoted more time to [both of] the latter.[293] I
did not consider that the other works [of the *Organon*] needed
protracted praise, since everyone thinks highly of them. Although
the [*Sophistical*] *Refutations* have been attacked because they contain
poetical verses,[294] this is, of course, not a valid objection. At the
same time, it must be admitted that idioms cannot easily be translated with full adequacy from one tongue to another. Still it seems
to me that the [*Sophistical*] *Refutations* are preferable to the *Ana-*

[289] Thierry of Chartres; cf. *Met.*, i, 5, n. 64, and iii, 5, n. 223.
[290] *Topica non Aristotilis sed Trecasini Drogonis irridebat.* A. Hofmeister and C. C. J.
Webb are of the opinion that this passage should be translated: "Master Theodoric . . .
derided the *Topics* as the work of Drogo of Troyes rather than of Aristotle." Thus
A. Hofmeister (Studien über Otto von Freising, ii, in *Neues Archiv für ältere deutsche
Geschichtskunde*, XXXVII, 665) says that Theodoric derided Aristotle's *Topics* as more
worthy of Drogo of Troyes, and that we are not to suppose a work of Drogo on the
Topics. Webb, in his edition of the *Metalogicon* (p. 191), follows Hofmeister. I have,
however, translated this passage in accordance with Clerval (*Les Écoles de Chartres*,
pp. 170 and 245), and Schaarschmidt (*Johannes Saresberiensis*, p. 78), and in what I
take to be the more literal sense of this passage. Schaarschmidt says that Drogo's *Topics*
were an adaptation of Cicero's *Topics*. However, since Schaarschmidt cites no authority
for his statement, he may only be surmising that Drogo wrote an adaptation of Cicero's
Topics, which (adaptation) is the object of John's present reference. The Hofmeister-
Webb theory may be correct, and is allowed by my somewhat ambiguous English, which
corresponds to John's ambiguous Latin.
[291] Cf. *Met.*, iii, 5, n. 223.
[292] Aristotle's *Topics*.
[293] Namely to the *Topics* and *Categories*.
[294] Cf. Aristotle, *Soph. El.*, 4, 166 a, 36 ff.

lytics. For the *Refutations,* while they exercise a student equally as much as the *Analytics,* are more easily understood and more effectively promote the development of eloquence.

CHAPTER 25.   *The fact that Cornificus is even more contemptible than Bromius, the buffoon of the gods. Also how Augustine and other philosophers praise logic.*

Since logic has such tremendous power, anyone who charges that it is foolish to study this [art], thereby shows himself to be a fool of fools. In the *Marriage of Philology* Pallas[295] rebukes [and checks] Bromius,[296] who had been deriding [and villifying] logic[297] as a sorcerer[298] and a poisoner, and with a long eulogy she formally admits the latter into the company of the gods.[299] In mythology, Bromius is consigned the ignominious position of buffoon of the gods. Our Cornificius, opponent of logic, may likewise be deservedly despised as the clown of philosophers. Not to mention Plato, Aristotle, and Cicero, who, as our forefathers relate, initiated [the science of] philosophy and brought it to perfection, Father Augustine, with whom it is rash to disagree, praised logic so highly that only the foolhardy and presumptuous would dare to rail against it. In his second book *On Order,* Augustine says: "After the work of completing grammar and organizing it [into a science] had been accomplished, reason was led to investigate and scrutinize the very power whereby it had begotten this art [of grammar]. For when reason [this power] formulated the definitions, drew up the classifications, and concluded the [general] principles of grammar, it not only

[295] Pallas Athene, Greek goddess of wisdom.
[296] A surname of Bacchus, the Roman god of wine and the vintage, who is represented by Martianus Capella as the jester of the gods.
[297] *eam,* namely dialectic or logic.
[298] *Marsicam,* a Marsian; the Marsi were a people celebrated as soothsayers and charmers of serpents.
[299] See Martianus Capella, *De Nupt.,* iv, §§ 331 ff.

arranged and organized the art, but also fortified the latter against any possible intrusion of falsehood. Was it not fitting, then, that, before reason would proceed to the construction of additional arts and sciences,[300] it should first distinguish, observe, and classify its own processes and instruments, and thus bring to light that discipline of disciplines called dialectic? For dialectic teaches both how to teach and how to learn. In dialectic, reason discloses its own identity, and makes manifest its nature, purpose, and potentialities. Dialectic alone knows [how] to know, and it alone both wills and has the power to make men learned." [301] What does Cornificius reply to the aforesaid? He does just what one would expect of a feeble-minded sluggard given to snoring during exhortations to virtue: he yaps at what he cannot attain.

CHAPTER 26.   *What tactics we should employ against Cornificius and [other like] perverse calumniators [of logic]*.

Against Cornificius and his fellow sluggards (for already he has companions in error), we may well follow the procedure which Augustine, in his first[302] book *Against the Academicians,* outlines as among the many things he learned from dialectic. In Augustine's [own] words: "Dialectic has taught me that when that which is being discussed is evident, one should not argue over words. It has also convinced me that when a disputant quibbles over words, if he does so from lack of learning or experience,[303] he should be

---

[300] Literally: to other things.

[301] Augustine, *De Ord.,* ii, 13 (in Migne, *P.L.,* XXXII, 1013). The Migne text of Augustine has *irreptione* instead of John's *irruptione* (192, 20); *distinguere* instead of *distingereret* (192, 22); *dirigeret* instead of *digereret* (*ibid.*); *demonstrat; atque aperit que sit, quid velit, quid valeat; scit scire; sola scientes facere* . . . instead of *demonstrat atque aperit que sit, que uelit; quid ualeat scit scire sola, scientes facere* . . . as in the Webb text (192, 25–26). I have translated according to the Migne (rather than the Webb) punctuation. Cf. MSS A, B, and C.

[302] This is found in Augustine's third, rather than first book *Against the Academicians* (*Contra Academicos*).

[303] *ex imperitia.*

instructed, but if he does so from malice, we should refuse to argue
any further with him. If [in the first instance] he cannot be instructed, then he should be warned that he ought to make better use
of his time and energies, instead of wasting them on what is superfluous. If he still does not comply, there is no point in paying more
attention to him. On the other hand, the rule for dealing with
captious and fallacious little arguments is brief: If conclusions are
inferred from premises which should never have been granted in
the first place, we should bring the discussion back to a reëxamina-
tion of what was previously conceded. If the conclusion contains conflicting truth and falsehood, then we should accept what is intelligible, but reject what cannot be explained. Finally, if the mode[304]
in given instances utterly defies human comprehension, we should
not worry about seeking scientific knowledge of it." [305]

CHAPTER 27.   *Although he has been mistaken on several
points, Aristotle is preëminent in logic.*

What we have so far said has been directed against Cornificius.
Against those who, in their conservatism, exclude the more efficacious books of Aristotle,[306] and content themselves almost exclusively
with Boethius,[307] much could also be said. There is, however, no
necessity to advance any arguments on this point. The inadequacy
of the knowledge[308] of those who have consumed all their time and
energies studying Boethius, with the result that they hardly know
anything, is so universally apparent that it excites compassion. I do
not claim that Aristotle is always correct in his views and teaching,

[304] *modus,* manner, mode, sense.
[305] Augustine, *Contra Acad.,* iii, 13, § 29 (in Migne, *P.L.,* XXXII, 949).
[306] This may be also translated: Against those who exclude the books of Aristotle that
were held in higher esteem by the ancients. Reference is apparently made to Aristotle's
Topics, Analytics, and *Sophistical Refutations.*
[307] Reference is apparently made to those who confined themselves, as did their predecessors in the earlier Middle Ages, to the *Categories* and the *Interpretation,* as translated and
commented on by Boethius.
[308] *imperfectum,* literally: the imperfect state; cf. Psalms, cxxxviii, 16.

as though everything he has written were sacrosanct. It has been
proved, both by reason and by the authority of faith, that Aristotle
has erred on several points. Thus, for example, Aristotle asserts
that not only anyone who so desires, but even God himself can do
evil.[309] He also denies that God's providence extends as far as the
region of the moon, and, to disprove the possibility of divination and
foreknowledge, he maintains that things below [the moon] are not
regulated by divine providence.[310] He further asserts that angels
cannot help us, and that demons have no special insight[311] relative
to these[312] or future things.[313] At the same time, even though Aristotle has made several mistakes, as is evident from the writings of
Christians and pagans alike, his equal in logic has yet to be found.
Hence he should be regarded as a [learned] master of argumentative
reasoning, rather than of morals, and he should be recognized as a
teacher whose function is to conduct the young on to more serious
philosophical studies, rather than [directly] to instruct in ethics.

CHAPTER 28.   *How logic should be employed.*

Although this art of logic has manifold utility, still, if one is learned
only in it, and ignorant of aught else, he is actually retarded, rather
than helped to progress in philosophy, since he becomes a victim
of verbosity and overconfidence. By itself, logic is practically useless.
Only when it is associated with other studies does logic shine, and
then by a virtue that is communicated by them. Considerable indulgence should, however, be shown to the young,[314] in whom
verbosity should be temporarily tolerated, so that they may thus
acquire an abundance of eloquence.[315] The minds of the immature,

---

[309] See Aristotle, *Top.*, iv, 5, 126 a, 34, 35.

[310] According to Chalcidius, Aristotle maintains that God's providence does not extend
to things below the moon.

[311] *perspicientiam*. Chalcidius has *prospicientiam*, or foreknowledge.

[312] This word, "these," evidently refers to "things below," mentioned above.

[313] Cf. Chalcidius, *Comm. in Tim. Plat.*, § 250.

[314] Literally: for tender age.

[315] Cf. Quintilian, *Inst. Orat.*, ii, 4, §§ 4 ff.

even as their [growing] bodies, must first be [well] fed, lest they become emaciated. Thus, by means of plenty of nourishing food, they can put on weight and acquire strength. During this stage, the flesh is allowed to luxuriate to a degree that might [otherwise] be considered excessive. At a later age, the surplus fat of the young will be sufficiently burned out and purified by the exertion of labor, the burden of responsibility, and the strain of work. As students mature and grow in understanding, our tolerance of unrestrained verbosity should diminish, and the impudence of sophistry (which Aristotle calls "contentious," [316] but we refer to as "deceitful" or "cavilling") [317] should be suppressed. It is the duty of those who have the title and function of teachers to see to this. However, rules alone are useless. Theoretical principles must be consolidated by practice and assiduous exercise, except perhaps where a disposition has already been transformed into a habit. [318]

CHAPTER 29.   *That the temerity of adolescence should be restrained; why eloquence[319] weds philology; and what should be our main objectives.*

Our tolerance of these exercises of the schools, which are, so to speak, games in the gymnasium of philosophy, indulged in for the purpose of developing proficiency [in the young], should not, however, be extended into more mature years and more serious studies. Facetious folly,[320] noisy [volubility], empty loquacity, and puerile silliness, should all be set aside, as soon as the first soft beard begins to appear on one's face.[321] To indulge in the foregoing [on reaching maturity] is to throw away one's birthright as a philosopher, and to class oneself as a fool. According to the lesson of the allegory, as soon as he reached adolescence. Mercury, the god of

---

[316] John's *ditatiuam* here is probably a slip for *litatiuam,* and so I have translated.

[317] *cauillatoriam;* see Boethius, *Comm. in Top. Cic.* (in Migne, *P.L.,* LXIV, 1045).

[318] Cf. Quintilian, *op. cit.,* viii, pref., § 28.

[319] Literally: Mercury.

[320] Buffoonlike, trifling, facetious silliness.

[321] *cum prima lanugine,* that is, as soon as the age of puberty is reached.

eloquence, in accordance with the exhortations of his mother, wed
Philology. For "the fact that his cheeks were already beginning to
show the down of manhood [322] meant that he could no longer go
about half naked, with only a short cape[323] over his shoulders, without provoking Venus to peals of laughter." [324] Venus,[325] who represents the happy combination[326] of wisdom and eloquence, derides
the foolishness of nude, unarmed, windy eloquence. The secret
and most excellent nature of the three things which are most desirable, is hidden from the senses of man. For man, preoccupied with
earthly things, is weighted down by his terrestrial environment.[327]
The aforesaid three things, which we should prefer to aught else,
are genuine goodness, unadulterated truth, and sound, trustworthy
reasoning. Human nature, "to whose heart," God, as we read in the
book of the son of Sirac, "has given vision, so that the greatness of
his own works may become manifest," and that He may be praised
in his goodness, and glorified in his wonders,[328] [human nature]
desires both to know the truth, and to apprehend and hold fast to
what is good. This appetite [for truth, goodness, and reason] has
been implanted in man's nature by God; but it cannot obtain its
objectives by nature alone, for it also needs the assistance of grace.
According to ancient pagan allegory,[329] there were three sisters,
Love of Reason, Love of Wisdom, and Love of the Beautiful,[330]
who were all daughters of Prudence. Augustine explains the nature
of Love of Wisdom and Love of the Beautiful,[331] Martianus expounds on that of Love of Reason,[332] and Aesop[333] indicates the

[322] *pubentes,* showing fuzzy down, denoting the age of puberty.

[323] *clamide:* χλαμύς: chlamys, a short cloak or cape.

[324] Martianus Capella, *De Nupt.,* i, § 5.

[325] *Cipris,* the Cyprian; a poetical name for Venus.

[326] *mixtura.* In *"Mythogr. III,"* in *Class. Auct.* (ed. Maius), III, 250, concerning Venus
we find: "She is called the Cyprian, which means a mixture."

[327] Cf. Wisdom, ix, 15.

[328] Ecclesiasticus, xvii, 7, 8. John's wording differs slightly from the Vulgate, although the
sense is the same.

[329] Or mythology.

[330] Literally: Philology, Philosophy, and Philocaly.

[331] Augustine, *Contra Acad.,* ii, 3, § 7 (in Migne, *P.L.,* XXXII, 922).

[332] Martianus Capella, *op. cit.,* ii, § 114.

[333] This evidently refers to the above-quoted passage in Augustine, where he says ". . .
for suddenly I have become Aesop . . ." Augustine apparently means merely that he is
speaking allegorically, that is, telling a fable, rather than that he actually attributes the
latter to Aesop, as John seems here to misinterpret him.

inter-relationship existing between the three. Although human infirmity dares not arrogantly promise these [three] to itself, it continually seeks after them, namely, after true goodness, wisdom, and
reason, and it is occupied in loving them, until, by the exercise of
love with the help of grace, it [ultimately] attains the objects of its
affection. Prudence it is that elicits this affection [for reason, wisdom,
and beauty], as their savour increases in sweetness, and begets an
appetite for what is true and good. The Greek *frono* [the root of
Fronesis] means "I relish," and refers more to appetitive delight than
to wisdom,[334] which consists in the contemplation of divine things.
The latter [contemplation of divine things] is called *Sophia* [Wis-
dom] rather than *Fronesis* [Prudence].[335]

CHAPTER 30.   *The fact that philology precedes its two sisters.[336] Also what investigation by categories[337]
is appropriate in a discussion of reason and
truth.*

Among the aforementioned three sisters, Philology comes first, inasmuch as it discloses the nature, power, and counsels of each of the
others. Since there are many probabilities on every hand (for, as
Pythagoras observes, it is possible to defend the contrary of practically any proposition),[338] Philology strives to attain certitude, and
exercises great caution to avoid error. For

> Flight from vice is virtue's initial act,
> And emancipation from folly is the beginning of wisdom.[339]

[334] *sapientiam.*
[335] See how Cicero, *De Off.,* i, 43, § 153, distinguishes Σοφίαν (Wisdom) and Φρόνησις
(Prudence).
[336] Philosophy and Philocaly.
[337] *predicamentalis inspectio.*
[338] See Seneca, *Ep.,* 88, § 43; cf. *Met.,* iii, 10. Here, again, John speaks of Pythagoras,
apparently with reference to Protagoras.
[339] Horace, *Ep.,* i, 1, 41, 42.

Thus the sister which has the function of guarding against error naturally precedes the other two, which confer virtues.[340] To quote Juno, or more precisely Martianus,[341] "Is there anyone who will confess that he is unacquainted with the laborious vigils of Philology and the pallor begotten during persevering toil by lamp light?" By her silent, powerful supplication, Philology constrains even the resting gods to come to her aid. A little before [in Martianus], the first sister [Philology] searches the heavens, earth, and seas, and scrutinizes everything in them:

> Toiling without stint the whole night through, Philology[342] unlocks the secrets of the unknown,
> And by her learned labors gains the power to foresee all that will come to pass,
> As do the gods themselves; in fact she frequently not only comes to rule over us [mortals],
> But even compels the very gods to comply with her bidding. Nor is this all,
> As she even knows how to accomplish, against the will of mighty Jove,
> What none of the other deities, however powerful, would dare attempt.[343]

Indeed, as another author, not inferior to Martianus, observes: "Persevering labor overcomes all obstacles." [344]

It is evident from what was said above, that many factors concur to produce sensation. These include the external object, with which the spirit, which is sensation's servant, comes in contact, and the spirit itself, which brings to the attention of the conscious soul the quality of the external object. There are thus three requisites [for sensation]: the conscious soul, the spirit whereby the soul senses, and the external object it perceives. By these, the deliberative force which we have above[345] called "reason," [346] is, as previously noted,[347] stimulated to action. Whereupon reason exercises its judgment,

---

[340] That is, Philology precedes Philosophy and Philocaly.
[341] Martianus Capella, *De Nupt.*, i, § 37.
[342] Literally: she.
[343] Martianus Capella, *op. cit.*, i, § 22.
[344] Vergil, *Georg.*, i, 145 and 146.
[345] *Met.*, iv, 16.
[346] *ratio.*
[347] *Met.*, iv, 16.

which is likewise called "reason." The latter is sometimes [unequiv-ocally] true, sometimes probable. True reason is sure and un-wavering. The word itself, "reason," signifies certitude. Only that which is firmly established can be called *ratum*.[348] Consequently, according to the great Augustine: "True reason is possessed only by God, and by those to whom God grants the privilege of genuine certitude and secure judgment." [349] Investigation[350] by categories,[351] the first step in seeking philosophical [scientific] knowledge of anything, consists in considering what the thing [in question] is; wherein it differs from, or is similar to other things; and whether it has, or can have contraries. Once these questions have been answered, the thing [in question] is more accurately determined, and thus becomes a part of our knowledge. I myself have chosen to imitate this method, because it is so suitable, despite the fact that, in the investigation of such an extensive subject, I have not been able to follow this plan as [closely as] I would have wished. There is no more fitting occasion for an examination of the substance of reason and truth, than when one is discussing the power of logic. For the latter [logic], as Augustine observes, professes to be the science of truth:[352] would that it could [fully] attain what it promises! However [although it falls short of perfection], logic certainly has very great efficacy, and provides both a method and a faculty for the invention and examination[353] of reasoning.

---

[348] *ratum*, ratified, established, secure, sure.

[349] It is uncertain what passage in Augustine's works John here refers to; cf. Plato, *Tim.*, 51 E.

[350] *inspectio*, inspection, investigation, consideration, theory, that is θεωρητική; cf. Quintilian, *Inst. Orat.*, ii, 18, § 1.

[351] *predicamentalis*, categorical.

[352] Perhaps John here refers to Augustine's *De C.D.*, viii, 4, where concerning "rational philosophy," Augustine says: "by which the truth is distinguished from falsehood." Also cf. the *De Spiritu et anima*, chap. 37 (in Migne, *P.L.*, XL, 808), sometimes attributed to Augustine.

[353] *inueniendi examinandique*.

CHAPTER 31. *The nature of original reason, and some observations concerning philosophical sects.*

Reason in creatures is a spiritual force that examines the natures of things and acquires a knowledge, not only of material entities, but also of concepts perceptible by the intellect alone.[354] In addition to reason in creatures, there is also that original reason which efficaciously[355] comprehends all things, whether they be material or perceptible only by the intellect. Fully and accurately, that is without any error whatsoever [this] original reason determines the exact nature and precise power of everything. If I describe [this] original reason as the divine wisdom or power, and the firm foundation of all things, I am undoubtedly correct. This original reason embraces the nature, development,[356] and ultimate end of all things. It is the sphere, which Martianus, speaking under a veil of poetical fiction, describes[357] as comprised of all the elements, and lacking nothing of which any nature may be conceived to consist. It includes all heaven and air, the seas, the various parts of the earth, the infernal regions,[358] and towns as well as crossroads, with their [manifold] activities and fortunes, as well as every sort of thing, particular or general,[359] that may be mentioned. This sphere is evidently an image, as well as an idea of the world. Plato raises the question whether there is but one idea or [there are] several ideas.[360] If, on the one hand, we consider the substance of scientific knowledge or reason, there is only one idea. But if, on the other hand, we consider the numerous diverse things that reason contemplates in its

[354] *intelligibiles,* intelligibles, as opposed to sensible things; things perceptible only by the intellect.
[355] *uirtute,* by its virtue, power, efficacy.
[356] *processus,* progress, development, evolution.
[357] Martianus Capella, *De Nupt.,* i, § 68.
[358] *claustraque Tartarea,* the Tartarean confines, the infernal regions.
[359] The Webb text here should be corrected to read *in genere,* instead of *in genera;* cf. MSS A, B, and C.
[360] Plato, *Tim.,* 31 A.

council chamber,[361] ideas are countless. In view of the aforesaid
[unity of scientific knowledge or reason] the Stoic reveres *Pronoen*,[362] which we may translate as "Providence," and maintains
that all things are bound by its necessary laws.[363] Epicurus, on the
other hand, impressed by the mutability[364] of [the numerous] things
[reason considers], does away with Providence, and relieves everything from subjection to necessary laws. The Peripatetic, for his
part, shuns the precipice of error on either side. He will fully accept
neither the "paradoxical teachings" [365] of the Stoic, nor the "authentic dogmas" [366] of Epicurus. While he admits the Providence of the
Stoics, he explains it in such a way that he does not bind things by
necessity. And while, with Epicurus, he frees things from the
shackles of necessity, he does so without denying the reality of
Providence. The Peripatetic thus maintains that, although things
are, on the one hand, partly necessary, they are also, on the other
hand, partly subject to natural changes[367] and to free will. The
Academician, however, wavers. He will not presume to state definitely what is true in each and every case.[368] His sect [of the Acad-
emicians] is divided into three camps. By excessive caution, the
right to be called philosophers has been forfeited [by some]. A
[second] group admit only knowledge of things that are necessary
and self-evident, namely, things that one cannot fail to know. A
third type [of Academicians] consists in those of us who do not
[venture to] precipitate an opinion concerning questions that are
doubtful to a wise man.[369]

[361] Literally: within itself (though they are not merely internal things).
[362] *Pronoen*, evidently from προνοέω to foresee, provide beforehand; Providence.
[363] Cf. Cicero, *De N.D.*, i, 8, § 18; also John's *Policraticus*, vii, 1, 2, with Webb's commentary *ad loc.*
[364] *facilitatem*. John evidently refers here to the ease with which change occurs, or in which man wills and accomplishes this or that: flexibility; easy mutability.
[365] *paradoxas*, paradoxes, doctrines contrary to those generally accepted, startling doctrines; see Cicero, *Acad. Prior.*, ii, 44, § 136; and *De Fin.*, iv, 27, § 74.
[366] *kirriadoxas*, that is, κυρίας δόξας, chief, or principal, or authentic doctrines; see Cicero, *De Fin.*, ii, 7, § 20.
[367] *facilitati nature*, the flexibility or mutability of nature.
[368] *in singulis*, in particular instances, or in each and every case.
[369] Cf. John's *Policraticus*, vii, 2; and *Met.*, Prol.

CHAPTER 32.   *What is opposed to reason, and the fact that the*
word "reason" has several different senses, as
well as that reasons are eternal.

Original and true reason is, as we have said,[370] divine. It does not admit of the slightest error. For there is nothing that seems more opposed to reason than error. Whereas reason builds up and confirms,
error, on the other hand, tears down and subverts, thereby replacing
reason's solid structure with its own flimsy instability.[371] With regard
to the meaning of the word "reason," just as "sensation"[372] at one
time means the power to sense, and at another the act of sensing;
and just as "imagination" at one time signifies the power to imagine,
and at another the act of imagining; so "reason" has various meanings. At one time "reason" refers to a faculty, at another to the
activity and operation of this power, and still again to the objects
of reason's activity. In the latter category are included inherent connections[373] in [logical] consequences, proportions between numbers,
and principles whereby absolutely necessary truths are demonstrated. Augustine, in his books *On Order* and *On Free Will*,[374] as
well as in his *Hypognosticon*,[375] and on several other occasions, states
that such "reasons" are incorruptible and eternal. "The *ratio*" he
says, "of one to two, as well as that of two to four [etc.], is most
true, and it is no less true today than it was yesterday. Its truth
does not vary one bit with the passage of days or years."[376] This

[370] *Met.*, iv, 31.
[371] *lubricitate*, slipperiness, inconstancy, insecurity.
[372] *sensus*.
[373] *inherentie*.
[374] Augustine, *De Ord.*, ii, 19, § 50, and *De Lib. Arbit.*, ii, 8, § 21 (in Migne, *P.L.*,
XXXII, 1018 and 1252.
[375] Perhaps John here refers to pseudo-Augustine's *Hypognosticon*, vi, 4, § 6 (in Migne,
P.L., XLV, 1660). This book, not really written by Augustine is also cited by John in
Met., iv, 34, as well as in his *Historia Pontificalis*, chap. 13 (ed. Poole, p. 32).
[376] The literal translation here is: It was no truer yesterday than it is today, nor will
it be any truer tomorrow, or a year from now. See Augustine, *De Ord.*, ii, 19, § 50 (in
Migne, *P.L.*, XXII, 1018).

ratio would not cease to hold true, even if the whole world were to perish." Likewise [true is the principle that] the existence of a body necessarily involves the existence of a substance.[377] While other sorts of things that are contemplated by the eye of divine reason are true, still, owing to their mutability, they may not by any means be termed "reasons." Because of the intimate association of truth and reason, some philosophers have held that if a thing is once true, it is forever true. Their view seems to be supported by the reason that Augustine advances to show that our faith is the same as that of our forefathers, even though we do enjoy in somewhat fuller measure what they anticipated. For Augustine says: "Our faith is the same [as theirs], even though we live in a different age." [378] Despite the fact that we preach it to different listeners, and in different words, we embrace the same truth.

CHAPTER 33.   *The imperfection of human reason; and the fact that the word "true" has various senses.*

The nature of the angels, which is not retarded by the contaminating presence of a body,[379] and is more closely akin to the divine purity, flourishes with the acumen of incorrupt reason.[380] While the angels do not enjoy an insight into all reality which is equal to that possessed by God, still angelic reason does enjoy the privilege of exemption from error. Human weakness, on the contrary, both as a result of the limitations[381] imposed on it by nature, and in punishment for sin, is exposed to many errors. Fettered by the latter, it slips and falls from original and subsequent purity,[382] and is handicapped in the investigation of reality by means of its reasoning

---

[377] *Simili modo substantiam esse si sit corpus non esse non potest.*

[378] See Augustine, *Tract. in Joann.,* xlv, 10, § 9; *Enarr. in Ps.,* i, § 17 (in Migne, *P.L.,* XXXV, 1722; XXXVI, 596).

[379] Cf. Vergil, *Aen.,* vi, 731.

[380] Cf. Augustine, *De C.D.,* xi, 29; xii, 1.

[381] Literally: condition.

[382] Reference is evidently made both to original loss of primary purity by our first parents, and to subsequent loss of acquired purity by their individual descendants.

processes. Slipping about in a mire of incertitude, man apprehends as much as he can. At times his opinions are true, inasmuch as they constitute accurate representations of reality. At other times, however, they are fallacious, since they are vitiated by empty, deceptive illusions. An opinion is true if it perceives things as they actually are. Speech is true if it presents things as they really are. In view of this, some philosophers have held, with probability, that[383] the truth because of which an opinion or speech is called true, is, as it were, an inter-relationship of things that are examined extrinsic to reason.[384] If reason is solidly based on these realities in its investigations, it possesses certitude, and it does not flounder in error. Accordingly speech termed "true" is called "modal" from the mode it indicates. Likewise a true opinion [is called "modal"] from its mode of perception, and true reason from the quality of its examination.[385] Particular things are called "true," as when we speak of "a true man," or "true candor," provided that, in taking them to be such, our opinion is not deceived by any phantasy of the imagination.[386] Accurate apprehension of reality, which is the basis for calling things "true," is generally proved to be such in one of two ways: either from the form of the substance [of things], or [at least] from the effects of this form. A being is a true "man" if this being has true humanity, that is, is conscious of reason and of the capacity to be affected by external things.[387] True "whiteness" is that which makes white; true "justice" is that which makes just. If you do not believe me, heed at least [what] the great Hilary,[388] towering in his Gallican buskin,[389] and exceeding the comprehension of the simpleminded [has to say on the subject].[390]

[383] *probabiliter,* or: that probably.
[384] *quasi medium quendam habitum esse rerum que examinantur extrinsecus ad rationem.*
[385] This may also be translated: Accordingly speech that is called "true" is so called from the mode the modal expression indicates. Likewise an opinion that is called "true" is so called from its mode of perception, and reasoning from the quality of its examination.
[386] *imaginis phantasmate,* an imaginary phantasm.
[387] *conscia rationis et passibilitatis.*
[388] See Hilary, *De Trin.,* v, 3, 14 (in Migne, *P.L.,* X, 131, 137).
[389] *Gallicano coturno [cothurno] attolitur.* Reference is evidently made to Hilary's solemn style. The buskin was a high-heeled, thick-soled boot worn by actors in tragedies.
[390] See Jerome, *Ep.* lviii, 10 (in Migne, *P.L.,* XXII, 585).

CHAPTER 34.   *The etymology of the word* uerum *["true"],
the nature of truth, and what is contrary to
truth.*

In imitation of the Stoics, who are much concerned about the etymology or resemblance of words,[391] we observe that [Latin] *uerum*
[true] comes from the Greek *heron,* which means secure and stable
or certain and clear. Hence those who had attained a state of
security and stability by being associated and classed with the gods
in ancient mythology were called "heroes." [392] Such "demigods" [393]
"came to be known as 'heroes,' " according to Martianus,[394] "because
the ancients also referred to the earth as *'heram,' "* owing to their certitude as to its stability. We, however, do not call anyone a "demi-
god," since no one is [really] such; nor do we refer to anyone as a
"hero," since the name connotes perfidy.[395] Rather, we refer to
the transfer of the elect from this world's inconstancy and emptiness to the glory of true certainty and security by a catholic[396] word,
and call them "saints," owing to the confirmation[397] they have
attained. For "to sanction" [398] means "to confirm" [ratify]. A
"saint" [399] is one who is "confirmed" [400] in [his possession of] virtue or glory.[401] One who is a saint is free from vanity, and abides
in the truth. The word "true" [402] itself also indicates confirmation,

[391] Literally: the analysis or analogy of words. Cf. Augustine, *Contra Cresc.,* i, 12, § 15
(in Migne, *P.L.,* XLIII, 455).
[392] *heroes,* ἥρωes.
[393] *hemitei,* demigods, lesser deities.
[394] Martianus Capella, *De Nupt.,* ii, § 160.
[395] Or deception.
[396] *catholico,* catholic, universal, orthodox.
[397] *confirmatione, confirmation,* state of firm, established, and ratified security.
[398] *sancire.*
[399] *sanctus,* saint.
[400] Or firmly established.
[401] Cf. Augustine, *De C.D.,* x, 21.
[402] *uerum.*

and signifies the security of a reality upon which reason may confidently depend. The word "truth"[403] likewise denotes certitude and stability. The fact that in Latin the consonant *v* relaces the Greek aspirate [*h*] constitutes no objection [to our etymological argument], since the Aeolian digamma [F][404] and the [Latin] consonant are closely related.[405] Just as the power of sensation requires some real object if it is to function usefully and efficaciously, so reason, too, must have an object to provide a solid basis for its processes. Otherwise it will slip and fall. If light is eliminated, sight stops; if sound ceases, we hear nothing; if odor and flavor are absent, our senses of smell and taste fail to function; while if our sense of touch does not come in contact with some solid object, it feels nothing. It may be objected that we say that we "see the darkness," "hear the silence," or "feel the emptiness"; but it would be more correct, in such cases, to say that these senses do not perceive anything. Augustine, both *Against the Manicheans,*[406] and in his *Ipognosticon,*[407] as well as in several of his other books,[408] teaches that not merely these, but all privations[409] are really nothing. Aristotle, however, asserts that they are something. He says that, in addition to being privative, they dispose subjects to themselves in a certain way.[410] In any event, our reason, just as our senses, requires a solid foundation. Otherwise its activity is futile, from its failure to lay hold of something definite. For when [our] reason strives to grasp something, and fails in its purpose, its labor has been fruitless, and it will be deceived by its own errors. Just as we have characterized error as the contrary of reason, so we also say that

---

[403] *Veritas.*

[404] *digamma,* the double gamma, written like an English *f,* but equivalent to the English *w* or *v.*

[405] See Priscian, *Inst. Gram.,* i, 20 (Keil, *G.L.,* II, 15); cf. *ibid.,* i, 25, 46 (Keil, *G.L.,* II, 19, 35).

[406] Perhaps John here refers to Augustine's *Libri de Nat. Boni c. Manichaeos,* chaps. 15, 16 (in Migne, *P.L.,* XLII, 556).

[407] *Ipognosticon.* Augustine's *Hypognosticon,* i, 4, 5 (in Migne, *P.L.,* XLV, 1616 ff.); cf. *Met.,* iv, 32, n. 375.

[408] Augustine, *Conf.,* xii, 3 ff.; *Enarr. in Ps.,* vii, chap. 19; *Op. Imperf. c. Julianum,* chap. 44 (in Migne, *P.L.,* XXXII, 327 ff.; XXXVI, 109; XLV, 1480, 1481).

[409] *priuationes,* privations, negations.

[410] Aristotle, *In Phys.,* ii, 1, 193 b, 20; see Boethius, *De Divisione* (in Migne, *P.L.,* LXIV, 883).

BOOK IV 257

emptiness[411] is the contrary of truth. Although false and empty are different words, they add up, in a way, to the same thing. Emptiness and falsehood [both] amount to nothing. What is false is absolutely nothing. It is not [even] an object of knowledge. As Augustine teaches in his *Soliloquies*,[412] and *Against the Academicians*,[413] as well as on several other occasions,[414] all the ancients, including even the Academicians, accepted the principle that it is impossible to have [scientific] knowledge of falsehood.[415] He proves [in his work] against the Academicians, that there cannot be any [scientific] knowledge of things that are false, for the [simple] reason that they are utterly non-existent. Where some translators[416] have taken the Scriptures to say that in the beginning the earth was empty and void,[417] others have interpreted them to assert that it was as yet nothing, and had not yet been constituted. By the law of contraries, what is true is opposed both to what is empty and to what is false, since the last two are the same. In my estimation, the fact that something which exists is opposed to something that is non-existent does not jeopardize this principle. Such evidently happens in propositions that are opposed in a contradictory manner. Does not Aristotle teach that one of these [contradictorily opposed propositions] must always be [true], while the other must, of necessity, not be [true]?[418] Cannot the existence of one thing indicate the non-existence of another? A ruddy sky may bespeak calm and undisturbed weather, as well as a tempest, in accordance with the saying:

> A blushing sky at dawn forebodes a storm,
> But at set of sun promises smooth sailing.[419]

[411] *uanitatem*, emptiness, vanity.
[412] Augustine, *Solil.*, ii, II, § 20 (in Migne, *P.L.*, XXXII, 894).
[413] Augustine, *Contra Acad.*, iii, 3, § 5; 4, § 10 (in Migne, *P.L.*, XXII, 936, 939).
[414] For example, Augustine, *De Trin.*, xiii, 10, § 17 (in Migne, *P.L.*, XLII, 1070).
[415] Augustine, *Contra Acad.*, iii, 4, § 10 (in Migne, *P.L.*, XXII, 939).
[416] *interpretes*, interpreters, translators, commentators.
[417] Genesis, i, 2.
[418] Aristotle, *De Interpr.*, 7, 17 b, 26 ff.
[419] Cf. Matthew, xvi, 2, 3. Margalits (in the *Florilegium*, p. 469), notes two other sayings of this kind: "A red sky in the evening foretells a fair morrow"; and "He who laughs on a sunny morning, is frequently found weeping in the evening."

CHAPTER 35.   *More about truths, and the fact that things,*
words, and truths are said to exist in different
ways, with an explanation of the latter.

All that is vain,[420] is, precisely because of its emptiness, illusory.
After deluding minds, which it dupes by its false pretensions, it
vanishes like a phantasm [of the imagination]. Because of this ephemeral nature of what is transitory and perishable, Ecclesiastes, in
his discourse concerning all earthly things, declares: "Everything
under the sun is vain." [421] He does so in such forceful and impressive
language, and with such authoritative probability,[422] that his saying
has become commonplace among all peoples, and has passed into
all languages. Penetrating the minds[423] of all who have ears to hear,
it shakes their souls to their very depths. In explaining the difference
between things which really exist and those which only seem to
exist, Plato states that intelligibles are impervious both to external
incursion and to internal passion. They cannot be injured by any
force, nor can they be wasted away by the wear and tear[424] of time.[425]
Rather, they persevere continually in the unimpaired vigor of their
[impregnable] state.[426] Hence they truly exist [in a strict sense], and
are second only to the first essence in their right to existence. This is
the sure, secure state that is denoted by a substantive word,[427] when
the latter is correctly used. Temporal things seem to exist, since they
are representative images of such intelligibles. But temporal things
are not fully worthy of being called by substantive names, for they
pass away with time. They are forever changing, and vanish like

---

[420] *omnia uana,* all vanities, emptiness, or falsity.

[421] Or empty. See Ecclesiastes, i, 14.

[422] *probabilitate sententie,* probability of authoritative opinion.

[423] *corda,* literally, the hearts. The heart was considered the seat of understanding and
feeling.

[424] *dispendium.*

[425] See Apuleius, *De Plat. et ejus Dogm.,* i, 6, 193.

[426] Cf. Boethius, *Inst. Arithm.,* i, 1 (ed. Friedlein, pp. 8, 3, 4).

[427] Or noun.

smoke. As Plato observes in his *Timaeus,* "They take flight without even waiting to receive names." [428] Plato divides true existence into three categories, which he posits as the principles of [all] things: namely, "God, matter, and idea." For these are, by their nature, unchangeable. God is absolutely immutable, whereas the other two are in a way unchangeable, even though they mutually differ in their effects. Coming into matter, forms dispose it,[429] and render it in a way subject to change. On the other hand, forms themselves are also to some extent modified by contact with matter, and, as Boethius observes in his *Arithmetic,*[430] are [thereby] transformed into a state of mutable instability. However, Boethius denies that ideas, which he posits as the first essence after God, are in themselves intermingled with matter or infected by change. Instead, [he states that] from these ideas proceed native forms,[431] which are images of their original exemplars [namely, of the ideas], and are created together with all particular things by nature. In his book *On the Trinity,* Boethius explains that "From forms that transcend matter, have come the forms which are found in matter and efficaciously constitute bodies.[432] Practically the same opinion has been put into verse by Bernard of Chartres, the foremost Platonist of our time:

I say that the cause of particular existences is to be found,[433]
Not in the intimate union of matter and form,
But rather in the fact that one of these [the form] perdures,[434]
Being called by the Greek[435] *"Idea,"* even as he called matter *hyle.*[436]

Although the Stoics believe that [both] matter and the "idea" are coeternal with God, while others, with Epicurus, would eliminate providence, and entirely dispense with the "idea," Bernard,[437] as a

---

[428] Plato, *Tim.,* 49 E, according to the version of Chalcidius.
[429] Cf. Gilbert de la Porrée, *Comm. in Boet. de Trinitate* (in Migne, *P.L.,* LXIV, 1274).
[430] *in Arismeticis;* see Boethius, *Inst. Arithm.,* i, 1 (ed. Friedlein, pp. 8, 10, 11).
[431] *forme prodeunt natiue;* see Gilbert de la Porrée, *op. cit.* (in Migne, *P.L.,* LXIV, 1267); also cf. *Met.,* ii, 17.
[432] Boethius, *De Trin.* (ed. Peiper, pp. 154, 49 ff.).
[433] Literally: that what is exists.
[434] Namely, the form.
[435] *Acheus,* namely, Plato.
[436] *ilen,* that is, ὕλην (prime) matter; Bernard could have learned from Chalcidius (*Comm. in Tim. Plat.,* §§ 123, 268), that Plato used this word (although he did not use it in this philosophical sense).
[437] *iste,* he: Bernard of Chartres.

[true] philosopher, used to say that neither [matter nor the idea] is "coeternal" with God. For Bernard accepted the teaching of the Fathers, who, as Augustine testifies, explained that, in making all things from nothing, God created their matter.[438] At the same time [while denying its coeternity with God] Bernard did hold that the idea is "eternal." For he admitted the eternity of [divine] providence, wherein God has jointly established all things at one and the same time, determining each and everything that was or is to come to be in time, or to endure throughout eternity. On the other hand, coeternity is possible only among entities that are neither greater nor less than one another in dignity, power, and authority.[439] Bernard accordingly concluded that only those three persons,[440] whose nature, power, and operation are one, singular, and inseparable, are coequal and coeternal, as among them [alone] there exists absolute parity. The idea cannot measure up to an equal status with the divinity. For the idea is, in a certain way, subsequent[441] in nature to the divinity, and a sort of effect which subsists in the inner sanctuary of the divine mind,[442] without needing any extrinsic cause. Consequently, although Bernard dared call the idea "eternal," he refused to say it was "coeternal." As he remarks in explaining Porphyry, the works of the divine mind are of two kinds. The first sort are created out of, or together with matter; the second are made out of and contained within the divine mind itself, without need of anything external. Thus the divine mind from the very beginning conceived the heavens in its understanding, nor did it need to employ any matter or form extrinsic to itself for this mental conception. As Bernard says elsewhere:

> Even though time eventually devours all its own offspring,
> Under compulsion of necessity, and despite temporary reprieve,
> It is still powerless to destroy, nor can it demolish,
> A principle based solely and directly on the divine will.

[438] See Augustine, *Conf.*, xii, 7, 8; and *Adv. Leg. et Proph.*, i, 8 (in Migne, *P.L.*, XXXII, 828, 829; and XLII, 609, 610).

[439] Literally: in the nature of their majesty, the privilege of their power, or the authority of their activity.

[440] That is, of the Divine Trinity.

[441] Posterior.

[442] Literally: the [divine] counsels.

Wherefore if one bewails the aforesaid condition
Clearly he does so with no or little reason.

Others, while admitting that some things are true from [all] eternity, deny that the latter are really eternal. They argue that only living things can be eternal, since Augustine[443] tells us that eternity is a state of interminable life. From what has been said, it is clear that the Platonists held, with Solomon, that all things under the sun are vain,[444] and that only those things which do not disappear like figments of the imagination, but remain definitely sure and always the same in the state of substances, are true.

CHAPTER 36.   *The difference between things that are true and things that only seem to be true,[445] according to the Platonists.*

While opinions, speech, and things may all be referred to as "false," this term is most correctly applied to opinions vitiated by fallacy. For it is opinion which is really deceived by falsehood.[446] Speech derives falsity from the fact that it expresses a false opinion. And something that is false is so called from the fact that only a mind that was empty and void would conceive of such a thing. In like manner, in medicine,[447] not merely animals, but also symptoms, and even causes[448] as well, are referred to as "healthy" or "unhealthy." To descend a bit with the Peripatetics from the lofty concepts of Plato, things are said to be true or false, with reference to the meanings of the words combined [into propositions], according as they perceived with valid [objective] or vain [empty] understanding. For the Peripatetics, who philosophize in a more human manner, refrain from

443 Or rather Boethius, *Cons. Phil.*, v, prosa 6.
444 Or empty; Ecclesiastes, i, 14.
445 This may also be translated: things which truly exist and things which only seem to exist.
446 *fallitur.*
447 *in phisicis*, in physical or natural science, among physicians, in medicine.
448 *cause*, causes or causal things. This could also mean cases.

being mentally transported for themselves and for God,[449] as do the
Platonists. On the contrary, they remain sober for [the sake of their
fellow] men, and place truth or falsity,[450] in whether or not the
understanding formulated in examination and comprehension is accurate or erroneous. If our understanding conceives of something as
being what it actually is, or as not being what it is not, then its
judgment is sure and correct. But if our understanding opines that
something that really exists, does not exist, or that something that
does not exist, really exists, doubtless it is deceived and erroneous.
The same holds true with regard to speech. As for things, a thing
that is represented in our understanding as it actually is, is true,
whereas a thing that is represented otherwise is vain and false. The
truth or falsity of both opinions and things accordingly depends on,
and is judged by, our mode of perception (namely, the way in which
our opinions perceive, or in which things are perceived); while the
truth or falsity of speech depends on, and is judged by its meaning.
As God cannot be deceived by falsehood, beyond doubt the more
accurate and sure our knowledge is, the less falsehood it contains,
since God recognizes the latter as false. What is true cannot be concealed from that [absolute] truth which contemplates all things.
Primary truth, that is to say original certitude, stability, and clarity,
subsists within the essence of God, and from this flows, in one way
or another, everything that is correctly called "true." God alone
perceives with certitude all mutual agreement and disagreement,
whether between things or words. All men yearn for certitude, for
the love of truth is not only kindred to, but also inborn in reason.
With Philology, man, as Martianus says,[451] "wholeheartedly be-
seeches that truth which exists, but derives its existence from non-
existent things." [452] This objective is realized only when some drop
of divine wisdom, derived from the effluence of grace, illumines a
mind that seeks and loves it. This, according to Martianus, is the "all

[449] Cf. II Corinthians, v, 13; also I Corinthians, xiv, 28.
[450] The comma before *hominibus* in the Webb text should apparently be transferred to
follow *hominibus*. Otherwise, the translation would read: ". . . they remain sober, and
place truth or falsity for men in whether or not . . ."
[451] Martianus Capella, *De Nupt.*, ii, § 206.
[452] *illam existentem ex non existentibus ueritatem.*

pure fountain"[453] whence flows the aforesaid truth.[454] Nothing becomes truly known unless it flows forth from this fountain, nor does the latter emit anything false. For this spring, which Martianus envelops in a veil of poetical imagery, is virgin pure, and knows neither corruption nor falsity.

CHAPTER 37. *That things, opinions, and speech are called "true" or "false" in different senses; and why such expressions are called "modal."*[455]

God, who is immune from composition, sees[456] all things, including both the future, which is not absent from God's knowledge, and the past, which does not fade from His consciousness. He weighs the mutual conformity and disagreement of things, and judges surely and accurately concerning what exists and what does not exist. What God sees from the very beginning is certain, and is called "true," since it does not vanish into nothingness. Such are verily the thoughts of the Most High, whose depths no man can probe:[457] the words said once and for all, and realized in the course of time, in accordance with the decrees of divine providence. Who will call God's mind idle, and [dare] assert that He has not contemplated all from the outset? If truths are, so to speak, the thoughts of God, who, except the presumptuous, will maintain that they vanish into nothingness? And who will be so impudent as to assert that they have not always existed in the mind of Him, Who, from [all] eternity, has prearranged and known everything? Does God, like man, conceive new thoughts and initiate new projects? At the same time, even though truths have been true from all eternity, neither they, nor anything

[453] *uirgo fontana,* the fountain-virgin or virgin-fountain, the all-pure fountain.
[454] Martianus Capella, *op. cit.,* ii, § 205.
[455] *modales,* modal (plural adjective), or modals (plural noun).
[456] Literally: the eye of the divine simplicity beholds.
[457] Literally: no man can explain. Cf. Psalms, xcii, 5; Numbers, xxiv, 6; and Romans, xi, 33.

else, can be called "coeternal" with the Creator. For, as we have
already observed, nothing whatsoever can ascend to an equality with
God. In fact, it is to God that eternal truths owe their truth and
certitude. When it is said that everything is either Creator or creature,
universal reality[458] is, on the authority of the Fathers, in a way reduced to substances and their attributes.[459] For the meanings[460] of
propositions are not included in this classification in view of the
context.[461] This division was formulated [462] with reference merely
to the meanings of uncombined words.[463] There are, therefore, some
truths which exist in the mind of God, but which are not creatures,
since they have existed from eternity. There is no question but that
some things are not eternal, unless one would argue, as do some, that
the statement of Ecclesiasticus to the effect that: "He who lives eternally has created all things together," [464] refers, not only to the
Trinity's activity in contemplating and disposing Itself, but also to
its creation of primordial matter. All things are either created out of
this original matter, or created together with things created in it. To
exist,[465] in the case of eternal truths, means that they belong to the
original knowledge of reason, and that they have being in such a
way as to be the objects of sure, direct judgment. Their existence consists in being known. Similarly, existence, in the case of human words,
consists in being uttered or remembered. Of the one [and only]
word,[466] Augustine says: "This is the Word, not because it is a temporary utterance, but because it is eternally begotten." [467] Such a dis-

---

[458] *uniuersitatis complexio*, the complex of universality.

[459] Literally: things present in substances.

[460] *significatio* in the Webb text should read *significata;* cf. MSS C and A (MS B does not
come to this point).

[461] *nam enuntiationum significata non contingit urgente aliqua ratione sermonis*, literally:
for this [classification or division] does not extend to [or concern] the things meant by
propositions, in view of the manner of speech. This passage is also susceptible of other
translations.

[462] *si partiti* in the Webb text should evidently be *sic partiti;* cf. MSS A and C (MS B
does not come to this point).

[463] *incomplexorum significationes*, words or terms is understood.

[464] Ecclesiasticus, xviii, 1.

[465] *esse*, to be, to exist, existence.

[466] *unico*, the one word (par excellence), namely, the Word of God.

[467] The exact words which John quotes here have not been found in Augustine's works;
see nevertheless Augustine, *De Gen. imp. lib.*, 5, § 19; and cf. *In Joann. tract.*, xiv, 3,
§ 7; *Enarr. in Ps.*, xliv, § 5; *Serm.*, xxxviii, 5; cxix, 7; clxxxvii, 3; ccxv, 1; *De Fide et
Symb.*, § 3; *De Trin.*, ix, 7, § 12; xv, 11, § 20; 13–16, §§ 22–26 (in Migne, *P.L.*, XXXIV,

tinction would seem in a way inappropriate, if words did not subsist through utterance. Since the terms "to exist" and "one" and "thing" may be used in varying senses, everyone should be careful in interpreting the meaning of statements. Things (that is, natures and the operations of natural things),[468] thoughts and speech, words and reasons, each have their own modes of existence. Correct statements should hence be interpreted according to the proper modes of their particular subject matter. Accordingly, I am unconcerned whether truths are said to exist or not to exist, when the meanings of words are carefully considered, provided simply that they are not considered to be nothing whatsoever. On the other hand, untruths have no existence at all, since they are absolutely nothing. This both the ancient philosophers and the catholic Fathers have declared. God's memory and speech are His knowledge, for His recollection or word or reason is His wisdom. The word whereby Omnipotence speaks is one, although the words He speaks are numberless. He says [of Himself]:[469] "The beginning of your words is truth;" [470] for, in "the inaccessible light" wherein He dwells,[471] God possesses a knowledge of all things. This light, I am sure, is identical with[472] His substance.

227; XXXV, 1506; XXXVI, 497; XXXVIII, 184, 185, 675, 1002, 1096; XL, 183; XLII, 967, 1072, 1073, 1075 ff.). In the margin MS A has *Augustinus: Fulgentius.* See Fulgentius, *Ad Monimum,* iii, 7 (in Migne, *P.L.,* XV, 204). The statement here attributed to Augustine may also be translated: "This is the Word: not an ordinary, passing utterance, but the Word which is forever [being] born."

[468] *nature scilicet uel naturalium opera* may be translated: natures or the works of natural things, or: the works of nature or of natural things.

[469] Or of the Word.

[470] Psalms, cxviii, 160.

[471] See I Timothy, vi, 16.

[472] Literally: not foreign to.

CHAPTER 38.   *The intimate connection*[473] *between reason and truth, with a brief explanation of the nature of each.*

Let us now, with all reverence, contemplate the happy and intimate connection between reason and truth. And let us, at the same time, implore the assistance of these two, without which we are powerless to comprehend or even to investigate them. Reason is, in a way, the eye of the mind.[474] Or to put it more broadly, reason is the instrument whereby the mind effects all its cognition. Reason's special function is to investigate and apprehend the truth. The contrary of the virtue of reason is imbecility and [consequent] lack of the power to investigate and determine the truth. The contrary of the activity of investigating the truth, which we have above called "reason," is error. In God, this virtue [of reason] is absolutely perfect, and in angels it is relatively perfect, according to their [angelic] nature. But in man it is either entirely or for the most part imperfect, although it may be [said to be] "perfect" in a person temporarily or comparatively, in contrast to less perfect reason.[475] Wherefore man lays claim, not to reason, but to the appetite for reason, as is indicated by the term "philology" [love of reason]. For the modesty of philosophers has tempered the names "philology" [love of reason], "philosophy" [love of wisdom], and "philocaly" [love of beauty]. Reason itself has no contrary. Divine reason is an immutable substance, whereas angelic reason and human reason are not substances.

[473] *coherentia,* coherence, cohesion, intimate connection.
[474] Cf. Claudianus Mamertus, *De Statu Animae,* i, 27 (ed. Engelbrecht, p. 98).
[475] Cf. *Met.,* iii, 3, 10.

CHAPTER 39.   *A continuation of the aforesaid [discussion].*
               Also [the fact] that neither reason nor truth
               has contraries.

Truth is both the light of the mind and the subject matter of reason.
God and the angels see truth directly, God beholding universal truth,
and the angels particular truths. But man, no matter how perfect,
glimpses the truth only in part, and to a [definitely] limited degree.
However, the more perfect a man is, the more ardently he desires to
comprehend the truth. For truth is the basis of certitude, in which
reason's investigations flourish and thrive. In the absence of light
and of solid objects [our senses of] sight and touch cannot operate.
Our other senses are put in a similar plight if sound and scent and
flavor are not present. In like manner, reason's perception is frustrated
when truth is withdrawn. The contrary of truth is vanity, falsity, or
emptiness,[476] all of which are proved by philosophy to be nothing.
Whence some have opined that the letter *a* in inanity [emptiness]
should be changed to *u,* so that the word would read "inunity," [477]
or that which is not [any] one thing. For what is not [any] one
thing, is nothing. Original truth is found in the divine majesty.
There is also other truth, which consists in an image or likeness of
the divinity. The truth of anything is directly dependent on the
degree in which it faithfully reflects the likeness of God. The more
deficient anything is in this respect, the more it fades into falsity
and nothingness. It is in this sense that [it is said that] "Man has
become like unto vanity," and "His days have faded as shadows." [478]
A shadow occurs only when "the light of a body" is cut off by some
intervening obstacle, and the absence of light thus induces an area of
darkness. As the light of truth is withdrawn, the darkness of error
grows, and this error deceives us. The contrary of truth is called "false-

---

[476] *inane,* the inane, empty, or void.
[477] *inune* = *in* (not) and *unum* (one thing or any one thing, something).
[478] Psalms, cxliii, 4.

hood" [479] from the word *fallendo* [deceiving]. One who walks in darkness [falters and] knows not whither he is going. Truth properly fosters, enlightens, and corroborates reason, just as reason properly seeks, attains, and embraces truth. As has been said, external light nourishes vision; [and] solid objects provide an object for the sense of touch. In God, however, reason and truth are one. He, Who is both the Reason and the Word eternal, says of Himself: "I am the truth." [480] He is self-sufficient, and has need of nothing external. His reason illumines itself, and His truth contemplates itself. In creation, on the other hand, truth is one thing, reason another. For in creation, truth is an image of the divinity, which is sought and found by reason in created things. Reason is a virtue or activity of the mind, whose object is to discern truth. Truth, like reason, does not have any contrary, and this for the same cause that was given and explained above in regard to reason.

CHAPTER 40.   *The proper aim of the Peripatetics, as well as of all who philosophize correctly, and the eight obstacles to understanding.*

If the purpose of the Peripatetics is to reject all empty illusions, determine objective reality, and seek after, venerate, and live according to the truth of God in every respect, they do not labor in vain. But if such is not their aim, then their efforts and pains[481] are wasted. The human heart[482] is so seduced that it but rarely succeeds in attaining knowledge of the truth. The many impediments to understanding include invincible ignorance[483] of such things as the mysteries[484] of the Holy Trinity, which reason cannot explain; the frailty

---

[479] *falsitas*, falsity, falsehood.
[480] John, xiv, 6.
[481] *impensa*, expenses, pains.
[482] The heart was regarded as the seat of both understanding and feeling.
[483] *inuincibilis ignorantia;* cf. Abelard, *Eth. s. Scito teipsum,* chap. 14 (in *Opp.,* ed. Cousin, II, 619).
[484] *archana*, literally: secrets, hidden things.

of man's condition; the brevity of human life; the neglect of what is useful and [corresponding] concern with what is unprofitable; the [perplexing] conflict of probable opinions; sin, which makes one unworthy of seeing the light; and finally the great multitude and vast expanse of subjects to be investigated. None of the aforesaid eight impediments is a greater obstacle to understanding those things that should be known than is sin. For sin separates us from God, and bars us from the fountain of truth, for which nevertheless, our reason does not cease to thirst. "My heart," exclaims the soul [485] which realizes its sin, "has forsaken me; the very light of my eyes has failed me." [486] Indeed, unless one refers [487] what he knows to the service of God, his knowledge is not only of no benefit, but even becomes a handicap. For it is futile to know many things, if the one thing which is the most necessary of all, [488] and is made manifest through understanding creatures, be lacking. Holy Solomon says: "I proposed to ascertain and investigate wisely everything under the sun. This is a most wretched occupation, which has been allotted to man by God." [489] The pagan philosophers were thus occupied. For, according to the Apostle, they suppressed the truth of God by falsehood, and became vain in their thoughts through their own fault. While boasting of their wisdom, they fell into foolishness, since they failed to return thanks to the author of [all] good things. [490] It is a waste of time to be curious about useless questions, yet this concern preoccupies not only the Peripatetics, but almost the whole world. Noting this vice, Lucan invites the curious to determine the hidden causes of the ocean waves [491] and reveal to him this inscrutable secret. "Investigate this," he says, "you who fret about the workings of the world." [492] When the mind is overoccupied with numerous questions that do not greatly concern it, it wanders far afield from itself,

---

[485] *mens,* mind, soul.
[486] Psalms, xxxvii, 11.
[487] Namely, turns back, returns, reflects.
[488] Luke, x, 42.
[489] Ecclesiastes, i, 13.
[490] Cf. Romans, i, 18, 21, 24.
[491] *estuantis Occeani,* of the tossing ocean, or of the ocean's waves, storms, movements, or tides.
[492] Lucan, *Phars.,* i, 417. The sense here is: "I leave this inquiry to those who study the workings of the world."

and often even becomes oblivious of itself. But no error can be more
pernicious than this. "To know oneself is," according to Apollo,
"practically the highest wisdom." [493] Of what use is it to understand
the nature of the elements and of things composed of the elements,[494]
to study the principles of quantitative and numerical proportion, to
speculate about the opposition of virtues and vices, to pay careful
attention to inferences in reasoning, and to dispute with probability
on all sorts of points, if, meanwhile, one remains ignorant of himself? Can one who, while he makes ready[495] the lodgings of others,
yet forgets whither he must betake himself in order to provide for
his own needs, be regarded as anything short of a fool? A person who
becomes so concerned about other people's business that he neglects
his own affairs, is not only excessively curious, but also fails in his
duty to himself. However, he who converts external things to the
betterment of his own life,[496] so that he may know and venerate
their author; takes into account his own imperfection, which is
scarcely able to understand a few things; uses transitory things, along
with which he himself will also pass away, merely as a short-term
loan;[497] checks, represses, or extinguishes the lusts of his flesh; endeavors diligently to form again [in himself] the image of God,
which has been disfigured by vice; and bends every effort to the
cultivation and practice of virtue: [such a one] is most truly philosophizing. If one first [of all] thoroughly studies himself, and [then]
carefully examines beings that are inferior to himself, gives due
consideration to those equal to himself, and reverently contemplates
those that are superior to himself, such a one is investigating with
proper moderation. He is not thrusting himself precipitously and
rashly into questions that exceed his comprehension. He is not inflated with pride. Neither does he covet the various [corruptible]
furnishings of this world, save so far as this is necessary or permissible. He is charitable to his neighbors, reveres and loves the heavenly
beings who stand in constant attendance before God, and thanks,

---

[493] Cicero, *De Fin.*, v, 16, § 44.
[494] *elementorum aut elementatorum*. John here apparently refers to the four elements
and things composed of these elements.
[495] *lustrat*, purifies, makes ready, surveys.
[496] *ad usum uite*, for the use or benefit of life or conduct.
[497] Literally: as a gift or loan, and for the hour.

praises, and glorifies for all good things the Divine Majesty, whose
immensity precludes our full comprehension, but whose creatures
would prevent us from entirely ignoring it, were it not for the fact
that we are handicapped and oppressed by our own weakness.[498] For
all creatures, as if by public attestation [witness to and] proclaim the
glory of their Creator. "Lift not your eyes to riches that you cannot
have," says Solomon in Proverbs, "for they will take wings like the
eagle and fly off into the sky."[499] As Augustine observes in his book
On Order, "Our best knowledge of God is [of a] negative [na-
ture]."[500] If a person who is ignorant of natures and morals and
reasons,[501] and who is a puppet of his passions, and an addict to perishable things, or who perhaps lives chastely although he is ignorant
of the various branches of knowledge, imagines that he can find God
by processes of investigation and argumentative reasoning conducted
by the faculties of his own [unaided] mind, he is doubtless making
the greatest possible of all mistakes.[502] Augustine remarks elsewhere:
"What [we realize that] we do not know about God constitutes our
truest wisdom concerning Him."[503] He also says: "No small part of
our knowledge of God consists in knowing what He is not, as it is
absolutely impossible to know what He is."[504]

[498] Literally: we labor under the infirmity which oppresses us.
[499] Proverbs, xxiii, 5.
[500] Literally: God is best known negatively, namely, by not knowing.
[501] Namely, one who is ignorant of natural, moral, and rational (logical) philosophy.
[502] Augustine, *De Ord.,* ii, 16, § 44 (in Migne, *P.L.,* XXXII, 1015).
[503] *Ignorantia Dei eius uerissima sapientia est.* Augustine, *Serm.,* cxvii, 3, § 5 (in Migne,
P.L., XXXVII, 663).
[504] Augustine, *De Trin.,* viii, 2, § 3; cf. *Ep.,* cxx, 3, § 13 (in Migne, *P.L.,* XLII, 948;
XXXIII, 458–459).

CHAPTER 41.[505]   *[The limitations of reason and the function
of faith.]*[506]

Many things exceed our comprehension: some because of their august dignity, some because of their great number or vast extent, some
because of their mutability and instability. Accordingly, Ecclesiasticus
instructs us as what should be our principal concern, and what is to
our greatest advantage. "Seek not" he says, "things that are beyond
your reach, and do not fret over questions that exceed your comprehension." [507] Note how he restrains the rashness of those who,
with irreverent garrulity, discuss the secrets of the Divine Trinity
and mysteries whose vision is reserved for eternal life.[508] While the
impression may be created that knowledge is increased by such a
procedure, devotion is certainly diminished. "Refrain," Ecclesiasticus
warns us, "from being inquisitive about numerous unnecessary things,
and do not be curious about too many of the divine works. . . . For
consideration of such things has caused the fall of many, and has
enslaved their minds to vanity." [509] The holy writer[510] represses the
audacity of those who stick their nose into everything, and want to
account for all things. We know, on the authority of Solomon in
Ecclesiastes, that man cannot fully explain the least object on earth,
much less give a complete account of heavenly and supracelestial
things.[511] The son of Sirac makes clear to what the philosopher
should direct his mental abilities: "Ever bear in mind God's commandments, and you will not be curious about too many of his
works." [512] We know that our knowledge flows ultimately from our

[505] This chapter, which is omitted in the list of chapters in MSS C, B, and A, although
not in their texts, lacks a title.
[506] Title in brackets supplied by the translator.
[507] Ecclesiasticus, iii, 22.
[508] Reference may be made here to attempts to rationalize the Divine Trinity, such as
those of Abelard in his *Theologia Christiana* (in Migne, *P.L.,* CLXXVIII, 1113–1330).
[509] Ecclesiasticus, iii, 24 and 26.
[510] Literally: he (*hic*).
[511] Ecclesiastes, viii, 17.
[512] Ecclesiasticus, iii, 22.

senses, which are frequently misled, and that faltering human infirmity is at a loss to know what is expedient. Accordingly, God, in
His mercy, has given us a law, to make evident what is useful, to
disclose how much we may know about Him, and to indicate how
far we may go in our inquiries concerning Him. This law displays
the divine power in the creation, the divine wisdom in the orderly
plan, and the divine goodness in the conservation of the world. The
latter [attributes of God] are especially evident in the redemption of
man. This law further clearly discloses God's will, so that everyone
may be certain about what he should do. Since not only man's senses,
but even his reason frequently err, the law of God has made faith
the primary and fundamental prerequisite for understanding of the
truth. Which is appropriately epitomized by Philo[513] in the Book
of Wisdom: "Those who trust[514] in the Lord shall understand the
truth, and those who persevere faithfully in love shall rest tranquil
in Him. For God's elect shall enjoy grace and peace." [515]

CHAPTER 42.   *How the fact that the world is subject to vanity
is confirmed by visible proofs, and why this
book is now concluded.*

But enough of this [discussion]. The present day[516] is more suited to
weeping than to writing. What I see about me convinces me that the
world is subject to vanity. We had hoped for peace, but what has
befallen us? The tempestuous whirlwind which rages at Toulouse[517]
has everywhere stirred up the English and the French. Kings whom

[513] Certain ancient writers maintained that the book entitled "The Wisdom of Solomon"
was really written by Philo, as Jerome states in his preface to the books of Solomon; cf.
Augustine, *Op. Imperf. c. Julianum,* iv, 123 (in Migne, *P.L.,* XLV, 1420).

[514] *confidunt,* trust or believe.

[515] Wisdom, iii, 9.

[516] This chapter seems, from what it says, to have been written in October, 1159. Cf.
Poole, "The Early Correspondence of John of Salisbury," p. 10.

[517] In 1159 Henry II endeavored to assert the claims of his wife, Eleanor, to Toulouse,
but was foiled by the intervention of Louis VII. News of the raising of the siege of
Toulouse at the close of September, 1159, probably reached England about, or shortly
after, the middle of October, by which time the Metalogicon was obviously completed.

we had seen the best of friends, have become each other's implacable
enemies. In addition, the death of our Sovereign Pontiff, Lord
Adrian,[518] has further distraught all Christian peoples and nations.
Among these, it has saddened most our own England, his native
country, and it has watered our own soil with the most copious tears.
While Adrian's death has been a cause of poignant grief to all good
men, it has been so to no one more than to myself.[519] For, despite the
fact that he had his mother,[520] together with a half-brother,[521] born
of this same mother,[522] I was even closer to his heart than they were.
Indeed, he used to declare, both in public and private, that he loved
me more dearly than [he did] any other mortal. So great was his esteem for me, that as often as he had the opportunity, he took pleasure
in revealing to me his inmost conscience.[523] Even after he became
Roman Pontiff, it was his delight to have me eat with him at his
very own table, where, against my protestations, he willed and
ordered that we use together a common cup and plate. It was in
acquiescence to my petitions that Adrian granted and entrusted
Ireland to the illustrious king of the English, Henry II, to be possessed by him and his heirs, as the papal letters still give evidence.[524]
This was by virtue of the fact that all islands are said to belong to the
Roman Church, by an ancient right, based on the Donation of Constantine, who established and conceded this privilege.[525] By me
[Pope] Adrian dispatched a golden ring, set with a magnificent
emerald, whereby he invested [our] Henry II with the authority to

[518] Pope Adrian IV died August 31, 1159.

[519] Cf. Horace, Carm., i, 24, 9, quoted in Priscian's Inst., vii, 18 (Keil, G.L., II, 302).

[520] Concerning Adrian's mother, cf. John of Salisbury's Ep. cxxxiv (in Migne, P.L., CXCIC, 114).

[521] Concerning Adrian's brother Ranulfus (Ranulph), see Edward Scott, "Nicholas Breake-speare," Athenaeum, No. 3453 (Dec., 1893), 915–916.

[522] Concerning Adrian's youth, cf. R. L. Poole, "The Early Lives of Robert Pullen and Nicholas Breakespeare," in Essays Presented to T. F. Tout, pp. 64 ff.

[523] His conscience, in the sense either of his moral conscience, or of his inmost thoughts.

[524] Concerning this passage and the corresponding papal bull Laudabilitur, cf. H. W. C. Davis, England under the Normans and Angevins, App. vi, pp. 531–532.

[525] In the Donation that Constantine was supposed to have made to Pope Silvester I, we do not read anything about all islands belonging to the Roman Church. Pope Urban II, however, wrote in 1091 to Bishop Daimbertus of Pisa: "Just as all islands are possessed according to the statutes of public law, it is also certain that they were made the property of blessed Peter and his Vicars by the liberality and special concession of the devout emperor Constantine . . ." (in Migne, P.L., CLI, 350, 351). Cf. Döllinger, Die Pabstfabeln des Mittelalters (ed. 1863), pp. 61–106, esp., pp. 78–80.

rule Ireland.[526] It was [subsequently] ordered that this ring be kept
in the public treasury, where it is still to be found. An attempt to
render an account of all of Adrian's virtues would result in a book
of great volume. Yet Adrian's death is not all. The worst catastrophe
which perturbs all minds is the schism in the Church,[527] which broke
out, in punishment for our sins, as soon as our great father was withdrawn. Satan, who has lusted to lay hold of the Church that he might
sift her like grain,[528] is [now] sowing bitterness and scandal on every
side by means of his tool, that perfidious second Judas.[529] Wars have
broken out that are worse than civil,[530] for they are sacerdotal and
fraternal. "Now the world is judged," [531] and it is to be feared lest,
in his fall, the ambitious traitor will drag down with him some of
the stars.[532] "Woe to him by whom this scandal cometh!" Certainly
"it would have been better for him had he not been born!" [533] The
aforesaid are causes of public sorrow. At the same time, another griev-
ous affliction has struck closer to home, and is just as distressing to me
as [is] any of the others. For my father and lord, who is yours also,[534]
Theobald, the venerable Archbishop of Canterbury, is gravely ill, so
much so that it is doubtful what can be hoped, or what should be
feared.[535] Since he is no longer capable of administering his office
as of yore, Theobald has committed to me this weighty responsibility.[536] Upon my shoulders he has set the [well nigh] insupportable
burden of supervising all [his] ecclesiastical affairs. Accordingly, for
many reasons, "my spirit within me is rent with anguish." [537] Nor
can I adequately describe the torments of my crucifixion. In the

[526] About September 30, 1155.
[527] Concerning the schism after Pope Adrian's death, cf. John's *Epp.* lix, in his own name, and xliv, xlviii, lxx, in the name of Archbishop Theobald (in Migne, *P.L.,* CXCIX, 38–43, and 27–28, 30–31, 50).
[528] See Luke, xxii, 31; cf. John's *Ep.* lxv (in Migne, *P.L.,* CXCIX, 50).
[529] John evidently refers to Octavian "Victor IV," the antipope set up by Emperor Frederick I in opposition to Alexander III.
[530] *bella plusquam ciuilia;* cf. Lucan, *Phars.,* i, 1.
[531] Cf. John, xii, 31.
[532] Cf. Apocalypse, xii, 4. Reference is evidently made here to the German part of the Church, which upheld Victor.
[533] Cf. Matthew, xviii, 7, and xxvi, 24.
[534] John is here speaking to Thomas Becket.
[535] Theobald had apparently weakened both mentally and physically.
[536] *prouinciam,* may refer either to Theobald's ecclesiastical province or to his duties as archbishop of the same. I have preferred the latter interpretation.
[537] Psalms, cxlii, 4.

midst of all these tribulations, there still remains one resource. This is to pray to the God-man, the Son of the undefiled Virgin, Who is [even] now, as it were, sleeping in the boat. All that is necessary is that He be awakened by the prayers of the faithful. He will then calm the raging storm which threatens His Church with shipwreck.[538] And He will mercifully deliver my Lord [Theobald] from all mental and physical infirmity, so far as He foresees this to be expedient for Himself and us. May He, through Whom kings reign and princes rule,[539] set over the universal Church a pastor who is worthy and acceptable to Himself. May He also defend our kings and princes from all adversity, and bring about that they watch over, and preserve in safety, for the honor and glory of His name, the flock entrusted to their care. Meanwhile, I piously beseech my reader and audience to intercede for me, a vain and miserable wretch, with the Virgin's Son, Who is "the way, the truth, and the life." [540] Let them pray that, dispelling the darkness of [my] ignorance, and uprooting [my] love of empty vanity, He [Christ] may enlighten me with His knowledge, and make me a zealous investigator, lover, and observer of the truth.

END OF BOOK FOUR

[538] Cf. Mark, iv, 36 ff.
[539] Cf. Proverbs, viii, 15 and 16.
[540] John, xiv, 6.

BIBLIOGRAPHY

BIBLIOGRAPHY

PRINCIPAL MSS OF THE METALOGICON OF JOHN OF SALISBURY

Cambridge, Corpus Christi College Library, Codex 46, fols. 184^r–239^r: "Iohannis Sarisburiensis Metalogicon": known as the *Cantuariensis* [Canterbury] or "C" MS.: probably of the twelfth, or, at latest, the thirteenth century.

Oxford, Bodleian Library, MS. Lat. misc., c. 16, pp. 272–340 [fols. 136^v–170^v]: "Iohannis Saresberiensis Metalogicon": known as the *De Bello* [From Battle Abbey] or "B" MS. [breaks off at the beginning of Chap. 36, Bk. IV]: of the thirteenth, or, at latest, the fourteenth century.

London, British Museum, Reg. [Old Royal] MS. 13, D, IV, fols. 161^v–208^v: "Iohannis Saresberiensis Metalogicon": known as the *S. Albani* [St. Alban's] or "A" MS.: probably of the twelfth century.

PRINTED EDITIONS OF THE METALOGICON

Ioannes Saresberiensis, *Metalogicus e codice MS. Academiae Cantabrigiensis nunc primum editus* (Paris, Hadrian Beys, 1610).

Ioannis Saresberiensis, *Policraticus . . . Accedit huic editioni ejusdem Metalogicus cum indice copiossissimo* (Leyden, J. Maire, 1639).

Ioannis Saresberiensis, *Policraticus . . . Metalogicus . . .* (Amsterdam, 1644).

Ioannis Saresberiensis, *Metalogicus,* in Ioannis Saresberiensis . . . , *Opera Omnia, nunc primum in unum, colligit et cum codicibus manuscriptis contulit* (ed.) I. [J.] A. Giles. 5 vols. (Oxford, 1848).

Ioannis Saresberiensis, *Metalogicus,* in *Patrologiae cursus completus, series latina,* ed. J. P. Migne. 221 vols. (Paris, 1844–1864). CXCIX, 823–946. (Herein cited as *P. L.*)

Ioannis Saresberiensis Episcopi Carnotensis, *Metalogicon Libri IIII,* ed. Clemens C. I. Webb (Oxford, 1929).

OTHER WORKS OF JOHN OF SALISBURY

Joannes Saresberiensis, *Entheticus de dogmate philosophorum,* ed. Christian Petersen (Hamburg, 1843).

Joan[nes] Saresberien[sis], *Epistola . . . Alexandro Papae . . . ,* in *Foedera . . . ,* ed. Thomas Rymer . . . (see below), 10 vols. I, 6–7.

Joannes Saresberiensis, *Epistolae,* in *P. L.,* CXCIX.

Ioannes Saresberiensis, *Historia pontificalis quae supersunt*, ed. R. L. Poole (Oxford, 1927).

Ioannes Saresberiensis, *Policraticus, sive de nugis curialium et vestigiis philosophorum libri VIII*, ed. Clemens C. I. Webb, 2 vols. (Oxford, 1909).

John of Salisbury, *Frivolities of Courtiers and Footprints of Philosophers, Being the First, Second, and Third Books, and Selections From the Seventh and Eighth Books of the Policraticus*, translated by J. B. Pike (Minneapolis, 1938).

John of Salisbury, . . . *The Statesman's Book, Being the Fourth, Fifth and Sixth Books, and Selections From the Seventh and Eighth Books of the Policraticus*, translated by John Dickinson (New York, 1927).

Joannes Saresberiensis, *Vita sancti Anselmi archiepiscopi Cantuariensis*, in *P. L.*, CXCIX.

Joannes Saresberiensis, *Vita sancti Thomae Cantuariensis archiepiscopi et martyris*, in *P. L.*, CXCIX.

SOURCES DRAWN ON, DIRECTLY OR INDIRECTLY, BY JOHN OF SALISBURY

Petrus Abaelardus, *Dialectica, II*, . . . *Analytica Priora, I*, in *Ouvrages inédits* . . . , ed. Victor Cousin (Paris, 1836). (Herein cited as *Ouvr. Inéd.*)

———, *Dialectica, II*, . . . *Analytica Priora, II*, in *Ouvr. Inéd.*

———, *Dialectica, II*, . . . *Analytica Priora, III*, in *Ouvr. Inéd.*

———, *Dialectica, III*, . . . *Topica*, in *Ouvr. Inéd.*

———, *Dialectica, IV*, . . . *Analytica Posteriora, I*, in *Ouvr. Inéd.*

———, *Dialectica V*, . . . *Liber divisionum et definitionum*, in *Ouvr. Inéd.* . . . *De Generibus et speciebus*, (falsely attributed to Abelard) in *Ouvr. Inéd.*

———, *Ethica sive liber dictus Scito teipsum*, in *Opera* . . . , ed. Victor Cousin, 2 vols. (Paris, 1849, 1859), I.

———, *Introductio ad theologiam*, in *Opera* . . . , I.

———, *Invectiva in quemdam ignarum dialectices* . . . , in *Opera* . . . , I.

Adam du Petit Pont, *Ars disserendi*, [fragment] in *Fragments philosophiques. Philosophie scholastique*, ed. Victor Cousin (2d ed.; Paris, 1840), 417–424.

Alcuinus, *De Dialectica*, in *P. L.*, CI.

Sanctus Ambrosius . . . , *Hexaemeron*, in *P. L.*, XIV.

Angelomus Luxoviensis, *Commentarius in Genesin*, in *P. L.*, CXV.

Lucius Apuleius, *De Platone et eius dogmate*, in *De Philosophia libri*, ed. Paulus Thomas (Leipzig, 1908).

———, Περὶ ἑρμηνείας, in *De Philosophia libri*.

Aristotle, *Analytica priora*, in *The Works of Aristotle translated into English* . . . , ed. W. D. Ross, 11 vols., (Oxford, 1908–1931). (Herein cited as *Works*, ed. Ross, I, [1928].)

Aristotle, *Analytica posteriora*, in *Works*, ed. Ross, I.

——, *Categoriae*, in *Works*, ed. Ross, I.

——, *De Interpretatione*, in *Works*, ed. Ross, I.

——, *Physica*, in *Works*, ed. Ross, II (1930).

——, *De Sophisticis elenchis*, in *Works*, ed. Ross, I.

——, *Topica*, in *Works*, ed. Ross, I.

Sanctus Aurelius Augustinus . . . , *Contra Academicos* . . . , in *P. L.*, XXXII.

——, *Contra Adversarium legis et prophetarum* . . . , in *P. L.*, XLII.

——, *De Civitate Dei*, ed. B. Dombart (Leipzig, 1877).

——, *Confessiones*, ed. P. Knoll (Leipzig, 1898).

——, *Contra Cresconium* . . . , in *P. L.*, XLIII.

——, *Principia Dialecticae*, in *P. L.*, XXXII. (Falsely attributed to Augustine.)

——, *De Diversis quaestionibus* . . . , in *P. L.*, XL.

——, *Enarrationes in Psalmos*, in *P. L.*, XXXVI.

——, *Epistolae*, in *P. L.*, XXXIII.

——, *Contra Faustum* . . . , in *P. L.*, XLI.

——, *De Fide et symbolo* . . . , in *P. L.*, XL.

——, *De Genesi ad litteram* . . . , in *P. L.*, XXXIV.

——, *De Genesi ad litteram imperfectus liber* . . . , in *P. L.*, XXXIV.

——, *Hypomnesticon* . . . *vulgo liber Hypognosticon*, in *P. L.*, XLV. (Falsely attributed to Augustine.)

——, *In Joannis Evangelium tractatus*, in *P. L.*, XXXV.

——, *De Libero arbitrio* . . . , in *P. L.*, XXXII.

——, *De Magistro, liber unus*, in *P. L.*, XXXII.

——, *De Natura boni contra Manichaeos* . . . , in *P. L.*, XLII.

——, *Opus imperfectum contra Julianum*, in *P. L.*, XLV.

——, *De Ordine*, in *P. L.*, XXXII.

——, *Sermones*, in *P. L.*, XXXVIII–XXXIX.

——, *Soliloquiorum* . . . , in *P. L.*, XXXII.

——, *De Spiritu et anima*, in *P. L.*, XL. (Falsely attributed to Augustine.)

——, *De Trinitate*, in *P. L.*, XLII.

Venerabilis Beda, *De Schematibus et tropis sacrae scripturae*, in *P. L.*, XC.

Sanctus Benedictus, *Regula monachorum*, ed. E. Woelfflin (Leipzig, 1895).

Bernardus Carnotensis [John refers to and even quotes certain writings of Bernard of Chartres, apparently no longer extant, e.g., in *Met.*, iv, 35].

Biblia sacra, Vulgatae editionis, ed. P. M. Hetzenauer (Innsbruck, 1906).

The Holy Bible. (Various versions in English.)

Anicius Manlius Boethius, *In Categorias Aristotelis* . . . , in *P. L.*, XLIV.

——, *Commentaria in Porphyrium*, in *P. L.*, LXIV.

——, *Commentarii in librum Aristotelis* ΠΕΡΙ ΕΡΜΗΝΕΙΑΣ [*De Inter-*

Anicius Manlius Boethius (*cont.*)
    pretatione] *I et II*, ed. Carolus Meiser, 2 vols. (Leipzig, 1877 and 1880).
——, *De Consolatione philosophiae* . . . , in *P. L.*, LXIII.
——, *De Differentiis topicis*, in *P. L.*, XLIV.
——, *Liber de Divisione*, in *P. L.*, LXIV.
——, *Contra Eutychen et Nestorium de Trinitate*, in *Philosophiae* . . . *accedunt* . . . *opuscula sacra*, ed. R. Peiper (Leipzig, 1871).
——, *De Institutione arithmetica libri duo* . . . , ed. G. Friedlein (Leipzig, 1867).
——, *Interpretatio Elenchorum sophisticorum Aristotelis*, in *P. L.*, LXIV.
——, *Interpretatio Posteriorum analyticorum Aristotelis*, in *P. L.*, LXIV.
——, *Interpretatio Priorum analyticorum Aristotelis*, in *P. L.*, LXIV.
——, *Interpretatio Topicorum Aristotelis*, in *P. L.*, LXIV.
——, *In Porphyrii Isagogen Commentaria*, in *P. L.*, XLIV.
——, *In Porphyrium Dialogi* . . . , in *P. L.*, XLIV.
——, *De Syllogismo categorico* . . . , in *P. L.*, XLIV.
——, *De Syllogismo hypothetico* . . . , in *P. L.*, XLIV.
——, *Commentaria in Topica Ciceronis*, in *P. L.*, XLIV.
——, *Quomodo Trinitas unus Deus* . . . , in *P. L.*, XLIV.
Caius Julius Caesar, *De Analogia libri duo*. (Not extant.)
Martianus Capella, *De Nuptiis Philologiae et Mercurii*, ed. F. Eyssenhardt (Leipzig, 1866).
Magnus Aurelius Cassiodorus, *De Anima*, in *P. L.*, LXX.
——, *De Artibus ac disciplinis liberalium litterarum*, in *P. L.*, LXX.
——, *Expositio in Psalterium*, in *P. L.*, LXX.
Q. Valerius Catullus, *Carmina*, ed. L. Mueller (Leipzig, 1877).
Chalcidius, *Commentarius in Platonis Timaeus*, in *Platonis Timaeus interprete Chalcidio cum ejusdem Commentario* . . . , ed. I. Wrobel (Leipzig, 1876).
M. Tullius Cicero, *Academicorum* . . . *prior liber*, in *Scripta quae manserunt omnia*, ed. C. F. Mueller and G. Friedrich, 48 fasciculi (Leipzig, 1878–1933), fasc. 29.
——, *Academicorum* . . . *posterior liber*, in *Scripta* . . . , fasc. 29.
——, *De Amicitia*, in *Scripta* . . . , fasc. 47.
——, *De Fato*, in *Scripta* . . . , fasc. 33.
——, *De Finibus bonorum et malorum* . . . , in *Scripta* . . . , fasc. 33.
——, *De Inventione* . . . , in *Scripta* . . . , fasc. 2.
——, *De Natura Deorum*, in *Scripta* . . . , fasc. 32.
——, *De Officiis*, in *Scripta* . . . , fasc. 48.
——, *De Oratore*, in *Scripta* . . . , fasc. 3.
——, *Orator* . . . , in *Scripta* . . . , fasc. 5.
——, *Paradoxa*, in *Scripta*, fasc. 47.

M. Tullius Cicero, *De Partitione oratoria dialogus*, in *Opera quae supersunt omnia*, ed. C. L. Kaiser and J. G. Baiter, 11 vols. in 9 (Leipzig, 1860–1869), I.

——, *Ad Herennium de arte rhetorica*, in *Scripta* . . . , fasc. 1. (Falsely attributed to Cicero.)

——, *De Senectute*, in *Scripta* . . . , fasc. 47.

——, *Topica*, in *Scripta* . . . , fasc. 6.

——, *Tusculanae disputationes*, in *Scripta* . . . , fasc. 31.

Claudianus Mamertus, *De Statu animae libri tres*, ed. A. Engelbrecht, in *Corpus scriptorum ecclesiasticorum latinorum*, XI (Vienna, 1885).

——, *Digesta*, ed. Theodorus Mommsen, in *Corpus Iuris Civilis*, ed. Paul Kreuger and Theodore Mommsen, 2 vols. (Berlin, 1877), I.

Dionysius Areopagita, *De Divinis nominibus*, in *Patrologiae* . . . *graeca*, ed. J. P. Migne, 162 vols. (Paris, 1886–1912), III. (Herein cited as *Patrologia graeca*.) (Falsely attributed to Dionysius the Areopagite.)

Aelius Donatus, *Ars grammatica*, in *Grammatici latini*, ed. H. Keil, 7 vols. (Leipzig, 1855–1870), IV. (Keil's *Grammatici latini* herein cited as *G. L.*)

——, *Commentum Terenti*, ed. P. Wessner, 3 vols. (Leipzig, 1902–1908).

——, *Vergilii vita*, in *Vitae Vergilianae*, ed. J. Brummer (Leipzig, 1933).

Sanctus Fulgentius, Episcopus Ruspensis, *Ad Monimum* . . . , in *P. L.*, LXV.

Galenus, Τέχνη ἰατρική, in *Mediocorum graecorum opera*, ed. K. G. Kühn (Leipzig, 1821), I.

Galfridus Monumentensis, *Historia Britonum* . . . , ed. J. A. Giles (London, 1844, and Halle, 1854).

Aulus Gellius, *Noctium Atticarum libri XX*, ed. C. Hosius, 2 vols. in 1 (Leipzig, 1903).

Gilbertus Porretanus, *Commentaria in Boetii librum de Trinitate*, in *P. L.*, LXIV.

——, *De Sex principiis*, in *P. L.*, CLXXVIII.

Sanctus Gregorius Magnus, . . . *Homiliarum in Evangelia libri duo*, in *P. L.*, LXXVI.

Sanctus Hieronymus, *Commentariorum in Danielem prophetam* . . . *liber*, in *P. L.*, XXV.

——, *Commentarius in Ecclesiasticen*, in *P. L.*, XXIII.

——, *Epistolae*, in *P. L.*, XXII.

——, *Praefatio in Salomonis libros*, in *P. L.*, XXVIII.

Sanctus Hilarius, Episcopus Pictaviensis, *De Trinitate*, in *P. L.*, X.

Hippocrates, *Aphorismi* . . . , ed. E. Littré (Paris, 1839–1861).

Q. Horatius Flaccus, *De Arte Poetica liber*, in *Carmina*, ed. F. Vollmer (Leipzig, 1925).

——, *Carminum libri IV*, in *Carmina*, ed. F. Vollmer (Leipzig, 1925).

Q. Horatius Flaccus, *Epistularum, libri II*, in *Carmina*, ed. F. Vollmer (Leipzig, 1925).

——, *Satirarum, libri II*, in *Carmina*, ed. L. Mueller (Leipzig, 1890).

Hugo de S. Victore, *In Salomonis Ecclesiasten homiliae XIX*, in *P. L.*, CLXXV.

——, *Didascalion de studio legendi*, ed. C. H. Buttimer (Washington, D.C., 1939).

——, *Eruditionis didascalicae libri VII*, in *P. L.*, CLXXVI.

——, *De Sacramentis Christianae fidei*, in *P. L.*, CLXXVI.

——, *De Sacramentis legis naturalis et scriptae*, in *P. L.*, CLXXVI.

——, *Summa sententiarum*, in *P. L.*, CLXXVI.

Ioannes Saresberiensis, *Policraticus* . . . , ed. C. C. I. [J.] Webb, 2 vols. (Oxford, 1909). [The *Metalogicon* includes references to the *Policraticus*.]

Ioannes Scotus Erigena, *Versio operum Dionysii Areopagitae: liber tertius: de Divinibus nominibus*, in *P. L.*, CXXII.

Isidorus Hispalensis Episcopus, *Differentiarum . . . libri duo*, in *P. L.*, LXXXII.

——, *Etymologiarum sive originum libri XX*, ed. W. Lindsay, 2 vols. (Oxford, 1911).

D. Iunius Iuvenalis, *Satirarum libri quinque*, ed. C. F. Hermann (Leipzig, 1926).

John of Salisbury. *See* Ioannes Saresberiensis.

John Scotus Erigena. *See* Ioannes Scotus Erigena.

Juvenal. *See* Iuvenalis.

Marcus Annaeus Lucanus, *Pharsalia* . . . , ed. C. Hosius (Leipzig, 1913).

Ambrosius Theodosius Macrobius, *Commentariorum in Somnium Scipionis* . . . , in *Macrobius*, ed. F. Eyssenhardt (Leipzig, 1893).

——, *Conviviorum primi diei Saturnaliorum*, in *Macrobius*.

M. Valerius Martialis, *Epigrammaton libri*, ed. W. Heraeus (Leipzig, 1925).

"Mythographys tertius," in *Mythographi tres* . . . , in *Classicorum auctorum e vaticanis codicibus editorum*, III, ed. Angelo Mai (Rome, 1831).

Nemesius Episcopus, *Premnon physicon* . . . , a N. Alfano archiepiscopo Salerni in latinum translatus, ed. C. Burkhard (Leipzig, 1917).

P. Ovidius Naso, *Amores*, in *P. Ovidius Naso*, ed. R. Ehwald, from the edition of R. Merkel (Leipzig, 1916–1932), I.

——, *De Arte Amatoria libri tres*, in *P. Ovidius Naso*, I.

——, *Fastorum libri VI fragmenta*, ed. F. W. Lenz (Leipzig, 1932).

——, *Heroides epistulas*, in *P. Ovidius Naso*, I.

——, *Metamorphoses*, in *P. Ovidius Naso*, II.

——, *Ex Ponto libri* . . . , in *P. Ovidius Naso*, III.

Rutilius Palladius, *Opus agriculturae*, ed. J. C. Schmitt (Leipzig, 1898).

BIBLIOGRAPHY

A. Persius Placeus, *Satirarum liber,* ed. C. F. Hermann (Leipzig, 1897).

Plato, *Rei publicae libri decem,* ed. C. F. Hermann (Leipzig, 1936).

———, ΤΙΜΑΙΟΣ, in *Dialogi,* ed. C. F. Hermann, IV (Leipzig, 1924).

Titus Maccius Plautus, *Comoediae,* ed. G. Goetz and F. Schoell, 2 vols. (Leipzig, 1893–1896).

———, *Aulularia sive Querolum,* ed. R. Peiper (Leipzig, 1875). (Falsely attributed to Plautus.)

C. Plinius Secundus, *Naturalis historiae libri XXXVII . . .* , ed. C. Mayhoff, 5 vols. and Index (Leipzig, 1898–1906).

Porphyrius, *Isagoge et in Aristotelis Categorias Commentarium,* ed. A. Busse (Berlin, 1887).

Priscianus, *De Figuris numerorum . . .* , in *G.L.,* III.

Institutionum grammaticarum libri XVIII, in *G.L.,* II.

Publilius Syrus, *Sententiae,* ed. G. Meyer (Leipzig, 1880).

M. Fabius Quintilianus, *Institutionis oratoriae libri duodecim,* ed. E. Bonnell, 2 vols. (Leipzig, 1905–1906).

Remigius Antissiodorensis, *In Artem Donati minorem commentum,* ed. W. Fox (Leipzig, 1902).

Salernitanum Regimen sanitatis, ed. C. Daremberg and C. M. Saint-Marc (Paris, 1880).

[L. Annaeus] Seneca (filius), *Epistularum . . .* , in *Opera . . .* , ed. F. Haase, 3 vols. (Leipzig, 1887–1892), III.

———, *Naturalium questionum libri VII,* in *Opera,* ed. F. Haase, 2 vols. (Leipzig, 1897–1898), II.

[M. Annaeus] Seneca (pater), *Controversiarum liber I,* in *Oratorum et rhetorum sententiae divisiones colores,* ed. A. Keissling, (Leipzig, 1872).

Servius Grammaticus, *Commentarius in Artem Donati,* in *G.L.,* IV.

C. Sollius Apollinaris Sidonius, *Epistularum . . .* , in *C. Sollius Appollinaris Sidonius,* ed. P. Mohr (Leipzig, 1895).

Publius Papinius Statius, *Thebais,* ed. A. Klotz (Leipzig, 1908).

C. Suetonius Tranquillus, "C. Caligula," in *De Vita Caesarum. Libri VIII,* in *Opera,* I., ed. M. Ihm (Leipzig, 1933).

Publius Terentius Afer, *Andria,* in *Comoediae,* ed. A. Fleckeisen (Leipzig, 1916).

———, *Eunuchus,* in *Comoediae.*

———, *Hauton Timorumenos,* in *Comoediae.*

———, *Phormio,* in *Comoediae.*

Theinredus Doverensis, De Legitimis ordinibus pentachordorum et tetrachordorum, MS Codex 842 in the Bodleian Library of Oxford University.

Theodoricus Carnotensis, Heptateuchon, siue Bibliotheca septem artium liberalium, MS Codex 497 (Nos. 141 and 142) in the Library of (the Ville de) Chartres.

Theodulus Monachus, *Eclogam* . . . , ed. J. Osternacher (Ripariae prope Lentiam, 1902).

Valerius Maximus, *Factorum et dictorum memorabilium libri novem,* ed. C. Kempf (Leipzig, 1888).

Flavius Vegetius Renatus, *Epitoma rei militaris,* ed. C. Lang (Leipzig, 1885).

P. Vergilius Maro, *Aeneidos,* in *Opera,* ed. G. Ianell (Leipzig, 1930).

―――, *Eclogae,* in *Opera.*

―――, *Georgicon,* in *Opera.*

Marius Victorinus, *In Librum I de Inventione,* in M. Tullius Cicero, *Opera* . . . , ed. J. C. Orellius, 12 vols. (Zurich, 1826–1838), V, part 1.

―――, *Liber de diffinitione,* (wrongly attributed to Anicius Manlius Boethius) in *P. L.,* LXIV, 891 ff.

Willelmus de Conchis, *Dialogus de substantiis confectus a Willelmo anenonymo philosopho* (Strassburg, 1567).

Willelmus Malmsberiensis, *De Gestis pontificum Anglorum,* ed. . . . from the MS. of N. E. S. A. Hamilton, in *Rerum britannicarum medii aevi scriptores* [*LII*] (London, 1870).

ADDITIONAL SOURCES

Annales monasterii de Theokesberia [A.D. 1066–1263], in *Annales monastici,* ed. H. R. Luard, 5 vols. (London, 1864–1869), I, in *Rerum Britannicarum medii aevi scriptores* [XXXVI].

The Ante Nicene Fathers: Translations . . . , ed. A. Roberts and G. Donaldson . . . , 10 vols. (Buffalo, 1885–1897).

Aristotle, *Problemata,* ed. E. S. Forster, in *The Works of Aristotle,* ed. W. D. Ross, 11 vols. (Oxford, 1908–1930), VII.

Sanctus Bernardus, Abbas primus Clarae-Vallensis, *Epistolae,* in *P. L.,* CLXXXII.

Bibliotheca scriptorum graecorum et romanorum teubneriana (Leipzig, B. G. Teubner and Company, 1811 ff.).

Concessio summi pontificis Adriani IV regi Anglorum Heinrico II facta de occupanda Hybernia . . . [1155], in *Corps universel diplomatique du droit des gens* . . . , ed. J. Dumont, 8 vols. (Amsterdam, 1726–1731), I, p. 80.

Conradus Hirsaugiensis, *Dialogus super auctores sive Didascalion,* ed. G. Schepss (Würzburg, 1889).

Conventio facta inter Henricum regem Angliae et Ludovicum regem Franciae, per quam uterque tenetur ire in servitium crucis [1177], in *Foedera* . . . , ed. T. Rymer et al., I, 16–17.

Corpus scriptorum ecclesiasticorum latinorum, 70 vols. in 78 (Vienna and elsewhere, 1866–1942).

Foedera, conventiones, litterae et cujuscunque generis acta publica inter reges Angliae et alios . . . , ed. T. Rymer and R. Sanderson . . . , 4 vols. in 7 (London: 1816–1869).

Gallia Christiana in provincias ecclesiasticas distributa. Begun by the Benedictines of St. Maur, and continued by the Académie des inscriptions et belles-lettres, 16 vols. (Paris, 1715–1765).

Grammatici Latini, ed. Heinricus Keilus, 7 vols. (Leipzig, 1855–1870). (Herein cited as *G.L.*)

Guernes de Pont-Saint-Maxence, *La Vie de Saint Thomas le martyr,* ed. E. Walberg (Lund, 1922).

Iocelinus de Brakelonda, *Memorials of St. Edmund's Abbey,* ed. Thomas Arnold, in *Rerum britannicarum medii aevi scriptores* . . . , XCVI.

The Loeb Classical Library [*Greek Authors*], 237 vols. (London, 1912–1947).

The Loeb Classical Library [*Latin Authors*], 139 vols. (London, 1912–1946).

Menko, *Chronicon,* in *Monumenta Germaniae historica,* ed. G. H. Pertz, T. Mommsen, et al. (Berlin and elsewhere, 1826–1896), *Scriptorum:* XXIII.

Monumenta germaniae historica, ed. G. Pertz, T. Mommsen, et al. (Berlin and elsewhere, 1826–1896).

Necrologium . . . *ecclesiae Beatae Mariae Carnotensis,* in *Cartulaire de Notre Dame de Chartres,* ed. E. de Lépinois and L. Merlet, 3 vols. in 2 (Chartres, 1862–1865), III (in II).

Otto Frisingensis, *Gesta Friderici I* . . . , ed. G. Waitz (3d ed.; Hannover and Leipzig, 1912).

Patrologiae cursus completus . . . , *series graeca,* ed. J. P. Migne, 162 vols. (Paris, 1886–1912). (Herein cited as *Patrologiae* . . . *graeca.*)

Patrologiae cursus completus . . . , *series latina,* ed. J. P. Migne, 221 vols. (Paris, 1844–1864). (Herein cited as *P. L.*)

Petrus Blesensis, *Opera* . . . , in *P. L.,* CCVII.

Petrus Cellensis, *Epistolae,* in *P. L.,* CCII.

Rabanus Maurus, *De Institutione clericorum libri tres,* ed. Aloisius Knoepfler (Munich, 1900).

Ragewinus, *Gesta Friderici imperatoris* . . . , ed. G. Waitz (3d ed.; Hannover and Leipzig, 1912).

Rerum britannicarum medii aevi scriptores, 98 vols. in 250 (London, Public Record Office, 1858–1896).

Sacrorum Conciliorum nova et amplissima collectio . . . , ed. J. D. Mansi and others, 53 vols. in 57 with introductory vol. (new ed.; Paris and Leipzig, 1901–1927).

Select Library of Nicene and Post-Nicene Fathers, trans. and ed. by P. Schaff and H. Wace, 14 vols. (2d series, New York, 1890–1900).

Thomas Magister sive Theodulus Monachus, *Ecloga vocum atticarum,* ed. Fridericus Ritschelius (Halle, 1832).

Urban II, Pontifex Romanus, *Epistola ad Daimbertum*, in *P. L.*, CLI.

Willelmus Filius Stephani, *Vita et passio sancti Thomae*, in *P. L.*, CXC.

SECONDARY WORKS

Abelson, Paul, *The Seven Liberal Arts* (New York, 1906).

Aspinwall, W. B., *Les Écoles épiscopales et monastiques de l'ancienne province écclésiastique de Sens du VIe au XIIe siècle* ... (Paris, 1904).

Baldwin, Charles Sears, *Medieval Rhetoric and Poetic* . . . (New York, 1928).

Baldwin, James Mark, *History of Psychology*, 2 vols. (London, 1913), Vol. I.

Baur, Ludwig, "Die Philosophie des Robert Grosseteste Bishofs von Lincoln," in *Beiträge zur Geschichte der Philosophie des Mittelalters*, Bd. XVIII, Heft 4–6 (Münster, 1917).

Baxter, J. H., and C. Johnson, *Medieval Latin Word-List from British and Irish Sources* . . . (London, 1934).

Beddie, J. Stuart, "Libraries in the XIIth Century, Their Catalogues and Contents," in *Anniversary Essays in Medieval History by Students of Charles Homer Haskins* . . . , ed. Charles Homer Haskins (Boston and New York, 1929).

Brett, George Sidney, *A History of Psychology*, 3 vols. (London, 1921), Vol. II.

Britton, John, *The History and Antiquities of the Cathedral Church of Salisbury* . . . (London, 1814).

Bulaeus, Caesar E., *Historia universitatis Parisiensis a Carolo Magno ad nostra tempora*, 6 vols. (Paris, 1665–1673), Vol. II.

Buonaiuti, E., "Giovanni de Salisbury e le scuola filosofiche del suo tempo," in *Rivista storico-critica delle scienze teologiche*, IV (Rome, 1908).

Burlaeus, Gualterus, *Liber de vita et moribus philosophorum*, ed. H. Knust (Tübingen, 1886).

Carlyle, R. W., and A. J. Carlyle, *A History of Medieval Political Theory in the West*, 6 vols. (London, 1903–1936), III.

A Catalogue of the Manuscripts Preserved in the Library of the University of Cambridge, 5 vols. with an *Index* . . . vol. by H. R. Luard (Cambridge, 1856–1867), III and *Index*.

Cave, Gulielmus, *Scriptorum ecclesiasticorum. Historia literaria a Christo nato usque ad saeculum XIV* . . . [1–1300 A.D.], 2 vols. and *Appendix* vol. [1300–1517] (Basel, 1741–1745).

Chenu, M. D., O. P., "Grammaire et théologie aux XIIe et XIIIe siècles," in *Archives d'histoire doctrinale et littéraire du moyen âge*, X (Paris, 1935–1936).

Clerval, A., *Les Écoles de Chartres au moyen âge du Ve au XVIe siècle* (Paris, 1895).

Clerval, "L'Enseignement des arts libéraux à Chartres et à Paris dans la première moitié du XIIᵉ siècle d'après l'*Heptateuchon* de Thierry de Chartres," in *Congrès scientifique internationale des catholiques tenu à Paris, 1888*, 3 vols. (Paris, 1888–1891), II.

Comparetti, Domenico, *Vergil in the Middle Ages* . . . , trans. E. F. M. Benecke (London, 1908).

Davis, H. W. C., *England Under the Normans and Angevins, 1066–1272*, in *A History of England*, ed. C. W. C. Oman, 7 vols., II (5th ed.; London, 1918).

Delisle, Leopold, "Les Écoles du xiiᵉ et du xiiiᵉ siècle," in *Annuaire-Bulletin de la Société de l'histoire de France*, VII (1869), 139–154.

Demimuid, Maurice, *Jean de Salisbury* (Paris, 1873).

Denis, Léopold, "La Question des universaux d'après Jean de Salisbury," in *Revue des sciences philosophiques et théologiques*, no. 16 (Paris, 1927).

Dodsworth, William, *An Historical Account of the Episcopal See and Cathedral Church of Sarum or Salisbury* . . . (Salisbury, 1814).

von Döllinger, Johann J. I., *Die Pabst-Fabeln des Mittelalters* (Munich, 1863).

Doyen, M. [Guillaume], *Histoire de la ville de Chartres, du pays Chartrain et de la Beauce*, 2 vols. (Chartres, 1788), I.

Drane, Augusta T., *Christian Schools and Scholars* . . . (new ed.; New York, 1910).

Du Cange, Carolus, *Glossarium mediae et infimae latinitatis* . . . , 10 vols. (new ed. by L. Favre; Niort, 1883–1887).

Engelhardt, George, "Die Entwicklung der dogmatischen Glaubenspsychologie in der mittelalterlichen Scholastik vom Abaelardstreit (um 1140) bis zu Philipp dem Kanzler (gest. 1236)," in *Beiträge zur Geschichte der Philosophie und Theologie des Mittelalters*, Bd. XXX, Heft 4–6 (Münster, 1933).

Essays in Mediaeval History Presented to Thomas Frederick Tout, ed. A. G. Little and F. M. Powicke (Manchester, 1925).

Fabricius, J. A., *Bibliotheca latina sive notitia auctorum veterum latinorum* . . . , 3 vols. (Hamburg, 1721–1722).

Faral, Edmond, *Les Arts poétiques du XIIᵉ et du XIIIᵉ siècle* (Paris, 1925).

Fisquet, Honoré, *La France pontificale (Gallia Christiana) Histoire chronologique et biographique des archevêques et évêques de tous les diocèses de France . . . Metropole de Paris* (Paris, 1864).

Fornicellinus, Aegidius, *Totius latinitatis lexicon* . . . (revised by Vincentius De-Vit), 6 vols. (Prato, 1858–1875).

Gennrich, Paul, "Zur Chronologie des Lebens Johanns von Salisbury," in *Zeitschrift für Kirchengeschichte*, XIII (Gotha, 1892).

——, *Die Staats- und Kirchenlehre Johanns von Salisbury* (Gotha, 1894).

de Ghellinck, J., *Le Mouvement théologique du XIIᵉ siècle* (Paris, 1914).

Gilson, Etienne, *Les Idées et les lettres* (Paris, 1932).

——, *La Philosophie au moyen-âge*, 2 vols. (Paris, 1922), I.

——, *The Spirit of Medieval Philosophy*, trans. A. H. C. Downes (New York, 1936).

Grabmann, Martin, *Die Geschichte der scholastischen Methode*, 2 vols. (Freiburg im Breisgau, 1909–1911), II.

Graesse, J. G. Th., and Friedrich Benedict, *Orbis latinus* . . . (Berlin, 1922).

Haskins, Charles Homer, *The Renaissance of the Twelfth Century* (Cambridge, Mass., 1927).

——, Review of "Ioannis Saresberiensis . . . , *Metalogicon* . . . , ed. Clemens C. J. Webb (Oxford, 1927)," in *English Historical Review*, XLV (London, 1930).

——, *The Rise of Universities* (New York, 1923).

——, *Studies in the History of Medieval Science* (2d ed.; Cambridge, Mass., 1927).

Hauréau, B., *Histoire de la philosophie scolastique*, 2 parts in 3 vols. (Paris, 1872–1880), I.

Helinandus Frigidi Montis Monachus, *Opera*, in *P. L.,* CCXII.

Histoire littéraire de la France . . . . Begun by the Benedictines of St. Maur and continued by the Académie des inscriptions et belles-lettres, 37 vols. (Paris, 1733–1927), IX and XIV.

Hofmeister, Adolf, "Studien über Otto von Freising[ii]," in *Neues Archiv der Gesellschaft für ältere deutsche Geschichtskunde* . . . , XXVII (Hannover and Leipzig, 1912).

Hublocher, Hans, *Helinand von Froidmont und sein Verhältnis zu Johannes von Salisbury* (Regensburg, 1913).

James, Montague Rhodes, *The Ancient Libraries of Canterbury and Dover* (Cambridge, 1903).

——, *A Descriptive Catalogue of the Manuscripts in the Library of Corpus Christi College, Cambridge*, 6 parts in 1 vol. (Cambridge, 1909–1912).

——, *The Sources of Archbishop Parker's Collection of Manuscripts at Corpus Christi College, Cambridge* (Cambridge, 1899).

Jourdain, Amable, *Recherches critiques sur l'âge et l'origine des traductions latines d'Aristote et sur les commentaires grecs ou arabes* . . . , revised and augmented by Charles Jourdain (new ed.; Paris, 1843).

Krey, August C., "John of Salisbury's Knowledge of the Classics," in *Transactions of the Wisconsin Academy of Sciences and Letters*, XVI, 2 (1909–1910).

Leach, A. F., *The Schools of Medieval England* (London, 1916).

Lelandus, Joannes, *Commentarii de scriptoribus Britannicis* . . . , ed. A. Hall, 2 vols. (Oxford, 1709).

BIBLIOGRAPHY

Liebermann, F., "Magister Vacarius," in *English Historical Review*, XI (London, 1896).

Liscu, M. O., *Étude sur la langue de la philosophie morale chez Cicerón* (Paris, 1930).

Lloyd, Roger Bradshaigh, *The Golden Middle Age* (London and New York, 1939).

Lloyd, Rev. Roger, "John of Salisbury," in *The Church Quarterly Review*, CVIII (1929).

Madan, Falconer, and Others, *Summary Catalogue of Western Manuscripts in the Bodleian Library at Oxford* . . . , 6 vols. in 7 (Oxford, 1895–1937), VI.

Maigne d'Arnis, W. H., *Lexicon manuale ad scriptores mediae et infimae latinitatis* . . . (Reprint; Paris, 1890).

Maître, Léon, *Les Écoles épiscopales et monastiques de l'occident depuis Charlemagne jusqu'à Philippe-Auguste (768–1180)* (Paris, 1866).

Manitius, M., *Geschichte der lateinischen Literatur des Mittelalters*, 3 vols. (Munich, 1911–1931). Bd. III with collaboration of P. Lehmann.

Masius, Herman, "Die Erziehung im Mittelalter," in *Geschichte der Erziehung vom Anfang an bis auf unsere Zeit*, 7 vols. (Stuttgart, 1884–1902), II.

McGarry, Daniel D., "Educational Theory in the *Metalogicon* of John of Salisbury," in *Speculum*, XXIII (1948), 659–675.

McKeon, Richard P., *Aristotelianism in Western Christianity* (Chicago, 1939). [Reprinted for private circulation from *Environmental Factors in Christian History*.]

———, "Glossary," in *Selections from Medieval Philosophers*, ed. Richard P. McKeon, 2 vols. (New York, 1929).

———, "Rhetoric in the Middle Ages," in *Speculum*, XVII (1942), 1–32.

Metais, M. Le Chan, *Eglise de Notre-Dame de Josaphat d'après les documents historiques et les fouilles récentes* (Chartres, 1908).

Neckam, Alexander, *De Naturis rerum, libri duo* . . . , ed. Thomas Wright (London, 1863), in *Rerum britannicarum medii aevi scriptores*, XXXIV.

Norden, Eduard, *Die antike Kunstprosa vom 6ten Jahrhundert vor Christus bis in die Zeit der Renaissance*, 2 vols. (Leipzig, 1898), II.

Norgate, Kate, *England under the Angevin Kings*, 2 vols. (London, 1887).

Ogle, Marbury B., "Some Aspects of Mediaeval Latin Style," in *Speculum*, I (1926).

Oudin, Casimir, *Commentarius de scriptoribus ecclesiae antiquis illorumque scriptis* . . . *ad annum MCCCCLX* . . . , 3 vols. in 2 (Leipzig, 1722).

Painter, Sidney, "John of Salisbury and the Renaissance of the Twelfth Century," in *The Greek Tradition*, ed. George Boas (Baltimore, 1939).

Paré, G., A. Brunet, and P. Tremblay, *La Renaissance du XIIe siècle, les écoles et l'enseignement* (Paris, 1933).

Pauli, Reinhold, Preface to his edition of fragments "Ex Iohannis Saresberiensis libris," in *Monumenta Germaniae historica, Scriptorum,* XXVII (Hannover, 1885).

Picavet, François, *Esquisse d'une histoire générale et comparée des philosophies médiévales* (Paris, 1907).

Poole, Reginald Lane, "The Early Correspondence of John of Salisbury," in *Proceedings of the British Academy,* XI (London, 1925).

——, "The Early Lives of Robert Pullen and Nicholas Breakespeare," in *Essays in Medieval History Presented to Thomas Frederick Tout,* eds. A. G. Little and F. M. Powicke (Manchester, 1925).

——, *Illustrations of the History of Medieval Thought* . . . (London, 1884; 2d ed. revised; London, 1920).

——, "John of Salisbury," in *Dictionary of National Biography,* ed. Sidney Lee, 21 vols. and 2 supplementary vols. (London, 1908–1913), X.

——, "John of Salisbury at the Papal Court," in *English Historical Review,* XXXVIII (London, 1923).

——, "The Masters of the Schools at Paris and Chartres in John of Salisbury's Time," in *English Historical Review,* XXXV (London, 1920).

Prantl, K., *Geschichte der Logik im Abendlande,* 4 vols. in 2 (2d ed.; Leipzig, 1855–1870), I, ii.

Putnam, George Haven, *Books and Their Makers During the Middle Ages* . . . , 2 vols. (New York, 1896–1897).

Raby, F. J. E., *A History of Christian-Latin Poetry from the Beginning to the Close of the Middle Ages* (Oxford, 1927).

Rand, Edward Kenneth, *Ovid and His Influence* (New York, 1928).

Rashdall, Hastings, *Universities of Europe in the Middle Ages,* eds. F. M. Powicke and A. B. Emden, 3 vols. (Oxford, 1936).

Reuter, Hermann, *Johannes von Salisbury: zur Geschichte der christlichen Wissenschaft in zwölften Jahrhundert* (Berlin, 1842).

Ritter, Heinrich, *Geschichte der Philosophie,* 12 vols. (Hamburg, 1829–1853), VII.

Robert, Gabriel, *Les Écoles et l'enseignement de la théologie pendant la première moitié du XIIe siècle* (Paris, 1909).

Rose, Valentin, "Die Lücke im Diogenes Laërtius und der alte Uebersetzer," in *Hermes, Zeitschrift für classische Philologie,* I (Berlin, 1866).

Sandys, J. E., *A History of Classical Scholarship,* 3 vols. (Cambridge, 1903–1908), I.

Savage, Ernest A., *Old English Libraries: the Making, Collection, and Use of Books during the Middle Ages* (London, 1911).

Schaarschmidt, C., *Johannes Saresberiensis nach Leben und Studien, Schriften und Philosophie* (Leipzig, 1862).

Schmidt, Julius, *Johannes Parvus Sarisberiensis, quomodo inter aequales antiquarum litterarum studio excelluerit* (Breslau, 1839).

Schneider, Arthur, "Die Erkenntnispsychologie des Johann von Salisbyry," in *Abhandlungen aus dem Gebiete der Philosophie und ihrer Geschichte. Eine Festgabe zum 70 Geburtstag George Freiherrn von Hertling . . .* (Freiburg im Breisgau, 1913).

Schubert, Ernst, *Die Staatslehre Johannes von Salisbury* (Berlin, 1897).

Scott, Edward, "Nicholas Breakespeare," in *Athenaeum*, no. 3453 (Dec. 30, 1893).

Siebeck, H., "Zur Psychologie der Scholastik: II. Johannes von Salisbury," in *Archiv für Geschichte der Philosophie* (Berlin, 1888).

Sikes, J. G., *Peter Abailard* (Cambridge, University Press, 1932).

The Social and Political Ideas of Some Great Medieval Thinkers, ed. F. J. C. Hearnshaw (New York, 1923).

Souchet, J. B., *Histoire du diocèse et de la ville de Chartres*, 4 vols. (Chartres, 1866–1873), II.

Spörl, Johannes, *Grundformen hochmittelalterlicher Geschichtanschaung: Studien zum Weltbild der Geschichtsschreiber des 12 Jahrhunderts* (Munich, 1935).

Stiglmayr, Joseph, "Dionysius the Pseudo-Areopagite," in *The Catholic Encyclopedia*, 15 vols. and *Index* (New York, 1908–1914), V.

Stubbs, William, "Literature and Learning at the Court of Henry II," Lectures VI and VII in *Seventeen Lectures on the Study of Medieval and Modern History and Kindred Subjects* (3d ed.; London, 1900).

Tanner, Thomas, *Bibliotheca britannico-hibernica: sive de scriptoribus qui in Anglia, Scotia, et Hibernia ad saeculi XVII initium floruerunt . . .* (London, 1748).

Taylor, Henry Osborn, *Medieval Mind*, 2 vols. (London, 1927).

Thompson, James Westfall, *The Medieval Library* (Chicago, 1939).

Thorlacius, Bigerus, "Qualem literarum classicarum cognitionem seculo XIImo Johannes Sarisberiensis habuerit," in *Prolusiones et opuscula academica . . .*, 5 vols., V (Copenhagen, 1822).

Tougard, l'Abbe A., *L'Hellenisme dans les ecrivains du moyen-âge du septième au douzième siècle* (Paris, 1886).

Ueberweg, Friedrich, *Grundriss der Geschichte der Philosophie*, 4 vols. (10th ed.; Berlin, 1905–1909).

Waddell, Helen J., "John of Salisbury," in *Essays and Studies by Members of the English Association*, XIII (Oxford, 1928).

———, *The Wandering Scholars* (London, 1927).

Webb, Clement C. J., "Corrigenda et addenda . . . ," in *Mediaeval and Renaissance Studies*, I, no. 2 (London, 1943), 232–236.

———, "John of Salisbury," in *Proceedings of the Aristotelian Society*, II, no. 2, part II (London, 1894).

———, *John of Salisbury* (London, 1932) [in *Great Medieval Churchmen*, ed. Leonard Elliott Binns].

———, "Notes on John of Salisbury," in *English Historical Review*, XLVI (London, 1931).

———, "Tenred of Dover," in *English Historical Review*, XXX (London, 1915).

White, Gleeson, *The Cathedral Church of Salisbury . . . and a Brief History of the See of Sarum* (London, 1911) [in Bell's Cathedral Series].

Willmann, Otto, *Didaktik als Bildungslehre nach ihren Beziehungen zur Socialforschung und zur Geschichte der Bildung*, 2 vols. (2d ed., rev.; Brunswick, 1894–1895).

———, *The Science of Education in Its Sociological and Historical Aspects*, trans. Felix M. Kirsch, 2 vols. (Beatty [Penn.], 1921).

Wright, F. A., and T. A. Sinclair, *History of Later Latin Literature . . .* (New York, 1931).

de Wulf, Maurice, *History of Medieval Philosophy*, trans. E. C. Messenger, 2 vols. (New York, 1935–1938).

INDEX

INDEX

INDEX

259; *Republic* (*The State*), 219, 226–228, 230; *Timaeus*, 229 and n. *190*, 230 and n. *197*, 259
Platonists, 29, 134, 135, 259, 261, 262
Plautus, Pseudo-, xxiii, 236 n. *257*
Pleasure, 108
Pliny, xxiii, 145 and n. *26*, 188 n. *361*
Poetry and poets, 51–52, 52–68 *passim;* and grammar, 51–52, 60, 67, 68; and philosophy, 63; purpose, 92
Political science, 46
Porphyry, xxiii, 76, 110–111 and n. *161*, 118, 146–150 *passim* and nn. *30, 36, 41, 49,* 179 and n. *282*, 180; *Isagoge,* 111, 146, 149
Position. *See* Thesis
Predicaments, 138–139, 149, 151–164 *passim,* 166, 173. *See also* Categories
Premonstratensians, 24
Prepositions, 53
Priority, 136, 163
Priscian, 44 n. *195,* 45 n. *201,* 48 n. *217,* 57 and n. *276,* 68 n. *354,* 121 n. *348,* 126 n. *381,* 128 n. *386,* 135 n. *438,* 176 n. *258,* 256 n. *405,* 274 n. *519*
Probability (probable reasoning, principles, and conclusions), 79, 83, 84–107, 109, 171, 188, 201, 210–211, 238–239. *See also* Dialectic
Problems, 173–174, 179
Pronoun, 43, 128
Pronunciation, 61
Property, 180–181
Propositions, 39–50, 165–170, 173, 176, 207–209; categorical, 43, 207; dialectical (probable), 107–109, 207; modal, 166; Augustine's three considerations in, 175; syllogisms and, 207–208
Proverbs, 10 n. *5,* 57 n. *271,* 75 n. *14,* 92 n. *130,* 200 nn. *463, 464,* 271 n. *499,* 276 n. *539*
Providence (*Pronoen*), 222, 251
Psalms, 64 nn. *319, 320,* 68 n. *353,* 208 n. *36,* 231 n. *217,* 243 n. *308,* 263 n. *457,* 265 n. *470,* 267 n. *478,* 269 n. *486,* 275 n. *537*
Prudence, 74–75, 78–79, 221–222, 224, 229, 246, 247
Publilius Syrus, xxiii, 176 n. *264*
Punctuations, 58–59
Pythagoras and Pythagoreans, 77, 85, 181, 201, 247

Quadrivium, xvii, 16, 20, 36, 67, 97
Questioner, 190–198. *See also* Disputation

Quintilian, xxiii, 5 n. *15,* 44 and n. *196,* 72 nn. *380, 381,* 46 n. *204,* 47 n. *214,* 50 n. *223,* 56 n. *269,* 57 and nn. *273, 280,* 60 nn. *293, 295, 296,* 61 nn. *298, 300, 302, 63, 69* nn. *355, 356, 360,* 81 n. *51,* 91 nn. *119, 122,* 93 n. *142,* 190 nn. *380, 381,* 199 n. *458,* 206 n. *22,* 243–244 nn. *315, 318,* 249 n. *350;* praises grammar, 61 and nn. *381–382,* 72; condemns Seneca, 62–63 and nn. *306, 308, 313;* on teaching grammar, 65–66 and nn. *328, 330;* quoted on Aristotle, 77 and n. *29;* on dialectic, 81 and n. *51;* a story concerning Timothy the music-teacher, 89–90 and nn. *106–109, 111; On the Education of an Orator,* 72; *Preparatory Training,* 81

Rational philosophy. *See* Logic; Philosophy
Reading, 64, 65–66, 69
Reason, 9, 16, 224–230, 248–254, 256; nature and, 9–11 *passim,* 82–83; and arts, 33–37 *passim; methodon,* 33; logic and, 82–83; and truth, 76, 224, 249, 253, 266–268; Aristotle on, 176, 235 and n. *248;* a spiritual force, 225, 250, 252; Cassiodorus on, 226; Plato on, 226–227; Hebraic concept of, 227–228; Seneca on, 228; function of, 228 ff., 242, 266; imagination, 229; ideas and, 232; Augustine on, 249, 252–253; limitations of, 253–254, 256, 272–273. *See also* Dialectic; Logic
Reasoning, 76, 78, 176–179, 187–188, 190–201, 204, 207–211, 214–215, 235–236, 239, 249. *See also* Dialectic; Disputation; Reason; Syllogism
Regimen sanitatis Salernitanum 18 n. *46*
Remigius of Auxerre, xxiv, 80 and n. *48*
Rhetoric, 16, 67, 79, 97–98, 102, 191, 206
Richard l'Evêque, xvii, 71 and n. *370,* 97 and n. *174*
Robert of Melun, xvi, 96–97 and n. *158,* 240
Robert Pullen, xvii, 23, 99
Romans, 10 n. *8,* 86 n. *83,* 109 n. *245,* 232 n. *225,* 263 n. *457,* 269 n. *490*
Romulus, 71
Roscelin, 112
Rudolf of Laon, 22

Saints, 255
Salernitanum Regimen sanitatis, xxiv
Salerno, 17–18
Salisbury (Sarum), xvi
Scaurus Rufus, 30
Schemata, 53, 54, 55, 56, 59, 66

More Titles about Books, Reading, and Writing
from Paul Dry Books

The Trivium: The Liberal Arts of Logic, Grammar, and Rhetoric
SISTER MIRIAM JOSEPH
MARGUERITE McGLINN, *editor*

Shakespeare's Use of the Arts of Language
SISTER MIRIAM JOSEPH

The Book Shopper: A Life in Review
MURRAY BROWNE

The Fiction Editor, the Novel, and the Novelist
THOMAS McCORMACK

**Literary Genius: 25 Classic Writers Who Define English
and American Literature**
JOSEPH EPSTEIN, *editor*

My Business Is Circumference: Poets on Influence and Mastery
STEPHEN BERG, *editor*

The Secret of Fame: The Literary Encounter in an Age of Distraction
GABRIEL ZAID, *trans. by Natasha Wimmer*

So Many Books: Reading and Publishing in an Age of Abundance
GABRIEL ZAID, *trans. by Natasha Wimmer*

Style: An Anti-Textbook
RICHARD A. LANHAM

Writers on the Air: Conversations about Books
DONNA SEAMAN

Look for these titles at your favorite bookstore or
online bookseller. Or order directly
from our website, where shipping is always free!
www.pauldrybooks.com

BOOKS TO
AWAKEN,
DELIGHT,
EDUCATE

PAUL DRY BOOKS
Philadelphia, PA
215.231.9939